GEOGRAPHY IN EDUCATION

Viewpoints on Teaching and Learning

Edited by

Ashley Kent

David Lambert

Michael Naish

Frances Slater

CAMBRIDGE
UNIVERSITY PRESS

Published by the Press Syndicate of the University of Cambridge
The Pitt Building, Trumpington Street, Cambridge CB2 1RP
40 West 20th Street, New York, NY 10011-4211, USA
10 Stamford Road, Oakleigh, Melbourne 3166, Australia

First published 1996

Printed in Great Britain at The University Press, Cambridge

A catalogue record for this book is available from the British Library

ISBN 0 521 47796 4

Cover photograph © Tony Stone Images

Acknowledgements
Every effort has been made to reach copyright holders; the publisher would be
glad to hear from anyone whose rights they have unwittingly infringed.

Figs. 1.1, 1.2, Gardner, R.A.M. & Hay, A.M. (1992); Figs. 6.1, 6.2, 6.3, 6.4,
OFSTED; Fig. 6.23, Worldaware; Fig. 6.25, The Institute of British
Geographers; Fig. 6.26, Blackwell Publishers; Fig. 6.27, Deanne Boydell; Fig.
6.29, Curriculum Council for Wales; Fig. 6.30, Journal of Geography in Higher
Education; Fig. 7.6, Butterworth-Heinemann Ltd; Fig. 7.10, Routledge and
Kegan Paul; Fig. 8.3, University of Leeds; Fig. 8.8, Midland Examining Group;
Fig. 9.8, HMSO; Fig. 10.1, *Research Intelligence*, Bera Newsletter; Fig. 11.1,
Macmillan Education/Routledge; Fig. 11.2, Open University Press.

Contents

Section Four Research and Research Methods 289

Contributors

Anthony Ghaye

Tony Ghaye is currently Reader in Educational Research and Director of Studies for the Advanced Modular In-Service Scheme at Worcester College of Higher Education. He has taught in both primary and secondary schools in England and Australia and worked with a wide range of professional groups. He is an action researcher committed to working to improve the quality of the educational experiences of learners in a variety of workplaces in both more developed and economically developing countries. Tony is a graduate of the Institute of Education, University of London, at both the Master's and PhD levels.

Norman Graves

After teaching in schools, Norman Graves taught at the University of Liverpool and then at the Institute of Education, University of London, where he became Head of the Geography Department and subsequently Pro-Director for Professional Studies. He has written and edited many books on geographical education and on education in its wider context, such as *Initial Teacher Education: Policies and Progress*. In 1993, Norman was awarded the Victoria Medal of the Royal Geographical Society for his services to geographical education.

Keith Hilton

Currently Head of the Geography Department at Chester College, Keith is a graduate of Bristol and McGill Universities. For a number of years, Keith was a member of the Geography Department of the Institute of Education, University of London. He has had a long-term interest in the teaching of physical geography and has written a number of texts including *Process and Pattern in Physical Geography* and *Understanding Landforms*. He also has an interest in promoting the educational use of remote sensing and has produced *The Earth Below*, and was involved in the TV series *Spaceship Earth*.

David Job

David Job worked for many years with the Field Studies Council, most recently at Slapton Ley Field Centre where he was involved in the development of fieldwork for the Geography 16–19 Project. While at Slapton he undertook research on coastal processes in Start Bay, leading to the award of MPhil from Huddersfield University in 1987. After a period of exploration in Asia and teaching geography at the Godolphin and Latymer School in Hammersmith, he was appointed Lecturer in Physical Geography at the Institute of Education, University of London in 1991. At the Institute he now runs the Earth Science Process Centre, which offers active learning experiences in physical geography to visiting school groups.

Ashley Kent

Ashley Kent is Senior Lecturer in Geographical Education at the Institute of Education, University of London, where he is Co-ordinator for Geography. He taught geography at Haberdashers Askes School, Elstree, and was Head of Geography at John Mason High School, Abingdon. Since becoming Associate Director of the Geography 16–19 Project, Ashley has directed a number of curriculum projects, the latest being concerned with remote sensing. He has long-standing professional interests in curriculum development, post-16 geography, fieldwork strategies, technology, and the professional development of teachers. He is currently Junior Vice-President of the Geographical Association.

David Lambert

David Lambert is Senior Lecturer in the Geography Section at the Institute of Education, University of London. Before joining the Institute he taught for twelve years, becoming Head of Geography and Acting Deputy Head at a comprehensive school in Hertfordshire. He is Course Tutor for the PGCE (Geography) and an Area Co-ordinator for the Institute's Partnership Scheme for Initial Training in East London. David is the series editor of the *Cambridge Geography Project* for Key Stage 3 (for 11 to 14 year-olds) which includes *Jigsaw Pieces*, which won the 1992 *Times Educational Supplement* Schoolbooks Award.

John Morgan

John Morgan graduated with a degree in Geography from University College, Swansea, in 1987. He has taught in schools and colleges in London, and in 1992 graduated with a Master's degree in Geography and Education from the Institute of Education, University of London. He is currently carrying out research on the implications of postmodern social theory for geography education, particularly the role of popular culture in curriculum planning.

Michael Naish

Michael Naish is University Reader in Education at the Institute of Education, University of London, and an education consultant. He was Head of Geography in two London schools before joining the Institute, where he has been Head of Geography, Chairperson of the Department of Economics, Geography and Business Education, Senior Tutor for Initial Courses, and Course Tutor of the MA in Geographical Education. Michael initiated and directed the Geography 16–19 Project and is co-author of *Geography 16–19: the Contribution of a Curriculum Project to the 16–19 Curriculum*. He has written widely on curriculum development, geographical education and teacher education, and has co-authored and edited various school geography books. Michael has also directed research into teacher education and edited research reports on geographical education.

Eleanor Rawling

From 1976 to 1985, Eleanor Rawling was a member of the University of London Institute of Education's Geography Section, working on the Geography 16–19 Project, first as a team member, then as Associate Director. At the time of writing for this volume she was a consultant in geographical education and Honorary Research Associate at the University of Oxford Department of Educational Studies. Eleanor was President of the Geographical Association in 1991/92 and Chair of the Council of British Geography 1993/95. Eleanor is now Professional Officer (Geography) with the School Curriculum and Assessment Authority. She received an MBE for services to geography education in 1995.

Margaret Roberts

Margaret Roberts is a Lecturer in Education at Sheffield University's Division of Education. Since 1989 she has been carrying out research into the implementation of geography in the National Curriculum at Key Stage 3, investigating different interpretations in case-study schools and relating this to survey data. Margaret is responsible for the Geography Curriculum course of the PGCE at Sheffield University. She works closely with students developing and exploring different classroom approaches to teaching and learning. At the time of writing for this volume Margaret is also the External Examiner for the Institute of Education's MA in Geographical Education.

Frances Slater

Frances Slater, MA (Otago), PhD (Iowa), is a Senior Lecturer in the University of London Institute of Education. Until recently she was Chairperson of the Department of Economics, Geography and Business Education. Frances has taught in schools and universities in New Zealand, Australia, the USA, Canada and the United Kingdom. She is currently Director of the Earth Science Process Centre. Her book, *Learning Through Geography*, first published by Heinemann in 1982, was updated and published by the National Council for Geographic Education (USA) in 1993. Frances has also written texts at the primary and secondary levels, and two particular interests – language and learning, and values in geography education – have been the subject of recent writing.

Preface

This book is concerned with the steadily growing interest, nationally and internationally, in how geography as a school discipline can act as a medium for education. The book is written by staff of the Geography Section of the University of London Institute of Education and some colleagues who are currently or have recently been linked with them. It could be regarded as the latest in a long tradition of books related to the value of geography in education which have emanated from the Institute of Education since *Geography in School* was published in the 1920s by the first geographer in post at the Institute, James Fairgrieve.

The book is divided into four sections. In Section One *Developments in Geography Education*, some recent developments in geography as an academic subject are discussed, and possible implications for school curricula are considered. Section Two *The Geography Curriculum – Principles, Practice and Evaluation*, discusses the study of curriculum thinking as it has impinged upon geography in schools, and the impact of current national policy. In Section Three *The Geography Curriculum – Issues and Concerns*, attention is given to particular issues relating to the implementation and practice of geography education. Finally, in Section Four *Research and Research Methods*, issues regarding research ideologies and methods are explored and in the course of this exploration some research findings and their implications are discussed.

SECTION ONE | Developments in Geography Education

In organising this volume we were aware that, to some extent, recent writing on geography's development, particularly in human geography over the past two or three decades, already exists. The decision was therefore taken to highlight in this section three areas less frequently covered: physical geography, environmental education including geographical fieldwork, and postmodernism in relation to geography.

The place and contribution of physical geography has been and always will be of importance. Keith Hilton opens the first chapter of this section, therefore, with an account of physical geography in education today. He justifies physical geography and its potential for education in science, and reviews the focus and nature of physical geography in education at all levels. Science or extinction: his subtitle suggests an uncomfortable polarity and challenge.

Chapter 2, by David Job, picks up a theme which has continually teased physical and human geographers and which derives much of its voice from the social movements of environmentalism and green concerns. Geography and environmental education are perhaps always destined to be in some sort of uneasy relationship, geography's dominant ideologies never being quite caring enough, critical enough, holistic enough for many environmentalists. David Job sets the scene on environmental education and then draws out challenges and possibilities for environmental education in fieldwork and field teaching in geography.

The chapters on physical geography and environmental matters consider themes, ideas and concepts with which we are familiar, even if that familiarity needs provoking and discussing from time to time.

John Morgan's final chapter in this section takes us into worlds and ideas which have been impinging on geographical thought and practice for a shorter time. The relevance and impact of postmodern beliefs and concepts need untangling from the new (to the uninitiated) language in which they are embedded. We should not ignore the movement and its development but try to clarify and understand the terms and 'big ideas' around which it is structured. 'Paradigm' was a much denigrated word and concept in the 1960s and 1970s and yet we handle it now with sophistication. The structure and agency debate threw up terms people disliked, but perhaps in clarifying them through discussion, further reading and then further discussion, certain geographical debates were honed. Environmental determinism and the like were given a fresh perspective. Much of the excitement of education comes from something which initially puzzles, throws one off, even annoys and brings protests of defence: 'jargon', 'rubbish', 'nonsense'. The 'big ideas' and language of postmodernism will be part of our vocabulary and concepts in an easier and more familiar way in the future when we will no doubt be assimilating and accommodating new structures of thinking and philosophical movements. In the meantime, John Morgan, one of our recent MA graduates, gives us geographers in education a start.

1 Physical geography: science or extinction?

Keith Hilton

> During the past two decades, natural disasters have been responsible for about 3 million deaths and have adversely affected at least 800 million people through homelessness, disease, serious economic loss and other hardships, including immediate damages in the hundreds of billions of dollars.
>
> UN resolution 42/169 (quoted in Jones, 1993)

The statement above refers to the designation, by the United Nations, of the 1990s as the International Decade for Natural Disaster Reduction (IDNDR). It indicates that physical geography has potentially a general, global and indeed political significance. It is the first of three quotations from disparate sources illustrating the themes which underpin this section.

The second was from Patrick Bailey, the then editor of *Teaching Geography*, writing in 1985 for a British educational readership in the *Times Educational Supplement* about physical geography as an essential foundation, who warned of the risks of an 'arrogantly man-centred [sic] world view' in a geographical education which focused mainly on the 'processes and patterns in the socioeconomic sphere'.

Thirdly, in the broadsheet media, notably at the time of the annual British Association meetings, came comment on the place of science in education and the public awareness of science; for example in 1994:

> The content of the National Curriculum is so full that it could result in the development of science understanding coming to a halt because of pressure and time, with the result that students view science as formal and objective rather than as something that can be relevant to life and questioned.
>
> Melkie and Alexander, 1994

An editorial in *The Guardian* at the same time stated:

> And yet a familiar problem remains : a self-feeding spiral of fewer science sixth form students, lower university entrance requirements, poor quality science graduates, particularly those entering teaching

and it continued:

How does a democracy achieve a rational debate on such crucial scientific issues as pollution, energy, and drugs in such an ill-informed society?

The Guardian, Comment, 5 September 1994

These extracts signal three cases for the continuing and enhanced relevance of physical geography as a part of geography that matters – to people, to teachers and to those who worry about the social effects of a limited scientific understanding: firstly at the global scale in respect of its relevance to the understanding and amelioration of disasters which reflect the interplay of natural and social systems; secondly at the level of the geography curriculum because without it geography can become placeless; and thirdly physical geography could potentially help to improve the general public's understanding of science and contribute to an enhancement of the quality of science education.

Contemporary physical geography: higher education

Geography as researched and taught in higher education has traditionally had an influence on the nature and content of school geography. The strength of that influence has varied through time, as have the 'lags' between innovations in the academic sphere and their reflections in school geography.

The contemporary concerns of geography in British universities are difficult to ascertain in any comprehensive way. In connection with teaching, no comprehensive survey of curricula exists. However, it is possible to monitor research activity and publications output which may illuminate teaching content. Within the more than 3,000 geographical research publications a year there is an immense diversity, reflecting various phases in the development of the discipline: the interests, time-frame and resources of researchers, the proclivities of journal editors and publishers, and other factors internal to the subject. External factors such as public and governmental concerns also shape the research agenda, notably research assessment exercises (Curran, 1994) and the decisions of funding agencies.

Gardner and Hay (1992), in their report on the state of geography in the United Kingdom for the 27th International Geographical Congress, presented the results of a survey of research in university geography departments. In terms of physical geography the results of this survey, involving a total of 845 papers published between 1988 and 1991, gave a picture of research activity. Only about a third of this reflected research interests abroad. The diversity of output was collapsed into the seven categories shown in Figure 1.1:

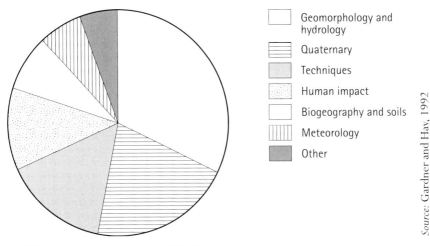

Geomorphology and hydrology

Quaternary

Techniques

Human impact

Biogeography and soils

Meteorology

Other

Source: Gardner and Hay, 1992

Figure 1.1 Research output 1988–91 by category

Geomorphology and hydrology accounted for a third of research output (see Figure 1.1). The growth of geographical hydrology as a feature of enquiry in physical geography, noticeable from the 1970s, is confirmed and this is likely to remain a significant area of activity.

Within this category the survey revealed catchment studies as being particularly significant (Figure 1.2), especially those investigations concerned with the sources and transport pathways of sediment and solutes. This work was largely United Kingdom based. The place of vegetation and soils in such investigations inevitably involves linkages with biogeography–biogeomorphology, demonstrating the problem of allocating research activity to any simple classification category. Figure 1.2 also illustrates the other topic concerns, the second ranking being concerned particularly with the dynamics of glaciers and meltwater and their associated bedforms. Arid and coastal subgroups follow in rank order, whilst massmovement occupies seventh place. Given scientific, popular and political concerns about the prediction of environmental change consequent on human activities, this spread of investigation is surprisingly traditional.

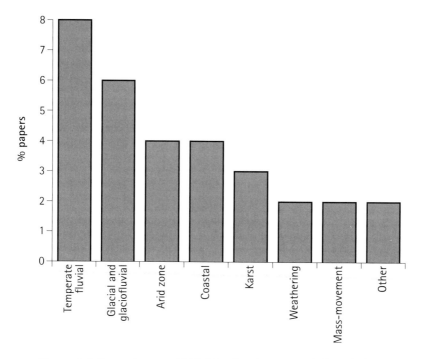

Source: Gardner and Hay, 1992

Figure 1.2 Research output 1988–91 within the geomorphology/hydrology
subgroup

Returning to the broader view, the Quaternary category accounted for
a fifth of all research (Figure 1.1). Much of this work has been concerned
with the elucidation of the history of environmental change using strati-
graphic records, and has been largely United Kingdom based. The innovative areas within this category relate to the development of techniques
and dating (aminostratigraphy, radiocarbon, uranium series and thermo-
luminescence) for palaeo-environmental reconstruction and the linkage of
ocean and terrestrial sequences running back over the last 500,000 years.

Of the techniques category (15 per cent of published research output),
more than half has been devoted to remote sensing. This is in line with the
significance of this technology identified by Gregory (Gregory, 1985) in
his overview of physical geography published some seven years before the
Gardner and Hay survey. Remote sensing and GIS have the demonstrated
capability to collect, collate and analyse the kind of global change data
required for environmental monitoring and the modelling of future
environments.

The human impact category accounts for 12 per cent of research output. The last decade has seen an increase in both scientific and public interest in environmental issues and environmental systems at both regional and global scales. In academic physical geography research this has been translated to a concern with areas such as environmental degradation, increasing hazard vulnerability (Degg, 1992) and the problems of global climatic change (Parry, 1990). Within the United Kingdom, wetlands and uplands have been particularly fruitful research environments. Issues connected with surface water acidification have also been investigated, the Surface Water Acidification Project (Battarbee *et al.*, 1990) being a notable example. In terms of global climatic change, work has involved refinement of global climatic models (GCMs) and the exploring of issues such as eustatic changes, ice-sheet response to global climatic change, and non-linear changes in ice budgets in the west Antarctic. The question raised by the survey authors was whether such work would transfer to macroscale environmental management. Their doubts were stated: 'In terms of substantive pure and applied research and environmental management at the global scale geographers in Britain have, with few notable exceptions, played a relatively minor role' (Gardner and Hay, 1992). They pointed out that ongoing tasks involve traditional synthesis, monitoring and modelling, together with the development of transdisciplinary work.

An example of the last is the MEDALUS Project, which began in 1991. MEDALUS (*Me*diterranean *Des*ertification *a*nd *L*and *Us*e) is a research programme funded by the EC Directorate General XII for Science Research and Development. Its aim is to identify and understand the effects of desertification in southern Europe. Nineteen teams from universities and research institutes across Europe are involved in the programme, which has five components:

- climatology
- physical processes of desertification
- modelling change
- the use of remote sensing and GIS to identify process response units
- linked socio-economic studies.

The structure and scope of the project are illustrated in Figure 1.3.

Biogeography and soils accounted for 8 per cent of research output. The significance of soils and organisms in geomorphological processes has received increased attention, in terms of weathering, stabilisation and hydrological response. On the other hand, meteorology produced only a small output (6 per cent). This reflected its declining professional base within university geography departments and the kind of 'competition' from other disciplines like physics, which, in the National Curriculum, has parallels with the geography curriculum.

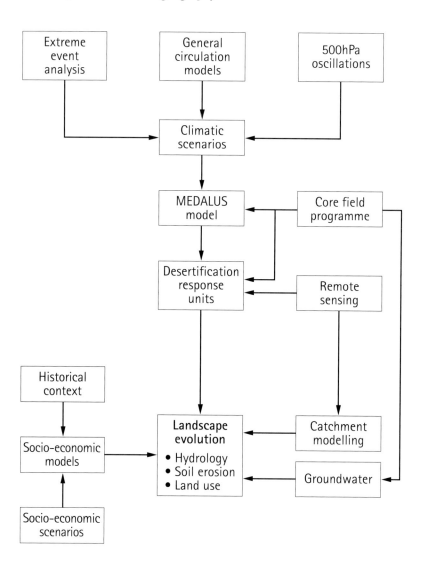

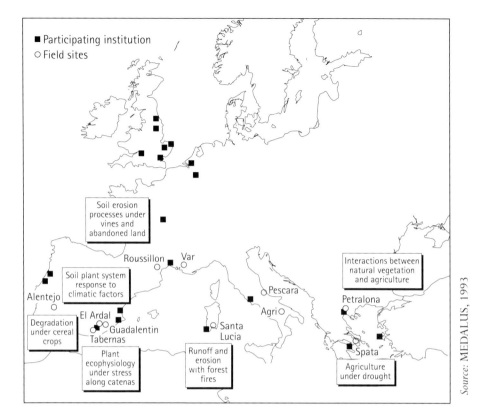

Figure 1.3 The MEDALUS Project

Process studies were mentioned as a distinguishing feature in an earlier overview (Hilton, 1985). Garner and Hay note that little research is reported in mass-movement, periglacial features, weathering, coastal dynamics, humid tropical geomorphology, community dynamics in bio-geography, or in pedology, but increased interest in arid zones was noted (Cooke *et al.*, 1992).

The information summarised above gives a partial view of intellectual effort in university physical geography. This division of the subject has not been characterised by the kind of theoretical debate affecting human geography. Positivist underpinnings are perhaps universally accepted in pure research, although increasing recognition is given to alternative frameworks when interdisciplinary work and prediction or management issues are being explored.

Traditionally, it has been claimed that research enlightens and informs teaching. The linkage of this picture of research output to undergraduate teaching is, however, unknown. The 1994–95 Assessment of the Quality of Education in departments of geography in Higher Education Funding Council for England (HEFCE) institutions may be significant in this context. This has required the production of self-assessment statements and related documentation (including curriculum and assessment). At the time of writing, however, it is difficult to see how the documentation produced by individual institutions and focused on the awarding of grades of satisfactory or excellent teaching can be surveyed to give a comprehensive picture of undergraduate geography curricula.

Contemporary physical geography: schools

A school-level publication survey was undertaken to allow the concerns of school physical geography to be compared with those of the higher education sector. Analysis was confined to two Geographical Association journals which have wide readership in secondary schools: *Geography* and *Teaching Geography*. As with the Gardner and Hay survey, the significance must be treated with caution given the actual 'personal' process of article conception and writing, the 'group' or 'institutional' context of editorial acceptance and the subsequent appearance of an article. There is also the unanswered question of whether such articles actually influence geography teaching! It was decided to extend the survey over a longer period, mainly to detect a more representative number of physical geography articles in the two selected journals with their non-specialist readership, but also to cover two of Rawling's 'Periods of Geographical Education' (Rawling, 1993).

Figure 1.4 indicates the proportion of physical geography articles in *Teaching Geography* and *Geography*. Since 1980 the *Teaching Geography* proportion has averaged 10 per cent and the *Geography* 7.6 per cent. There is no evidence of an underlying trend. It is considered that no significance can be placed on the fact that some of the lows in *Geography* coincide with above-average figures in *Teaching Geography*. Such variations reflect the normal pattern of article acceptances mentioned earlier.

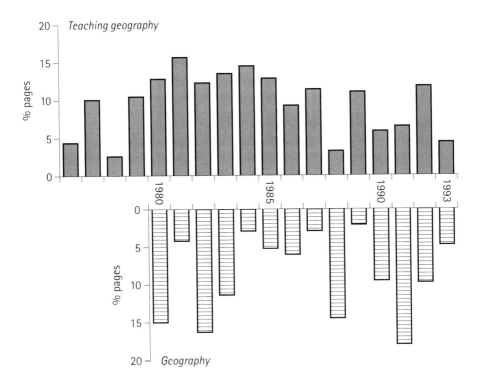

Figure 1.4 Articles on physical geography in *Teaching Geography* and *Geography*

Figure 1.5 shows for both journals the breakdown of content focus, using the same categories as Gardner and Hay. In *Teaching Geography* meteorology accounted for three times the proportion of the university-level survey. Equivalent proportions were noted for soils, geomorphology/hydrology and techniques, although there are significant differences in sophistication of the latter. Quaternary/glacial and human impact categories were smaller in *Teaching Geography*. In the case of *Geography*, meteorology was again larger, as was biogeography; geomorphology/hydrology was slightly less, and Quaternary/glacial and techniques much less.

Within geomorphology/hydrology (Figure 1.6), *Geography* reflects academic concerns less than its sister journal. *Teaching Geography*'s 'temperate fluvial' category matched the ranking observed in the university research (Figure 1.2). This reflects the deployment of ideas and techniques promoted in the earlier developments in geographical hydrology.

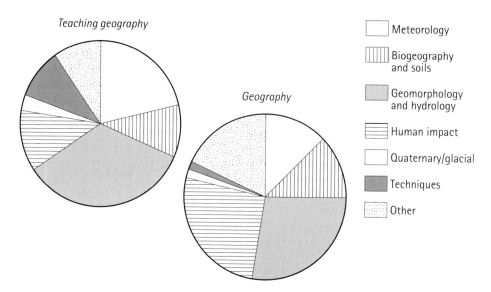

Figure 1.5 Types of articles on physical geography in *Teaching Geography* and *Geography*

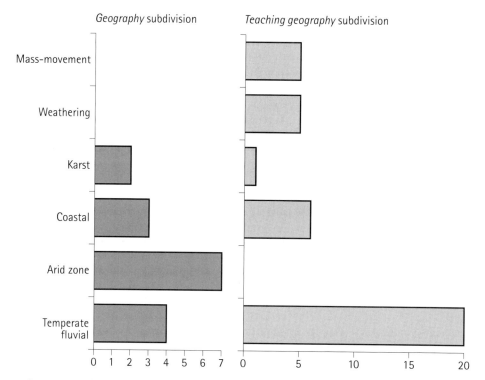

Figure 1.6 Articles on physical geography in *Teaching Geography* and *Geography* within the geomorphology/hydrology subgroup

Weathering and mass-movement are of limited weight in all three contexts. The primacy of arid zone work within *Geography* is surprising, but it reflects the contributions of a small number of individuals.

The interpretation which may be placed on the similarities and differences shown in this analysis must be cautious. However, the content coverage of *Teaching Geography*, with the exception of meteorology, more closely resembles the higher education profile than that detectable in *Geography*. If the two teacher-oriented journals are combined, the physical geography teacher can be seen to have received a fairly well-balanced 'update' coverage.

Lest a false impression be created that schools always lag behind higher education, there are some areas where the reverse is the case. In computer-assisted learning (CAL) the production of exchangeable teaching materials for the university sector only began in 1993, with the Computers in Teaching Initiative (CTICG, 1994). Similarly the clarification of objectives, assessment criteria and so on came to some universities only after the arrival of the 'Quality Industry' (Johnston, 1994a) and the 1994/95 HEFCE assessment of teaching quality in geography departments. The publication of the results of this exercise in the form of a Subject Overview Report and Quality Assessment Reports for individual departments will place universities in the kind of 'league table' world familiar to schools, whose examination performances are published.

Science and physical geography

Physical geography in higher education has, for at least three decades, been both perceived and practised as a science. The continuities and discontinuities between the content areas of higher education and school geography have been reviewed in the earlier sections of this chapter. It is now appropriate to discuss the process of enquiry and learning in physical geography.

Science, in the context of physical geography, can be considered as a way in which knowledge about the living and non-living world is progressively established. The method used is the generation and testing of ideas and theories (scientific method). The goal is the explanation of connected events leading to generalisations which permit reliable predictions about future events – in other words, science is a law-seeking activity. The inductive process was weak in generalisation. The deductive route, whose wider exposure to geographical educators might be linked to Harvey's book (Harvey, 1969), is more central to our concern.

Prior to the development of the National Curriculum, much secondary school science for older pupils had been undertaken within the frame of separate physics, biology and chemistry. For younger pupils, integrated science was frequently offered. Apart from its educational justification, it eased timetabling and the frequently cited shortage of physics teachers. It would be fair to summarise that there was little linkage with geography.

The National Curriculum 1989 Statutory Order for Science stated in connection with Attainment Target 1 (the Exploration of Science): 'activities should encourage the ability to plan, hypothesise and predict; design and carry out investigations; interpret results and findings; draw inferences; communicate exploratory tasks and experiments'.

This view of science education had been signalled some four years before with the publication of DES Policy Document 'Science 5–16' with its requirement that an expanded science provision should be balanced, broad, relevant and problem-solving. The requirement that future science teaching be experimental, investigational and concerned with problem-solving had thus been clearly signalled. The four characteristics of balance, broadness, problem-solving and relevance were to be significant for geography in secondary education. The emphasis on breadth and relevance led to extensions of science into various environmental and earth-science content areas previously regarded as the domain of school geography. With the onset of the National Curriculum, secondary school science was also required to pay more overt attention to the scientific method. This has encouraged interest in field work as an augmentation of traditional laboratory-based experimentation. In terms of both content and method the boundaries between science and physical geography in schools were set to change.

The period since the mid-1980s has thus been marked by a concern with the relations of science and geography in the school curriculum. King, writing from the perspective of the Association of Teachers of

Geology, noted that he was 'surprised to find so few physical geographers working with us' (King, 1986). Perhaps he should not have been surprised! By the late 1970s the Geography and the Young School Leaver (GYSL) (Avery Hill) project had, from one caustic view, 'led half a generation of 14–16 year olds to believe that environmental factors can be virtually ignored in geographical enquiry' (Hopkin, 1986). Human geography with its models, quantification and perceived 'relevance' was seen to have all the fruits of the conceptual revolution which could transform school geography. The revision of the GYSL and the arrival of the GCSE 16+ examination (1986) reflected an awareness of such criticisms, but none the less confirmed the weakened position of physical geography. Physical geography in GCSE was treated in a people–environment frame which omitted consideration of physical processes.

Such treatment is not surprising given the generally weak rationale produced for the teaching of physical geography at this time. Not only was the rationale ill-developed and badly promoted, but there was also a lack of concern with a conceptual base and issues like progression. Some arguments were proposed for a holistic (systems) approach where the ecosystem, for example, was also seen as an organising concept which emphasised linkages between physical and social systems (Hopkin, 1986). Mottershead (1987) noted that a modern process-oriented physical geography could promote the development of transferable skills, notably throughout the scientific method and the deployment of appropriate information technology. He also argued for an environmentally aware populace to tackle long-term societal and environmental problems. He saw the achievement of an understanding of environmental processes coming through a systematic study of physical geography. He listed seven objectives that a process-oriented physical geography, capable of being taught at a range of scales, could demonstrate. They are that:

1 environmental resources are essentially finite

2 environment alone provides both the energy and material resources utilised by humankind

3 the existence of the human race, and its activities of production and consumption, are based on environmental energy supply

4 human life and activity exist inescapably in an ecological context

5   environment is holistic in kind, and is characterised by complex connections between disparate phenomena, an objective that emphasises the limitations of studying selected isolated phenomena such as hazards, or environmental deterioration, without setting them in a wider context

6   all environmental resources exist in the form of flows or stores of energy or materials

7   there are environmental consequences of tapping into these flows and stores, and there are limits to the extent to which they can be tapped without producing exhaustion or irreversible degradation.

Such discussion, signalling the intellectual and pedagogic utility of systems thinking, reflected concerns raised earlier in academic geography. The issue of investigative method – how we should study physical geography – was referred to a little later in the decade: 'Physical geography taught through the medium of scientific method can provide for the investigative, experiential and problem solving approaches to study' (Catling, 1989). The place of physical geography in exposing pupils to scientific method was vigorously put by Burt. He stated: 'Physical geography is an excellent vehicle for teaching science: it deals with the kind of everyday objects and issues to which pupils can relate, and it provides a means of integrating several aspects of science at a scale relevant to the issues involved' (Burt, 1989).

Central to erecting a case for physical geography has been, firstly, a restatement of geography's traditional synthesis role in integrating the study of social and environmental systems. Secondly there has been a restatement of the positive role of fieldwork. This has been particularly the case when the whole deductive path is the organisational base underpinning learning – when exploratory and tentative solutions are advanced (using pupils' observations) prior to the formulation of hypotheses and the subsequent planning of investigation. This involves stress on ideas, on generating multiple working hypotheses, for example, and – after the data gathering and testing stages – on the evaluation of the whole project and the placing of its results in a wider context. Much fieldwork in physical geography had always been organised in this way. It is this experience which physical geography teachers have, in combination with exposure to new teaching ideas and techniques (through the kind of articles in *Teaching Geography* surveyed earlier), which has provided a positive base for transition to a more explicit focus on scientific method in the late 1990s. In comparison with school-based laboratory investigation, the uncertainty and complexity of the field situation could lead to the generation of more ideas from pupils, in a less formal learning context and, of course, with no forced closure when the lesson ends.

The detail of the geography–science interface became more apparent towards the end of the 1980s. The Geographical Association's Geography/Science Working Group (Mottershead and Hewitt, 1989) pointed out the convergence between geography and science; for example, that of the 16 Attainment Targets (ATs) concerned with the knowledge and understanding of science, five were of traditional concern to geographers, and that at Key Stages 3 and 4, a third of the science curriculum contained earth science and environmental material of interest to geographers. Whilst the science curriculum document was subsequently rewritten (ATs reducing from seventeen to four) and the National Curriculum Council (NCC), recognising the convergence issue, claimed a 'removal of

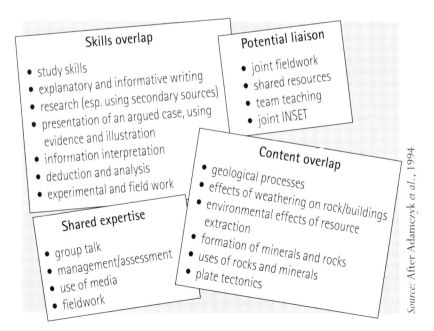

Figure 1.7 Science and geography curriculum overlap

Source: After Adamczyk et al., 1994

a small amount of unnecessary duplication of material in the science and geography orders' (NCC, 1991), content convergence remains an issue.

The resolution of this overlap of interest and content remains a problem for the 1990s and beyond. Examples of collaborative practice across the curriculum are rare. Its incorporation in school-based teacher education would seem a useful priority. The production of a geology unit described in a recent *Teaching Geography* article (Adamczyk *et al*, 1994) is of particular significance in this context.

Summary

In conclusion, a SWOT (Strengths, Weaknesses, Opportunities and Threats) analysis of physical geography in geographical education reveals the following. As the first section of this chapter demonstrated, physical geography remains a vigorous part of academic geography. It is involved with socially and scientifically relevant research with many links to other disciplines. This variety is reflected in schools, where physical geography remains a minority interest but with no evidence of recent decline or a role restricted purely as a service to human geography. Physical geography's content is recognised in the National Curriculum and the public examinations. It exploits systems thinking and is able to employ relevant information technology in the consolidation of transferable skills (Figure 1.8).

There are weaknesses: the image of geography as a humanity remains strong, and geography does not carry the status and resources of science. In terms of threats, the diminution of geography's role at Key Stage 4 will result in few favours for physical geography, whose earth and environmental content will continue to exist in the core science National Curriculum area. In spite of the weaknesses and threats there are, however, significant opportunities. Public awareness of environmental issues is unlikely to diminish, and the integrative tradition of the subject combined with experience of systems analysis should serve physical geography teachers well. Secondly, physical geography is well placed to contribute to cross-curricular themes.

Finally, there is the opportunity presented by the lack of public aware-

Transferable skills	Realisation in school-level physical geography
The ability to:	
• locate, appreciate and synthesise the salient materials on a topic →	Limitations imposed by time, school resources and teachers' knowledge, but good basis for development at a range of levels
• critically evaluate arguments presented (orally or in writing) by others →	A shift from content (the physical phenomena) to processes of learning required
• solve/resolve problems involving	
– design of a critical experiment →	Not well developed – teacher/ text dominated
– collection of relevant information(qualitative and quantitative) to operationalise the experiment →	Data gathering skills exist
– analysis →	Exists
– evaluation →	Less well developed, time and pupil maturity
• work in a team and manage the work of others →	Particularly well developed in field situations
• present material to a critical audience, through a variety of media	
• use information and other technology. →	Dependent on schools resourcing and IT

Source: After Johnston, 1994b

Figure 1.8 Transferable skills and their relationship to school-level physical geography

ness of science, and concern over the quality of science teaching. A physical geography that could signal itself to parents, headteachers and pupils as an effective science would have an assured and worthwhile educational niche in the most crowded curriculum. The kind of media quotes presented at the beginning of this chapter would then become a thing of the past.

BIBLIOGRAPHY

Adamczyk, P., Binns, T., Brown, A., Cross, S. and Magson, Y. (1994) 'The geography–science interface: a focus for collaboration', *Teaching Geography*, 19(1):11–14.

Bailey, P. (1985) 'Physical geography – the essential foundation', in *The Times Educational Supplement*, 8 December 1985.

Battarbee, R.W., Mason, J., Renberg, I. and Talling, J.F. (eds.) (1990) *Palaeolimnology and Lake Acidification*, London: The Royal Society.

Burt, T. (1989) 'Science and fieldwork in physical geography', *Teaching Geography*, 14(4):151–5.

Catling, S. (ed.) (1989) 'Physical geography and the school curriculum', in *Some Issues for Geography within the National Curriculum*, Geographical Association.

Clark, M.J., Gregory, K.J. and Gurnell, A.M. (eds.) (1989) *Horizons in Physical Geography*, Macmillan.

Cooke, R.U. (1992) 'Common ground, shared inheritance: research impera-tives for environmental geography', *Transactions of the Institute of British Geographers*, 17(2):131–51.

Cooke, R.U., Warren, A. and Goudie, A.S.G. (1992) *Desert Geomorphology*, UCL Press.

CTICG (1994) *Newsletter* and *Geocal*, CTI Centre for Geography, University of Leicester.

Curran, P. (1994) 'The slope of the playing field', *Area*, 26(3):249–60.

Degg, M.R. (1992) 'Natural disasters: recent trends and future prospects', *Geography*, 77(3):198–209.

Gardner, R. A. M. and Hay, A. M. (1992) 'Geography in the United Kingdom 1988–92', *Geographical Journal*, 158(1):13–30.

Gregory, K. J. (1985) *The Nature of Physical Geography*, Arnold.

The Guardian, Comment, 5 September 1994.

Harvey, D. (1969) *Explanation in Geography*, Arnold.

Hilton, K. (1985) 'Physical geography: perspectives, problems and prospects' in *Geography and Education Now*, 2nd edn, Bedford Way Papers 13, University of London/Heinemann.

Hopkin, J. (1986) 'A new physical geography', *Teaching Geography*, 12(1):32–3.

Johnston, R.J. (1994a) 'The quality industry in British higher education', *Professional Geographer*, 46 (4):491–7.

(1994b) 'Resources, staff student ratios and teaching quality in British higher education: some speculations aroused by Jenkins and Smith', *Transactions of the Institute of British Geographers*, NS 19:359–65.

Jones, D.K.C. (1993) 'Environmental hazards in the 1990s: problems, paradigms and prospects', *Geography*, 78(2):161–5.

King, C. (1986) 'Will physical geography join the sciences?', *Teaching Geography*, 12(1):32.

MEDALUS (1993) Executive summary, EC Directorate General XII.

Melkie, J. and Alexander, S. (1994) 'Pupils find science an uphill struggle', *The Guardian*, 5 September 1994:8.

Mottershead, D. (1987), 'Physical geography … the debate continues' *Teaching Geography*, 12(2):80–1.

Mottershead, D. and Hewitt, M. (1989) 'Geography and the Science National Curriculum', *Teaching Geography*, 14(1):156–7.

NCC (1991) *National Curriculum: Non Statutory Guidance (Science)*, HMSO.

Parry, M.L. (1990) *Climatic Change and World Agriculture*, Earthscan.

Rawling, E. (1993) 'School geography: towards 2000', *Geography*, 78(2):110–16.

2 Geography and environmental education – an exploration of perspectives and strategies

David Job

> People who start to think about green matters usually begin at the shallow level
> – cleaner rivers, protect the ozone layer. Then, if they go much deeper: what
> ways of *thinking*, what ways of *being*, have led us to mistreat the earth and abuse
> each other?
>
> Damian Randle, *Teaching Green*

> As a minister responsible for education in Britain, it has been my job to ensure
> that our schools help young people understand the complexity of our environ-
> ment and appreciate the balance that has to be struck between our prosperity
> and our ecological health.
>
> Angela Rumbold MP, former Minister of State for Education and Science

These two observations on environmental education provide a clear demonstration that there is no single vision of the nature and aims of environmental education, just as there is no consensus on a single environmental perspective or ideology. The second quotation, taken from the National Curriculum Council guide on environmental education, presents us with a view of environmental education which, while implying some need to reconsider our relationship with the earth, does not appear to require any major rethinking of either our world view, or how we see ourselves in relation to others, or the nature of learning experiences in the environment. The objectives in such an approach are probably attainable through fine-tuning of existing curricula within the context of existing structures and patterns of organisation within schools and without any major overhaul in the prevailing Western world view. The questions posed by Randle (1989) raise issues which cannot be accommodated by the 'business as usual' viewpoint. The means to adjusting our lives to avoid abuses of the planet appear to entail not merely different ways of doing, but different ways of being.

This chapter begins by offering a review and critique of some of the main strands in environmental thinking, then explores how the different genres within environmental education have been and might be informed by these differing perspectives. In order to reflect more specifically on the implications of this debate for geography education, the chapter then focuses on the range of approaches used by geographers in undertaking fieldwork with students, reviewing the strengths and weaknesses of each strategy in relation to the range of environmental perspectives previously examined.

Environmental perspectives reviewed

There are several sources which offer thorough reviews and critiques of the numerous perspectives on environmentalism and their ideological underpinnings (Pepper, 1984, 1993; O'Riordan, 1981; Eckersley, 1992). It can become confusing when exploring the many genres of environmentalism when different criteria are used by different authors to make distinctions. Two sets of criteria are commonly applied in drawing out such distinctions.

One relates to the world view regarding the relationship between people, nature and the earth, often with a spectrum of positions being identified. At one end of this spectrum, positions can be distinguished which several authors refer to as representing the *technocentric* perspective. It is characterised by a view of the earth as a machine whose operation can be understood, predicted and managed using the tools of classical science. It is a perspective that is normally linked with a people-dominant (anthropocentric) view of the earth in which the significance of resources, landscapes and other life forms are evaluated (and valued) largely from a human viewpoint. The opposing genre of environmentalism is generally labelled *ecocentric* and encompasses a collection of positions that are based on a sustainable earth with an equality of rights which includes all species, landscapes and resources.

A second set of criteria is dominantly political and relates both to the perceived causes of environmental degradation and to the social, political and economic changes which are thought to be required in order to rectify the harm done to the earth and to achieve sustainability. Again a spectrum of positions can be distinguished, with free-market environmentalists drawing inspiration from the political right at one pole and an amalgam of ecosocialist and ecoanarchist perspectives at the other. Some analyses of environmental perspectives imply that these two spectra may be viewed in parallel, with technocentrics tending to be free-market environmentalists and ecocentrics tending towards the political left or anarchist traditions. Such a simplification is not always helpful, as examples are quoted of deep ecologists (ecocentrics) drawing on political thought from the right, the left and anarchist traditions as a means of achieving harmony with the earth. Equally, examples are quoted of studies from socialist societies of both benign and destructive instances of environmental policy.

The following two subsections take a closer look at the distinctions between technocentric and ecocentric perspectives, and open up the implications of each for environmental education. Figure 2.1 presents a summary of some of the distinctions that have been drawn. (This synthesises and complements the more detailed environmental positions in Figure 7.6 on pages 212–13.)

TECHNOCENTRIC PERSPECTIVES

The view of the earth as a mechanistic structure whose behaviour can be understood in cause–effect terms, whose responses to change can be predicted, and whose direction can be manipulated by decisions and management towards desirable ends, is so familiar as to be unremarkable. It is a view that has dominated much of physical geography and underlies most interpretations of the physical world, as outlined in Keith Hilton's account of physical geography in schools and higher education (see Chapter 1). What seems remarkable to critics of the technocentric position (Pepper, 1984; Eckersley, 1992) is that this view has rapidly become the dominant world view despite its growth from a restricted and relatively recent period of development in human thought, namely the emergence of classical science in the Western world over the past four hundred years or so.

A central feature of a technocentric outlook concerns the nature of progress. This is seen largely in terms of material advancement with increasing levels of consumption and development of high technology as key indicators of progress. Technological optimism is expressed in a belief that if certain resources become depleted, human ingenuity will find alternatives (resource replacement) and pollution can be controlled through technology-based processes.

	Technocentric	Ecocentric
Earth view	*Mechanistic / Reductionist* The earth and its subsystems can be likened to a machine whose behaviour is predictable in cause–effect terms. The whole is viewed as the sum of the parts.	*Gaianist / Holistic* The earth is likened to a single living organism which adjusts its environment in ways that sustain life. The whole is greater than the sum of the parts. The complexity of its feedback mechanisms and the possibility of chaos are constraints on understanding and predictability.
Knowledge and understanding of the earth	The functioning of the earth machine can be understood by scientific investigation of its parts. Future states can be predicted and changed through environmental management.	Understanding of the earth is not limited to scientific knowledge based on logical positivism. Sensory, emotional and spiritual ways of knowing have equal validity.
Perspective on resource depletion and pollution	Human ingenuity can solve environmental problems through resource replacement. Technical solutions can be used to control pollution.	Fundamental changes in lifestyle are needed to live in a compatible way with the earth, involving restraint on energy and resource use. Pollution can be solved by eliminating waste and using natural processes to purify water.
Perspective on development issues	Poverty can be eliminated by limiting human numbers and developing industrial technology to increase production and relieve people from drudgery.	Excessive consumption in rich countries is the main cause of degradation of the earth. Poor countries in debt are forced to over-exploit their resources.
Social/ political perspective	Technology extends and amplifies human experience, freeing people from mundane tasks and liberating creativity.	Inner, personal ecology is linked to outer ecology. Abuses of nature by people are seen as extensions of social patterns of domination. Excessive consumption attempts to compensate for inner emptiness. Solving environmental problems lies within ourselves and society.

Figure 2.1 Ecocentric and technocentric ideologies compared – a summary

Pepper (1984) suggests that technocentrism constitutes a major component of the cultural filter in the Western world and that it informs, affects and determines our conception of nature at all levels. In terms of ideology, science is regarded as having replaced myth, folklore and natural magic in our understanding of the world. The technocentric perspective has implications for how decisions are made as well as determining the nature of those decisions. Since it is supposed that an understanding of the mechanics of the earth requires specialised knowledge and skills, then decisions are best left to those experts who possess the necessary level of understanding. Clearly there are education implications here in that specialists in the sciences and technology are needed to fulfil the key roles of researching, advising and decision-taking.

In reflecting on our own approaches to environmentalism with students, how can we distinguish the degree to which we are consciously or otherwise projecting a technocentric interpretation of the earth? First we might consider the kinds of knowledge that we use and refer to in our understanding of environmental issues. Are the kinds of knowledge we use based only on scientific materialism or are other 'categories of knowing' (Beare and Slaughter, 1993) admissible? A useful checklist of the types of knowledge specific to scientific materialism is referred to by Beare and Slaughter (1993), drawing upon the work of Harman (1988).

Reductionism The way to understanding is to break things down into their component parts. An understanding of the whole can be achieved by building up our knowledge of the individual pieces.

Positivism Extending our knowledge about the earth and the universe depends only upon what we can observe. Verifiable truth is achieved by experimentation and measurement using the physical senses and the technology that extends them.

Materialism The empiricist works only with what is substantial and real, insisting on evidence that can be examined.

Objectivity There is a clear distinction between the objective world, which any observer can perceive and which all observers will read in the same way, and subjectivity, which is limited to the privacy of one's own brain and consciousness. What is objective is reliable; what is subjective can be dismissed unless the subjectivities of several people agree and therefore confirm an objective conclusion.

Rationalism   The application of reasoning, rigorous logic, dispassionate (and therefore value-free, or unemotional) rationality – especially when based upon observed phenomena – is the only safe method whereby to advance knowledge.

Quantitative analysis   Qualitative properties are best reduced to quantitative ones, to properties that can be weighed, measured, rendered objective and assessable.

It is the fragmentation implicit in scientific materialism, together with the exclusion of other categories of knowing that rest on values, feelings and emotions, which critics of the technocentric perspective have focused upon. Furthermore, the dominance of this world view as a basis for making environmental decisions and as a basis for exploring knowledge in schools is seen as a root cause of current ecological disharmony:

> What develops from this approach is a fragmented, fractured view of the cosmos and of our part in it. We encourage people so much in the 'bits' approach that they do not identify with the whole. How else can we explain the expenditure of huge sums on armaments while children starve? Why do industries concentrate on producing materials and their own private riches with so little concern about the pollution of streams and atmosphere resulting from their own waste? How else can we explain destruction parading as growth; consumption being called development …?
>
> Beare and Slaughter, 1993

Technocentric perspectives continue to dominate many of our approaches to teaching geography, particularly our interpretations of the physical world. Can a postmodern orientation of geography change these emphases in our approaches? (See Chapter 3.)

ECOCENTRIC PERSPECTIVES

Key elements of the ecocentric perspective recognise that the rate of resource use is very uneven between the developed and less developed world, and that the earth has both insufficient resources and a limited capacity to absorb waste to enable all its inhabitants to consume at the rates current in the developed world. Consequently it is considered that

global development policies need to be directed towards reducing consumption and waste in rich countries in order to allow poor countries
their fair share of the earth's resources.

Some adherents to the ecocentric view base their thinking on aspects of
James Lovelock's Gaia hypothesis (Lovelock, 1979). Lovelock proposes
that:

> the earth's living matter, air, oceans and land surface form a complex system
> which can be seen as a single living organism which has the capacity to keep our
> planet a fit place for life.

The way in which the planet is thought to regulate conditions to sustain
life is a familiar one to us in geography and depends on the idea of feedback. One of the observations that brought Lovelock to his conclusions
(and serves to illustrate the general principle of self-regulation) was the
discovery that over many millions of years the heat output from the sun
had increased to a level which should have made the earth too hot for life.
However, as the earth heated up, Lovelock suggests that plants evolved
and spread over the earth, taking in carbon dioxide from the atmosphere
and so cooling the earth by allowing more outgoing radiation. Thus life
systems and the physical components of the earth are seen to be involved
in complex interactions which maintain an environment that enables life
to continue. Superficially such a thesis could be interpreted as assuming
that whatever abuses humans inflict upon the planet, the earth will
bounce back and regulate itself. Not so, say the Gaianists. If human activity threatens life on earth then Gaia will respond by eliminating the human
species to allow life in its broader sense to continue:

> Any species (that is, any part of Gaia) that adversely affects the environment is
> doomed; but life goes on . . . Gaia is not purposefully antihuman, but so long as
> we continue to change the global environment against her preferences, we
> encourage our replacement with a more environmentally seemly species.
>
> Lovelock, 1979

Thus far the Gaia hypothesis may appear to represent a somewhat
mechanistic view of the earth. Many ecocentrics, however, would propose that the number and complexity of interactions among the feedback
mechanisms may be beyond our conceptual powers and our ability to
model and predict. The response to such a world view is to recognise this
complexity, and as far as possible to avoid disturbing it. Others have

placed a more spiritual interpretation on Lovelock's ideas, suggesting that once we have established contact with the earth and its energy flows, we know intuitively how to behave appropriately towards her.

The view of an earth which in detail is beyond complete explanation, understanding and prediction, is reinforced by perspectives emerging from the theories of chaos (Gleick, 1987) in which very subtle differences in initial conditions are thought to result in large and unpredictable responses. As Eckersley proposes (1992):

> An ecocentric perspective… recognises that nature is not only more complex than we presently know but also quite possibly more complex than we can know – an insight that has been borne out in the rapidly expanding field of chaos theory.

Many adherents to the ecocentric perspective would not wish to reject scientific explanation as a means of trying to understand the earth. Rather, they would seek to make explicit the achievements and limitations of scientific explanation while opening the way for other means of knowing about the earth based on our senses, feelings and emotions. McDonagh (1986) summarises this view from an educational standpoint:

> We need to tell children a new story about the universe, based upon what we know from science but also imbued with the wonder and mythological colourings that are the natural offspring of reverence.

In contrast to technocentrism, decision-taking is not seen as the preserve of an all-knowing scientific elite but is regarded as a collective endeavour involving devolved power, with many decisions being taken at community level. This clear distinction in the process of decision-taking between the technocentric and ecocentric perspective is perhaps the most significant in educational terms. While a technocentric position only requires the education process to deliver a small, highly trained scientific elite with the skills to understand, model, predict and make decisions on our behalf, ecocentrism requires an ecologically informed world citizenry who are also in touch with themselves, their community and the earth.

One of the streams of thought within ecocentrism which has considerable implication for education rests on the proposal that our outer world view arises from our own inner ecology, our feeling of self-worth and our relationships with those around us. To explore this proposed link between our inner and outer ecologies we might return to the question posed by Randle:

> What ways of thinking, what ways of being, have led us to mistreat the earth and abuse each other?

Capra (1982) and Bookchin (1980) explore this idea by suggesting ways in which social and personal behaviour may become models which influence and inform our values and attitudes towards the natural world:

> Inner fragmentation mirrors our view of the world 'outside' which is seen as a multitude of separate objects and events. The natural environment is treated as if it consisted of separate parts to be exploited by different interest groups. The fragmented view is further split into different nations, races, religious and political groups. The belief that all these fragments – in ourselves, in our environment and in our society – are really separate can be seen as the essential reason for the present series of social, ecological and cultural crises.
>
> Capra, 1982

An extension of the idea that inner fragmentation influences our outer view of the world is proposed by Bookchin. It is suggested that hierarchical social structures imply domination of certain groups and individuals by others. An acceptance of these underlying hierarchical structures within the social context is seen as nurturing the view that people also occupy a position of domination over nature:

> ...the domination of nature first arose within society as parts of its institutionalization into gerontocracies that placed the young in varying degrees of servitude to the old and in patriarchies that placed women in varying degrees of servitude to men – not in any endeavour to 'control' nature or natural forces. Various modes of social institutionalization, not modes of organizing human labor (so crucial to Marx), led to domination hence, domination can be removed only by resolving problematics that have their origins in hierarchy and status, not simply class and the technological control of nature.
>
> Bookchin, 1987; reported in Eckersley, 1992

The implications of such a thesis are far-reaching and would extend environmental education into critiques of how families, workplaces, schools and governments are organised and function. Its implications for environmental education involve confronting the issue that to lead us away from ideas of people being dominant over nature we have first to question certain political, social and personal relationships and the underlying structures that influence them.

There is therefore a viewpoint among some environmentalists that education for environmental change starts with the individual and her or his world view. Since the dominant world view – characterised by consumerism, rationalism, utilitarianism, and reductionism – is identified as lying at the root of environmental problems, then strategies for environmental education would need to challenge these precepts. Not all involved in environmental education would agree, however, and the following section distinguishes three distinct approaches.

Education 'about', 'through' or 'for' the environment?

Several writers draw distinctions between education about, through and for the environment (Fien, 1992), with the different approaches having links with the varying genres of environmental ideology.

Education *about* the environment is generally interpreted as promoting a technocentric perspective. There is an assumption that by knowing more clearly the functioning of the earth as a machine through positivist scientific and economic approaches, appropriate environmental management, often with the aid of new technology, can obviate harmful human impacts without major redirection of political, economic or personal value systems. O'Riordan (1981) suggested that (at the time) this was the dominant form of environmental education. Huckle (1985) proposes that much environmental education has focused on science and geography to teach pupils about the environment, emphasising ecological concepts and technical solutions to environmental problems at the expense of their human causes and of the changes in social systems necessary for solving them.

Fien (1992) sees education *through* the environment as using students' experiences in the environment as a medium for education. Episodes involving direct contact with the environment are considered to offer reality, relevance and practical experience as well as developing an appreciation of places and providing opportunities to acquire a range of practical skills. A fusion of education about and through the environment is characteristic of much common practice in the UK in outdoor education. The approach is typified in the sorts of experiences offered by many field study centres. The potential for fostering environmental concern is recognised if students come to feel the significance of ecosystems and the beauty of landscapes.

Education *for* the environment is viewed as having a more explicit agenda of values education and social change. The educational goals are seen in terms of promoting lifestyles that are compatible with the sustainable and equitable use of resources. The 'for' mode is seen as building on education about and through the environment in order to develop informed concern for the environment, a sensitive environmental ethic and the skills for participating in environmental action. The approach also involves challenging and exploring alternatives to many of the assumptions that are central to the technocentric world view. 'Business as usual' – in economic, social and political terms – is no longer an option in education *for* the environment. Fien (1992) summarises as follows:

> Education *about* and *through* the environment are valuable only in so far as they are used to provide skills and knowledge to support the transformative intentions of education *for* the environment.

Geographical fieldwork as environmental education

A number of traditions within geography have the potential to provide major inputs into programmes of environmental education *about*, *through* and *for* the environment. It is debatable whether any accomplish all three. Geography's endeavours in attempting to understand and explain the earth as a dynamic, holistic system can provide a strong conceptual input into programmes of education *about* the environment, though in a postmodern world we perhaps need to adjust our view of an entirely predictable, 'explainable' earth. Fundamental principles such as the role of feedback in natural systems are frequently explored in physical geography, as are examples of the tendency for human activity to interfere with and disrupt the negative feedback loops which normally maintain natural systems in some sort of equilibrium state.

The fieldwork tradition in geography is strongly reflected in the skills and understanding which Fien (1992) associates with education *through* the environment, as well as offering the potential to increase sensitivity to environments and lead to the building of a personal environmental ethic.

Finally, the learning processes which characterise geographical enquiry, especially if they are rooted in fieldwork, can provide a framework which is able to deliver some, but perhaps not all, of the aims which distinguish education *for* the environment. As the field tradition is central to geography's contribution to environmental education, some further exploration of the varying approaches to field-based activity is required.

In view of the diversity of fieldwork strategies which have evolved over the past thirty years or so, we must ask ourselves what sort of field experiences are most appropriate in the context of environmental education. Personal reflection of our own experiences of geography fieldwork – as school pupils ourselves, as undergraduates, at field study centres and on field courses we have organised for our pupils – may well reveal at least two or three quite distinct approaches. The following sections offer a brief if somewhat personal review of five distinct *genres* of fieldwork. Figure 2.2 attempts to show these different approaches to fieldwork in a diagrammatic form. The vertical axis ranges from more structured, teacher-led approaches to heuristic, pupil-centred activities, while the horizontal axis distinguishes quantitative and qualitative approaches. There are parallels here with the examples of fieldwork strategies identified by Margaret Roberts (Chapter 8) to exemplify teaching styles.

THE FIELD EXCURSION

Those of us of sufficiently advanced years who are of a nostalgic disposition and find it difficult to jettison possessions from the past, may be able to unearth field notebooks from twenty or more years ago whose contents reveal something of the nature of the field excursion. If we were fortunate to have been guided through the landscape by a skilled practitioner who took care to ensure that observations and detail were carefully recorded, we might open a stoutly bound notebook whose pages record in notes and sketches something of the essence of the landscapes we were exploring. Places would have been carefully grid-referenced and then described in what today would be considered a somewhat holistic approach. A record of the landscape as a palimpsest would often emerge, with geology and structure as the underlying influence but bearing mantles of soil, vegetation and human use, both past and present. Locations might well have been organised in the form of a transect perhaps from

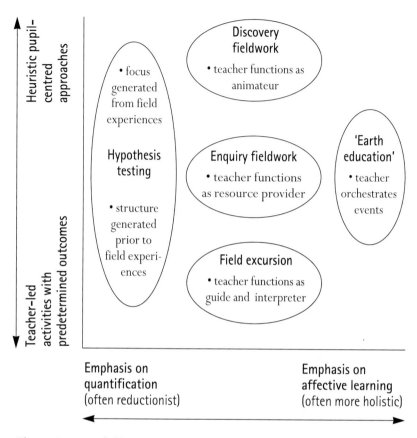

Figure 2.2 Some fieldwork strategies

north to south across Purbeck or the Weald, or from east to west across one or other flank of the Pennines in order to bring out regional diversity and landscape change across a variety of underlying geological formations. Landscape descriptions would be illuminated with the pencilled outlines of annotated field sketches, the execution of which developed skills in observation, recording and interpretation. Goudie (1994) recognises the value of such landscape studies as a stimulus to an interest which engages the lay person as much as the student of geography, and quotes Wooldridge in support of the landscape tradition:

> By what right can we withhold a knowledge of how our terrestrial home is constructed, the meaning of its scenery and the patterns of its sky. The world contains not only factories, farms, railway sidings, market places, etc., but the blue hills on the skyline, the winding valleys which traverse them, russet bracken

covered slopes, and heather fells and the ever changing incident of long and varied coastlines.

> Wooldridge, 1949: 14–15

It is easy to criticise the traditional field excursion from a present-day
pedagogic standpoint: the relatively passive role of the student; the role of
the field leader as the omniscient provider of knowledge; the lack of input
of the student into the learning process; the somewhat uncritical interpretation of landscape as if it were devoid of environmental, social or
political conflict. But for those who experienced this type of fieldwork,
most would recall the pleasure and satisfaction of acquiring the skills to
'read' and interpret a landscape in its wholeness and thereby to grasp
something of the essence of place.

MADE TO MEASURE – FIELDWORK AND THE QUANTITATIVE REVOLUTION

It is interesting to reflect upon whether the changing strategies adopted in
geographical fieldwork have been driven by changing paradigms in the
subject or by new thinking in pedagogy and ideas concerning the nature of
learning. Was the enthusiasm with which fieldwork practitioners
embraced quantification and hypothesis testing in the 1970s a response to
the power of the quantitative revolution in geography as a whole, or was
the new methodology perceived to offer fresh opportunities for different
ways of learning in the field which obviated the traditionally passive role
of the student? Perhaps both explanations are necessary to account for the
startling redirection of much geographical fieldwork during the 1970s.
The adoption of the hypothetico-deductive system as the dominant
framework for the organisation and practice of field-based activities
proved instantly popular with many school teachers and tutors in field
study centres, while students experiencing this fresh approach tended to
respond positively to their more active roles in the field. Fitzgerald *et al.*
(1970) offered early examples of hypothesis testing applied to fieldwork
in human geography.

The establishment of hypotheses before venturing forth into the field
to measure and collect data provided a tangible structure and purpose to
the field day. Pupils felt a degree of ownership of the field study, having
had at least some input, albeit on occasions a somewhat illusory one, into

the hypotheses to be tested. Most field leaders of the time would probably admit to some degree of manipulation in the process of hypothesis generation. It is remarkable how few pupils seemed surprised that both the equipment and recording sheets miraculously matched the variables which they had identified as being of importance in 'their' hypotheses!

The nature of the hypotheses upon which field data were then collected was normally based on *a priori* models, rather than on ideas which had arisen from a pupil's own experience of the field environment. It was fun on occasions to deliberately encourage hypotheses which were based on now discredited models, hypotheses which the field leader knew would be negated by the field data. 'Davis bashing', for example, became a popular pursuit not only because the measurement of stream velocity in increasingly higher-order streams was recreationally enjoyable for most (but not all) pupils, but because the discovery that river velocity does not generally decrease downstream was a revelation to pupils previously fed on the Davisian model of Youth, Maturity and Old Age. There was an element of self-satisfaction in the iconoclastic toppling of old ideas.

From a pedagogic standpoint the new quantitative approach encouraged a high level of student involvement and physical activity which, at least superficially, created the impression of active learning in the heuristic tradition. Yet, in retrospect, and in the broader context of education *for* the environment (and for all pupils), a number of limitations became apparent. An inventory of such criticisms might focus on the following concerns.

- The reliance of the hypothetico-deductive methodology on logical positivism denied the validity of non-quantifiable forms of knowledge and experience. Feelings, emotions, sensations and opinion were negated because the prevailing way of thinking only permitted quantifiable forms of evidence to be valid.
- The *a priori* models which were often used in the process of hypothesis formation were often reductionist and narrow, focusing on either form *or* process, and on either physical *or* human systems.
- This reductionism reinforced the implicit view of a mechanistic earth which could be broken down into convenient compartments. Each of these often provided a theme for a day's fieldwork which ensured focused and manageable units of study but failed to deliver

a holistic and integrated landscape view in which interactions between the subsystems were vital to an understanding of the functioning of the whole.

- Basing studies on models and hypotheses together with the search for generally applicable explanations of processes, forms or patterns in the landscape led us away from any sense of the uniqueness of place. Did this approach contribute to growing placelessness by not revealing and valuing the idiographic or place-unique tradition in geography? The nomothetic, law-seeking approach contrasted with the strong sense of place previously engendered by the traditional field excursion.

- As with the field excursion, the quantitative approach did little initially to provoke a critical appraisal of what was being studied. Hypothesis testing and explanation of patterns and processes became ends in themselves. Studies of rivers explored channel relationships, while graphs and correlation coefficients helped us to see how channels were adjusting towards an equilibrium state along their course. Consideration of human modifications to the system and the consequences thereof, tended to be introduced retrospectively if at all. In urban environments it was felt to be sufficient to compare the real land-use distributions in towns and cities with predictions derived from largely economically based models. There was often little focus on the implications of the patterns which were revealed in terms of inequality, quality of life or aesthetic values.

ENQUIRY-BASED FIELDWORK

While fulfilling some worthwhile educational objectives, some disquiet with the purely quantitative approach to fieldwork was developing by the late 1970s. This paralleled development and change in both geography and geography education. The search for relevance and application in physical geography and the emergence of humanistic and more behaviourally oriented approaches in human geography coincided with the desire in geography education to foster greater student autonomy. These changes in geographical paradigms and pedagogy were also contemporaneous with a burgeoning concern over human mistreatment of the earth and its resources. The scene was set for new ways of learning in geography which addressed these emerging concerns.

Enquiry-based strategies which adopted more heuristic approaches are evident in much of the fieldwork guidance written in the 1960s. Long and Roberson (1966), Archer and Dalton (1968) and Dilke (1965) all favour approaches which embrace enquiry to a lesser or greater degree and thereby go some way to achieving the objective of education *through* the environment. It was not until the emergence of fieldwork geared to the Geography 16–19 Project that enquiry methods were combined with investigations into people–environment issues. Hart (1983) outlines early examples of enquiry-based investigations which were also focused on issues. Some of these examples began to achieve some of the transformative intentions of education *for* the environment, though often implicitly rather than explicitly.

In practice, some enquiry-based fieldwork continued to suffer from somewhat reductionist perspectives, often through failing to ask the most important questions at the outset. Slater (1982), in the context of scientific, humanistic and more critical viewpoints, focuses on question identification as the key to successful learning through geography:

> Question identification can be usefully adopted as the first procedure in planning a learning activity. Questions are thus the initial and continually guiding signposts which help us to organise and plan pathways leading students to meaningful learning through geography.

These questions should not be too narrowly focused thereby giving limited scope for exploring the wider context and more far-reaching causes and consequences surrounding people–environment issues. In practice, some examples of fieldwork enquiries were often based on narrowly defined locational questions. 'Which is the best site for a reservoir?', 'Which is the best route for the motorway?' and 'Where is the best location for the new superstore?' were the kinds of question frequently asked. Enquiries arising from these sorts of questions fulfilled most of the criteria for enquiry-based investigations and provided scope for factual and values enquiries, but they left more fundamental questions not only unanswered but also unasked. By asking such narrow questions there was no encouragement to explore the demand side of resource issues, only the 'where' of the supply side. For example, alternative strategies to water resource use which recognise the finite nature of the resource and ways of reducing demand need never be confronted in an investigation which only considers where the next reservoir should be built. Similarly, the social causes and resource consequences of unbridled consumerism need never be explored in a study which is only concerned with where the next superstore should be located.

DISCOVERY FIELDWORK

The emergence of the discovery approach to outdoor learning arose from a sense that to be truly heuristic, not only should pupils be finding out for themselves during the investigative phase of an activity, but the entire direction and focus of a study should arise from a pupil's spontaneous interaction with an environment.

Thus in its purest form, discovery fieldwork commences with an entirely unstructured and undirected exploration of an environment. The teacher would ideally not lead but follow the inclinations of a group of pupils, functioning as *animateur*, waiting to be asked questions about features that are encountered in which pupils express a spontaneous interest, then countering questions from pupils with further questions. In reality those who have taken on the role of *animateur* with pupils in the field would admit to a degree of stage management through subtle intervention using body language and facial expression.

On return from the discovery walk, students would then brainstorm memorable experiences and observations from the day. Individuals or small groups would be encouraged to pursue a more in-depth investigation of some aspect of the locality which they found particularly memorable or interesting. These investigations might be based on scientific enquiry, compiling and editing a video or sound recording, artwork, drama or poetry. The culmination of these endeavours would take the form of some sort of programme of presentations and reflection, during which the larger group would re-unite and show appreciation of the work of individuals or small groups.

While offering a highly pupil-centred approach to learning which draws on pupils' own experience of environments at all stages, discovery learning is not without its critics. As education *for* the environment, the approach has a number of limitations in that the restricted opportunity for the *animateur* to guide both the focus and process of learning may result in outcomes which are superficial and lack both depth and a critical element. An example from a residential experience in south Devon which adopted the discovery approach serves to illustrate some of the constraints. Brainstorming after a day of unstructured discovery gave rise to a rich assemblage of experiences drawing from diverse environments which included lake, marsh, woodland, farmland, coasts and settlements and touched on geography, ecology, local history, social factors and folklore. The most memorable feature for most students, however, was a Second World War Sherman tank which had been restored and put on display as a reminder of military activity in the area prior to the D-Day landings. When the range of resources available for use in investigations was described, which included video equipment, and pupils were then asked to select their topic and approach, making a video about the tank proved to be the exclusively popular option. While an investigation involving the tank had the potential to provide an opening into an important and dramatic period of local history, the popularity of the topic, together with the selection of video as the favoured medium of study, highlighted the influence that a dominantly technocentric perspective was having on students' decisions. Consequently, students remained unaware of many of the more subtle ecological and social issues in the local environment, which only a more teacher-led approach would have revealed.

EARTH EDUCATION

The approaches to environmental education which have become known as 'earth education' have not in general been developed by geographers. They are included here because the techniques go some way to achieving that elusive balance between learning activities which engage the emotions and the senses on the one hand, and understanding of ecological and geographical principles on the other. The approach owes much to the pioneering work of Steve Van Matre and colleagues (Van Matre, 1979) while working with children in summer camps in North America where the 'Sunship Earth' programme was developed. It has been adopted extensively in the UK by countryside rangers working with children in country parks and on nature reserves, through the sensory experiences of 'Earthwalks'. As originally developed by Van Matre, the programmes represent highly integrated activities which fulfil many of the criteria of learning *about*, *through* and *for* the environment. The aims focus on both cognitive and affective learning, enabling participants to develop a clear view of their place in the universe, as well as developing a sense of wonder about natural processes.

> ...we wanted to cast a point of reference for each of our learners – to convey something about their place in the universe. We hoped to establish this sense of place forever in their understandings, or perhaps more accurately in their *feelings*, for we wanted it to become embedded inside them, where it would be a continued source of awareness about who and where they were. Second, like a friendly wizard, we wanted to convey to them a feeling for life's wondrous mysteries in which they are bound up with every other living thing on earth. And we hoped that this recognition of miraculous interrelationship would become a mental touchstone against which they could forever check their actions.

Van Matre justifies a largely non-quantitative approach in the following terms:

> ...we feared entrapment by the idea that things are only real if they can be measured. Many of life's most rewarding, enriching and heartfelt experiences can barely be put into words, let alone placed on a scale. If we relied too much upon the usual processes of collecting and testing, what would happen to our goals of instilling a sense of wonder, a sense of place, and a reverence for life? If we failed to develop appreciations in our haste to convey understandings, if we overemphasised analytical skills at the expense of deep natural experiences, what would we gain – people who could take life apart, but cared nothing for keeping it together?
>
> Van Matre, 1979

The aims of earth education are distinctive among the many genres of environmental education in that they combine a scientific understanding of ecosystem processes with a somewhat pagan reverence for nature. The approach also aims to embody some of the 'transformative intentions' which Fien distinguishes as being a key feature of education *for* the environment, though these intentions are often implicit rather than explicit.

Randle (1989) provides a useful précis of earth education, summarising the 'whys, whats and ways' of the approach, and offers a checklist of criteria which characterise the method. Further examples of activities using the earth education approach are provided by Cornell (1979).

A critique of fieldwork practice – evidence from recent research

When developing field-based activities, it is not uncommon to experience a tension of purpose. On the one hand there is a concern to ensure that students come away from the field experience with a clear understanding of geographical concepts, of the processes at work in the landscape, the interdependency between a range of variables and the interplay between people and the environment. Though often not clearly stated in our aims and objectives, there may also be the implicit intention or hope that students will return from their direct contact with the outdoors with memories of a less tangible kind. Phrases such as 'an appreciation of sense of place', 'a sense of wonder', 'new insights into the way other people live' spring to mind. Much of the discussion about both fieldwork in geography and the development of activities in environmental education focuses on this balance between cognitive and affective learning.

There are several examples in research into the outcomes of environmental education experiences where researchers have reported some degree of frustration among students with the limited opportunities for them to express their feelings about places and events during fieldwork. Harvey (1991) undertook detailed evaluations of the experiences of Advanced level (16 to 19 year-old) students during and after their residential fieldwork. A number of tensions emerged between the cognitive and affective dimensions of the activities, which are well illustrated by the following quotation from a student:

> …I found myself getting really annoyed at what had been done to this village. I'm not sure that geographers are supposed to get worked up. They're just supposed to analyse. But this was the reason that I got enthusiastic about what we were doing.

The source of this revealing reflection was the diary kept by one of a group of students who had been asked by Harvey to record not only the day-to-day activities on the field course but also her feelings about those activities. She was referring to the ruined village of Hallsands in south Devon where offshore dredging of gravel is thought to have brought about a reduction in the level of a shingle beach leading to the destruction of the adjacent settlement in subsequent storms. The field experience at the ruined village had taken the form of a loosely structured, somewhat anecdotal visit in which local folklore had been used to convey some of the hardships experienced by villagers as their village was destroyed by the sea. This took place within what was otherwise a highly structured quantitative approach which aimed to develop explanations of coastal processes and sediment movement on the Start Bay coast.

The significance of the student's remarks lie partly in her perceptions of the nature of geography. The subject was seen as being rather coldly analytical, with little space for emotion and feeling about events and places. Moreover, the source of her interest in what was otherwise a very quantitative investigation based around tightly drawn-up hypotheses, was her feeling of anger about past abuse of an environment. Would students whose feelings were not aroused in this way experience the study purely as a scientific investigation from which they remained emotionally detached?

In his evaluation of field activities where the prevailing methodology was based on the hypothetico-deductive system, Harvey distinguishes a range of positive outcomes but also identifies some major limitations which he regards as arising largely from the nature of the fieldwork methodology. Among the positive outcomes, Harvey distinguished the following:

- increased motivation and enthusiasm for the subject aided by novel milieu
- technical competency in a range of field, laboratory and data-handling skills
- opportunity to relate to peers and teachers in a new physical and social setting
- exemplification of theoretical ideas and provision of case studies
- some increase in conceptual understanding
- creation of intellectual and physical challenges
- strengthening of technical and specialised vocabulary
- contribution to personal and social development, and growth in self-confidence and self-esteem
- growth in respect for others and emphasis on collaboration rather than competition.

Harvey also identifies a number of limitations of the fieldwork experience. These focus on the limited opportunities for students to determine the direction of the course, and an overemphasis on conceptual understanding to the detriment of affective learning. He includes the following observations:

- foci of studies predetermined rather than arising from students' own field experiences and perceptions
- restricted opportunities for students to clarify their own values positions on issues
- reinforcement of students' perception that the teacher is primarily responsible for the organisation of learning
- tension of purpose between thorough and clear treatment of concepts, and equipping students with the skills to carry out independent investigation
- dependency of conceptual understanding on processed data rather than direct field experiences
- weak links between observations in the field and subsequent data processing
- opportunities for transferring field experiences into examination answers often missed
- environmental decisions considered only in the light of objective and neutral facts emerging from hypothesis testing
- environmental issues tending to be considered from a techno-centric perspective
- environmental planning and management tacked onto a study, not central to it
- lack of integration of subsystems/themes into a holistic view.

In summary, Harvey's interpretation of his findings was that a greater balance needed to be struck between attention to conceptual understanding and consideration of the neglected area of affective learning and experience.

Pocock (1983) expresses similar reservations concerning fieldwork based upon rigid hypothesis testing. It was seen to be overprescriptive and teacher-dominated. While pupils were active in the field collecting data, their interaction with that environment was reduced to operationalising a set of instructions and not directed to environmental exploration, personal reflection and discovery.

Further reservations about highly quantitative field activities focus on the limited opportunities for pupils to develop a sense of place. Brough (1983), reflecting on village fieldwork over a number of years, recognised that even after the whole repertoire of fieldwork techniques had been practised, *the essence of the place remained elusive*.

Other research (Mackenzie and White, 1982) focuses on the importance of episodes in producing memorable experiences from fieldwork. An episode has the capacity to make a connection between a memorable event in which an individual participated, and a principle or concept under investigation. The concept becomes memorable through its association with an event which involved active participation.

In critically reviewing the range of approaches which have been used in geographical fieldwork and in the broader context of environmental education, a number of key questions can be applied if we are interested in dealing with some of the limitations identified by Harvey:

- To what extent is the approach based on a technocentric or ecocentric perspective?
- To what extent is the experience drawing on students' own direct experience of an environment?
- To what extent does the experience involve emotional engagement as well as cognitive understanding?
- To what extent is understanding based on forms of experience other than the quantifiable?
- Does it provide opportunities to use the senses and develop a personal relationship with the natural world?

Conclusion

If after considering our current approaches we feel the need for change, where do we look for inspiration? Philosophically and pedagogically, some of the answers may come from an approach to education which consciously brings together the cognitive and the affective – understanding and feeling – so that the two interact and refine each other. L.A. Reid (Reid, 1986) has given us a basis for this kind of thinking, as Slater (1994) has recently reminded us. If we accept that few activities in education are value free, then our sources of inspiration are inevitably linked to the ideological perspectives with which we feel most comfortable.

If we feel content with a technology-centred view of the earth and are confident in the power of science to offer understanding, explanations and solutions, then we might imagine that we need look no further than the abundant materials on hypothesis-based research designs, quantitative techniques and analytical statistical methods.

If we are interested in pursuing some of the implications of an overtly ecocentric perspective then we may have to search more widely and diligently if we are to unearth the more imaginative and innovatory ideas. We may need to delve into projects and resources which may not initially appear to be primarily geographical or educational in their purpose. The most interesting ideas may come from small-scale innovations which are happening in spite of rather than because of centralised decisions from the educational establishment. These are often in remote places and the outcomes may not always see the light of day in conventional published form.

Damian Randle's *Teaching Green* (Randle, 1989) typifies the eclectic approach. In exploring and linking 'inner' and 'outer' ecologies, and in drawing together all the themes which inform a holistic educational view, Randle brings together ideas and activities from teachers with roots in every area of the curriculum. A similarly critical and holistic perspective is taken in a number of recent publications from the World Wide Fund for Nature. These include the companion volumes *Greenprints for Changing Schools* (Greig, Pike and Selby, 1989) and *Earthrights – education as if the planet really mattered* (Greig, Pike and Selby, 1987), as well as the stimulating resources and activities tackling education for sustainability from John Huckle (Huckle, 1988, 1993).

In terms of educational projects and activities *for* the environment, one could point to residential centres such as the eco-cabin operation at the Centre for Alternative Technology in Wales, where environmental fieldwork can be integrated with personal, practical involvement in resource and energy use in the domestic setting during a field course. In such settings, students are able to retreat from the city with its seemingly linear throughputs of energy and materials, and are able to have the experience of using energy which has been generated benignly from renewable sources on the doorstep. Links are re-established with the soil and biological productivity through using facilities such as composting toilets, an experience which can then be compared with conventional urban systems of wastewater treatment which disrupt nutrient cycles.

One could point to the visionary work of Satish Kumar, peace campaigner and environmental educator, initially in setting up the first Small School in north Devon with its integration of craft skills and domestic operations into the conventional curriculum, and more recently, the establishment of Schumacher College at Dartington, which offers alternative higher education opportunities firmly rooted in the ecocentric perspective (Kumar, 1992).

To take an example from the less developed world, the work of Helena Norberg-Hodge in Ladhak represents an essentially educational initiative which challenges the stifling of a formerly sustainable traditional culture beneath the onslaught of environmentally and socially degrading consumerism (Norberg-Hodge, 1991). From North America we might draw on the approaches adopted by David Orr who set in motion an autonomous student project to investigate the energy and resource implications of the operations of the campus canteen, initiated through an analysis of the kitchen invoices (Orr, 1993). A rich source for innovatory practical fieldwork is Bill Mollison's work on permaculture, in which physical geography can contribute to the design of productive and diverse sustainable landscapes (Mollison, 1991).

The distinctive feature of these diverse projects are that they involve people doing practical things within the contexts of sustainability, discovering through doing, and challenging a world view which has resulted in the abuses of people and planet.

BIBLIOGRAPHY
Archer, J.E. and Dalton, T.H. (1968) *Fieldwork in Geography*, Batsford.
Beare, H. and Slaughter, R. (1993) *Education for the Twenty-first Century*, Routledge.
Bookchin, M. (1980) *Toward an Ecological Society*, Black Rose Books.
Booth, R. (1990) *Ecology in the National Curriculum – A Practical Guide to Using School Grounds*, Learning through Landscapes Trust.
Brough, E. (1983) 'Geography through art', in Huckle, J. (ed.) *Geography Education: Reflection and Action*, Oxford University Press.

Cade, A. (1991) *Policies for Environmental Education and Training: 1992 and Beyond*, English Nature.

Capra, F. (1982) *The Turning Point – Science, Society and the Rising Culture*, Flamingo.

Carwardine, M. (1990) *The World Wide Fund for Nature Environmental Handbook*, Macdonald Optima.

Cornell, J. (1979) *Sharing Nature with Children – A Parents and Teachers Nature Handbook*, Exley Publications.

Dilke, M.S. (ed.) (1965) *Field Studies for Schools*, Vol.1 The purpose and organisation of field studies, Rivingtons.

Eckersley, R. (1992) *Environmentalism and Political Theory: Towards an Ecocentric Approach*, UCL Press.

Fien, J. (1993) *Education for the Environment: Critical Curriculum Theorising and Environmental Education*, Deakin University Press, Australia.

Fitzgerald, B. *et al.* (1970) 'Hypothesis testing in the field', *Teaching Geography*, no. 11, Geographical Association.

Gleick, J. (1987) *Chaos*, Heinemann.

Greig, S., Pike, G. and Selby, D. (1987) *Earthrights – Education as if the Planet Really Mattered*, World Wide Fund for Nature/Kogan Page.

 (1989) *Greenprints for Changing Schools*, World Wide Fund for Nature/Kogan Page.

Goudie, A. (1994) 'The nature of physical geography: a view from the drylands', *Geography,* 79(3).

Harman, W. (1988) *Global Mind Change: The Promise of the Last Years of the Twentieth Century*, Indianapolis: Knowledge Systems Inc.

Hart, C. (1983) *Fieldwork the 16–19 Way*, Occasional Paper no. 4, Schools Council.

Harvey, P.K. (1991) 'The role and value of A-level geography fieldwork: a case study', unpublished PhD thesis, University of Durham.

Huckle, J. (1983) *Geography Education: Reflection and Action*, Oxford University Press.

 (1985) 'Geography and schooling', in Johnson, R.J. (ed.) *The Future of Geography*, Methuen.

 (1988) *What We Consume*, World Wide Fund for Nature/Richmond.

 (1990) 'Environmental education: teaching for a sustainable future', in Dufour, B. (ed.) *The New Social Curriculum*, Cambridge University Press.

 (1993) *Our Consumer Society*, World Wide Fund for Nature/Richmond.

King, A. and Clifford, S. (1985) *Holding your Ground – An Action Guide to Local Conservation*, Wildwood House.

Kumar, S. (1992) *No Destination*, Green Books, Devon.

Lacey, C. and Williams, R. (1987) *Education, Ecology and Development*, World Wide Fund for Nature/Kogan Page.

Long, M. and Roberson, B. (1966) *Teaching Geography*, Heinemann.

Lovelock, J. (1979) *Gaia – A New Look at Life on Earth*, Oxford University Press.

Lovelock, J. (1991) *Gaia: The Practical Science of Planetary Medicine*, Gaia Books.

Mackenzie, A.A. and White, R.T. (1982) 'Fieldwork in geography and long-term memory structures', *American Education Research Journal*, 19(4).

McDonagh, S. (1986) *To Care for the Earth: A Call to a New Theology*, Geoffrey Chapman.

McPartland, M. and Harvey, P.K. (1987) 'A question of fieldwork', *Teaching Geography*, 12(4).

Mollison, W. (1991) *Introduction to Permaculture*, NSW Australia: Tagari Publications.

National Curriculum Council (1990) *Curriculum Guidance Series no. 7. Environmental Education*, National Curriculum Council.

Norberg-Hodge, H. (1991) *Ancient Futures*, Rider Books.

O'Riordan, T. (1981) 'Environmentalism and education', *Journal of Geography in Higher Education*, 5(1):3–18.

Orr, D. (1993) *Earth in Mind – On Education, Environment and the Human Prospect*, Washington DC: Island Press.

Pepper, D. (1984) *Roots of Modern Environmentalism*, Croom-Helm.

(1987) 'The basis of a radical curriculum in environmental education', in Lacey, C. and Williams, R. (eds) *Education, Ecology and Development*, World Wide Fund for Nature/Kogan Page.

(1993) *Eco-socialism, from Deep Ecology to Social Justice*, Routledge.

Pike, G. and Selby, D. (1988) *Global Teacher, Global Learner*, Hodder and Stoughton.

Pocock, D. (1983) 'Geographical fieldwork: an experiential perspective', *Geography*, 88:319–25.

Randle, D. (1989) *Teaching Green – A Parent's Guide to Education for Life on Earth*, Green print, Merlin Press.

Reid, L.A. (1986) *Ways of Understanding and Education*, Heinemann.

Seabrook, J. (1990) *The Myth of the Market – Promises and Illusions*, Green Books, Devon.

Slater, F. (1982) *Learning through Geography*, Heinemann.

(1994) 'Education through geography: knowledge, understanding, values and culture', *Geography*, 79(2).

Van Matre, S. (1979) *Sunship Earth – An Acclimatization Program for Outdoor Learning*, Martinsville, Indiana: American Camping Association.

Wooldridge, S.W. (1949) 'On taking the Ge out of Geography', *Geography*, 34:9–18.

Young, K. (1990) *Using School Grounds as an Educational Resource*, Winchester: Learning Through Landscapes Trust.

3 What a Carve Up!
New times for geography teaching

John Morgan

Towards the end of Jonathan Coe's novel *What a Carve Up!* (1994) which is, amongst other things, a social history of Thatcherism, the narrator, Michael Owen, experiences a moment when he realises how seemingly distant events in fact impinge directly on the quality of his life. His sick girlfriend is waiting in vain for a hospital bed, which is unavailable partly because hospital wards are being commandeered for wounded soldiers from the impending war in the Gulf. Michael discovers that the family of capitalists about whom he is writing a biography, have had a great impact on his personal world. Thomas Winshaw's swindling of the pension scheme of the firm that his father worked for led to his redundancy and subsequent depression, before his death through eating junk food from Dorothy Winshaw's torture-chamber of a farm, and Henry Winshaw played his part in the running-down of the National Health Service and the death of Michael's girlfriend.

For this leftward politically inclined geography teacher in the 1990s, Coe's novel is interesting reading. It touches on many of the themes I taught about during the 1980s – inequality between rich and poor, modern capital-intensive agricultural systems, the decline of the welfare state, the geography of peace and war. In this sense the novel serves as social realism, a rage against material injustice and a society in which welfare is rejected in the name of profits. But in Coe's novel, the criminals get their come-uppance, gruesomely murdered in a manner that befits their activities in late capitalism. This, the reader knows, is a dream of narrative closure, a utopian impulse for a world where everything can be explained and solved. The governing elite of Britain is not a family, and cannot be called to answer for their crimes. Things are not so simple.

In this essay I want to discuss my own struggle as a geography teacher with the two messages of Coe's novel. Specifically, to register my shift from social realism with its claim to be able to provide a coherent account of events and processes, to a less confident, less all-embracing view of the social world, one that is sceptical of claims of large-scale social change. To do this, I first provide here some context for this work.

Susan Smith (1989) points out that, over the last two decades, geography as an academic discipline has provided an alternative to the apolitical quantitative 'revolution' and the unqualified individualism of classical economics and behavioural science. The initial impetus came from Harvey (1973) and Peet (1977), and the idea that capitalist societies are the product of a power struggle between competing interest groups over the control of the means of producing and distributing material resources is an established theme in critical geographical work. Growing out of this 'conflict' perspective were welfare studies (Smith, 1977; Knox, 1989) which showed a concern with poverty, and studies concerned with the gender divisions within cities (Women and Geography Study Group, 1984) and the role of racism in structuring residential segregation (Jackson, 1987). Additionally, this tradition embraces studies that seek to explain the social and economic causes of environmental degradation, resource depletion and maldistribution (Emel and Peet, 1989).

There is no simple relationship between developments in academic geography and school geography, but the conflict tradition has found a space within schools (Huckle, 1983, 1988; Fien and Gerber, 1988). Teachers within this tradition are likely to draw upon critical social theories associated with feminism, neo-Marxism and environmentalism to design lessons which encourage students to reflect critically on forms of development that meet social needs and promote environmental welfare. The 1980s was a difficult time for such geography teachers, as they struggled to come to terms with the social and political upheavals associated with the continued success of Thatcherism and the seeming decline of working-class politics (see Hall, 1988). Leadbeater (1989) argues that the Thatcherite project served to erode the old Left's sense of collectivism, including a loss of trust in the state's ability to act as guardian of collective social interests; the decay of traditional work-based solidarities and communality; and the revolt against centralising sameness. Smith argues that within academic geography, the authority of the conflict approach has been undermined as the political consensus on the immorality of inequality and the role of state intervention dissolved. The conflict sociology theories of the 'old' Left are increasingly questionable as a means to analyse the 'New Times', and Smith urges geographers to join the struggle to realise an alternative. Thrift (1992), too, discusses the questions posed by Thatcherism for critical social theory, and documents the responses. It is part of this response that I discuss in this essay, namely the supposed shift to 'postmodernity'.

'Postmodernity' and 'postmodernism' are terms routinely used to refer to a variety of changes in architecture, the arts, culture and social life more generally. Dear (1988) regards postmodernism as a 'revolt against the rationality of modernism' (p.265), a search for a philosophy freed from ultimate foundations, and a world-view which rejects 'totalizing discourse' or 'metanarratives' that seek to explain complexity with few variables. Following Featherstone (1991), my discussion here distinguishes between 'postmodernity' as a new *epoch* in economic, social and cultural life, and 'postmodernism' as a style and by extension a *method* of studying social science. I discuss two recent geographical texts that make sense of the condition of postmodernity in different ways, before outlining the challenge postmodernism poses for current forms of social science, making reference to geography. In conclusion, I offer some comments about what all this means for geography teachers working in schools and colleges.

David Harvey and the condition of postmodernity

The concept of place has enjoyed a revival in human geography in recent years (Jackson and Penrose, 1993). For geography teachers, the primary concern is to describe what goes on in places and explain the processes at work. For instance, how can we explain the influx of inward investment by Japanese companies in Britain, or why did some parts of some British cities experience civil unrest in 1991? One approach to answering these questions is to apply the 'new Right' analysis of society to places. In this view, the 'structures', markets and institutions of a place are reduced to the uncoordinated actions of individuals, and social and economic order is the result of spontaneous accumulations of rational choices. Places are to be regarded as no more than the sum of their parts. Hence places that are economically prosperous are reaping the rewards of their inhabitants applying market forces, along with the necessary characteristics of self-interest, hard work, flexibility, self-reliance, private property, patriarchal family values and the distrust of state interference. Similarly, social patterns such as residential differentiation are the result of rational decisions which individuals or families take in the housing market. New Right economics thus tries to create the 'isotropic plain' beloved of the 'quantitative revolution' of the 1960s, long after geographers realised the world is not an isotropic plain (Johnston, 1991). This form of analysis, with its associated political agenda, is unacceptable for geographers raised in the tradition of conflict theory. The evidence is that such an approach is inadequate as an attempt to explain changes occurring within and between places. Instead, we can turn to developments in economic and social theory for more convincing accounts of the new times.

In Western intellectual circles, the last decade has been characterised by debates which have focused on various transformations of economic and political life, involving the shift from 'Fordist' to 'post-Fordist' society (Murray, 1989), from 'organised' to 'disorganised' capitalism (Lash and Urry, 1987), from an 'industrial' to a 'post-industrial' society, or from an 'industrial' to an 'information' society. In each case it is argued that a particular form of society rooted in an early part of this century is undergoing transformation. Following Harvey I shall refer to this new condition as one of 'postmodernity', and my discussion here will be limited to his account.

Harvey (1989), in *The Condition of Postmodernity*, documents the shift from Fordism to a new regime of 'flexible accumulation'. He retrospectively dates the sea-change in the political economy of advanced capitalism as 1972. Symbolically the change was marked by the demolition of a modernist architectural project in Paris which was designed for housing low-income people but then condemned as uninhabitable. According to Harvey, the post-1972 era is marked by profound changes in the way capital accumulation is achieved. The new regime is characterised by flexibility with respect to labour processes and markets, products and patterns of consumption. The 'new regime of accumulation' has been called 'post-Fordism', because one of its main features is a move away from assembly-line production techniques to smaller-scale 'just-in-time' production. Greater geographical mobility is a feature of this regime as firms switch production to zones of easier labour control. Other features of this new regime include mergers, increasing centralisation of ownership, intensified rates of innovation and the increasing autonomy of banking and finance capital.

According to Harvey, what makes this latest transformation of capitalist social relations disturbing is the intensity and depth of this new burst of 'time–space compression' – the speeding-up of global processes, so that the world feels smaller and distances shorter, so that events in one place have an immediate impact on people and places a long distance away. As Harvey describes it:

> As space appears to shrink to a 'global' village of telecommunications and a 'spaceship earth' of economic and ecological inter-dependencies – to use just two familiar and everyday images – and as time horizons shorten to the point where the present is all there is, so we have to learn to cope with an overwhelming sense of compression of our spatial and temporal worlds.
>
> 1989:240

Harvey argues that a whole range of cultural changes is linked to this new regime of flexible accumulation. In what follows I will summarise some of the consequences of the new round of 'time–space compression' and their implications for places. This discussion is based on Lash and Urry (1994).

The speeding-up of economic and social life ushers in a whole set of changes, best summarised by the idea that 'I want the future now' and the search for instantaneous gratification (Adam, 1990:140). This results from the way in which geographically distant events are brought into our everyday lives, and leads to the development of the three-minute culture or video time in which events come thick and fast and appear to have no particular connection with each other. The future is no longer something in which people appear to trust. We are witnessing the advent of a disposable, 'throwaway society' marked by ephemerality and volatility in fashions, products, labour, ideas and images – in short a society in which the 'temporary contract' is everything.

In addition, people have more control over their use of space and time. Standard life patterns are increasingly replaced by personalised, subjective 'life calendars' (Giddens, 1991:Ch.6). Trust and commitment over time are less geared to institutions and more a matter of subjective choice.

People are less tied-in with the needs of family, generation, place, kinship, religion, and so on which used to give order and structure to life. Morality becomes a private matter, less related to social roles (Giddens, 1991: 146–8). The 'time–space' paths of individuals are desynchronised. There is a greatly increased variation in people's times. Life is less collectively organised as mass consumption gives way to more varied and segmented patterns. Indicators of this process include the increased significance of 'grazing': that is, not eating at fixed mealtimes in the same place with the family or workmates; the rapid growth of free and independent travel; the growth in flexitime working patterns; the development of VCR culture which erodes any sense of an authentic shared watching of events; and the emphasis placed on 'quality time' in many people's lives, those short but sweet moments of uninterrupted interaction between people (for example, the romantic dinner or short-break holiday).

Harvey paints a picture of a postmodern dystopia, characterised by a depthlessness and a flattening of effect as places are transformed into images by the acceleration of people and objects. All objects, including townscapes and landscapes, become homogenised, flattened and disposable, while social relationships are empty and meaningless and lack long-term commitment. Other analysts share Harvey's view. Soja (1989) is also disturbed by what he calls the 'theme park' nature of urban areas echoing Jameson's (1984) picture of a postmodern society in the grip of an orgy of artificial and superficial consumption. We can see postmodern landscapes as increasingly important sites of consumption (the cathedrals of capitalism). Examples might include Main Street in EuroDisney, or the themed Mediterranean village at the MetroCentre near Gateshead. Sharon Zukin (1992) describes how property developers have constructed new 'landscapes of power' for visual consumption. These artificial landscapes signal the victory of the market over the vernacular, and pose problems for people's social identities which have historically been founded on place, on where people have come from or moved to. Postmodern landscapes are consumed; they are not places that people come from or live in. Postmodernity involves the conquest of space by instantaneous time and leads to a form of placelessness. The effect of this is to dislocate places from their traditional, local identities, and to impose identities related to the requirements of the marketplace.

I would like now to discuss some of the debates that have raged since the publication of *The Condition of Postmodernity*. Leaving aside the question of whether or not a condition of postmodernity best describes contemporary economic and social life, and the general pervasiveness of the trends described here, a number of issues have been raised about Harvey's account. First, Harvey's view of postmodernity must be seen as an attempt to re-assert the relevance and theoretical primacy of the conflict tradition within social theory. He is concerned that 'new social movements' organised around axes of race, gender, sexuality and the environment threaten the coherency of a meta-theory based around class-based struggles. Hence Harvey seeks to show that Marxist analysis is as useful now as it ever has been in providing an understanding of the condition of our lives. Harvey's analysis is appealing because it provides a totalising account of the myriad problems created by late capitalism.

Second, Harvey has been criticised for providing a gender-blind account of postmodernity (Morris, 1992). He provides the example of Frédéric Moreau, hero of Flaubert's *L'Education Sentimentale*, who, armed with money, 'glides in and out of the differentiated spaces of the city' (Harvey, 1989:263). Doreen Massey asks whether or not Frédéric also had the little advantage of being male (Massey, 1991). Gillian Rose (1993) considers Harvey's masculine vision as endemic of the disciplinary procedures of geography. She notes that the desire to provide a fully coherent account of the social world is a peculiarly male pursuit, whereas the accounts of feminist geographers are more content to live with difference, complexity and fragmentation. In a similar vein, Keith and Cross (1993) suggest that Harvey ignores the centrality of racial divisions of labour to the labour processes that characterise the condition of postmodernity.

Third, and related to these points, Harvey's account underplays the role of culture in the formation of identity. As Cosgrove and Jackson (1987:95) argue, 'culture is not a residual category, the surface variation left unaccounted for by more powerful economic analyses; it is the very medium through which social change is experienced, contested and constituted'. Caroline Mills (1993) provides an example of this in her study of gentrification in Vancouver, Canada. She shows how the gentrified parts of the city are produced by planners, architects and developers who shape the site; the sales people and advertisers who code the built environment into consumption codes; and the purchasers who interpret the urban environment according to their own identities and personal narratives. In this case, the gentrifiers self-consciously defined themselves as 'city- people', in sharp antipathy to the perceived banality of suburban life. The interpretations of landscape imagery are examples of what Jackson (1989) calls 'maps of meaning'.

Fourth, we can take issue with Harvey's view of 'place'. Morris (1993) argues that Harvey views places as small communities with long memories living in the same area for a long period of time. From this standpoint, identities based on place usually emphasise tradition and nostalgia, and veer towards fascism. As well as being 'essentialist', this view of place obscures the internationalised flows of capital, commodities and people that put our dinner on the table. Massey questions the view that our 'sense of place' must always be backward-looking in the search for a lost authenticity. Taking the example of Kilburn High Road in west London, she illustrates the blending of the global in the local; how places do not have single unique identities but are full of internal contradictions and differences; and how places do not have boundaries. Bhatt (1994:152) recomposes this example for any urban street in London:

> An 'Indian' restaurant here, run by a Bangladeshi family whose relatives may have been recent flood victims in Bangladesh, an East African newsagency there, part of a national chain run by a family of refugees from Uganda, descendants of indentured Indian labourers, whose immediate fortunes are bonded into the recession of the British economy and the actions of the German Bundesbank, and whose children are spoken to by an African-American expressive culture. Overhead, a plane carries (if she is lucky) a Somali woman, who has lived in border refugee camps for several years, and who may seek housing in Camden, the housing officer perhaps being the son of a Jamaican woman who arrived in Britain in the 1950s to work on the buses. In another street, a heterosexual black man visits an AIDS project, staffed by gay men who were inspired to establish the project through the political activism of American groups.

So much for the criticisms of Harvey's work. In the next section I consider another account of the condition of postmodernity.

Allan Pred and Michael Watts: reworking postmodernity

In *Reworking Modernity: Capitalism and Symbolic Discontent*, Allan Pred and Michael Watts (1992) take a different approach to the process of 'time–space compression' described by Harvey. Though they prefer to use the term 'hyper-modern', they cover the same terrain, where industrial capitalism is characterised:

> ...by a furthering of 'time–space compression,' by a temporal and partial shrinking of the world, by advances in transportation and communications technology that have increased the mobility of goods and capital, the spatial reach of investments, the ease with which everyday practices and power relations are transformed at a distance.

But where Harvey's interest is the circuits of capital through which these changes are travelling, Pred and Watts are more interested in exploring the new identities that have come about as a result of the multifarious restructuring of global capitalisms, or, as they put it, the 'cultural articulations associated with new forms of capital' (p.xiii). The emphasis is on a world of borders; borders that are increasingly crossed, where new transnationalisms and new identities are continually being made and reworked. For Pred and Watts (1992:195) it is the struggle to explain how people construct a sense of identity for themselves that is important: 'How these identities are cobbled together and contested in order to act?' How is it possible to approach the experience of 'the Korean Buddhist chemical engineer, recently arrived from three years in Argentina, who becomes a Christian greengrocer in Harlem?' Such an approach adopts a strategy of unsettlement and embraces the ideas of difference and hybridity. Pred and Watts, too, pay attention to the realm of culture in the broadest sense, as a form of 'symbolic creativity' (Willis, 1990) in which people create for themselves 'maps of meaning' through which to negotiate the difficult terrains of economic and social change. As a result, their studies are more successful in portraying the way in which people in actual places negotiate the faultlines of the local and global.

In a series of case studies they seek to describe the 'symbolic discontent that emerges as new forms of capital make their local appearance; as the agents and actions of capital intersect with already existing – more or less deeply sedimented – everyday practices, power relations, and forms of consciousness; as local residents simultaneously experience modernity and hegemony in new guises' (p.xiii). An example of their approach can be seen in Michael Watts' (1992) account of the Muslim reformist movement – the Maitatsine movement – which arose in the wake of the Nigerian oil boom of the 1970s. He describes the transformation of the city of Kano in northern Nigeria, after the influx of petrodollars, from a traditional Muslim mercantile centre with a population of 400,000 (in 1970) into a sprawling, anarchic metropolis of over one and a half million equipped with a workforce of 50,000 workers. New industrial estates sprang up on the periphery of the city, armies of migrants poured in, and the icons of modernity, massive state-sponsored building projects, dotted the urban area. In short, Kano experienced the 'shock of modernity'. The Muslim insurrectional activity of the 1980s that Watts seeks to explain is embedded in this context: that is, the collision of precapitalist and capitalist institutions, namely Islam and the fast capitalism generated by huge revenues earned for the state by oil, and the industrial development it brought. Maitatsine represented a fundamentalist reading of the codes of Islam that challenged the hegemony of the discourses of capitalist accumulation. The key word here is 'reading' of Islam because, as Watts points out, rather than being rigidly prescriptive, Islam is a text-based religion that is rendered socially relevant through 'enunciation, performance, citation, reading and interpretation' (p.197). The socio-economic changes made new subject-positions or identities possible and these were actively negotiated by different social groups.

I think Pred and Watts offer a solution to some of the criticisms made of Harvey's work. First, they pay attention to the way in which economic shifts are negotiated in the realm of culture. Second, rather than viewing places as points on the circuit of capital, their accounts highlight the provisionality of place-identities and the complex cultural links between the local and the global. Third, Pred uses an unconventional textual strategy that is intended to challenge the assumption of correspondence between words and what they seek to describe. A series of mis-spellings, hyphenations and word-couplings serve to highlight multiple meanings of words, whilst unconventional sentence structures remind readers of the limitations of linear sentences for representing the diversity and complexity of the world. This approach goes some way to answering Gregory's call for human geography writing strategies that celebrate the openness and complexity of 'day-to-day lives of particular people in particular places' (Gregory, 1989:89; but see Gregory, 1994:Ch.3). In the following section I discuss further the issue of representation in human geography.

Postmodernism, social science and geography teaching

The implications of 'postmodernism' as a method or way of doing things in the social sciences are far from clear. This is partly due to the confusing array of terms and concepts which congregate under the umbrella of postmodernism. The implications for geography teachers in schools and colleges are even less clear. In this section I sketch out some of the major challenges posed by postmodernism for the social sciences, and make some comments on their relevance for geography teaching.

Graham, Doherty and Malek (1992) argue that postmodernism challenges three facets of contemporary social science (which they regard as modernist). These are: the assumption of a sovereign subject or actor; the acceptance of a correspondence theory of truth; and the formulation of the idea of progress.

First, the assumption of an independent 'actor' as the basic component of society underlies most social sciences, including geography. In geographic models based on neo-classical economics, the abstract 'economic man' was characterised by self-interest and rationality. Geography teachers have incorporated critiques of such assumptions within their teaching of these models, but a much more sweeping critique is offered by postmodernism. The postmodern subject has no 'fixed, essential or permanent identity. Identity becomes a "moveable feast": formed and transformed continuously in relation to the ways we are represented or addressed in the cultural systems which surround us' (Hall, 1992:277). Let me suggest what this implies for geography teaching by way of an example.

Imagine a land-use conflict in a rural area. Within geography lessons concern is usually focused on the planning agencies and mechanisms available to reduce and manage conflict. This is generally achieved through discussing the 'needs' of various actors (for example, ramblers' need for 'quiet' and access, drivers' need for parking space), and the values and attitudes they hold. Armed with this knowledge about what people say they want or need, solutions or policies can be developed to minimise conflict or disruption. The tacit assumption is that individuals or groups of individuals have clear-cut and unitary 'attitudes' to the issue under review. But recent research on attitudes to countryside issues suggests that attitudes are often fluid, ambiguous and contradictory. Hence respondents could simultaneously be in favour of allowing drivers to use their cars freely in the countryside and in favour of strong restrictions on such traffic. The research points to the need to 'locate attitudes within particular social and historical contexts, but also points to the contradictions and variabilities of everyday discourse as the appropriate sites where world views come to be formed and produced' (CPRE, 1994:136). This points to the need to consider the specific context in which such issues arise, and to guard against an assumption that similar attitudes and values are transferred across contexts.

Second, and linked to the rejection of the notion of the rational subject, is the attack on the assumption of a correspondence theory of truth or the idea that knowledge is a representation of reality. Duncan and Ley (1993) suggest that within twentieth-century Anglo-American human geography there have been four modes of representation. The first mode dominated until the 1950s and was based on providing an accurate description of the world, before it was challenged by the 'new' geography which was concerned with models of spatial theory based loosely on positivist science. Though apparently different – the former favouring the concrete and particular, the latter valuing the abstract and general – these two types of geography were basically similar in that they both accept the goal of achieving mimesis; that is, the goal of providing as accurate a reflection of the world as possible. A third mode of representation is interpretive and its basis is hermeneutics. It recognises that a 'perfect copy' of the world is not possible since interpretation involves a dialogue between the data – other people and other places – and the interpreter. The fourth mode of representation is a postmodernism that makes a radical attack on mimetic theories of representation and their search for truth.

This typology provides a useful framework with which to analyse various forms of geographical education. The National Curriculum for Geography clearly promotes mimetic modes of representation (DES,

1991): places are empirical 'containers' made up of shops, transport systems, leisure facilities and workplaces. Geographical information systems and Landsat imagery offer a 'technical fix' which assumes that it is possible to have unproblematic access to 'reality' – the issue of representation and its relationship to the actual world is never allowed to become an issue. Then there is the type of geography that dominates most textbooks and classrooms, where the emphasis on 'models' does at least raise the issue of representation and its link to the real world. Here teachers are likely to draw upon criticisms of mimetic theories of representation. I discuss here some of these criticisms and how postmodernism develops them further.

Humanistic geography (Ley and Samuels, 1978) challenged the neutrality of positivist science and argued for the centrality of values in the construction of knowledge. Gillian Rose (1993) has applied feminist criticisms of Western representation to the academic discipline of geography. She notes the existence of two types of masculinity in geographical knowledge: social scientific masculinity, and aesthetic masculinity. The former is characterised by a quest for abstraction, for a detached objectivity which seeks to mask its value-ladenness. In the latter, male geographers have asserted their power by claiming a heightened sensitivity to human experience of place. As noted earlier, Marxist geography has not escaped criticism for adopting a gender-blind, patriarchal view of the world (Massey, 1991; Deutsche, 1990). Along with these critiques there is the issue of Eurocentrism in the representation of 'Other' people and places. European representations of 'the Orient' or 'darkest Africa' have been linked to notions of superiority and inferiority (Said, 1978; Jackson, 1989).

Postmodernism shares the critiques of mimetic representation described above, and goes further by questioning the ability of social science to provide analyses of the social world. There is no one true account but only many voices, each claiming its own validity. Dear has recognised and (guardedly) welcomed the inevitable relativism implied in the postmodernist assertion that 'reality' is not something to be discovered, but a social or cultural construction. According to Dear:

> The postmodern challenge is to face up to the fact of relativism in human knowledge, and to proceed from this position to a better understanding.
>
> 1988:271

Third, postmodernism rejects the idea of progress with its assumptions of historicism and developmentalism. Rob Gilbert (1984) has argued that school geography textbooks present a 'progressivist view of social change' by assuming that history is a process of society's increasing success in coming to terms with the environment. The classic model familiar to geography teaching is Rostow's (1960) *Stages of Economic Growth*. Though Rostow's model is conservative, even radical accounts contain this assumption of ultimate progress, despite periodic setbacks (Peet, 1991). With postmodernism's many voices, none of which is privileged over another, the achievement of any ideal society is rejected, and along with it any belief in the notion of progress.

Geography teaching and postmodernism

In this final section I attempt to set out some of the lessons that I have learned through my reading of postmodernism and how they relate to my work as a geography teacher. I should note here that I am using the term 'postmodern' in a loose way to denote a 'structure of feeling'. Most of the arguments I present here have grown out of the critiques of the assumptions of the social sciences, but a postmodern structure of feeling describes a weariness with the idea of progress and the search for truth. A postmodern structure of feeling recognises only fragmentation, mutability and change.

I will discuss five implications of a postmodern 'turn' for geography teaching. These are: a shift from a concern with general processes to a concern for the geographic and historical specifics of places; the recognition of the social constructedness of scale; the acceptance of relativism; the recognition of pluralism and diversity as features of social life; and the postmodern emphasis on culture and the associated view of regarding places as 'text'. Though none of these trends will be particularly surprising, and many teachers will recognise elements of their own practice within them, I suggest that, taken together, they mark a fundamental shift in the way geography is taught in schools.

First, there is a shift away from the claims of realist approaches. Ron Johnston (1985:336) sets out the task of a realist human geography:

> Our goal as geographers must be to foster appreciation of these social forma-
> tions, in all their diversity. But we must not fall into the singularity trap, focus-
> ing on the particulars of our chosen societies and failing to identify their
> relationships to the general processes. Our work must contain two major ele-
> ments, therefore: (1) a *theoretical appreciation* of the general processes of the cap-
> italist mode of production (or other modes where relevant); and (2) an *empirical
> appreciation* of the particular social formations.

Although much of Johnston's work is an engagement with positivist approaches to geography, his realist stance reproduces the positivist assumption that explanation consists of showing specific events to be the outcomes of wider processes (Warf, 1990). This is a fair summary of much radical geography, where places are studied in order to reveal some deep-seated structure or logic to the social world (my own favoured form of realism has been a form of historical materialism). In contrast, post-modernism marks the shift from the production of general theories which suggest that places can be explained with reference to processes or laws that operate independent of them. Places *are* caught up in 'universal processes', as Harvey (1987) insists, but these processes can only be made sense of in terms of places. Postmodernism does not reject explanation *per se*. Rather, theory must be adapted to the temporal and geographical specificities of place. The purpose of postmodern explanation is not to infer about wider processes, but to understand the dynamics of specific conjunctures.

For example, Beatrix Campbell's (1993) accounts of urban unrest in British cities in 1991 point to structural themes such as economic decline, unemployment, and economic and political marginalisation which are common to these localities. But this fails to explain why such unrest did not occur in dozens of other similar localities. What Campbell shows is the way in which these themes were articulated or linked in specific places with their own mix of gender and racial relations. Thus, argues Campbell, the events in the Meadowell estate in Newcastle were tied up in the com-plex relationship between the local state and political activists, which led to the political marginalisation of an already economically disadvantaged section of the community. Thus general processes were only expressed in specific micro-contexts, and the knowledge gained would not allow us to make assumptions about the way these processes are articulated in other contexts. This marks a scaling-down of the power of explanation.

Second, postmodernism raises the question of scale. Neil Smith (1992) argues that the social construction of scale is seldom theorised, but there is nothing 'natural' about the concepts of home and locality, urban and regional, national and global, which form the framework for geographical study. Indeed, events take on different meanings according to the scale at which they are studied. As Smith asks, 'Was the brutal repression of Tiananmen Square a local event, a regional or national event, or an international event? We might reasonably assume that it is all four...' (p.73). Smith (1993) proposes a scale which includes levels of the body, the home, the community, the region, the nation, and the globe. These various scales allow for an appreciation of places as having different (sometimes contradictory) meanings under different circumstances, including local labour markets, as products of gendered divisions of labour, as arenas of collective actions and consumption, or as spheres of everyday life or lived experience. Postmodernism implies that places are all these things, and more.

Third, postmodernism entails an acceptance of relativism. To the postmodernist, 'reality' is not out there waiting to be discovered. Instead, knowledge is a social or cultural construction. There are many realities, each with its own claims to 'truth'. For example, there are a number of 'Docklands' competing for dominance in the 1990s. These competing conceptions coincide with the distinctions drawn by Lefebvre (1991) in his work on 'the production of space'. The first category is that of 'spatial practice' – Docklands as a distinct place produced by the logic of the market. East London's riverside from the Tower of London to the Thames Barrier has been re-positioned within the circuits of international finance capital. Through the activities of the London Docklands Development Corporation (LDDC), the area became the testing ground for free-market intervention into what had previously been the preserve of democratically elected local councils and boroughs. The second category is that of 'representations of space'. These are the ideologies of space associated with Docklands. Bird (1993) notes how the publicity material produced by the LDDC presents an image of coherence and harmony, a unity of places and functions 'woven together by the meandering course of the river into a spectacular architectural myth of liberal *civitas*' (p.126). The iconography of Docklands paves the way for the post-industrial, upwardly mobile, credit-wealthy, information-rich future and presents this as the 'natural' function for a 'metropolitan water city' now that the original functions of the docks have passed. Bill Schwarz (1991) points out that the 'official' version of Docklands history omits any reference to the class struggles, to multicultural communities, and the campaigns over housing that have been central to London's Docklands. Against these 'official' representations of Docklands, a range of groups within Docklands challenged the claims of the LDDC. This often involved portraying Docklands in a different light, focusing on the existence of a 'real' Docklands inhabited by a range of social and ethnic groups, engaged in struggles to improve access to employment, housing and social amenities. The third category is that of 'representational spaces', the complex symbols and notions which entail opposition or hostility to dominant conceptions. Michel de Certeau has referred to the everyday practices of inhabiting the street as the 'tactics' of lived space. We use cities in the same way that we use language. In both cases we are constrained – by streets and buildings in the former, by grammar in the latter – but we adapt them to fit our own purposes. How can geography lessons be opened up to reflect these competing 'realities'? Is there a limit to how far teachers can embrace relativism? Does it promote a situation where 'anything goes'?

Fourth, postmodernism suggests that social life and social conflict have become more pluralistic. This entails attaching less importance to the class-based character of politics. Take the example of racial segregation within cities. Susan Smith (1989) argues that an emphasis on accounts that explain 'racial' differentiation as an outcome of labour market processes in a postcolonial era are insufficient in accounting for 'racial' segregation given that racialised minorities can no longer be classed as migrants, and in many cases are unable to sell their labour. Such explanations, which reduce social phenomena such as 'racial' segregation to the operations of the capitalist economy, fail to recognise the role of the state in allocating resources and the evidence that social policy in Britain has been 'racially' divisive; for example, through direct and indirect discrimination in the public housing sector. The point of Smith's example is to suggest that the allocation of welfare, political and civil rights is as important as economic processes in structuring the social arrangement of places. Geography lessons need to pay attention to the various spheres of social life through which places are created and re-created.

Fifth, postmodernism urges geography teachers to take culture seriously. Against accounts that associate popular culture with conformity, waste and passivity, certain forms of postmodernism emerge as optimistic of its ability to be used positively. A recent account is Willis's (1990) research on the leisure activities of young people, which revealed how cultural objects are actively used in the production of social identities. Peter Jackson's (1989) influential work on the 'maps of meaning' used by individuals and groups to make sense of their worlds makes the case for a reformed cultural geography which recognises the symbolic component of struggles over place and environment. For geography teachers, John Huckle's most recent work (1993) has displayed a concern with the cultural politics of consumption, most notably in an activity where students are encouraged to deconstruct the meanings at work in advertisements which use images of nature to sell their products. The work of Jacqui Burgess (1985, 1992) on the production and consumption of environmental meanings related to the Thames grazing-marsh in Essex, and the representation in the press of inner-city areas after the 1981 'riots', could be a useful source of ideas for geography lessons. A move in this direction would be to accept the notion of places as 'texts' to be interpreted or 'read' in different ways by different individuals and social groups (Barnes and Duncan, 1992). Treating social life as a 'text' would have significant implications for the form of geographical 'writing' undertaken in classrooms.

Conclusion

> If postmodernism … means the opening up to critical discourse of the lines of enquiry which were formerly inadmissible so that new and different questions can be asked and new and other voices can begin asking them; if it means the opening up of institutional and discursive spaces within which more fluid and plural social and sexual identities may develop; if it means the erosion of triangular formations of power and knowledge with the expert at the apex and the 'masses' at the base; if, in a word, it enhances our collective (and democratic) sense of possibility, then I for one am a postmodernist.
>
> Hebdige, 1988:226

Dick Hebdige's own comments about his relationship to postmodernism suggest one of the problems surrounding the use of the term.

Simply, his is a big 'if'. Postmodernism is a currently much contested cultural site which geographers and, eventually, geography teachers will find hard to ignore. The challenge is to shape it in ways that promote forms of social justice (even if postmodernism seems to negate this possibility) and open up spaces for new voices and identities to develop. The new times are challenging times for geography teaching.

BIBLIOGRAPHY

Adam, B. (1990) *Time and Social Theory*, Polity.

Barnes, T.J. and Duncan, J.S. (1992) *Writing Worlds: Discourse, Text and Metaphor in the Representation of Landscape*, Routledge.

Bhatt, C. (1994) 'New foundations: contingency, indeterminacy and black translocality', in Weeks, J. (ed.) *The Lesser Evil and the Greater Good*, Rivers Oram Press.

Bird, J. (1993) 'Dystopia on the Thames', in Bird, J., Curtis, B., Putnam, T., Robertson, G. and Tickner, L. (eds) *Mapping the Futures*, Routledge.

Burgess, J. (1985) 'News from nowhere: the press, the riots and the myth of the inner city', in Burgess, J. and Gold, J. (eds) *Geography, the Media and Popular Culture*, Croom Helm.

—— (1992) 'The cultural politics of nature conservation and economic development', in Anderson, K. and Gale, F. (eds) *Inventing places: Studies in Cultural Geography*, Longman.

Campbell, B. (1993) *Goliath: Britain's Dangerous Places*, Methuen.

Coe, J. (1994) *What a Carve Up!*, Viking.

Cosgrove, D. and Jackson, P. (1987) 'New directions in cultural geography', *Area*, 19: 95–101.

CPRE (1994) *Leisure Landscapes*, Council for the Protection of Rural England.

Dear, M. (1988) 'The postmodern challenge: reconstructing human geography', *Transactions of the Institute of British Geographers*, 13:262–74.

DES (1991) *National Curriculum: Draft Order for Geography*, HMSO.

Deutsche, R. (1990) 'Men in space', *Artforum*, February: 21–3.

Duncan, J.S. and Ley, D. (1993) *Place/Culture/Representation*, Routledge.

Emel, J. and Peet, R. (1989) 'Resource management and natural hazards', in Peet, J. and Thrift, N. (eds) *New Models in Geography*, Vol. 1, Unwin Hyman.

Featherstone, M. (1991) *Consumer Culture and Postmodernism*, Sage.

Fien, J. and Gerber, R. (eds) (1988) *Teaching Geography for a Better World*, Oliver and Boyd.

Giddens, A. (1991) *Modernity and Self-identity: Self and Society in the Late Modern Age*, Polity.

Gilbert, R. (1984) *The Impotent Image: Reflections of Ideology in the Secondary School Curriculum*, The Falmer Press.

Graham, E., Doherty, J. and Malek, M. (1992) 'Introduction: the context and language of postmodernism', in Doherty, J. *et al*. (eds) *Postmodernism and the Social Sciences*, Macmillan.

Gregory, D. (1989) 'Areal differentiation and postmodern human geography', in Gregory, D. and Walford, R. (eds) *New Horizons in Human Geography*, Unwin Hyman.

(1994) *Geographical Imaginations*, Blackwell.

Hall, S. (1988) *The Hard Road to Renewal*, Verso.

(1992) 'The question of cultural identity', in Hall, S., Held, D. and McGrew, D. (eds) *Modernity and its Futures*, Polity.

Harvey, D. (1973) *Social Justice and the City*, Blackwell.

(1987) 'Flexible accumulation through urbanisation: reflections on "postmodernism" in the American city', *Antipode*, 19:367–76.

(1989) *The Condition of Postmodernity: An Enquiry into the Origins of Cultural Change*, Blackwell.

Hebdige, R. (1988) *Hiding in the Light*, Routledge.

Huckle, J. (1983) *Geographical Education: Reflection and Action*, Oxford University Press.

(1988) *What We Consume*, Richmond Publishing.

(1993) *Our Consumer Society*, WWF-UK.

Jackson, P. (1987) *Race and Racism*, Allen and Unwin.

(1989) *Maps of Meaning*, Unwin Hyman.

Jackson, P. and Penrose, J. (eds) (1993) *Constructions of Race, Place and Nation*, UCL Press.

Jameson, F. (1984) 'Postmodernism, or the cultural logic of late capitalism', *New Left Review*, 146:53–92.

Johnston, R. (ed.) (1985) *The Future of Geography*, Cambridge University Press.

(1991) *A Question of Place: Exploring the Practice of Human Geography*, Blackwell.

Keith, M. and Cross, M. (1993) 'Racism and the postmodern city', in Cross, M. and Keith, M. (eds) *Racism, the City and the State*, Routledge.

Knox, P. (1989) 'The vulnerable, the disadvantaged and the victimized: who they are and where they live', in Herbert, D. and Smith, D. (eds) *Social Problems and the City*, Oxford University Press.

Lash, S. and Urry, J. (1987) *The End of Organised Capitalism*, University of Wisconsin Press.

(1994) *Economies of Signs and Space*, Sage.

Leadbeater, C. (1989) 'Back to the future', *Marxism Today*, May: 12–17.

Lefebvre, H. (1991) *The Production of Space*, Blackwell.

Ley, D. and Samuels, M. (eds) (1978) *Humanistic Geography*, Maaroufa.

Massey, D. (1991) 'A global sense of place', *Marxism Today*, June: 24–9.

Mills, C. (1993) 'Myths and meanings of gentrification', in Duncan, J. and Ley, D. (eds) *Place/Culture/Representation*, Routledge.

Morris, M. (1992) 'On the Beach', in Grossberg, L., Nelson, C. and Treichler, P. (eds) *Cultural Studies*, Routledge.

(1993) 'Future Fear', in Bird, J. *et al.*, *Mapping the Futures: Local Cultures, Global Change*, Routledge.

Murray, R. (1989) 'Fordism and post-Fordism', in Hall, S. and Jacques, M. (eds), *New Times*, Lawrence and Wishart.

Peet, R. (ed.) (1977) *Radical Geography*, Methuen.

(1991) *Global Capitalism: Theories of Societal Development*, Routledge.

Pred, A. and Watts, M.J. (1992) *Reworking Modernity: Capitalisms and Symbolic Discontent*, Rutgers University Press.

Rose, G. (1993) *Feminism and Geography: The Limits of Geographical Knowledge*, Polity.

Rostow, W. (1960) *The Stages of Economic Growth*, Cambridge University Press.

Said, E. (1978) *Orientalism*, Columbia University Press.

Schwarz, W. (1991) 'Where horses shit a hundred sparrows feed: Docklands and East London during the Thatcher years', in Corner, J. and Harvey, S. (eds) *Enterprise and Heritage: Crosscurrents of National Culture*, Routledge.

Smith, D. (1977) *Human Geography: A Welfare Approach*, Edward Arnold.

Smith, N. (1992) 'Geography, difference and the politics of scale', in Doherty, J. *et al.* (eds) *Postmodernism and the Social Sciences*, Macmillan.

(1993) 'Homeless/global: scaling places', in Bird, J. *et al.* (eds) *Mapping the Futures*, Routledge.

Smith, S. (1989) 'Society, space and citizenship: a human geography for the "new times"?', *Transactions of the Institute of British Geographers*, NS 14:144–56.

Soja, E. (1989) *Postmodern Geographies: The Reassertion of Space in Social Theory*, Verso.

Thrift, N. (1992) 'Light out of darkness? Critical social theory in 1980s Britain', in Cloke, P. (ed.) *Policy and Change in Thatcher's Britain*, Pergamon Press.

Warf, B. (1990) 'Can the region survive postmodernism?', *Urban Geography*, 11(6): 586–93.

Watts, M. (1992) 'The shock of modernity: petroleum, protest and fast capitalism in an industrializing society', in Pred, A. and Watts, M. (eds) *Reworking Modernity: Capitalisms and Symbolic Discontent*, Rutgers University Press.

Willis, P. (1990) *Common Culture*, Open University Press.

Women and Geography Study Group (1984) *Geography and Gender*, Hutchinson.

Zukin, S. (1992) *Landscapes of Power*, University of California Press.

SECTION TWO | The Geography Curriculum – Principles, Practice and Evaluation

This section focuses on change in curriculum thinking and how that and recent national-level policy have impinged on geography in schools.

In Chapter 4 Norman Graves reflects on post-war developments, with particular emphasis on changes in the 1980s and 1990s in the UK. He addresses the following three broad themes: a review of the way in which thinking about curriculum and curriculum development has evolved; where we stand now in our quest for curriculum change; and where this journey might take us in the foreseeable future, given present-day political, economic and social imperatives.

In Chapter 5, Eleanor Rawling explores three questions: What are the characteristics of school-based curriculum development and what did we learn from the curriculum development projects of the 1970s and 1980s? What impact has the geography National Curriculum had on these curriculum development activities and what might be the impact of the revised orders? What is the outlook for school-based curriculum development in the future? She identifies three levels of curriculum planning and suggests how their balance and significance have changed as schools have implemented a centralised National Curriculum.

Finally in this section, in Chapter 6, Ashley Kent focuses on the departmental level, having first outlined recent developments in the overall field of evaluation. There are sections on OFSTED inspections and departmental review; managing a department; staff appraisal; evaluating curricula and resources; and classroom observation. He ends with a plea to consider the views of students as a part of the evaluation process.

4   Curriculum development in geography: an ongoing process

Norman Graves

I am not sure that in the 1950s we really understood what curriculum development was about, though it was evident that no subject and its teaching could stand still for long. But how these changes could come about was not entirely clear, except perhaps through the interplay of ideas between subject teachers and between teachers and colleagues in higher education. Some of these people may have attended conferences, such as those of the Association for Science Education, the Historical Association, or the Geographical Association, to cite but three. Much seemed to depend on the individual efforts of teachers in individual schools. At that time, few of us had heard of Ralph Tyler's *Basic Principles of Curriculum and Instruction,* although it had been published in the USA in 1949. It is possibly a measure of the slowness with which, at that time, ideas crossed the Atlantic that his book was not published in the UK until 1971, when an initiative was taken by the Open University. The curriculum process was not an idea with which we were familiar. We tended to view the curriculum as an ensemble of subject syllabuses, and each subject syllabus as a collection of some of the content of that subject.

We have come a long way since those days, and presented here are, first, a review of the way thinking has evolved about curriculum and curriculum development; secondly, an analysis of where we are at present in our quest for curriculum change; and, finally, an attempt to see where we might be going given the political, economic and social imperatives of the time.

The development of thinking about curriculum and curriculum development

VIEWS OF THE CURRICULUM PROCESS

Understanding how curriculum development could take place involves having a workable model of the curriculum process. Whilst Ralph Tyler's model (1949) was a step forward, it had the disadvantage of being a linear model linking objectives to learning experiences to methods of teaching to evaluation (Figure 4.1), but not explicitly going on to indicate how the feedback mechanism operated, though it is implied in his chapter on evaluation.

? ⟶ Objectives ⟶ Content ⟶ Methods ⟶ Evaluation ⟶ ?

Figure 4.1 Tyler's linear model of the curriculum process
Source: After Tyler, 1949

Wheeler, on the other hand, suggested that a circular model was more appropriate to a dynamic situation in which the curriculum process was an ongoing one, where the feedback mechanism ensured changes in the objectives (Figure 4.2) (Wheeler, 1967).

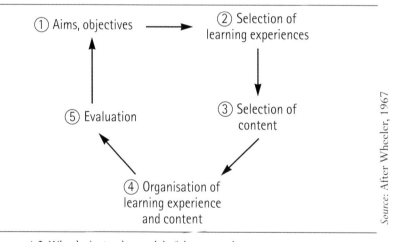

Source: After Wheeler, 1967

Figure 4.2 Wheeler's circular model of the curriculum process

I am convinced that much of the development that occurred in curricula in the 1960s and 1970s was in part the result of this new thinking about the curriculum process. Of course, the apparent simplicity of the idea becomes somewhat more complicated when it comes to be applied in practice. As Jack Kerr (1968) pointed out in his book *Changing the Curriculum*, someone has to decide what the aims and objectives should be: should these come from society, from the disciplines to be taught, or even from the pupils themselves? Which aspects of objectives should be stressed – the cognitive, the affective, the psychomotor or manual skills? These questions of the 1960s acquired a new vigour in the 1980s as some governments began to stress the need to emphasise the vocational aspects of education. This question is still with us. Kerr also pointed out that 'learning experiences' implied a whole host of decisions as to how these learning experiences could be structured. These clearly depended on the nature of the learners, on the resources available to the teacher and to the learner, and on the knowledge and skills of the teacher. Even the content of the discipline used was not unproblematic, since describing what to select from the total content of a discipline for use in schools is no easy task. Lastly, how to evaluate what had happened involved two related but distinct processes: evaluating student learning (and there are many ways of doing this), and evaluating the curriculum in action.

Kerr also provided a diagram to illustrate the curriculum process, which I have simplified (Figure 4.3) to show that this process was perhaps much more interactive in practice than either Tyler or Wheeler had allowed.

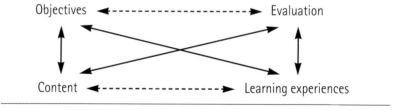

Source: After Kerr, 1968

Figure 4.3 Kerr's interactive model of the curriculum process

In other words, the curriculum process was not simply a circular system moving from objectives to evaluation and then on to new objectives and so on, but an interactive system in which every part affected every other part. There might not be a single starting point such as the objectives, but teachers might start at any point in the system: for example, an idea for learning methods (e.g. a game) might be used to trigger off the whole process.

In terms of geography, the process of planning a course could be the one shown in Figure 4.4 (Graves, 1979). From item 1 in Figure 4.4, 'Aims of schooling and education', one could select an appropriate paradigm of geography and from these two decide on what aims geographical

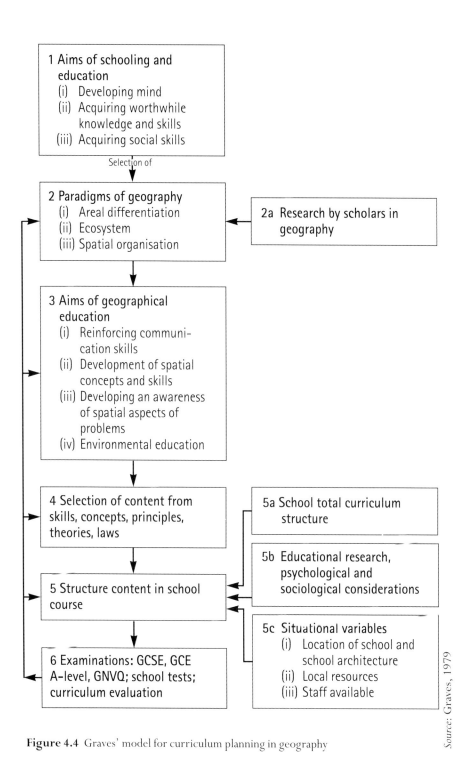

Figure 4.4 Graves' model for curriculum planning in geography

Source: Graves, 1979

education may have in schools. The input into the 'Paradigms of geography' (item 2) comes from geographical research. Given these aims of geographical education it will be necessary to select content that will achieve those aims. By content I mean the concepts, principles, theories and skills contained in the appropriate paradigm of geography, *not* the facts or areas which provide the context within which the content may be taught. This content needs to be structured in a progressive fashion throughout the school course. The nature of the total school curriculum will need to be noted in order to avoid duplication. Educational research which gives us information about concept hierarchies and the relative difficulty of ideas will give an input here. Similarly, such situational variables as the school location and its resources, including staff resources, will be taken into account. Lastly, evaluation of the output from school tests and examinations will need to be fed back to various stages of the process to improve it next time round. The teacher still has to plan individual lessons or teaching units.

CURRICULUM DEVELOPMENT PROJECTS

It is one thing to have a clear model of how the curriculum process works, but quite another to make it work so that curriculum development can take place. Perhaps it is worth pausing and reflecting on the meaning of and need for curriculum development. In the course of my work, I have sometimes been invited to visit other countries and observe and comment on what is going on in their schools. In one country, I saw the geography of Europe being taught from textbooks which described the Europe of 1939. But lest you think this only happens in developing countries, in England, the General Certificate of Education O-level examination in geography did not change to any substantial degree between 1950 and 1970, although geography as a research discipline in universities had developed to a considerable extent. There is an inevitable tendency for human beings and human organisations to stick with what they have and with what appears to be working well. Any proposal for change tends to meet what Donald Schon (1971) in his illuminating book *Beyond the Stable State* calls 'dynamic conservatism'. All sorts of ways are found of frustrating the initiative which will upset the 'stable state'. However, unless something is done about the curriculum, teachers find themselves teaching ideas and skills that are no longer relevant to the society in which they live. Some readers may be familiar with the fable of the prehistoric tribe whose elders insisted on the importance of teaching the skills of hunting and killing the sabre-toothed tiger, even though it was a species that had been extinct for hundreds of years.

So how did we attempt to undertake curriculum development? Early projects were influenced by the success of the natural sciences, in which ideas are tested in laboratories with experiments, and then perhaps subsequently used in industry and commerce. In the 1960s and 1970s, we had widespread experimentation with curriculum development in a range of subjects. In the USA, various foundations financed this experimentation, and the Earth Science Curriculum Project was set up, along with the High School Geography Project (HSGP) and Man a Course of Study (MACOS), for example.

In the UK, the Nuffield Foundation financed curriculum development in the Sciences, and the Shell Company did the same for Mathematics. Subsequently, in 1964, the Schools Council for Curriculum and Examinations was set up by the Department of Education and Science, local education authorities and the teachers' unions, to provide an institutional base for curriculum development. It was from the Schools Council that there emanated such projects as 'The Humanities Curriculum Project', directed by the late Lawrence Stenhouse, 'Project Technology', 'Geography and the Young School Leaver' (GYSL), 'Geography 14 to 18', and in 1976 the last of the big national projects for geography, 'Geography 16–19'. All these projects were developed by teams of teacher-researchers, who mapped out a course of action, tried it out in a number of schools, subsequently modified it and then launched it on the schools as a whole (Boardman, 1985). The launch was more of an offer, since no school was obliged to take it up, and different projects had different rates of success, depending on the extent to which they were taken up by schools. Thus the GYSL project was reckoned to be 'the jewel in the Schools Council's crown', since of all projects, it had the greatest number of schools taking it up. By contrast, 'History, Geography and Social Science 8–13' came very low down the list in terms of take-up by schools.

In the main phase of curriculum development up to the demise of the Schools Council in 1984, curriculum development projects took a number of forms and adopted different styles of working. Some – for example most of the science and mathematics projects – were straightforward developments of the curriculum of a major subject. Some were attempts at experimenting with combinations of subjects, as with the Integrated Studies Project based at Keele University. Yet others had as their remit the development of a course for a particular clientele, for example the GYSL project which was aimed initially at those pupils who would normally have left school at 15 but were being kept on for an extra year in 1972/73. Project directors adopted different styles of working; most in the early stages used a 'research, design and development' (or 'research, development and diffusion') – RDD – style of working, literally researching the subject area and its educational implications (what in other cultures is called *didactics*), designing a course based on appropriate materials, and then developing it in schools. Subsequently teachers were presented with a package of curriculum materials with instructions, and were asked to get on with it. For example, the GYSL project used this style of working. Another style, adopted by the Geography 14 to 18 project, was to use some teachers in schools as partners in the process of curriculum development. Here the argument was that 'there could be no curriculum development without teacher development', and so it was vital to involve teachers from the beginning and to get them to undertake the curriculum development process, since the ultimate aim was to develop a system of ongoing curriculum development which would not stop after a particular innovation had been adopted. The curriculum development project was seen more as a catalyst than as a means of handing down a ready-made curriculum innovation. This proved a difficult system to work in practice because of the constraints under which most teachers were working. Most teachers had neither the time nor the resources to give to radical curriculum development, no matter how much stimulus the project team provided. Not surprisingly, the third style of working, sometimes known as the *co-operative* style, was an attempt to marry the best features of the RDD model or intervention model with those of the catalytic or independence model. Teachers were consulted at many stages of the project, but they were not expected to undertake the total design and production of the new curriculum. The Geography 16–19 Project was developed along those lines at the Institute of Education in London (Naish *et al.*, 1987).

Although in the ultimate analysis, the number of schools actually taking up any of these projects may not have been a large percentage of the total number of secondary schools, the impact of the projects was much wider than might be indicated by their low take-up figures. In the first place, teachers often used part of the project's course even if they did not use the whole. Secondly, as teachers became aware of what the project advocated, so it affected their thinking, their own course design and their own teaching. Thus the influence of a curriculum development project is usually much greater than is sometimes estimated by its critics, as is evident when one looks at subsequent examination syllabuses, many of which were based directly on one or other of the projects.

CURRICULUM DEVELOPMENT AT DIFFERENT SCALES

The abolition of the Schools Council in England and Wales in 1984 corresponded to an ideological view of curriculum development which looked with suspicion at the independence of the National Curriculum projects, especially when these made recommendations which did not accord with Government or Department of Education and Science views (Lacey, 1984). The replacement of the Schools Council by two bodies – the School Curriculum Development Committee (SCDC) and the School Examinations Council (SEC) – was seen as a retrograde step by many, since separating curriculum development from examinations did not make much sense, given the interaction between evaluation and the other elements in the curriculum. Further, the resources available to the SCDC were very much smaller than those that had previously been available to the Schools Council. What funds were available were used to finance local curriculum development in certain local education authorities (LEAs) and, at an even smaller scale, in particular schools. There was also a view, traditionally held in the UK if not elsewhere, that the proper place – in fact the only place – where in the ultimate analysis curriculum development has to take place, is the individual school or college. The issue is debated in Malcolm Skilbeck's book *School-based Curriculum Development* (1984). However, while it is a truism that the only place where curriculum development can occur is the school or college, ideas and frameworks may come from elsewhere. Depending *only* on schools for ideas may not be wise if we are to learn from past experience. In any event, the debate about local versus central curriculum development was to be overtaken by events, as the Government decided that there should be a National Curriculum, and set up Working Groups to develop attainment targets and programmes of study for each subject as well as for cross-curricular themes. The Education Reform Act (ERA) of 1988 enshrined the National Curriculum in the law of England and Wales, with the National Curriculum Council (NCC) as an advisory body. The SEC was replaced by the School Examinations and Assessment Council (SEAC) with extended powers. In a sense, the ERA returned the control of the curriculum and curriculum development to a central body, but one that was very much under political and DES control compared with the Schools Council, and with the examinations body SEAC having the greater influence. There was no mention of development — the term seems to have been banned by the DES, rather as at an earlier date the term 'teacher training' was substituted for 'teacher education'.

The genesis of geography in the National Curriculum

THE EDUCATION REFORM ACT

The National Curriculum in England and Wales is embedded in an ideological and a legal context, the latter being very much influenced by the former. The ideological context is one that may be placed under the slogan of 'back to basics', which encompasses the idea that education in Britain has been led astray both by the misguided romantics who practised so-called progressive education, and by left-wing revolutionaries whose purpose was to undermine established authority; there was a need to return to the didactic teaching of basic fundamentals (Graves, 1993). The legal context is that of the 1988 Education Reform Act, which determined the parameters of the reform and its process. Thus the National Curriculum was defined in terms of subjects and certain cross-curricular areas. The Foundation Curriculum consisted of a Core Curriculum of English, mathematics and science, and other foundation subjects consisting of history, geography, a modern foreign language, art, music, physical education and technology. Religious education was also to be taught, except that parents could withdraw their children from such teaching if they were so minded. Cross-curricular themes such as economic and industrial understanding, careers education and guidance, health education, education for citizenship and environmental education were to be encouraged either by incorporating them in existing subjects or by giving them a separate place on the timetable of a school.

Another aspect of the ERA was the division of the teaching and testing of the National Curriculum into four Key Stages: Key Stage 1 covered years 1 and 2 (5 to 7-year-old pupils); Key Stage 2 covered years 3,4,5 and 6 (7 to 11-year-old pupils); Key Stage 3 covered years 7,8 and 9 (11 to 14-year-old pupils); and Key Stage 4 covered years 10 and 11 (14 to 16-year-old pupils). The ERA also specified that for each subject there would be attainment targets (ATs), programmes of study (PoS), and assessment arrangements. Attainment targets were defined as 'the knowledge, skills and understandings which pupils of different abilities and maturities are expected to have by the end of each key stage'. Programmes of study were stated to be 'the matters, skills and processes which are required to be taught to pupils of different abilities and maturities during each key stage'. It is useful to bear in mind that the ATs were formulated on the understanding that these could be categorised as belonging to one of ten different levels which were outlined in the report of the Task Group on Assessment and Testing (TGAT Report 1987/88).

The two separate bodies created to oversee the National Curriculum and the evaluation of its 'products' were, as already indicated, the National Curriculum Council (NCC) based in York and chaired by Duncan Graham, and the School Examinations and Assessment Council (SEAC) based in London and chaired by Philip Halsey. Why two bodies were required to carry out tasks which should in practice be closely linked is not clear, except that (see above) when the Schools Council was abolished in 1984, its curriculum and evaluation functions were then separated into two bodies, though no rationale was given for this separation. Duncan Graham believes that this was a political move to prevent a body such as the former Schools Council from having too much power (Graham, 1993).

DRAFTING THE GEOGRAPHY CURRICULUM

On 5 May 1989 the Secretary of State for Education and Science (Kenneth

Baker) set up a Geography Working Group (GWG) to advise him on ATs, PoS and assessment arrangements. The group consisted of eleven members and a chairman, the latter being Sir Leslie Fielding, Vice-Chancellor of Sussex University and a former diplomat. An Interim Report was to be delivered on 31 October 1989 and a Final Report on 30 April 1990. The Interim Report was duly delivered to a new Secretary of State, John MacGregor – earlier in 1989 Kenneth Baker had become Chairman of the Conservative Party. The Interim Report proposed eight attainment targets divided into the following groups:

Area Studies
AT1 The Home Area and Region
AT2 The United Kingdom
AT3 World Geography: Part 1
AT4 World Geography: Part 2

Geographical Themes
AT5 Physical Geography
AT6 Human Geography
AT7 Environmental Geography

Skills
AT8 Geographical Skills

It is inappropriate here to go into the details of the proposed curriculum (see Graves *et al.*, 1990a, 1990b) but for many it proved a great disappointment. There was a re-emphasis on area studies and locational knowledge which seemed to go back to an earlier stage of school geography. There was an absence of the consideration of values as a factor in locational decisions. Also the sheer number of statements of attainments (SoA) – there were over 250 of these – provided teachers with an almost impossible task. Not surprisingly, the GWG received many submissions from individuals and from professional groups suggesting modifications to the report. The Geographical Association played a key role in this by setting up regional meetings of teachers.

In the Final Report, not published until June 1990, the number of ATs was reduced and their grouping was changed to the following:

AT1 Geographical Skills (maps and diagrams, fieldwork skills, skills in using secondary sources)

AT2 The Home Area and Region

AT3 The United Kingdom within the European Community

AT4 The Wider World

AT5 Physical Geography (weather and climate, rivers, river basins and seas, landforms, animals, plants and soils)

AT6 Human Geography (population, settlements, communications and movements, economic activities)

AT7 Environmental Geography (use and misuse of natural resources, quality and vulnerability of environments, protecting and managing environments)

Each AT is made up of a number of statements of attainment (SoA), each SoA being allocated to one of the ten levels to which that SoA is deemed to belong. The programme of study (PoS) is described in greater detail and arranged in accordance with the contribution its elements make to each key stage. For each key stage, the PoS is divided into three sections, respectively: Geographical Enquiry, Geographical Skills, and Places and Themes.

The Final Report pleased more teachers than the Interim Report, which is what one would expect. The curriculum content had been reduced, choice had been increased, and more emphasis had been placed on enquiry learning. The three ATs based on areas still posed problems, though attempts had clearly been made to deflect the criticism that knowledge of an area cannot by itself be an intellectually respectable target, by wording the SoAs in such a way that the emphasis was on an intellectual process rather than on recall. For example, in AT2 (The Home Area and Region), an SoA at Level 9 states: 'Pupils should be able to evaluate the ways in which local and central government and other organisations have attempted to stimulate, plan and control the development of the local area and region'. Clearly the emphasis here is on the evaluation of planning and development and not simply on the facts of the area. However, another problem which was well known at the time when regional geography syllabuses were in vogue, is that the same general idea is repeated in several different regional contexts. For example the phrase, 'explain how landscapes have been changed by human actions', or some similar phrase, occurs in AT2, AT3 and AT4 and always at Level 4, so no intellectual progression is involved. Such repetitions are likely to prove tedious for pupils.

As required by the 1988 ERA, the Final Report of the GWG was submitted to the National Curriculum Council (NCC) whose function was to consult widely about the proposals in the report and to make recommendations to the Secretary of State. The NCC reported in November 1990 (NCC, 1990). Its main recommendation was that the number of ATs should be reduced to five by combining the three area-based ATs to one. The NCC proposals were thus:

AT1   Geographical Skills
AT2   Knowledge and Understanding of Places
AT3   Physical Geography
AT4   Human Geography
AT5   Environmental Geography

The NCC report made clear that its decision to collapse the three area-based ATs into one was to avoid the kind of duplication of SoAs illustrated above. The NCC report was submitted to yet another Secretary of State, Kenneth Clarke, who had replaced John MacGregor in a Cabinet re-shuffle following Sir Geoffrey Howe's resignation from the Government. Clarke, whilst accepting the NCC's reduction in the number of ATs, proceeded to emasculate some of the proposals by omitting under AT1 (Geographical Skills) 'the use of secondary sources' and 'enquiry skills', on the grounds that such skills were not specific to geography. Further the Secretary of State argued that in AT2, AT4 and AT5 dealing with 'Knowledge and Understanding of Places', 'Human Geography' and 'Environmental Geography' respectively, SoAs should not be concerned with economic and political issues nor with people's attitudes or views. Consequently such issues and views were removed from the Draft Orders laid before Parliament, thereby demonstrating the power vested in the Secretary of State to determine the detail of a curriculum which, many argue, should only have been the concern of professionals.

INSIDER VIEWS OF THE PROCESS OF DRAFTING THE
NATIONAL CURRICULUM

Eleanor Rawling (1992) has, in her presidential address to the Geographical Association, carried out a lucid analysis of the way the geography
National Curriculum was drawn up. Considerable pressure was put on
the GWG by officials and by their chairman to incorporate place knowledge in the ATs, on the grounds that geography had failed children in the
recent past by not teaching them such place knowledge. This became
known as a 'deficit view of geography'. In effect it negated and effectively disowned all the thinking and experimentation that had been undertak-
en by curriculum workers both at the theoretical level and in the practice
of curriculum development. The work of the Schools Council and of the
various curriculum development projects was ignored. A somewhat different perception of the outcome of the whole exercise of formulating the
geography National Curriculum comes from Rex Walford, who like
Eleanor Rawling was a member of the GWG. He agrees with Eleanor
Rawling that the influence of the chairman and the DES officials, including the Assessor (Andrew Wye) 'who acted as the eyes and ears of the
Secretary of State' (Walford, 1992), was very powerful. Walford writes:

> A small agenda committee of the Chairman, Vice-Chairman, Secretary, DES
> Assessor, and HMI Assessor often met before the main meetings, ostensibly to
> determine the order of business; some of us came to wonder if the ultimate
> decision-making might not rest in such a conclave. It was a group notably light
> on the 'professional' element of the Working Group, and perhaps it was
> designed to be so.

It was clear to him that the DES, as against the HMI who were represented by Staff Inspector Trevor Bennetts, was intent on demolishing the
conventional wisdom emanating from curriculum theory and curriculum
development.

> The Assessor (and the Secretariat) also had a trump card to play – would things
> be 'acceptable' to the Minister in the last resort? The Assessor brought news of
> changes of government thinking almost weekly, and this complicated the task
> already underway.
>
> Walford, 1992

Walford, unlike Rawling, believed that, in going along with the essentially political nature of the operation, he could safeguard the position of
geography in the National Curriculum. He writes:

> Most of us as members of the Working Group understood the political nature of the exercise in which we were involved. Certain major principles underlay the institution of the Group: work in schools was not satisfactory, geography's *distinctive* contributions must be focused, the curriculum model was assessment led. These principles were unlikely to be overturned …the exercise was not one in which the Group members were pawns, but it was one in working 'within the realms of the possible'.
>
> Walford, 1992

And geography's *distinctive* contribution appeared to the non-professionals to be place and locational knowledge. Walford had hoped that by agreeing to include area-based ATs in the National Curriculum (with which he agreed, because of his adherence to the notion of 'cultural literacy' [Dowgill and Lambert, 1992]), the GWG could also incorporate some of the more 'ambitious and controversial topics'. Alas this was not to be and the excisions undertaken at the behest of Kenneth Clarke 'underlined the important shift in curriculum power that the 1988 Education Reform Act had brought to the curriculum in England and Wales' (Walford, 1992). Walford does not say whether the 'major principles underlying the institution of the Group' were made explicit to the Geography Working Group or whether, on reflection, he had been right to go along with these principles. There is a hint in his 1992 article that he feels that power over the curriculum had shifted too far away from the professionals to the 'politicians'.

MODEL OF THE CURRICULUM PROCESS IMPLIED BY THE GEOGRAPHY NATIONAL CURRICULUM

In effect, what we now have is a much simpler model of the curriculum process than that proposed by Jack Kerr in 1968. It is much more akin to the original model proposed by Tyler in 1949. A set of attainment targets (*Objectives*) determined by the state are placed before teachers, who have to teach these to pupils using the programmes of study (*Content*) – also determined by the state; teachers may use their own teaching strategies (*Methods*) and then they have to evaluate the learning of their pupils, again using instruments – Standard Assessment Tasks (SATs) – decided by the state. There is no feedback loop from evaluation as in the Wheeler or Kerr models, though teachers could infer that if pupils had not reached the attainment targets set, then their methods were inappropriate and they would need to modify these.

But there could be no modification of the objectives or of the content. Thus the model is rather an inflexible one.

Although, as Walford indicates, this is an evaluation-led model of the curriculum, it is the evaluation which proved its undoing. The total weight of evaluation imposed on teachers was such that in 1993, an overwhelming majority of teachers in all subject areas refused to administer the tests.

Modifications to the National Curriculum

In April 1992, following the general election, the Secretary of State for Education changed once again. John Patten, a former geography lecturer at Oxford University, was appointed to the post by Prime Minister John Major. The department was renamed the Department for Education (DFE). But before that event, modifications had been effected in the National Curriculum. Whilst under Baker's original 1988 ERA all pupils from 5 years to 16 years would have to take the ten subjects of the National Curriculum and be tested in these at the end of each key stage, in August 1989 MacGregor announced that all pupils would take GCSE examinations in all ten subjects at the end of Key Stage 4. By January 1990, MacGregor indicated that art, music and physical education would no longer be compulsory for 14 to 16-year-olds, and that it would be permissible to design half-sized courses for technology, history, geography and foreign languages. In February 1991, Clarke announced that 14 to 16-year-olds need no longer take both history and geography; they could choose between them or study a combined course taking up the time of a single subject.

In the meantime all was not well with the NCC and SEAC. Both chairmen, Duncan Graham and Philip Halsey, left in 1991 within a week of one another. Duncan Graham left because he felt that the NCC was being circumscribed by DES civil servants (Graham, 1993) and, although we have no firm personal evidence from Philip Halsey, the fact that he resigned soon after Kenneth Clarke had rejected as 'elaborate nonsense' English SATs for Key Stage 3 submitted by him on behalf of the SEAC, gives some indication. Soon after, the two bodies were merged into the School Curriculum and Assessment Authority. By 1993 teacher protests about the excessive content and testing of the National Curriculum were so powerful that Ministers were forced to take action. Sir Ron Dearing, who had been appointed chairman of the new School Curriculum and Assessment Authority (SCAA), was asked by John Patten in April 1993 to review the National Curriculum and the framework for assessing pupils' progress. Broadly, in his Final Report which came out in January 1994, he recommended:

- reducing the volume of material required by law to be taught
- simplifying and reducing the programmes of study
- reducing prescriptions so as to give more scope for professional judgement
- ensuring that the Orders are written in a way that offers maximum support to the classroom teacher.

In terms of time allocation, it has meant some reduction of formal teaching time allocated to each subject, in order to give schools the freedom to use 20 per cent of teaching time in Key Stages 1, 2 and 3, as they see fit. For geography, assuming a 36-week teaching year, it means that the weekly time allocation will be 1 hour at Key Stage 1, and 1.25 hours at Key Stages 2 and 3. At Key Stage 4 there is an altogether different scenario, since both history and geography now become optional subjects alongside art, music, home economics, a second foreign language, classics, religious studies, economics and business studies. The statutory curriculum would consist of English, mathematics, and science as full courses, and a foreign language and technology as short courses, whilst physical education, religious and sex education should remain as statutory requirements. The Dearing Report also recommended the development of an Academic and a Vocational pathway in Key Stage 4 to link up with post-16 courses of a similar type, at the same time allowing for 'bridges' to be built between pathways. Thus the General National Vocational Qualifications (GNVQ) could be taken alongside GCSE.

The Dearing Report was accepted by the Government, and the SCAA proceeded to set up new Working Groups to undertake the slimming-down of the curriculum content of each subject; each Working Group was chaired by an SCAA officer. In the case of geography the chairman was Keith Weller, assistant chief executive of the SCAA. The expectation was that once the revised Orders were law, there would be no further changes for five years. With respect to Key Stages 1, 2 and 3, new Orders were published in January 1995, with matching GCSE criteria for each subject sent to examination boards. Draft GCSE syllabuses were sent to the SCAA in June 1995; the SCAA was to respond in September 1995; and modified syllabuses were to reach the SCAA in October 1995 and be given final approval by the SCAA in November 1995. The printed syllabuses were to be in schools in January 1996.

As a means of reminding ourselves of the significant events in education and in geography since the 1950s, the following table has been drawn up (Figure 4.5).

Brief chronology of educational developments, 1950–95	
General developments	Geographical education
1950 Schools develop within the frame-work of the 1944 Education Act	Curriculum based on regional geography
Some comprehensive schools created	Relative stagnation of geography curricula
1964 Schools Council founded	
Many curriculum development projects launched	
1965 CSE examination introduced	Impact of conceptual and quantitative revolution begins on school geography
	Reform of examination syllabuses
1969 First Black Paper published	Development of thematic non-regional syllabuses
1970 Growth in number of comprehensive schools	Curriculum development projects in geography launched: Geography 14–18; Geography for the Young School Leaver; History, Geography, Social Science
1973 School leaving age now 16	
1976	Geography 16–19 launched
1980 The accountability movement takes root	
1984 Schools Council abolished SCDC and SEC created	
1988 GCSE replaces GCE O-level and CSE	

General developments	Geographical education
1988 National Curriculum incorporated into Education Reform Act NCC and SEAC created	
1989	*May*: Geography Working Group set up
August: all pupils to take 10 NC subjects at GCSE	
	October: Interim report of GWG
1990 *January:* Art, music, PE no longer compulsory for KS4	
	April: Final report of GWG Emphasis on place knowledge
	November: NCC proposes amendments to report
1991 *February:* Either history or geography or a combination of both to be studied at KS4	
1992 *April:* John Patten becomes Secretary of State	
July: White Paper *Choice and Diversity* published	
NCC and SEAC abolished	
1993 *April:* Dearing invited to slim-down the NC	
October: School Curriculum and Assessment Authority replaces NCC and SEAC	
December: Final Dearing Report	
1994 Working Groups set up to modify the National Curriculum	Geography Working Group set up
1995 *January:* New curriculum orders published	
June: New GCSE syllabuses with SCAA	
September: SCAA responds	
November: Modified GCSE syllabuses available	
1996 Printed syllabuses in schools	

Figure 4.5 Brief chronology of educational developments, 1950–95

In case it should be thought that concern about the geography curriculum was exclusively an English and Welsh matter, let us turn briefly to an examination of international initiatives.

Other initiatives on geography education

THE INTERNATIONAL GEOGRAPHICAL UNION

The International Geographical Union (IGU) is a union of geographers on a worldwide basis which was created in 1871 in Antwerp (Anvers), where the first International Geographical Congress (IGC) was held. Its main function is to enable geographers from all over the world to meet and exchange research findings and views on the development of the subject. It holds congresses every four years – the 1992 Congress was held in Washington DC in the USA, and the 1996 Congress is to be held in the Netherlands. Between congresses the work of the IGU is carried on by various specialised commissions, usually consisting of six to twelve full members and any number of corresponding members. One of these Commissions is the Commission on Geographical Education, which was first created in 1904 but disappeared soon afterwards, not to re-emerge until 1952 at the Washington congress of the IGU (Wise, 1992). Since then the commission's mandate has been renewed at each IGC, although the chairperson of the commission usually changes after eight years, and its work has become well known. In 1988, the Executive Committee of the IGU accepted that the main objectives of the commission would be:

1   to develop international guidelines for teacher education, geography curriculum planning and geography instructional materials

2   to promote integrated programmes in geographical education at primary, secondary and post-compulsory levels

3   to collaborate with other organisations in the development of geography as a scientific discipline in the school curriculum by co-sponsoring conferences, workshops and symposia

4   to develop exemplary classroom instructional materials in

geography and to carry out research in geographical education directed towards an international audience of geography teachers

5   to address pertinent issues related to geography instruction in higher education, both as general education and as specialised scientific study.

Relevant to the present context is a study carried out between 1988 and 1990, of the impact of centralised education systems upon geography curricula (Naish, 1990). It was a questionnaire survey initiated by the British Sub-committee of the Commission on Geographical Education of the IGU, guided by Michael Naish. Whilst the survey was a wide-ranging one covering such issues as curriculum control, aims and objectives, resources, assessment, curriculum development and the opportunities and constraints of working in a centralised system, here only a brief summary can be given of what respondents believed to be the advantages and disadvantages of working in a centralised system of education.

The view was expressed by many that a centralised system encourages teachers to teach and learners to learn a common body of knowledge; this means that teachers know precisely what is expected of them, and it facilitates the process of monitoring the curriculum and how far pupils have learned what they are supposed to learn. In developing countries it was felt that a more economical use of resources resulted. Curriculum design could also benefit from using the services of highly competent professionals.

On the other hand, there was a fear that the creativity of teachers might be stifled and that too much time might be spent on the assessment of pupils, to the detriment of stimulating learning experiences. There was also the fear that too much control by the 'authorities' might be inimical to catering for the needs of pupils, and that tensions might arise, as we have seen in England and Wales, between teachers at the periphery and officials at the centre. One senses that many respondents thought that an acceptable situation was one where some measure of curriculum prescription was allied to freedom for teachers to interpret the curriculum in ways which they felt were suitable for their own students as well as freedom to experiment with both content and methods of teaching. The present chairperson of the Commission on Geographical Education of the

IGU, Professor Dr Hartwig Haubricht and his commission, published in 1992 an International Charter on Geographical Education which was adopted by the General Assembly of the IGU at its 27th IGC in Washington DC, in August 1992. In effect the charter reaffirms geography's contribution to education, and to international education in particular, and it specifies in some detail what that contribution can be, what the content and concepts of geography are, and what the strategies for implementation should be, as well as the importance of research in geographical education (IGU, 1992). It does not recommend any one method of structuring the geography curriculum, but recognises that it may be structured along regional or thematic lines:

> At their best, both regional and thematic studies are strongly theory-oriented. In the context of teaching children, theories are used to illuminate the real world. In their studies, children should be encouraged to adopt a questioning or enquiry approach which will lead them towards the statement and application of generalizations and principles.

In the details of the Charter, the outline of the Thematic Studies seems to indicate clearly where the substance of geographical study lies, whilst Regional Studies of the local community, the home region, the home country, the home continent, other continents and the world and global structures, provide the contexts within which such themes may be studied.

THE NATIONAL COMMISSION ON EDUCATION

In August 1990, Sir Claus Moser in his presidential address to the British Association for the Advancement of Science, suggested 'an overall review of the education and training scene: a review which would be visionary about the medium and long-term future facing our children and this country; treating the system in all its inter-connected parts; and last but not least, considering the changes in our working and labour market scenes' (National Commission on Education, 1993). He had wanted a Royal Commission to undertake this review, but the government which had undertaken educational reform on its own terms through the Education Reform Act 1988, turned down this idea. Fortunately the Paul Hamlyn Foundation agreed to fund what was to be called the National Commission on Education. The National Commission under the chairmanship of Lord Walton of Detchant worked for two years, hearing and reading evidence from numerous sources, and commissioning research on different aspects of its enquiry. Its report, called *Learning to Succeed*, was published in November 1993.

Learning to Succeed is a wide-ranging review of the educational scene in England and Wales, but it has very little to say about geography specifically. Essentially it sees the curriculum consisting of a compulsory core of English (and Welsh in Wales), mathematics, natural sciences, technology, citizenship and a modern foreign language, from Key Stage 2 through to Key Stage 4, and the rest of the curriculum being decided by the school, although at least one subject must be chosen from each of the expressive arts and the humanities, the last of these to include history and geography. There is no mention of curriculum development. In one sense geography is better catered for under the Dearing Report since it will be part of the foundation subjects at Key Stages 1, 2 and 3.

Taking stock: curriculum development in the present context

THE PRESENT CONTEXT

In talking about 'the present context', I am conscious that it is different in different countries and that the political, economic and social imperatives inevitably vary. Yet I am struck by the way in which dominant themes seem to pass from one country to another much more rapidly now than they did in the 1950s and 1960s. Whereas the 1960s and early '70s were periods of optimism about the possible achievements of education – hence the investment in curriculum development projects – in the late 1970s and '80s there was more concern with the accountability of those using educational resources than with further curriculum development. Thus in the early and mid-1980s such books as *School Accountability* (Elliott *et al.*, 1981), *The Incompetent Teacher* (Bridges, 1986) and *The Control of Education* (Lauglo and McLean, 1985) were published. The late 1980s and early '90s seem to be concerned with the extent to which education can deliver the kind of workforce fit for the economic and technological demands of the twenty-first century rather than with free-wheeling educational development. So one finds that, in the UK for example, the minor curriculum development projects financed in the '80s have titles like 'Understanding Industry', 'Geography, Schools and Industry', whilst one of the National Curriculum cross-curricular themes is called 'Economic and Industrial Understanding'.

Thus the aims of education have veered from the intrinsic to the instrumental end of the spectrum, and the control both of finance and of the curriculum framework is tighter, though I am conscious that in many countries the curriculum framework has always been tightly controlled. Over and above this there has been concern about the education of those with special needs, which includes the gifted as well as those whose progress may be slow in certain areas of the curriculum (Warnock, 1978). Perhaps all-important in the present context is the need to cater for the multicultural nature of societies.

UNDERSTANDING THE CURRICULUM PROCESS

I am not sure that we have made any spectacular strides recently in our understanding of the curriculum process as a whole. What has happened is that, first, we are much more conscious of what this curriculum process means in the context of each individual subject area. Thus in the languages area, whether the home language or a foreign language, we have agreed that the skills we must concentrate on are those of listening, speaking, reading and writing. In mathematics, the relevant areas are numbers, algebra, measures, shape and space, and data handling. In biology, the working group concerned with developing attainment targets for the National Curriculum has concentrated on such areas as the variety of life, the processes of life, genetics and evolution; and similar choices have been made in the physical sciences. It involves knowing what essential ideas and skills must be taught and leaving out the rest.

Secondly, within each area we are conscious of what ideas and skills may usefully be taught and learned at particular stages in the school course. Hence in the National Curriculum proposals the idea has been accepted that the content of particular disciplines may be placed at one or more of ten levels. Such placings are more an art than a science at the present time, but they are informed by developments in cognitive psychology including work on the 'mediation of meaning' by Reuven Feuerstein (1980), in which 'instrumental enrichment' is used to develop cognitive processes in children whose minds need developing in that direction.

Thirdly, we are conscious that curriculum development involves teacher development. Thus no curriculum development can succeed without a substantial input of in-service education in which the ideas as well as the materials involved in the curriculum process are stressed in an active workshop situation. One of my most recent learning experiences has been that of using a computer for electronic mail and word processing. The manual was useful, but the hands-on experience absolutely necessary. Without investment in INSET, curriculum development can become inoperative, no matter how much was invested in the original scheme. This is as relevant to a national curriculum as it is for a single curriculum development project.

Lastly, we are also conscious that sometimes demands are placed on teachers which it is unrealistic to expect them to fulfil. I am mindful of this in relation to the UK where secondary school teachers are not only expected to teach their own subject, but are also expected to permeate their delivery of that subject with such cross-curricular themes as Economic and Industrial Understanding, Technology including Information Technology, Personal and Social Education, Health Education, and Careers Education. It is as well to be realistic in our plans for curriculum change, otherwise we will be heading for failure. The Dearing Report is to a large extent a recognition of the danger of attempting to do too much.

Curriculum development: a prognosis

ECONOMIC AND SOCIAL IMPERATIVES

Looking forward is no easy task in any society. Yet one needs to plan on certain assumptions about society and its education system. These will throw up problems which will need to be tackled with energy and goodwill by all sections of society.

From my own perspective, it would seem to me that there is a need to ensure that the economy grows at a sufficient pace to allow all to share in its benefits, and to permit a substantial investment in education to ensure that an educated and skilled workforce is present to further develop the economy. This investment in education will need to be both in upgrading schools and, even more importantly, in the development of teacher education, both pre-service and in-service, to ensure that all teachers are as well qualified as those in the better schools. This will be no mean achievement if it occurs.

CURRICULUM DEVELOPMENT FOR THE FUTURE

Since time is of the essence, and the need is to ensure that educational change has a relatively rapid effect in society, I would see a need to stress the instrumental aims of education and therefore the instrumental objectives of school subjects in so far as these can have such objectives. This is easier in mathematics and the sciences than it is in geography. This does not mean a complete neglect of what may be seen as cultural subjects such as literature. But as the Geography, Schools and Industry Project has shown, it is possible within the field of geography to embark on work closely related to the 'world of work' (Corney, 1985). It is as well to remember also that attitude formation is as important as skill development, since the way an economy works is as much dependent on the work ethic as on skills and knowledge, as is evident in the cases of Japan and Singapore.

Further, the need to experiment will still be present to ensure that the curriculum in general – and the geography curriculum in particular – does not begin to ossify. The somewhat looser framework suggested by the Dearing review in England and Wales should make it easier for teachers to develop their curricula.

It will be vital to ensure that there is feedback to the curriculum developers, not just by consulting the teachers, but by undertaking a thorough evaluation of the curriculum process including a consideration of the students' view of the curriculum development. I have in mind here the kind of illuminative evaluation developed by Parlett in the 1970s, rather than the traditional evaluation involving tests and statistical analysis (see Simons, 1987). Lastly, if a new curriculum is to be successfully introduced, specific efforts will be needed to ensure its dissemination in all schools.

Conclusion

We are not living in particularly happy times for education. The kind of respect for and encouragement of teachers that were typical of an earlier generation have vanished. The hard-nosed accountability movement is with us and we need to face it. But the process of education and curriculum development must of necessity be optimistic and forward-looking, otherwise it loses all purpose. There is ahead of us a hard road to tread, but schools and colleges must make an effort to develop curricula that will address the needs of present and future society, so that we do not fail future generations of our citizens. The curriculum needs to be both practical and theoretical since these are but two sides of the same coin. It needs to consist of transferable knowledge and skills which will enrich our students intellectually and materially. When we enrich our students, we enrich society (Warnock, 1988).

BIBLIOGRAPHY

Boardman, D. (ed.) (1985) *New Directions in Geographical Education*, The Falmer Press.

Bridges, E.M. (1986) *The Incompetent Teacher*, The Falmer Press.

Corney, G. (ed.) (1985) *Geography, Schools and Industry*, Geographical Association.

Dowgill, P. and Lambert, D. (1992) 'Cultural literacy and school geography', *Geography*, 77(2):143–51.

Elliott, J., Bridges, D., Ebbutt, D., Gibson, R. and Nias, J. (1981) *School Accountability*, Grant McIntyre.

Feuerstein, R. (1980) *Instrumental Enrichment*, University Park Press, Baltimore.

Further Education Unit (FEU) (1979) *A Basis for Choice*, Further Education Curriculum Resource and Development Unit, Department of Education and Science, London.

Graham, D. (1993) *A Lesson For Us All*, Routledge.

Graves, N.J. (1979) *Curriculum Planning in Geography*, Heinemann Educational Books, London.

(1980) *Geographical Education in Secondary Schools*, Geographical Association.

(1993) 'The genesis of the geography curriculum in the English and Welsh National Curriculum', in Jäger, H., *Liber Amicorum Günter Niemz*, Internationale Beiträge zur Geographischen Fachdidaktik und zur Regionalgeographie, University of Frankfurt am Main.

Graves, N.J., Kent, A., Lambert, D., Naish, M. and Slater, F. (1990a) 'First impressions', *Teaching Geography*, 15(1).

(1990b) 'Evaluating the Final Report', *Teaching Geography*, 15(4):147–51.

IGU (1992) *International Charter on Geographical Education*, Commission on Geographical Education of the International Geographical Union.

Kerr, J.K. (1968) *Changing the Curriculum*, University of London Press.

Lacey, C. (1984) 'The Schools Council: an evaluation from a research perspective', in Skilbeck, M. (ed.) *Evaluating the Curriculum in the Eighties*, Hodder and Stoughton.

Lauglo, J. and McLean, M. (eds) (1985) *The Control of Education: International Perspectives on the Centralization-decentralization Debate*, Studies in Education No. 17, Heinemann Educational Books.

Naish, M. (ed.) (1990) *Experiences of Centralization, an International Study of the Impacts of Centralized Education Systems upon Geography Curricula*, Institute of Education, University of London.

Naish, M., Rawling, E. and Hart, C. (1987) *Geography 16–19. The Contribution of a Curriculum Project to 16–19 Education*, Longman.

National Commission on Education (1993) *Learning to Succeed: Report of the Paul Hamlyn Foundation National Commission on Education*, Heinemann.

NCC (1990) *National Curriculum Council Consultation Report: Geography*, National Curriculum Council.

Rawling, E. (1992) 'The making of a National Geography Curriculum', *Geography*, 77(4):337.

Schon, D. (1971) *Beyond the Stable State*, Temple Smith.

Simons, H. (1987) *Getting to Know Schools in a Democracy: The Politics and Process of Evaluation*, The Falmer Press.

Skilbeck, M. (1984) *School-based Curriculum Development*, Harper & Row.

Tyler, Ralph W. (1949) *Basic Principles of Curriculum and Instruction*, University of Chicago Press.

Walford, R. (1992) 'Creating a National Curriculum: a view from the inside', in Hill, D. A. (ed.) *International Perspectives on Geographic Education*, Center for Geographic Education, Department of Geography, University of Colorado at Boulder.

Warnock, M. (1988) *A Common Policy for Education*, Oxford University Press.

Warnock Report, The (1978) *Special Educational Needs*, Her Majesty's Stationery Office.

Wheeler, D.K. (1967) *Curriculum Process*, University of London Press.

Wise, M.J. (1992) 'International Geography: The IGU Commission on Education', in Naish, M. (ed.) *Geography and Education*, Institute of Education, University of London.

5 The impact of the National Curriculum on school-based curriculum development in secondary geography

Eleanor Rawling

The terms 'curriculum development' and 'school-based curriculum development' are both relative newcomers on the educational scene. It was not until the 1960s that the process of planning the experiences which pupils were to gain in school was recognised as something requiring a name, discussion and 'development' in the formal sense. Much of the impetus for this more formalised view of the curriculum came from education thinkers in the USA (for instance from Tyler, 1949, published in the UK in 1971). The establishment of the Schools Council in 1964 also gave considerable stimulus to work in the UK, and led to the setting-up of a number of curriculum development projects. These were large-scale national projects and although the early ones tended to focus their efforts on detailed subject advice and all-inclusive curriculum packages, by the 1970s the emphasis was more on curriculum frameworks, with clearly identified opportunities for schools and teachers to implement these in individual ways. Indeed, by 1980, such school-based curriculum development was considered to be so important that Eggleston could write, 'school-based curriculum development has, in the early 1980s, become the dominant form of the curriculum development movement' (Eggleston, 1980).

In geography, the 1970s and early 1980s were the key years for school-based curriculum development in England and Wales, in the sense that teachers (at least in the secondary curriculum) took on a substantial role in planning the content and character of their geography courses and, most significantly, in sharing this planning experience with other teachers. The three secondary geography projects (Geography and the Young School Leaver (GYSL), Avery Hill; Geography 14–18, Bristol; and Geography 16–19) were instrumental in ensuring that large numbers of teachers were either directly or indirectly influenced by these activities, so that there was a great flowering of curriculum thinking, articles and books about the geography curriculum, and opportunities for profession-al in-service teacher development linked to these activities.

It will be argued that these developments can be understood better by envisaging three levels of curriculum planning (Figure 5.1) for a subject:

1 The *general level* which results in the establishment of broad curriculum frameworks or guidelines, as outlined in Graves' general level of curriculum planning (1979).

2 The *school level* in which courses or schemes of work are prepared.

3 The *classroom level* resulting in strategies for the teaching and learning taking place in individual lessons or sequences of lessons.

The geography project teams were active at the general level, setting out clearly structured aims and frameworks for geography, and so giving project teachers confidence to plan courses, schemes of work and teach-ing strategies (levels 2 and 3) to suit their own schools and pupils.

The purpose of this chapter is to explore how far the balance and sig-nificance of these different levels of curriculum development have changed, given the current situation in which schools are faced with implementing a centrally prescribed National Curriculum. The existence of a centralised National Curriculum is not necessarily in conflict with continued professional creativity and involvement at the school and class-room level. Indeed, the Government has always stressed that the National Curriculum is not intended to dictate how schools and individual teach-ers 'deliver' the curriculum (DES, 1989). However, the 1991 geography National Curriculum with its 5 specific attainment targets, 183 state-ments of attainment, overlapping programmes of study, and highly pre-scriptive details of places and topics to be studied, was so weighty a structure that it seemed to make further professional interpretation unnecessary. For many teachers and educationalists, it seemed that the geography National Curriculum would result in a decline or even the demise of school-based curriculum development, so that level 2 (course planning) and even level 3 (lesson planning) would disappear as creative activities, while teachers became mere 'technicians' delivering centrally devised requirements (see Schofield, 1990 and Robinson, 1992).

Level	Who does it?	What questions are asked?	What does it provide?
LEVEL 1 General level	National bodies – curriculum councils, e.g. SCAA, SCCC – curriculum projects, e.g. Geography 16–19, GYSL (in consultation with the profession)	*What* contribution can/should the subject make to the education of young people? *What* broad areas of geographic knowledge and skill development are essential for pupils to acquire at school? *How* can the subject's contribution be best outlined so that schools can develop this potential? *What* targets might be set for pupil achievement and how might this be monitored?	• Broad aims for the subject • A framework of themes, concepts and skills fundamental to the subject • Procedures/guidance on interpreting and implementing the framework • Assessment requirements and arrangements
LEVEL 2 School level	The school geography department (using the stimulus of interdepartmental and teacher group discussions)	*How* do we translate the broad aims? What is the general purpose and character of geographical education appropriate to our pupils? *What* particular content emphases, key ideas, skills and learning experiences will we offer to particular age groups of pupils? *How* and *when* will we assess pupil progress and achievements? *How* will we evaluate the success of programmes offered?	• Specific objectives for geographic education in the school and for each age group • Course outlines and teaching programmes • Departmental assessment strategy and agreed policy on monitoring/reviewing courses
LEVEL 3 Classroom level	The individual geography teacher in discussion with colleagues	*What* particular sequences of activities and experiences do I provide for each element of the geography course? *What* teaching/learning approaches and resources shall I use in particular lessons? *How/When* shall I assess pupils' progress and achievements? *How* will I know how successful my lessons are?	• Detailed schemes of work • Detailed lesson plans and decisions about resources • Plans for preparing/administering assessment tasks and recording/reporting results • Commitment to collect evidence/review lessons

Figure 5.1 Levels of curriculum planning for geography

There was, of course, only a brief period (1991–94) in which the 1991 geography National Curriculum was implemented and from which evidence can be sought of the effects on schools. Also, as this chapter is being completed, the whole ten-subject National Curriculum has been reviewed by Sir Ron Dearing and the SCAA, and the resultant revised geography curriculum has just been published for implementation in September 1995 (SCAA, 1995b). It is thus difficult to do more than make some observations about school-based curriculum development and to highlight some pointers for the future – but I believe this is worth doing. Over the next few years, as teachers face the immediate demands of interpreting yet another set of curriculum requirements, it will be important to keep in view some longer-term objectives for the geography curriculum. Accordingly, this chapter aims to explore the following questions in relation to geography in the secondary curriculum:

> What are the characteristics of school-based curriculum development? What did we learn from the curriculum development projects of the 1970s and 1980s?

> What impact has the 1991 geography National Curriculum had on these curriculum development activities, particularly on level 2 (the school level), and why? What difference will the revised Geography Order make?

> What is the outlook for school-based curriculum development in the future? Will there be continuing opportunities for creative development work at school level?

The flowering of school-based curriculum development

School-based curriculum development may be defined as the process of making plans and developing strategies for teaching the subject, starting directly from the needs, enthusiasms and expertise of the school, the pupils and the teachers. It is a process which normally takes place in the school and involves creative interpretation to suit the particular context. In some cases, planning for change may start from a relatively 'clean slate'. Fien (1984) outlines a series of questions to be asked when a new geography course is being planned, and these include questions like: 'What geographic knowledge and skills are important for pupils at a particular age and ability level to acquire? What content exemplars are most interesting and appropriate?' However, he points out that school-based curriculum development does not deny the role of central authorities (whether project teams or government committees) to provide answers to some of these questions in central guidelines or syllabus frameworks. The guidelines then become the standard starting point (level 1 on Figure 5.1) for further interpretation by individual schools and teachers.

In England and Wales in the 1970s, the Schools Council Geography Projects provided the initial central stimulus (level 1 planning) for creative rethinking. At a broad level, each tried to answer the questions: 'What can geography contribute to the education of young people? What geographical knowledge, skills and abilities are appropriate for the age group?' This was partly a response to the changes that had taken place in academic geography in which, during the 1960s, university geographers had developed a more conceptual approach to the subject and a greater use of quantitative methods and techniques. There was concern about how suitable some of these innovations were for school geography. More significantly, the projects were a reflection of a general trend in education to reconsider how well the school curriculum was serving the needs of young people in a rapidly changing society. Curriculum development projects were seen as the vehicle for improving the quality of education by setting out the broad agenda for the subject and then encouraging individual schools and teachers to match the detail of content and teaching/learning approaches to the needs of their own pupils. Accordingly, each geography project set out aims, objectives and a rationale for the subject in the appropriate age group; provided various procedures for designing courses and lessons; and sought appropriate teaching, learning and assessment strategies.

By clarifying the curriculum system in this way, the projects helped teachers to appreciate their creative role. The amount of structure and support given by the projects varied. GYSL provided the relative security of the three themes (Man, Land and Leisure; Cities and People; People, Place and Work) and packages of well-designed curriculum materials as a 'jumping-off' point for teacher input, all in relation to an initially very specific target group of less motivated, lower ability 14- to 16-year-olds. Geography 14–18 encouraged teachers to develop their own professional skills by taking on the full process of reviewing, designing and evaluating their own curricula within some broadly framed project guidelines. Geography 16–19, as Graves points out (1979), took more of a middle path between the two earlier projects – consulting teachers about alternative approaches but then developing with them a curriculum framework encompassing a distinctive approach to geography (people/environment) and an enquiry approach to learning. Teachers were given help in interpreting the framework to produce courses, syllabuses, schemes of work and lessons. Figure 5.2 shows how the project summarised the way in which central guidelines and school-based curriculum development activity worked together.

By the mid-1980s, it was apparent that the geography projects were having a major influence on the kind of geography being taught in schools, on pupil achievements, and most significantly on teachers' perceptions of their creative role in school-based development work. At its best, the geography classroom of these projects combined exploration of real issues and real places with the development of conceptual understanding and the application of geographical models and theories. Teachers used their newly recognised freedom to draw on local issues and matters of topical concern. A much wider range of teaching and learning strategies was also characteristic – including for instance simulation, individual research, role play and group discussion as well as more formal teacher exposition and essay writing. By the end of the 1980s, there was growing evidence from GCSE and A-level examinations and from those in higher education receiving new students, that project pupils were responding to the variety of approaches. Many were competent not only in skills and abilities specific to geography (like map interpretation) but also in broader transferable skills of handling evidence, communicating ideas and problem solving. They also showed greater confidence in their own ideas and a wider awareness of the relevance of the subject to current concerns. Many of these impacts were difficult to quantify. However, the number signed up for the project examinations was one hard indicator of project influence. Boardman (1988) estimates that about 42,000 pupils entered for GYSL-based O-level and CSE courses in 1984, and for the Geography

Major questions arising in curriculum planning	Appropriate element of the curriculum framework	Resultant response and curriculum action
1 What kind of geography provides an effective basis for the 16–19 curriculum?	• Approach to geography • Approach to learning	Enquiry-based study focusing on questions, issues and problems arising from people–environment interrelationships
2 What kinds of questions, issues and problems should be chosen as the focus for geographical study?	Four themes • The Challenge of Natural Environments • Use and Misuse of Natural Resources • Issues of Global Concern • Managing Human Environments	Questions, issues and problems relating to these four broad areas of concern
3 How can the enquiry be made distinctively geographical?	• Key questions and guiding concepts	By ensuring that enquiry is directed to: 1 asking the questions which geographers ask 2 illuminating important geographical concepts
4 How can the choice of study topics be monitored to ensure a balanced coverage?	• Curriculum matrix diagram	By plotting enquiry topics and/or syllabus components on to curriculum matrix diagrams to check whether desired balance has been achieved for (a) scale and (b) regional examples
5 What kinds of classroom procedures and teaching strategies ensure that enquiry is developed in the most effective way?	• Route for enquiry	The route for enquiry acts as a guide to the development of enquiry sequences in teaching and learning and as an aid to planning individual enquiry activities
6 In what ways can student achievement and response be evaluated?	• Route for enquiry	The route for enquiry acts as a reminder about the broad areas of intellectual activity developed during enquiry which may also be identified in assessment and evaluation

Figure 5.2 Geography 16–19 Project: A guide to the use of its curriculum framework by schools
Source: Naish, Rawling and Hart, 1987

16–19 Project, A-level alone accounted for about 14,000 candidates in 1994. As David Boardman has pointed out in relation to GYSL, the actual impact was much greater than this because many mainstream GCSE syllabuses after 1986 took on project characteristics not only in terms of content, but also by recognising a greater role for teachers in course construction (e.g. optional and school-based units) and in assessment (e.g. coursework assessment and individual projects). In the 16–19 age range the influence of Geography 16–19 was similar, with many A-level revisions of the late 1980s taking on '16–19' characteristics. The new GCSE National Criteria (1985) and the A-level Common Core (1983) also showed that project's influence, both having more similarity to curriculum frameworks than to core lists of subject content, and both focusing on people–environment enquiry. The projects' desire 'to help teachers to appreciate their role as curriculum developers' (Geography 16–19 aim) did seem to be bearing fruit by the late 1980s.

But success in 'project' implementation did not result in uniformity of practice. There were many different emphases given to 'project' geography according to the importance attached by individual schools to particular aspects of the 'project' approach, and this was the case whether the starting point was the highly structured packages of GYSL or the more open curriculum system approaches of Geography 14–18 and Geography 16–19. Hall (1976) points out that GYSL materials were often used without changing the teaching method (p. 187), whilst all the projects were aware that new teaching strategies were often taken on without the associated consideration of their purpose (Rawling, 1991a). The corollary of greater teacher freedom in curriculum planning was greater diversity in outcome at levels 2 and 3. In any case, involvement in a project was not the only way to participate in school-based curriculum development. Many teachers found stimulus in innovative commercial textbooks (e.g. the *Oxford Geography Project* and *Reformed Geography*) or in new examination courses, whilst journals like *Teaching Geography* and *Classroom Geographer* were influential in promoting new ideas. Overall there was a feeling of confidence in what had been achieved, and what appears now to be an unwarranted sense of optimism about the future. In fact, the debate about geography's place in the curriculum was already under way in the early 1980s, couched in more strident and instrumental terms. Rex Walford was warning in 1981 that geographic educationalists might have to trim their sails according to the changing direction of political winds (Walford, 1981). Looking back, it is easy to see that the project movement as a whole failed to react quickly enough to growing public unease about basic skills and place knowledge in geography. There was a tendency to find security in existing project themes and materials even while the more util-itarian tones of the educational debate raged. It was not that project frameworks were incapable of amendment. Each of the geography cur-riculum frameworks was flexible enough to allow a changed emphasis on place and some redirection of skill focus. A conference held in Oxford in 1980 (Rawling, 1980) brought the projects together for the very purpose of discussing their common messages and identifying strategies for the future. Indeed, it could be argued – as Michael Naish did at the Oxford conference – that the kind of professional development experience and attitudes to change which the projects had promoted, should have been ideally suited to a period of national rethinking and development of national guidelines. However, the educational debate was being conduct-ed in very different terms, and the Education Reform Act (1988) eventu-ally made it clear that there was to be a much greater degree of content prescription, a very different relationship between curriculum and assess-ment, and a diminished role for the teacher. The debate was not only about changing content but also about redefining curriculum control, and the resulting educational policies were inevitably going to have a profound impact on school-based curriculum development.

The conditions for creativity

Looking back over the core period of project activity, it is possible to iden-tify certain conditions in which school-based curriculum development flourished.

(a) *Control of the curriculum was seen as a shared responsibility*
Control of the curriculum was not an imposition by one dominant group. Thus the project teams took the lead in developing curriculum aims and broad content frameworks, providing only sufficient guidelines as were required for teachers to share the common project approach. The frame-

works established geographical themes, key ideas, generalisations, and guidance on selecting content. But they did not stray into levels 2 and 3 (school and classroom planning) other than in an exemplary capacity, leaving it to teachers to choose appropriate content examples and to decide on teaching/learning strategies. Borrowing terminology from European Community discussions, it might be suggested that this revealed a *principle of subsidiarity* in curriculum planning as an unspoken rule of the projects: leave curriculum decisions to be taken at the level closest to the school and pupils. In practice, this also meant that teachers were free to draw on local resources, contacts and current issues of relevance to the community in which the school was situated.

(b) *Within these levels of responsibility, curriculum development was seen as a co-operative team activity*

Project teams (particularly 14–18 and 16–19) involved teachers in working out aims and key ideas. At school level, members of the geography department were encouraged not only to work together (sometimes a new experience) but also to work in local teachers' groups or consortia. Groupworking fostered creative exchange of ideas and resources and, more significantly, the confidence to share problems and own up to mistakes in the non-threatening environment of a small informal group (Pitts, 1978). The Sheffield '16–19' co-ordinator, Elspeth Fyfe, writing in *Project News* 1982, commented:

> central to our work is a desire to cooperate at all possible opportunities. Five schools and eleven teachers are involved – a very special relationship has developed within the group. Curriculum development is not only hard work, it is also fun. Collectively, we can achieve so much more than individually.

Research carried out into the workings of these 16–19 teacher groups showed that much benefit was also gained from the involvement of college or university lecturers, like Fyfe, bringing stimulus or new ideas from academic geography or educational thinking (McElroy, 1980).

A major part of the dissemination strategy for all three secondary geography projects was the extension of these networks. For Geography 16–19, the 'working system of involvement' was crucial, ensuring that change was rooted in classroom practice, that teachers were involved in a continuous process of professional development, and that teachers themselves were able to act as the spearhead for dissemination (Naish *et al.*, 1987).

(c) *School-based curriculum development was seen as an evolutionary rather than a revolutionary process*

Teachers were encouraged to start from a review of existing provision and to build on the best of good practice as appropriate to the aims and objectives set for the subject. It did not require the abandonment of all existing content, resources and teaching strategies and their replacement by new ones. For instance, the Geography 14–18 Project referred to the need to analyse the existing situation and to 'review assumptions'; and the Geography, Schools and Industry Project (a smaller-scale national project operating in the 1980s and funded by the Geographical Association) put forward a 'process for planning and teaching schemes of work' which began with Stage 1 'Review existing schemes of work and students' existing knowledge, skills and understanding' (Corney, 1991). In practice, the work of all the projects did lead to substantial change in approaches and resources being adopted but what was significant was that teachers perceived this as building on their existing practice. The ideas had evolved from *their* work, they were part of the new look, not passive recipients of imposed ideas.

(d) *The different elements of the geography curriculum such as content, teaching/learning strategies and assessment, were thought of as integral parts of a curriculum system*

In this respect, change in any one part of the system was seen to have repercussions elsewhere. In particular, the importance of assessment was recognised. Unless the messages being given by the assessment and examination system were compatible with those being promoted by the curriculum, there was little chance of coherent and effective curriculum change. It is significant that all three secondary geography projects became involved with examination boards and project examinations as a means of influencing the complete curriculum system and of legitimising the changes they had made. Geography 16–19's insistence that a decision-making exercise should be part of the formal A-level examination, for instance, was initially greeted with some surprise. But it reflected the project's view that one good way to ensure that attention would be given to a full process of enquiry during the course, was to require students to use and apply it in the final examination.

(e) *A necessary part of curriculum development was seen as teacher development*
As Fien (1984) explains, 'school-based curriculum development and
teacher development are part of a single process – two sides of the same
coin, so to speak'. In order to plan and develop appropriate curricula for
their pupils, teachers use a wide range of professional skills and abilities.
At the same time, 'the very processes involved in such school-based curriculum development help to prepare those participating for the professional roles they will be required to undertake' (Naish *et al.*, 1987) – that
is, it is a form of professional development itself. All the projects appreciated this point and it is implicit in points (a) – (d) above.

Essentially, school-based curriculum development with all its perceived benefits, flourishes best in an atmosphere of professional trust and
confidence on all sides. Professional trust is not a bad foundation on which
to build a national curriculum. However, this was not to be the starting
point for the educational reforms of the 1980s, as numerous commentators have reported (e.g. Kelly, 1990) and as the experience of geography
has revealed.

The impact of the geography National Curriculum

The Statutory Order for National Curriculum Geography, published in
March 1991, presented geography teachers with a totally new situation –
a prescribed set of requirements for the subject from 5 to 16. The new
curriculum was to be implemented from September 1991 and the whole
process was to be made accountable by means of a system of statutory
national assessment at 7, 11, 14 and 16 years, although subsequently
assessment arrangements were considerably amended. The Order set out
five attainment targets (ATs), four of which focused on specific areas of
content and knowledge in geography (ATs 2 Places; 3 Physical; 4 Human;
5 Environmental) and one of which (AT1) outlined some narrowly
defined geographical skills, predominantly mapwork and simple fieldwork. For these attainment targets, the 183 statements of attainment
(SoA) at ten levels set out very specific details of topics to be known and
aspects to be covered. The programmes of study (PoS) repeated and elaborated these requirements with considerable detail on localities, regions

and countries to be studied. The geography National Curriculum put forward a highly prescriptive and very traditional view of the subject.

The initial reaction to the Order and indeed to the Geography Working Group's Interim and Final Reports which had preceded it (1989 and 1990) was one of concern and even disbelief. Many geography teachers feared that the clock was being turned back to give a traditional 'information about the world' view of geography and to reinstate a dusty 'capes and bays' style of regional geography (Schofield, 1990). Key ideas in geography were hard to find in the Statutory Order, and the Secretary of State (Kenneth Clarke) had intervened just before publication of the Draft Order to remove enquiry skills, issues and values. It seemed that the Order for Geography now presented 'a situation strangely out of line with current concerns and with best educational practice' as understood by geography teachers (Rawling, 1991b).

There is evidence that on the Geography Working Group, members were subjected to considerable pressure to ensure that geography addressed the utilitarian concerns for hard facts, place knowledge and traditional skills. For those minimalist thinkers in the Conservative Party, these were the main and only justifications of geography's place in the curriculum, and I have referred elsewhere (Rawling, 1992a) to the way in which the Working Group was steered by its chairman to a simple formula which placed those aspects 'up-front' in the attainment targets.

However, as evidence became available about the implementation of the geography National Curriculum over the years 1991–94, so other aspects of the Order's character assumed much greater significance than the traditional attainment target titles and detailed prescription.

Both the National Curriculum Council (1992) and the Curriculum Council for Wales (1994) carried out monitoring exercises in relation to the implementation of the original Geography Orders at Key Stages 1–3, whilst OFSTED, England (1993) and HMI Wales (1993) also published reports of the first years of the geography National Curriculum. The main conclusions from these sources bear a striking similarity. In each case, the response from school and local education authorities (LEAs) showed that the broad emphases of the Order (Skills, Places, Physical, Human and Environmental) were generally agreed to provide an acceptable if somewhat traditional base from which to develop courses and schemes of work. However, 'the way in which the AT/PoS structure has been inter-preted makes it difficult for teachers to plan and implement good-quality geographical work' (National Curriculum Council, 1992). The attain-ment targets and programmes of study did not work together in a com-plementary way.

> Because the PoS is largely made up of level-related content, there are substan-tial overlaps between the PoS for the four key stages. This causes problems for planning, results in repetition between the key stages and accounts to a large extent for the perceived overload at all key stages
>
> Curriculum Council for Wales, 1994

There was no clear content entitlement for each key stage. Consequently, teachers were confused as to the exact nature of their role in implementation and, indeed, uncertain as to whether they should start planning from ATs or PoS. In addition, the Order, whilst hinting at the importance of geographical enquiry, failed to make clear how this process of finding out in geography could be integrated with, or was even com-patible with, the predominantly descriptive SoA.

Given this situation, much depended on teachers' understanding of the problems and on their perceptions of how these difficulties might be addressed. The Geographical Association explicitly recognised these structural faults but took the line that constructive support to geography teachers on making the most of the National Curriculum (Rawling, 1991c) was the best way to promote high-quality geography, at the same time as continuing to campaign for change behind the scenes. Many LEAs also provided sound support aimed at imposing well-tried curriculum planning practice onto the Order (e.g. Staffordshire, Hampshire), and it is interesting to note that the most popular and well-used official Non-Statutory Guidance – that produced by the Curriculum Council for Wales (1992) – also took this compensatory approach. Inevitably, some publications aimed at the National Curriculum market went straight for specific SoA linkage or for comprehensive coverage of the AT require-ments direct from the Order, and for many teachers these seemed to pro-vide a quick and easy answer to 'delivering' requirements.

It is not surprising, then, that OFSTED and HMI Wales found a con-siderable diversity of practice in the early years of implementation of National Curriculum geography. The OFSTED report (1993) pointed out that high-quality geography teaching and learning was usually linked with sound school-based curriculum planning. Although some curriculum plans were based on amending existing practice and others had started afresh, the significant common factor was that teachers had perceived the need to impose their own planning approach to compensate for the problems of the Order. This then resulted in 'detailed discussion within departments, allowing geography specialists to contribute towards a team approach and reach a fully understood rationale and shared objectives'. Good practice was also characterised by the preparation of curriculum plans for the whole key stage, making clear the integrated nature of places, themes and skills and 'having specific objectives in mind, usually in terms of key ideas, skills and attitudes'.

Reports from individual teachers of their experience in planning National Curriculum geography seemed to reinforce this evidence. The Secondary Section Committee of the Geographical Association published a collection of case studies of Key Stage 3 planning (Fry and Schofield, 1993), revealing that all six contributors were aware of the faults and difficulties of the Order and had in various ways imposed their own philosophy and planning approach. Schofield, introducing the publication, stated his view that it was essential that geography teachers did adapt the Order to 'make it work in line with advances in geographical education that have been made since the 1960s', but he commented that this was 'an immense task' and one that would be made easier if structural amendments were made to the Geography Order. Otherwise, he inferred that good practice would be patchy, and 'good' departments would suffer from National Curriculum fatigue.

OFSTED visits found that the poorest quality of geography offered tended to be in departments that had perceived the teacher's role in more narrow terms as delivering some very specifically defined content. Invariably, this was characterised by focusing almost exclusively on attainment targets, neglecting the programmes of study and failing to consider any overall objectives or purpose for the courses. Such departments often relied exclusively on one textbook. HMI Wales reported finding a minority of cases where schools 'were using the Statutory Order in an unmodified form as the basis for a scheme of work'. In these cases, 'courses lack cohesion and contribute to schools falling behind targets set for the year'.

Schools' approaches to assessment showed a similar range. The best practice was found where departments had planned assessment tasks as an integral part of learning, including a variety of tests and tasks from which to gain evidence and concentrating on obtaining an overall view of the pupil's level in geography rather than recording results on every SoA. HMI Wales reported that this kind of curriculum-led approach contrasted markedly with schools which either made no reference to SoA at all or attempted to assess every single SoA, these two representing 'the extremes of indifference and overcomplexity in meeting NC requirements'.

A small-scale research survey of the way in which teachers in southeast England and south Wales were handling Key Stage 3 assessment arrangements in 1993 (Daugherty and Lambert, 1994) found that both creative (artistic) and more technical rule-following responses to planning National Curriculum assessment could be found amongst the sixty schools surveyed. The difference in approach could be strongly linked to the way in which the department perceived the spirit and purpose of the geography curriculum as a whole *and* its own role in implementation.

Research recently undertaken in south Yorkshire involved following the experience of three secondary schools in implementing the geography National Curriculum at Key Stage 3, between 1989 and 1994 (Roberts, 1995). The three schools were chosen for their distinctive philosophies and approaches to geography before the National Curriculum was imposed. Roberts characterises them as perceiving the curriculum either as content to be transmitted, or as a framework of ideas, skills and values to be expanded, or as a process of pupil development. She found that the way these schools responded to and implemented the Geography Order was related most directly to their pre-National Curriculum style. Thus the school which believed the curriculum to be most concerned with transmitting content found least adjustment to make with the content-based Geography Order. Conversely, the other two departments made major efforts to retain their distinctive approaches despite an apparently alien philosophy. From the evidence of these three schools, Roberts comments:

> Deeply held beliefs about what it is to teach and to learn are persistent. In these three schools, teachers' and students' roles have remained the same. Teachers

frame the new curriculum according to the ways they learned to frame the old curriculum.

Roberts, 1995

The conclusion which seems to be emerging from this limited evidence is that the extent to which schools continued to find a role for themselves in creatively developing the curriculum and assessment during the early 1990s (and so according to OFSTED and HMI Wales in maintaining high-quality geography teaching and learning) was directly linked to the way they perceive their professional role – and this despite the acknowledged problems of the original Order. Effectively, school-based curriculum development was 'hanging on', having given some teachers the ability to cope in their own way with the changed context of the National Curriculum. However, the task of maintaining one's own philosophy and developing the curriculum to suit the school was undoubtedly made much more difficult by the highly prescriptive and badly structured Geography Order. Despite Roberts' findings in the three schools, OFSTED/HMI evidence seems to indicate that some teachers may, initially at least, have given up the battle with the Order and assumed a 'delivery' mode rather than a 'creative' mode of operation.

Given this situation, what impact will the revised Geography Order make on this situation? Will it help to persuade more teachers to reconsider their role in this respect instead of merely delivering National Curriculum requirements, and how can school-based curriculum development be made more secure?

The Dearing National Curriculum review

In May 1993, Sir Ron Dearing was asked to undertake a complete review of the National Curriculum and Assessment arrangements. The Dearing Final Report, published in December 1993, made it clear that the broad-balanced curriculum was to be retained at Key Stages 1–3 but that all ten National Curriculum subjects (eleven in Wales) were to be considerably simplified in format and reduced in content, allowing greater room for professional input by teachers. At Key Stage 4, even greater flexibility was to be gained by reducing the statutory requirement to a smaller core.

The emphasis, particularly in the non-core foundation subjects, was to be on outlining a core of prescribed content whilst also recognising options for schools to develop work beyond the minimum. Assessment requirements were to be considerably reduced overall. Dearing envisaged that one way in which both curriculum and assessment could be simplified was by making a significant reduction in ATs and associated SoA for all subjects, although an amended ten-level scale was to be retained. During the spring of 1994, officers of the School Curriculum and Assessment Authority worked intensively at putting these proposals into practice, operating through appointed Key Stage groups and subject groups. The main curriculum proposals were distributed for consultation in mid-May 1994, amended in line with the main consultation messages during the autumn of 1994, and finally approved by the Secretary of State and published in January 1995 for implementation in September 1995. Amendments were made to the assessment arrangements for the core subjects of English, Mathematics and Science, but for all other subjects it was agreed that major decisions about the scale and nature of assessment would be held in abeyance until the new curriculum was implemented.

The impact of the Dearing review on the geography curriculum is substantial. The subject remains a statutory part of the 5–14 (Key Stages 1 to 3) curriculum although it is now optional at 14–16 (Key Stage 4). For Key Stages 1 to 3, the opportunity has been taken to address some of the faults of the original Order. Both the Geographical Association and the Council of British Geography campaigned strongly for structural changes to be made and indeed the Dearing Final Report contained a separate paragraph (4.39) which sanctioned such an approach, despite the fact that the whole Dearing exercise was publicised as merely slimming-down from existing requirements. In the new Geography Order, the programmes of study now present the main content to be studied at each Key Stage in the form of a much-reduced but more distinctive set of requirements. The broad emphases of the older Order (Skills, Places, Human, Physical and Environmental) are confirmed as important aspects of the subject but they appear as headings in the PoS, not as separate ATs. Although there may be some debate about the strength of commitment to geographical enquiry, it is referred to in each PoS and implied in the wording of both PoS and level descriptions – 'investigative' seems to be the code word.

Locational knowledge is set out in the PoS and reference is also made to awareness and understanding of the wider world as appropriate to all Key Stages. All in all, the emphasis, as far as curriculum planning is concerned, has now been redirected back to the programmes of study and the greater clarity about each Key Stage entitlement is reinforced by the introductory paragraphs to each Key Stage.

Alongside this, there is only one attainment target (Geography) with a set of eight level descriptions (plus one description of exceptional performance) rather than statements of attainment, to be used to summarise and report on pupils' progress in geography.

The initial reaction of the geography education world to the new Order is generally one of relief that structural amendments have been made, tempered by some concern at the specific detail of the reductions and disappointment at the Key Stage 4 situation. Roger Carter, writing in the *Times Educational Supplement* (November 1994) as Chair of the Geographical Association's Education Standing Committee, stated:

> The revised National Curriculum for geography is good news. Most of the problems identified in the earlier Order have been addressed, although some with more success than others. Teachers will now be able to work with programmes that are more realistic in content terms, more straightforward in presentation, and clearer about the relationship between Key Stages.

Of course, there are still some big issues to address for geography: the character of the level descriptions and their use in assessment; the development and success of new GCSE syllabuses; the opportunities for geography in vocational courses; and the whole future of geography assessment.

However, there is little doubt that requirements like those offered by Dearing provide a better basis for school curriculum planning. Though labelled as a core of geography — a term which sounds politically acceptable to Ministers — the new proposals may best be likened to a curriculum framework (level 1 on Figure 5.1) setting out the main topics and experiences to be covered but leaving considerable room now for school-based development or, as Carter put it, 'to refocus on the quality of teaching and learning'. The question is — will teachers see it in this way? The decision has been made not to allow the School Curriculum and Assessment Authority to produce non-statutory guidance for the new National Curriculum, although there will be some information and advice about the use of information technology (Spring 1995) and exemplification of the level descriptions for each subject (1996). The Geographical Association is planning substantial curriculum support which will start from well-tried curriculum planning principles. However, the evidence from three years of implementation of the original National Curriculum revealed that the key factor in all this is teachers' perception of their role. The amendments to the Order are a good start but it may be argued that many teachers will not find it so easy to return to a pre-National Curriculum atmosphere of professional confidence. The revised National Curriculum has been hailed as giving back the initiative to teachers and reinstating their professional contribution – for many educational commentators this was the crux of the Dearing review. But, as the details of the changes are digested and plans are made for implementation, the big question is – have the new proposals made a real and lasting impact on the conditions which have been outlined as essential for school-based curriculum development to flourish?

Re-establishing professional confidence?

Earlier in this chapter, five factors were identified as fundamental for school-based curriculum development and professional creativity (pages 108–11). These will now be reconsidered to see how far the National Curriculum developments of the last decade have diminished them, and what are the opportunities for re-establishing them in the post-Dearing era (Figure 5.3).

(A) SHARED CURRICULUM CONTROL

The experience of the curriculum development projects seems to confirm that creative school-based curriculum development flourishes when control of the curriculum is shared in a meaningful way. Effectively this means recognising the three levels of curriculum planning (Figure 5.1) and respecting the need for decisions to be made by the appropriate body or group. It is quite legitimate for governments to set out frameworks for curriculum and assessment at the general level. However, if education is to address the needs of individual schools and pupils, those frameworks must be interpreted and developed at the school level, and eventually

Important conditions	Characteristics of 1989–94	Characteristics post-Dearing
(a) *Shared curriculum control* • Recognition and respect for three levels of curriculum planning	— Curriculum control imposed by detailed Statutory Order — All levels of decision-making appeared to have been appropriated nationally	— Apparently greater recognition of school/teacher input [Dearing] — Geography proposals more clearly represent a national framework [May 1994]
(b) *Teacher teamwork* • Teachers work together in supportive environment on curriculum planning	— Focus on individual schools and teachers *delivering* requirements — Existing curriculum support networks wither (especially LEAs)	— Provision of Orders still seen as all that is required from central body — Still no coherent policy of curriculum support for schools or subjects
(c) *Building on good practice* • New developments draw on existing good practice and teacher commitment	— 'Deficit' view of geography as context for original proposals — Denial of curriculum project experience	— Greater emphasis on teachers and professional input — Character/extent of guidance still awaited
(d) *The curriculum system* • Content, teaching/learning approaches and assessment recognised as integral parts of one system	— Decisions about specific content made with no reference to impact on curriculum and assessment — Assessment matters ignored in original proposals	— New AT/PoS structure more clearly operates as a system — Level descriptions targeted to assessment purpose – but not trialled
(e) *Professional development* • Teacher development seen as an essential part of curriculum development • Confidence/trust	— National Curriculum development overall diminished teacher confidence and trust — Over-prescriptive Geography Order perceived as deskilling and demotivating	— Dearing review claims that professional input is being revalued

Figure 5.3 The conditions in which school-based curriculum development flourishes

translated into classroom teaching/learning situations at the individual teacher level. The 1991 geography National Curriculum did not respect this division of responsibility. In its over-prescription and misapplication of the AT/PoS structure it gave the impression that all levels of curriculum planning were appropriated by the centre. As already explained, the result was confusion in teacher role and the not surprising reaction of many that they were not required to plan the curriculum any more, only to 'deliver' requirements. Lambert (1994) suggests that the geography National Curriculum called into question the whole nature of 'teacher work'.

> There is a chasm between those who interpret teaching in craft/labour terms and those who see it as a professional or even artistic role involving critical reflection usually in a collegial setting. The National Curriculum is a device which some teachers imagine denies them certain kinds of decision. The direct message to these teachers seems to be less autonomy and more conformity.
>
> Lambert, 1994

It is interesting to look back at the final report of the Geography Working Group. I have elsewhere referred to this as 'a report within a report' (Rawling, 1992a) because the supplementary chapters recognise the teacher's role and are full of advice on curriculum planning, despite the narrowness of the AT/PoS proposals themselves which seem to be directly incompatible with such sentiments. Chapter 10, in particular, is all about helping teachers to appreciate their role in determining the 'content and teaching methods which they consider to be appropriate', and paragraph 10.5 sets out a process of curriculum planning which draws directly on the experience of the projects. As a member of the original Geography Working Group, I know that this attempt to raise the profile of school-based curriculum activity, even incongruously linked to a faulty Order, was a deliberate strategy – in the hope that subsequent amendments and implementation could pick up these hints.

How far is the 1995 Geography Order likely to reinstate school and teacher involvement in decision-making? As explained, with the requirements reduced to a much clearer and more concise set of Key Stage emphases and with level descriptions decoupled from specific content, the opportunities are apparently now there. But, as Carter has pointed out (1994), much depends on teachers recognising this role and being encouraged by curriculum guidance and support strategies to do so. The new Geography Order does not recognise core and options, as was originally intended – essentially the Order comprises a framework, so the onus is on teachers to develop and take ownership of the curriculum (Rawling and Westaway, 1994). The 'option' actually is to turn it into experiences and activities best suited to the school, not an option at all but essential to ensure geography's contribution to the whole school curriculum. For geography, given the history of the Order, it would have seemed that there was, at the least, a need for a lead from the centre about this interpretation. However, it is now clear that the new Order stands on its own as the main element of central responsibility, and that SCAA and ACAC (the Curriculum and Assessment Authority for Wales) will not be allocated funding for anything that sounds like 'classroom guidance'. After the over-prescription of the original Order, it is ironic that the central authorities are now drawing back from giving necessary help. It remains for other support providers to ensure that teachers appreciate their reinstated professional responsibilities.

Recognition of these responsibilities would also help to allay the fear circulating about the future of cross-curricular themes. 'Near disappearance of environmental education and other cross-curricular themes', announced the *Times Educational Supplement* (11 March 1994), suggesting that the reduction in content of the geography curriculum would automatically lead to a decline in attention to these themes. In fact, as geographers know, there is no shortage of possibilities even in a reduced curriculum specification to pick up environmental, political, social and economic issues. The important factor is the way in which teaching and learning activities are planned to emphasise the application of understanding and skills to real world issues (Rawling, 1991d) and to promote critical reflection by pupils. Geography's role in developing cross-curricular themes and dimensions will be assured if teachers take back their creative planning role, and hold on to the curriculum time needed to make links into the community and the world beyond school. Much will depend on the messages teachers receive about how far cross-curricular capabilities are valued; currently schools are getting little encouragement in this respect from central bodies, a situation contrasting markedly with that of five years ago when full NCC guidance was prepared (NCC Curriculum

Guidance series). However, there are signs that other education bodies (for example the World Wide Fund for Nature) and business and industry are attempting to fill the gap. A new (1995) 'Pathways to Working Life' initiative, sponsored by business and industry, is working with schools to develop new guidance and support for all cross-curricular themes.

At this point it is worth taking a sideways glance at another curriculum initiative, in progress at the same time as the National Curriculum review, but inevitably somewhat overshadowed by the Dearing debate. The Department for Education's IT in Schools unit has established a curriculum-led view of IT, taking advice from subject specialists that information technology is most likely to be used effectively in schools if it is seen as an integral part of good practice in the subject. The DFE has been working initially with four secondary school subjects (maths, science, technology and geography) and over the past eighteen months has refocused the Grants for Educational Support and Training (GEST) for IT and made funds available for curriculum support in all these subjects. The details of this work are written up elsewhere (Rawling, forthcoming). However, what is significant here is that for geography, the DFE has recognised that the most lasting curriculum change will be made if teachers are given a clear framework outlining the way in which IT can contribute to good-quality geographical learning and are then given adequate resources and guidance to implement the framework creatively in their own schools. The Geography/IT leaflet (1994) funded by the DFE sets out this approach succinctly, the final page presenting a curriculum planning diagram directly descended from 'project' philosophy. The new geography and IT Orders and subsequent guidance material from SCAA (1995a) reinforce this approach, so that curriculum planning ideas are at least permeating through one significant source.

(B) TEACHER TEAMWORK

An essential feature of creative school-based curriculum planning is that it is a co-operative team activity characterised by teachers working together in school departments and with other teachers in the local area to interpret central requirements. The general ethos of the 1988 Education Reform Act seemed to run counter to this atmosphere – stressing the responsibilities of individual schools and teachers to 'deliver' detailed requirements and to be 'accountable'. Other parts of the ERA (e.g. local management of schools, opting out, city technology colleges) were designed to dismantle all the structures (often LEA planned) which had given teachers the necessary support to work in curriculum groups. In addition, there is evidence that increasing administrative demands on heads of departments, other responsibilities given to department members, and increasing reliance on non-specialist staff, are collectively making an adverse impact on time available for subject planning work (Bowe *et al.*, 1992). For geography, a National Curriculum INSET Task Group surveyed the situation in 1991 and reported that 'the National Curriculum has initiated a major curriculum development exercise in geography. The publication of the Statutory Order is only the first step, the subsequent follow-up is crucial'. It went on to recommend the establishment of regional and local support structures providing opportunities for teacher interaction and 'shared interpretation of geography National Curriculum and clear messages about what is intended and required' (National Curriculum Council, 1991) (i.e. effectively a National Curriculum dissemination and support strategy). The report remained unpublished and apparently ignored.

The Geographical Association's series of nine regional INSET seminars which was run during 1991/92 revealed that the ERA reforms had already caused the demise of many existing courses, teachers' groups and curriculum consortia, and a reduction in the number of LEA subject advisory staff, just at a time when geography teachers needed these most. Their intended replacement by services offered in the new market-led situation had not yet materialised. The effect on geography teachers was noticeable: 'opportunities for genuine curriculum development activities and planning creatively are virtually non-existent'. The GA's response was to start establishing a regional support network which would 'provide coherence and support to geography INSET and to geographical education in general' (Rawling, 1992b). Although the DES (as it then was) showed interest in this initiative (1992), it was left to the Geographical Association (GA) to provide the funding for the network. A two-region pilot project went into operation for 1993/94 and an evaluation of the first year highlighted the beneficial impact being made on dissemination of ideas, shared development work and opportunities for new initiatives (Rawling, 1994). As a result the GA has now extended its pilot region network to cover all of England, Wales and Northern Ireland. The DFE's IT initiative specifically targeted regional and local curriculum activity with funding allocated for this purpose. What is more, management of the Geography/IT activity has been explicitly handed over to the Geographical Association in close co-operation with the National Council for Educational Technology, and the GA's regional strategy has been an added incentive in this respect.

The experience of geography seems to reveal a more general point about incompatibility between different elements of government policy. The establishment of a centralised National Curriculum has set in motion a major curriculum change affecting all levels of the system, and yet to implement it will require a co-ordinated programme of support which the new 'free market' structure is as yet unable to provide. Lawton (1992) suggests that this conflict of ideologies runs deep within government policy as a whole. For geography, the confusions and uncertainties of recent years mean that there is now a pressing need for teachers to talk through the experience and to share interpretation of the new Order. Without the support of this 'team' approach, however provided, the hard-won improvements to the Order's curriculum structure may yet fail to achieve the expected impact on the quality of geography offered in schools.

(C) BUILDING ON GOOD PRACTICE

As Graves commented (1979), 'it is much more likely that a gradualist approach will succeed in making curriculum changes, when an attempted revolution may cause chaos and little else'. A revolution seems to have been what the Conservative government had in mind for geography. When the original geography National Curriculum was being prepared, a 'deficit' view of geographical education was consciously promoted by Ministers and the DES. Kenneth Clarke, when Secretary of State, made it clear that he believed that geography was 'fading in importance and in strength ...in our schools' and that this was because geography needed to re-emphasise 'learning about places and where they are ...not just vague concepts and attitudes' (*Hansard*, 29 April 1991:123–4). The deficit view was extremely unhelpful as a context for the work of the Geography Working Group, leading to the feeling that any previous experience was equated with things going wrong and should therefore be ignored. In their unrelenting focus on specific content and the avoidance of key ideas, enquiry learning, and the role of the teacher in curriculum planning, both the Interim and Final Reports of the GWG seemed to deny the previous twenty years of curriculum development. I have pointed out elsewhere (1992a) that the professional geographical educators on the Group must take some of the blame for this situation, failing to present a common message about the significant points learned from curriculum project experience. Even given the refocused content required by Ministers, it should have been possible to ensure that the structure of the Order allowed a clear route for teacher involvement. In the event, teachers received the message from both the content and the structure of the Order that their experience was not required – they were to ignore the past and start again. Many of course did not do so – encouraged by the support materials from the GA and CCW in particular, to take ownership of the curriculum despite the unfriendly curriculum language. Equally however, as OFSTED/HMI reports showed, some teachers undoubtedly redefined their role in the early 1990s more as technicians and have abandoned previous curriculum planning processes based on key ideas, in favour of those delivering bundles of content-defined SoA.

The language and tone of the new Order are more friendly to teachers and there is no reason why geography teachers should not feel encouraged to draw on all their previous experience to apply to interpreting the new proposals. Hacking (1994) writing about initial teacher education and the National Curriculum explains that this has been the approach at the Oxford Department of Educational Studies, so that new teachers do not feel deskilled by recent developments. However, in one sense the damage has already been done. The 1989–94 National Curriculum experience was initially seen as a sharp change of direction, diametrically opposed to all that went before. The new-look 'technical manuals' covering SoA one by one, are already on the publishers' shelves and on pupils' desks vying for attention with the more curriculum-led approaches. Although, as Roberts (forthcoming) has shown, it is likely that some schools will assimilate the Order into their existing structures and philosophies, it may take some time before 'National Curriculum shock' is overcome so that geography education can move forward again in an evolutionary way.

(D) THE CURRICULUM SYSTEM

The Final Report of the Geography Working Group (DES, 1990) contained a diagram grandly entitled 'The Curriculum System for
Geography 5–16'. In fact this diagram was an afterthought included to
justify the Group's proposals and to suggest that curriculum issues raised
in the Interim Report consultation had been addressed. During the
Working Group deliberations, the integral nature of the different elements of this curriculum system were not recognised, although advice
was offered from within and outside the Group. The first five months of
the Group's work were spent entirely on attainment target emphases, as
an exercise in selecting content and in complete isolation from any consideration of their role in and likely influence on assessment. Daugherty
(1992) commented that the Group 'evidently did not see the design of
curriculum and assessment being closely interrelated', and in particular
he noted the unfortunate disregard for the assessment implications of
content-specific SoA. As Chair of SEAC's Geography Committee at the
time, Daugherty knew that SEAC advice had been given to the Geography
Working Group on this very topic (1990 and 1991), but it was ignored as
likely to delay the timetable. Assessment was anyway seen by some members of the Group (Walford, 1992) as something which could be attended
to later.

This failure to appreciate the integral nature of the curriculum system,
and particularly the importance of assessment, has caused continuing
problems for geography, as already mentioned. Teachers have struggled
to plan coherent courses whilst recognising the highly specific and numerous SoA; teacher assessment has turned into 'a nightmare' (Curriculum
Council for Wales, 1994); and the team established to develop national
Key Stage 3 tests in 1992/93 found that the lack of clarity and purpose
about assessment was one of the major problems with the Geography
Order. The new Order apparently presents a clearer picture. The PoS are
now presenting the material to be taught; the level descriptions are to be
used as 'best-fit' descriptions of pupils' progress regardless (within limits) of which Key Stage programme they are following. However, there
are still many unanswered questions crucial to the way in which geography will be interpreted in schools. How will teachers actually apply the
level descriptions? How will those descriptions relate to the work under-

taken for a Key Stage? Where will teachers find assistance with progression in key geographical ideas and skills, still essential to developing quality geographical work but not available in PoS or SoA or level descriptions? And probably most fundamental of all: What is the purpose of the new system? Are level descriptions to be used purely for reporting to parents? What weight will be given to a varied range of teacher assessment activities in this process? Where, if at all, do national tests fit into this picture? Materials that exemplify the geography level descriptions for Key Stage 3 and give some guidance on the process of making judgements about pupils' work will be available from the SCAA, but not until 1996, as preparation for the return of statutory teacher assessment for Key Stage 3 in 1997. Other decisions about tests and about reporting mechanisms remain to be made at the time of writing. However, all these matters will affect the status and quality of geography in schools, and ultimately they are fundamental to the value that teachers place on their creative role in curriculum development.

(E) PROFESSIONAL DEVELOPMENT AND TRUST

Many educationalists have pointed out that the National Curriculum developments of the past decade do not appear to have been focused on trust and confidence in the professionals. Ball (1990) comments:

> ERA ... is about control over teachers and teacher work. It rests upon a profound distrust of teachers and seeks to close down many of the areas of discretion previously available to them. In doing this, it brings into being a massively over-determined system of education.

In microcosm, the experience of geography in England and Wales in the years 1989–94 reveals just such a situation and the big question is: Will the new Geography Order really change all this? A more appropriate curriculum framework for geography has been designed; the rhetoric of Dearing is that of recognising professional input and professional responsibility. However, the extent to which this is more than a superficial change will only become apparent over the next few years. After all, the logic of the arguments put forward in this chapter is that greater teacher responsibility for levels 2 and 3 of curriculum planning will almost certainly provide a geographic education better suited to individual schools and pupils; however, it will also lead to greater diversity in the way that central guidelines (level 1) are interpreted. This may still be a situation which is unacceptable to Ministers. If greater scope for school-based curriculum development really is envisaged, then it will be signalled by the way further guidance is phrased, by the decisions made about assessment, and by the extent to which teachers really are given partnership with central bodies in developing curriculum and assessment. It will depend on re-creating some, at least, of the conditions in which school-based curriculum development can flourish.

Conclusion

I suggest in an article in *Geography* (1993) that the geography education profession had to believe, almost as an article of faith, that it was moving into a new era where its professional skills would be revalued even whilst recognising the greater political constraints. The experience of implementing the 1991 Geography Order may have helped to clarify how this more appropriate balance can be found. The establishment of central curriculum guidelines is not, in itself, a problem; indeed the NCC and CCW surveys showed that geography teachers overwhelmingly welcomed the existence of a National Curriculum in the changed socio-political context of the 1990s. The difficulties and confusions of the past five years have resulted from the lack of recognition given to professional input at the school and classroom levels (2 and 3) of curriculum planning. School-based curriculum development in geography has been damaged by the over-prescription and inadequate structure of the original 1991 Geography Order, by the lack of creative teacher time, by the poorly developed curriculum support structures for the National Curriculum, and by the decline in teacher confidence and morale; but it has not ceased to exist. OFSTED and HMI surveys show that competency in curriculum development is the one key factor which has allowed some geography departments to develop good geography despite the faults of the Order. The necessary commitment and expertise still exist. The reinstatement of school-based curriculum development and the revaluing of teacher creativity within an enabling national framework must be the best strategy to ensure high-quality geographical education for individual schools and their pupils.

BIBLIOGRAPHY

Ball, S. (1990) *Politics and Policy Making in Education: Explorations in Policy Sociology*, Routledge.

Boardman, D. (1988) *The Impact of a Curriculum Project: Geography for the Young School Leaver*, Educational Review Occasional Publication 14, University of Birmingham.

Bowe, R., Ball, S.J. and Gold, A. (1992) *Reforming Education and Changing Schools*: *Case Studies in Policy Sociology*, Routledge.

Carter, R. (1994) 'Feet back on firmer ground', Geography Extra, *Times Educational Supplement*, 18 November.

Corney, G. (1991) *Teaching Economic Understanding through Geography*, Geographical Association.

Curriculum Council for Wales (1991) *Geography in the National Curriculum; Non-Statutory Guidance for Teachers*, CCW.

(1992) *Geography Non-Statutory Guidance*, CCW.

(1994) *Monitoring Report on National Curriculum Geography in Wales 1993*, CCW.

Daugherty, R. (1992) 'The role of assessment in geographical education: a framework for comparative analysis', in Hill, D. (ed.) *International Perspectives on Geographic Education*, Center for Geographic Education, University of Colorado at Boulder.

Daugherty, R. and Lambert, D. (1994) 'Teacher assessment and geography in the National Curriculum', *Geography*, 79(4):339–49.

DES (1989) *National Curriculum: From Policy to Practice*, HMSO:Para.4.3.

(1991) *Geography in the National Curriculum (England)*, HMSO.

DES and Welsh Office (1985) *GCSE: The National Criteria, Geography*, HMSO.

(1990) *Geography for Ages 5–16: Proposals of the Secretaries of State for Education and Science and for Wales*, HMSO.

Eggleston, J. (ed.) (1980) *School-based Curriculum Development in Britain – A Collection of Case Studies*, Routledge and Kegan Paul.

Fien, J. (1984) 'School-based curriculum development in geography', in Fien, J., Gerber, R. and Wilson, P. (eds) *The Geography Teacher's Guide to the Classroom*, Macmillan (Australia).

Fry, P. and Schofield, A. (1993) *Teachers' Experiences of National Curriculum Geography in Year 7*, Geographical Association.

Fyfe, E. (1982) 'The Sheffield Experience', *Geography 16–19 Project News 17*, Geography 16–19 Project, Institute of Education, University of London.

GCE Examining Boards of England, Wales and Northern Ireland (1983) *Common Cores at Advanced Level (Geography)*.

Geography/IT Support Project (1994) *Geography: A Pupil Entitlement for IT*, Geographical Association and National Council for Educational Technology.

Graves, N. (1979) *Curriculum Planning in Geography*, Heinemann Educational.

Hacking, E. (1994) 'Beginning teachers and the National Curriculum', in Walford, R. (ed.) *Challenging Times. Implementing the National Curriculum in Geography*, Cambridge Publishing.

Hall, D. (1976) *Geography and the Geography Teacher*, Unwin Education.

HMI Wales (1993) *A Survey of Geography in Key Stages 1,2 and 3 in Wales 1992–93*, OHMCI.

Kelly, A.V. (1990) *The National Curriculum: A Critical Review*, Paul Chapman Publishing.

Lambert, D. (1994) 'The National Curriculum: What shall we do with it?' *Geography*, No.342,79 (1):65–76.

Lawton, D. (1992) *Education and Politics in the 1990s: Conflict or Consensus?* The Falmer Press.

McElroy, B.I. (1980) 'School-based curriculum development', unpublished MA dissertation, Institute of Education, University of London.

Naish, M., Rawling, E.M. and Hart, C. (1987) *Geography 16–19: The Contribution of a Curriculum Project to 16–19 Education*, Longman for SCDC London.

National Curriculum Council (1991) 'INSET for National Curriculum Geography', unpublished report of the NCC Geography INSET Working Party.

(1992) 'Implementing National Curriculum Geography', unpublished report of the responses to the NCC Questionnaire Survey, NCC.

OFSTED (1993) *Geography Key Stages 1,2 and 3. The First Year 1991–92*, HMSO.

Pitts, D. (1978) 'The Geography 16–19 Project: A case study of curriculum development in its formative stages', unpublished MA dissertation, Institute of Education, University of London.

Rawling, E.M. (ed.) (1980) *Geography into the 1980s*, Geographical Association.

(1991a) 'Innovations in the Geography curriculum, 1970–90: a personal view', in Walford, R. (ed.) *Viewpoints in Geography Teaching*, Longman.

(1991b) 'Spirit of enquiry drops off the map', Second Opinion, *Times Educational Supplement*, 25 January.

(1991c) 'Making the most of the National Curriculum', *Teaching Geography*, 16(3) July:130–1.

(1991d) 'Geography and cross-curricular themes', *Teaching Geography*, 16(4):147–54.

(1992a) 'The making of a national geography curriculum', *Geography* No.337,77(4):292–309.

(1992b) 'Supporting the implementation of National Curriculum Geography: A role for the Geographical Association', Geographical Association paper.

(1993) 'School geography: towards 2000', *Geography* No.339,78 (2):110–16.

(1994) 'The Geographical Association Regions: present and future', unpublished paper presented to the Geographical Association Council, March 1994.

(forthcoming) 'Geography and Information Technology: a minimum pupil entitlement', in Villiers, M. de (ed.) *Primary Geography Matters*, Geographical Association.

Rawling, E.M. and Westaway, J. (1994) 'Choose your destination', Geography Extra, *Times Educational Supplement*, 18 November.

Roberts, M. (1995) 'Interpretations of the Geography National Curriculum: a common curriculum for all?' *Journal of Curriculum Studies*, 27 (2):187–205.

Robinson, R. (1992) 'Facing the future: not the National Curriculum', *Teaching Geography*, 17 (1):31–2.

Schofield, A. (1990) 'Geography Extra', *Times Educational Supplement*, 13 April.

School Curriculum and Assessment Authority (1993) *The National Curriculum and its Assessment, The Final Report / Sir Ron Dearing*, SCAA.

(1994) *Geography in the National Curriculum, Draft Proposals*, HMSO.

(1995a) 'Geography and Information Technology' leaflet in *Key Stage 3, Information Technology and the National Curriculum*, HMSO.

(1995b) *Geography in the National Curriculum*, HMSO.

Slater, F. and Spicer, B. (1971) 'Objectives in sixth-form geography: towards a consensus', *Classroom Geographer*, December.

Tyler, R. (1949) *Basic Principles of Curriculum and Instruction*, University of Chicago Press.

Walford, R. (1981) 'Language, ideologies and geography teaching', in Walford, R. (ed.) *Signposts for Geography Teaching*, Longman.

(1992) 'Creating a National Curriculum: a view from the inside', in Hill, D. (ed.) *International Perspectives in Geographic Education*, Center for Geographic Education, University of Colorado at Boulder, USA.

Welsh Office (1991) *Geography in the National Curriculum (Wales)*, HMSO.

6 Evaluating the geography curriculum

Ashley Kent

Evaluation in general

As Scriven (1991) put it, evaluation is the 'determination of the worth or value of something judged according to appropriate criteria, with those criteria explicated and justified'. An eminent geography educator, Bill Marsden, similarly defined evaluation as 'the making of qualitative and quantitative judgements about the value of various curriculum processes' (Marsden, 1976). In education, the ultimate purpose of evaluation is to improve the quality of student learning. Evaluation is to be anticipated, since there is a human tendency to reflect upon experience, to assess the value of one's actions and intentions, and to relate consequences to aims.

Simple, early objectives-led models of the curriculum process (such as Wheeler, 1967) probably caused evaluation to be 'tagged onto' the end of the process, and this is still a temptation. As Bruner (1966) reminds us, 'it would seem much more sensible to put evaluation into the picture before and during curriculum construction, as a form of intelligence operation to help the curriculum maker in his [sic] choice of material, in his approach, in his manner of setting tasks for the learner'. Marsden (1976) agrees that evaluation is 'critical at each stage of the curriculum process, from the first stage of evaluation of the broad aims of a course, to the late stage of evaluating which instruments of assessment to use and the final one of making judgements anew on the basis of the evidence which these instruments provide'. However, even in relatively recent writings (Curriculum Council for Wales, 1991) this 'end of a process' description is given. Here it is said that 'evaluation is an essential part of the "Plan–do–review" cycle of curriculum development', and takes place when judgements are made about the value of the work that *has* been done.

Evaluation then is an umbrella term, with assessment as one of its elements, and is concerned as much with classroom processes as with learning outcomes. This is important since evaluation is often confused with assessment, which is just one subset of its meanings.

Educational evaluation has become a new industry in the last thirty years, and following House and Scriven in the USA, a number of UK evaluators have gained eminence. These include D. Hamilton, D. Jenkins, B. McDonald, R. Walker and H. Simons. As House (1993) remarked, 'when I began a career in evaluation more than 25 years ago, I tossed all the papers I could find about the topic into a small cardboard box in the corner of my office and read them in one month'. Evaluation now has its own books, journals, awards, conferences and standards. In North America alone, there are approximately 3,000 members in the American Evaluation Association, and 1,500 in the Canadian Evaluation Society. As House remarks, he could envisage this profession in fifty years' time being 'a much larger enterprise around the globe, playing a central role in decision making in many countries!' (1993).

According to Nisbet, quoted in Skilbeck (1984), there have been the following trends in evaluation over the last three decades: Phase 1 in the 1960s was a time when evaluation was an integral part of curriculum development but without a separate identity and often tagged onto curriculum projects. The contrasts and opposites of formative–summative, hard–soft were debated. By the 1970s evaluation had become a profession, and was institutionalised, since there was massive expenditure on innovation, and evaluation was seen as a control mechanism. Finally, in the 1980s there was greater participation in evaluation – often self-evaluation – as the centre–periphery model of curriculum development was criticised as a cause of the policy–practice gap. Hopkins' 1989 publication represents this phase.

Evaluation must always consist of two elements: data collection, and judgements. Judgements concern curricula and what constitutes curricula – that is, syllabuses, units of work, lessons, lesson plans, teaching strategies and resources. Questions are asked about the feasibility, educational value, quality, acceptability, durability and effectiveness of curricula. However, first, some questions need to be raised about the form that an evaluation might take. For example:

- What is the purpose of the evaluation?
- What is being evaluated?
- What evaluative criteria should be used?
- Who is going to evaluate?
- What will be done with the evidence?

The whole exercise of evaluation can be seen as political, and the overarching political question apart from 'Who undertakes it, of whom, for whom?' is 'Whose interests does the evaluation serve?' Recently there has been a trend to involve the 'stakeholders' more, as the people who have a 'stake' in the programme under review. Equally political is the type of evaluator and the consequent approach taken. McDonald has spoken of bureaucratic, autocratic and democratic evaluators, for instance.

In the early days of evaluation, the dominant or 'classical' paradigm was the 'agricultural-botany' approach which used a hypothetico-deductive methodology derived from the experimental and mental-testing traditions in psychology. Such evaluations assess the effectiveness of an innovation by examining whether or not it has reached required standards on pre-specified criteria. A relatively more recent alternative has been the 'social anthropology' paradigm. Such illuminative evaluation relates more to social anthropology, psychiatry and participant observation research in sociology, and its main concern is with description and interpretation rather than measurement and prediction.

As the latter alternative became established, debates ensued around these two so-called 'extremes'. There is now seen to be a place for both in different circumstances, and 'triangulation' is often regarded as a pragmatic compromise. After all, there are now – as House (1993) puts it:

> pluralistic conceptions of evaluation in which multiple methods, measures, criteria, perspectives, audiences and interests are recognised. Conceptually evaluation has moved from a monolithic to a pluralist conception, reflecting the pluralism that had emerged in the larger society.

Most recently evaluation has become a part of the widespread accountability movement leading to teacher and school improvement and the related quality assurance impetus. Mirroring these recent and rapid directions for the evaluation profession, the Institute of Education established in January 1989 a Centre for Educational Evaluation; *Quality Assurance (QA) in Education*, a new journal for those concerned with quality assurance within the educational sector, was first published in 1993; and 1994 saw the establishment of an International School Effectiveness and Improvement Centre, again at the Institute of Education.

More and more – and in this writer's view rightly – there has been a stress on the vital need to develop skills of self-evaluation. In Skilbeck's view (1984), 'there is a need for educators everywhere to pay greater attention to the goals, values and processes of self-evaluation. Education needs to become a critically reflective community.' This teacher self-evaluation surely has to be one of the most effective long-term ways of securing educational improvement.

Departmental reviews and OFSTED inspections

Evaluations can be undertaken at all levels of an educational system, from HMI national-level reports to those of the individual teacher or class-room, and even of specific resources. This chapter focuses primarily on the geography department level of evaluation. Good departments have always reviewed their workings on a regular basis, but in a new climate of concern for quality and school improvement, formal departmental reviews are an expectation of senior management in a school. Departmental goals and targets are reviewed regularly, and annual meet-ings take place between headteachers and departmental heads on the publication of external examination grades. The arrival of an OFSTED inspection team once every four years provides an external stimulus, val-idation and cutting-edge for an ongoing departmental review process. Not surprisingly, a number of books have rapidly hit the market to aid departmental reviews and OFSTED inspections. Woods and Orlik (1994) rightly offer 'a practical guide to school inspection within the con-text of continuous school review', but often the titles of such books reflect the concern (some would say neurosis) of staff with inspection. *Inspection: A Preparatory Guide for Schools*, by Ormston and Shaw (1993), is a good example.

Woods and Orlik challenge departmental heads to look at ways of improving attainment through organisational curriculum change and teaching and learning strategies. Approaches include:

- improving the classroom climate/learning environment
- more precise diagnosis of learning needs
- better monitoring and record keeping
- extra reinforcement of learning
- more opportunities for individuals to discuss their work with teachers
- enrichment strategies
- coursework and homework 'clinics'
- review of teaching styles
- raising pupil expectations.

This amounts to a clear departmental review checklist!

1993/94 saw the start of a new system of school inspection in England. For the first time independent teams of inspectors, led by registered inspectors authorised by and under contract to Her Majesty's Chief Inspector (HMCI) visited and reported on schools under the new arrangements created by the Education (Schools) Act 1992.

The *Handbook for the Inspection of Schools* was first published in 1993 but clearly this new and complex system is still settling down, so it is no surprise that considerable modifications were made to the handbook in May 1994. Further substantial changes are expected once the first four-year cycle of inspections has been completed (by 1997).

Simplification and streamlining of the system was promised by Anthea Millett, Director of Inspection, in early 1994 at a public meeting on 7 February. Indeed, many professionals within the education system complain that the present system is unwieldy, stifling and bureaucratic. Others would agree that the framework provides a model for excellence in the provision of education.

This inspection system is driven by 'standards of achievement' and 'quality of learning'. The evaluation criteria for standards of achievement are:

- the evidence of what pupils know, understand and can do
- their competence in the key skills of reading, writing, speaking and listening, number and information technology, in the curriculum as a whole.

The evaluation criteria for the quality of learning are:

- progress made in knowledge, understanding and skills, including those used in reading, writing, speaking and listening, number and information technology
- learning skills, including observation and information-seeking, looking for patterns and deeper understanding, communicating information and ideas in various ways, posing questions and solving problems, applying what has been learned to unfamiliar situations, evaluating work done
- attitudes to learning, including motivation, interest and the ability to concentrate, co-operate and work productively.

The judgements on quality of learning are based mainly on direct observation of lessons during the period of the inspection (see Figure 6.1), whereas judgements on standards of achievement are based on assessment records held by the school as well as evidence in geography lessons of:

- students' knowledge of where places are and what they are like, including an appreciation and understanding of the lifestyle of the inhabitants
- their understanding of patterns and processes in physical and human geography
- their appreciation of the application of geography to environmental, social and political issues
- their ability to carry out a geographical enquiry, applying skills and techniques in doing so, particularly the skills required for the effective use of maps and diagrams, fieldwork and information technology.

Quality of teaching should be judged, according to the OFSTED system, against 'good teaching' which presents pupils with sound and appropriate information in a suitable variety of forms (maps, films, photographs, diagrams and written texts) and should:

- use a range of teaching methods to ensure that pupils can interpret information and assimilate knowledge
- focus, as appropriate, on the knowledge of places
- develop an understanding of geographical patterns and processes
- explore geographical relationships

- make possible the learning of skills and techniques
- provide opportunities to carry out geographical enquiries to seek explanations
- link teaching across the range of attainment targets, as appropriate, showing how they interrelate.

OFSTED inspectors use a variety of forms for the collation of evidence. Most important for departments are Figure 6.1, the lesson observation proforma, Figure 6.2, the subject evidence form, and Figure 6.3, the judgement recording form: subject.

At the end of a week of inspection, a departmental head in geography can expect a full *oral* feedback on the work of the department, but in the written report the subject is covered in as little as two or four paragraphs in summary concerning the department's work. Two examples are shown in Figure 6.4.

Managing a department

In a secondary school the department is often the vitally important 'home' for most teaching staff. The professional and personal interactions which take place within that unit are probably the most intensive and significant for any teacher. So setting up, managing and, in this context, evaluating the workings of a department are of considerable importance.

The key role within a department is normally, but not always, the head of that department. Such middle managers arguably underpin the success or otherwise of a school, and their responsibilities are certainly onerous. The sample job description given by Bob Carr in 1990 (Figure 6.5) confirms that. An even more formidable list of responsibilities of the head of a geography department was published in 1982 in Kent LEA's Geography Newsletter. Figure 6.6 lists those responsibilities concerning teaching staff, but other headings were curriculum, pupils, parents, and facilities.

Over the years the role has changed in a more bureaucratic and administrative direction. Subject documentation has expanded (see Figure 6.7) as the National Curriculum and OFSTED inspections have been implemented.

LESSON OBSERVATION FORM

(see Handbook Part 3)

Inspector's Number:				DFE School Number:		/
Subject/Activity [2]:	Ability	Upper:	Middle:	Lower:	Mixed:	
Year Group(s):	NoR:	Present	Boys:	Girls:	All:	
Accreditation [2]:	Time in Lesson:		minutes			

CONTENT:

ACHIEVEMENT (age-referenced)

Grade [1] ⸬

ACHIEVEMENT (taking account of pupils' abilities)

Grade [1] ⸬

QUALITY OF TEACHING

Grade [1] [:]

CONTRIBUTION TO KEY SKILLS

Grade [1] [:]

CONTRIBUTION FACTORS Any positive or negative effects should be indicated with "+" or "-"

Support staff: _____ Resources: _____ Accommodation: _____

COMMENT:

OVERALL LESSON GRADE [:]

[1]Grades: see grade descriptors in Part 3 of the Handbook.   [2]Use subject and accreditation codes from the appendix to Part 3 of the Handbook

Figure 6.1 Lesson observation form from the *Handbook for the Inspection of Schools*

Source: OFSTED, 1994

[Expand sections as required]

Subject or aspect inspected:

Inspector: **Days in school:**

Time spent observing lessons during the inspection

Key Stage	Pre-1	1	2	3	4	6th form
Lessons seen	:	:	:	:	:	:
Total (hours)	:	:	:	:	:	:

Paragraph for the report

Text:

3.1 Standards of achievement

Achievement in relation to national norms

Grade	1	2	3	4	5	6
No. KS:	:	:	:	:	:	:
No. KS:	:	:	:	:	:	:
No. KS:	:	:	:	:	:	:

Achievement in relation to capability

Grade	1	2	3	4	5	6
No. KS:	:	:	:	:	:	:
No. KS:	:	:	:	:	:	:
No. KS:	:	:	:	:	:	:

Text:(with reference to Key Stages)

3.2 Quality of learning

Learning

Grade	1	2	3	4	5	6
No. KS:	:	:	:	:	:	:
No. KS:	:	:	:	:	:	:
No. KS:	:	:	:	:	:	:

Text: (with reference to Key Stages)

7.1 Quality of teaching

Teaching
Grade   1   2   3   4   5   6

No. KS: :   :   :   :   :   :

No. KS: :   :   :   :   :   :

No. KS: :   :   :   :   :   :

Text: (with reference to Key Stages)

7.2 Assessment, recording and reporting

Text:

7.3 Curriculum content: subject quality and range; equality of opportunity

Text:

7.4 Provision for pupils with special educational needs

Text:

7.5 Management and administration of the subject, aspect or department

Text:

7.6 Resources and their management

(i) Teaching and non-teaching staff

Text:

(ii) Resources for learning

Text:

(iii) Accommodation

Text:

Other points

Text:

Source: OFSTED, 1994

Figure 6.2 Subject evidence form

A COPY SHOULD BE COMPLETED FOR EACH SUBJECT INSPECTED

NAME OF SCHOOL

TYPE OF SCHOOL (REFER TO HEADTEACHER'S FORM)

SCHOOL NUMBER

DATE OF INSPECTION

NAME OF RgI

1)   Judgements recorded on this form refer to the subject inspected.

2)   Refer to the *Framework, Guidance* and *Technical* sections of the *Handbook* when recording judgements.

3)   Circle the asterisk on the scale which reflects most clearly your general judgement about how far the statement applies. Where the statement is not applicable, indicate by circling N/A.

4)   The central point of the scales below is where there is an equal measure of strengths and weaknesses.

3   STANDARDS AND QUALITY

3.1 Standards of achievement

In relation to national norms

3.1.1 Pupils' standards of achieve- ment in the subject are:				
0 PreKS1	Very High	* * * * * * *	Very Low
1KS1		* * * * * * *	
2KS2		* * * * * * *	
3KS3		* * * * * * *	
4KS4		* * * * * * *	
5Post-16		* * * * * * *	

In relation to pupils' capabilities

3.1.2 Pupils' standards of achieve- ment in the subject are:				
0 PreKS1	Excellent	* * * * * * *	Very
1KS1		* * * * * * *	Poor
2KS2		* * * * * * *	
3KS3		* * * * * * *	
4KS4		* * * * * * *	
5Post-16		* * * * * * *	

3.1.3 Pupils' knowledge in the subject is:				
0 PreKS1	Excellent	* * * * * * *	Very
1KS1		* * * * * * *	Poor
2KS2		* * * * * * *	
3KS3		* * * * * * *	
4KS4		* * * * * * *	
5Post-16		* * * * * * *	

                                                            1 2 3 4 5 6 7

			1	2	3	4	5	6	7	
3.1.4 Pupils' understanding in the subject is:	**0 PreKS1**	Excellent	*	*	*	*	*	*	*	Very Poor
	1KS1		*	*	*	*	*	*	*	
	2KS2		*	*	*	*	*	*	*	
	3KS3		*	*	*	*	*	*	*	
	4KS4		*	*	*	*	*	*	*	
	5Post-16		*	*	*	*	*	*	*	
3.1.5 Pupils' skills in the subject are:	**0 PreKS1**	Excellent	*	*	*	*	*	*	*	Very Poor
	1KS1		*	*	*	*	*	*	*	
	2KS2		*	*	*	*	*	*	*	
	3KS3		*	*	*	*	*	*	*	
	4KS4		*	*	*	*	*	*	*	
	5Post-16		*	*	*	*	*	*	*	

3.2 Quality of learning – in relation to their age and abilities

			1	2	3	4	5	6	7	
3.2.1 The progress of pupils' learning is:	**0 PreKS1**	Excellent	*	*	*	*	*	*	*	Very Poor
	1KS1		*	*	*	*	*	*	*	
	2KS2		*	*	*	*	*	*	*	
	3KS3		*	*	*	*	*	*	*	
	4KS4		*	*	*	*	*	*	*	
	5Post-16		*	*	*	*	*	*	*	
3.2.2 Pupils' learning skills are:	**0 PreKS1**	Very Well	*	*	*	*	*	*	*	Very
	1KS1	Developed	*	*	*	*	*	*	*	Poorly
	2KS2		*	*	*	*	*	*	*	Developed
	3KS3		*	*	*	*	*	*	*	
	4KS4		*	*	*	*	*	*	*	
	5Post-16		*	*	*	*	*	*	*	
3.2.3 Pupils' attitudes to their learning are:	**0 PreKS1**	Excellent	*	*	*	*	*	*	*	Very Poor
	1KS1		*	*	*	*	*	*	*	
	2KS2		*	*	*	*	*	*	*	
	3KS3		*	*	*	*	*	*	*	
	4KS4		*	*	*	*	*	*	*	
	5Post-16		*	*	*	*	*	*	*	

7 FACTORS CONTRIBUTING TO THESE FINDINGS

7.1 Quality of teaching

			1	2	3	4	5	6	7	
7.1.1 Objectives for lessons are:	**0 PreKS1**	Very	*	*	*	*	*	*	*	Very
	1KS1	Clear	*	*	*	*	*	*	*	Unclear
	2KS2		*	*	*	*	*	*	*	
	3KS3		*	*	*	*	*	*	*	
	4KS4		*	*	*	*	*	*	*	
	5Post-16		*	*	*	*	*	*	*	

1 2 3 4 5 6 7

7.1.2 Teachers' command of
the subject is:

0 PreKS1	Excellent	*	*	*	*	*	*	*	Very
1KS1		*	*	*	*	*	*	*	Poor
2KS2		*	*	*	*	*	*	*	
3KS3		*	*	*	*	*	*	*	
4KS4		*	*	*	*	*	*	*	
5Post-16		*	*	*	*	*	*	*	

7.1.3 Lesson content and
activities are:

0 PreKS1	Very	*	*	*	*	*	*	*	Very
1KS1	Suitable	*	*	*	*	*	*	*	Unsuitable
2KS2		*	*	*	*	*	*	*	
3KS3		*	*	*	*	*	*	*	
4KS4		*	*	*	*	*	*	*	
5Post-16		*	*	*	*	*	*	*	

7.1.4 The challenge, pace and
motivation of lessons
are:

0 PreKS1	Very	*	*	*	*	*	*	*	Very
1KS1	Effective	*	*	*	*	*	*	*	Ineffective
2KS2		*	*	*	*	*	*	*	
3KS3		*	*	*	*	*	*	*	
4KS4		*	*	*	*	*	*	*	
5Post-16		*	*	*	*	*	*	*	

7.2 Assessment, Recording and Reporting

7.2.1 Statutory requirements
for assessment and
recording are met

1KS1	Fully	*	*	*	*	*	*	*	Not at all	N/A
2KS2		*	*	*	*	*	*	*		N/A
3KS3		*	*	*	*	*	*	*		N/A
4KS4		*	*	*	*	*	*	*		N/A

7.2.2 In taking account of the
pupils' achievements the
assessment and recording
system is:

0 PreKS1	Very	*	*	*	*	*	*	*	Very	N/A
1KS1	Effective	*	*	*	*	*	*	*	Ineffective	N/A
2KS2		*	*	*	*	*	*	*		N/A
3KS3		*	*	*	*	*	*	*		N/A
4KS4		*	*	*	*	*	*	*		N/A
5Post-16		*	*	*	*	*	*	*		N/A

7.2.3 Reporting about the
progress of pupils is:

0 PreKS1	Very	*	*	*	*	*	*	*	Very
1KS1	Effective	*	*	*	*	*	*	*	Ineffective
2KS2		*	*	*	*	*	*	*	
3KS3		*	*	*	*	*	*	*	
4KS4		*	*	*	*	*	*	*	
5Post-16		*	*	*	*	*	*	*	

1 2 3 4 5 6 7

7.3 CURRICULUM

7.3.i Quality and range

1) The subject meets the statutory requirements of the National Curriculum (or Locally Agreed Syllabus in the case of RE):

1KS1	Fully	*	*	*	*	*	*	*	Not at all N/A
2KS2		*	*	*	*	*	*	*	N/A
3KS3		*	*	*	*	*	*	*	N/A
4KS4		*	*	*	*	*	*	*	N/A

2) The contribution of the subject to the school's aims is:

Very Effective	*	*	*	*	*	*	*	Very Ineffective

3) The curricular planning and organisation of the subject are:

0 PreKS1	Excellent	*	*	*	*	*	*	*	Very Poor
1KS1		*	*	*	*	*	*	*	
2KS2		*	*	*	*	*	*	*	
3KS3		*	*	*	*	*	*	*	
4KS4		*	*	*	*	*	*	*	
5Post-16		*	*	*	*	*	*	*	

7.4 SEN

7.4.1 The progress that all pupils with SEN make in this subject is:

0 PreKS1	Excellent	*	*	*	*	*	*	*	Very Poor
1KS1		*	*	*	*	*	*	*	
2KS2		*	*	*	*	*	*	*	
3KS3		*	*	*	*	*	*	*	
4KS4		*	*	*	*	*	*	*	
5Post-16		*	*	*	*	*	*	*	

7.5 MANAGEMENT AND ADMINISTRATION

1) The quality of management and co-ordination of the teaching in the subject are:

Excellent	*	*	*	*	*	*	*	Very Poor

2) Guidance to teachers through the provision of a scheme of work or other methods is:

Excellent	*	*	*	*	*	*	*	Very Poor

7.6 RESOURCES AND THEIR MANAGEMENT

7.6.i Teaching and non-teaching staff

1) The deployment of teachers' specialist skills is:

Very Effective	*	*	*	*	*	*	*	Very Ineffective

2) The contribution of non-teaching staff to the quality of provision in the subject is:

Very Effective	*	*	*	*	*	*	*	Very Ineffective	N/A

1 2 3 4 5 6 7

7.6.ii Resources for learning (in terms of their effect on the quality of teaching and learning):

1) The quality of available books is:	Excellent	* * * * * * *	Very Poor
2) The quality of available equipment is:	Excellent	* * * * * * *	Very Poor
3) The quality of available materials is:	Excellent	* * * * * * *	Very Poor
4) The quality of learning resources is:	Excellent	* * * * * * *	Very Poor
5) The use of learning resources is:	Very Effective	* * * * * * *	Very Ineffective

7.6.iii Accommodation (in terms of its effect on the quality of teaching and learning):

1) The availability of accommodation, bearing in mind the need for specialist facilities, is:	Excellent	* * * * * * *	Very Poor
2) The use of accommodation is:	Very Effective	* * * * * * *	Very Ineffective
3) The condition of accommodation is:	Excellent	* * * * * * *	Very Poor
		1 2 3 4 5 6 7	

Source: OFSTED, 1994

Figure 6.3 Judgement recording form: subject

In Y9 pupils' achievements are generally satisfactory, while in Y10 and Y11 the standards achieved are generally high. The standard of writing, although over a fairly narrow range, is often good and the handling and representation of statistical information in a geographical context is particularly good. In the sixth form high standards of work are expected and achieved. Advanced-level examination results have been good. The quality of sixth-form students' individual fieldwork projects is high.

Teaching creates a good, relaxed working atmosphere in lessons. Practical activities in class and during fieldwork are a feature of the course. Provision of opportunities for discussion is a little limited.

The department has a very useful set of curricular documents which detail the work to be covered through to A level. A start has been made in Y9 on matching the content to the National Curriculum Attainment Targets and to the Programmes of Study. However, the time currently given to geography in Y9 to Y11 will not be sufficient to implement fully the requirements of the National Curriculum.

Overall this is a good, well-managed department whose pupils work hard and generally achieve well. There are clear priorities for development: deployment of rooms requires careful attention to reduce the difficulties for teachers using several rooms; and the current curriculum needs adaptation to match the needs of the National Curriculum.   (1993)

The quality of geography lessons was variable, with about half of a satisfactory standard. At Key Stage 3, standards of pupils' achievements are satisfactory on the whole, though there is some evidence that the grouping by ability needs adjustment. Poor planning rather than lack of time inhibits complete coverage of the National Curriculum requirements. At Key Stage 4, standards of achievement vary. Girls' work in exercise books shows a narrow range of methods of recording information, and in some cases inaccurate work is not corrected. Standards of achievement in sixth-form lessons are variable in A-level Geography and satisfactory in Travel and Tourism, though one of the examination targets for this course is at a low level for this age group.

Lessons are characterised by a didactic introduction, followed by questions and answers to develop some main points before pupils work individually on undifferentiated exercises. Though, occasionally, behaviour in lessons is poor, relationships are generally satisfactory as, in most cases, is the teacher's interpretation of the subject. Visual aids are used on occasion but a lack of resources is having an adverse influence on the quality of lessons, particularly at A level. Work in pupils' books is marked, though not always accurately, and the particular grading and reward systems are used only by history and geography. On the whole, pupils work with commitment and willingness and occasionally with enthusiasm. In general, however, the pace in lessons is rather too gentle and expectations too low.   (1993)

Figure 6.4 Two examples of OFSTED reports on the work of geography departments

Co-ordinator, initiator and supervisor of all the work of the subject/subject area. Regular communication of important trends, innovations, problems and discussion.

Contribute to the corporate life and management of the school as a whole.

Staff

Support, to be responsible for welfare and morale of subject staff.

Liaison with other heads of department.

In-service training.

Support and prepare initial assessment of probationers and students in liaison with head/deputies.

Deployment of subject staff in liaison with headteacher.

Regular meetings of subject staff.

Support overall school policies.

Support general school activities and Parents' Association.

Oversee and deploy laboratory technician/other ancillary staff as appropriate.

Oversee and make staff and pupils aware of health and safety regulations.

Pupils

Assessing and monitoring progress of pupils.

Writing reports and effort letters.

External examination entries and estimates.

Set and produce internal examinations.

Monitor homework.

Overseeing visits.

Curriculum

Overall syllabus, guidelines, teaching methods, research and development, internal and external liaison concerning subject matters.

Evaluation of work and control of standards on a regular basis.

Carefully consider development of well-monitored and researched courses in the subject area or linked with other subjects.

Examination policy in liaison with headteacher and pastoral staff.

Setting and options.

Open day and parents' meetings.

Liaising fully with the department of learning skills.

Considering their subject area in the context of the community and society.

Involvement in the development and categorisation of resources.

Giving particular support for the skills of language and numeracy across the curriculum, learning skills, health and safety education and community education.

Consultation with headteacher.

Collaborating in the preparation of interlinked courses, extra-curricular activities and presentations.

Curricular liaison with infant/junior schools/colleges concerning policy continuity and approach where relevant.

Rooms

The care and appearance of subject rooms and areas and adjacent corridors.

Control and upkeep of furniture.

Finance and stock

Using departmental finances to maximum efficiency.

Security and prudent use of stock and equipment in the department.

Upkeep of the inventories/stock records.

Any additional duties as agreed with the headteacher.

Source: Carr, 1990

Figure 6.5 Sample job description for a Head of Department or Acting Head of Department

Teaching Staff

1   To co-ordinate the work of the staff in the geography department.

2   To hold regular, minuted departmental meetings (encouraging involvement, commitment and cohesion).

3   To differentiate and to delegate various tasks (ensuring that the contributions of all members of the department are known, assessed and valued).

4   To guide departmental colleagues in the formulation of their personal schemes of work (ensuring that the approaches adopted are matched to the age, abilities and aptitudes of the pupils – particularly those with learning difficulties and the very able ones).

5   To make certain that when subject colleagues are absent, appropriate work is set for their classes.

6   To ensure that members of the department have the best possible provision of materials and accommodation so that they can teach to their maximum capacity (opportunities for staff to make suggestions and to discuss requisitions).

7   To be responsible to the headteacher for the teaching standards in his/her department, including (i) preparation and marking, and (ii) the mounting of induction programmes for probationary teachers.

8   To advise colleagues, as and when necessary, about their own professional development.

9   To consult the headteacher (and others) about the deployment of departmental staff, timetabling, and use of rooms.

10   To advise the headteacher about colleagues' views and suggestions, generally acting as spokesperson for the department.

11   To advise the headteacher about appointments to the geography department (including the preparation of job descriptions, short-listing, etc.).

Source: Kent LEA Geography Newsletter, September 1982

Figure 6.6 Guidelines on the responsibilities of the head of a geography department

The contents of departmental documentation should relate to whole school aims, objectives and policies.

Aim and objectives

These should include a statement on the philosophy of the department – this forms the basis on which decisions relating to curriculum provision, teaching and learning, and targets are agreed, and evaluation of effectiveness can be made.

Policy statements

- Assessment, recording and reporting – methods of assessment, formative assessment, standardisation procedures and marking policy
- Equal opportunities
- Homework
- Information technology
- Pupil entitlement in terms of quality of teaching and learning experiences, including those with learning difficulties and the more able; use of the learning support unit; approaches to differentiation.
- Teacher planning and record keeping

Departmental organisation and co-ordination

- Organisation of subject at KS3 and KS4 – time allocations; groupings of pupils; criteria for establishing teaching groups; syllabuses followed; management of programmes of study; continuity and progression
- Timetables
- Staff roles and responsibilities
- Staff development – INSET needs identification and dissemination; support for NQTs
- Decision-making processes – cycle of meetings and minutes; involvement of staff
- Accommodation

- Organisation of resources – stock control, list and location of stock; organisation within classrooms; display

- Teaching and learning – organisation and strategies; classroom management; role of the learner; support and extension

- Summary of end-of-key-stage results – i.e. examination and NC performances

- Visits – policy; organisation; charging

- Community links

- Liaison – primary and 16+

- Monitoring, evaluation and review procedures

Department development plan

- Prioritised, short and long-term targets

- Financial implications: capitation; staffing and staff development

- Success criteria

Scheme of work

By module, series of lessons, lesson

- Aims and objectives in terms of knowledge, understanding, skills, values and attitudes – reference to Programmes of Study and Attainment Targets

- Key ideas

- Content to be covered

- Teaching and learning strategies, including differentiation

- Resources

- Assessment opportunities

- Cross-curricular contribution: skills and themes

Source: Solihull Education Department

Figure 6.7 Subject documentation checklist

At a recent (October 1994) session, a part of a short course on 'Managing a Geography Department' at the Institute of Education generated several shared concerns. These included concerns over change; paper overload; administration; and coping with conflict. Juett (1989) suggested that a manager (head of department in this context) had five key functions to perform:

- leading
- decision-making
- planning
- monitoring
- evaluating.

To cope with this considerable and changing set of responsibilities requires certain qualities of a department head. Although some people undoubtedly possess such qualities, much relevant knowledge and skills need to be acquired. It is surprising then that so few INSET courses are available for heads of department.

Brighouse (1991) identified seven qualities of leadership from observations made in hundreds of schools over a five-year period in the 1980s. These were:

- to be cheerful and optimistic, e.g. to have a clear vision, be able to show humour in a crisis
- to be welcoming and ready to be enthusiastic
- to be a good listener
- to have a considered view and practice towards the use of time
- to celebrate others and blame themselves
- to have the ability to manage change
- to have a clear educational philosophy and to set a personal example.

Carr (1990) had a different list of the management abilities of a head of department, which he laid out as an assessment sheet (Figure 6.8). Bird (1992) spoke of the 'right' attitudes for leadership, and included:

- an awareness that people matter
- an understanding of many human characteristics
- a willingness to search for and analyse the facts
- readiness to make changes

- willingness to learn
- enthusiasm for training and development of subordinates
- a preference for working in a systematic way
- ability to set objectives and devise plans to meet them
- readiness to face problems and deal with them
- willingness to give up technical work in favour of managing human resources
- acceptance that management techniques may be more effective than instinct.

Bayne-Jardin and Hannam (1972) have suggested five qualities which might make for a good head of department. These are the abilities: to co-operate and communicate; to observe and listen; to manage resources efficiently; to delegate within the department; and to forward-plan. In summary, a successful head of department needs a mixture of personal

Administrative competence	1	2	3	4	5
Clear personal values and objectives	1	2	3	4	5
Personal creativity	1	2	3	4	5
Problem-solving ability	1	2	3	4	5
Commitment to personal development	1	2	3	4	5
Ability to influence others	1	2	3	4	5
Ability to supervise others	1	2	3	4	5
Ability to communicate effectively	1	2	3	4	5
Effective team leader and member	1	2	3	4	5
Commitment to professional development of others	1	2	3	4	5

1 = Skills are effectively demonstrated
3 = Satisfactory
5 = Skills need to be developed

Source: Carr, 1990

Figure 6.8 Some general management abilities of a head of department: assessment sheet

qualities (for example being supportive and accessible), professional qualities (for example effective teaching and record keeping) and leadership qualities (for example a clear focus or vision and ability to manage a team). These qualities contrast markedly with the views of student teachers who have just started on their one-year PGCE course. Over the years they have consistently identified enthusiasm, subject knowledge, communication skills, humour, efficiency, originality, charisma and flexibility as the qualities they consider make for a 'successful' teacher.

It is clear that individuals have different leadership styles. Traditionally (see Juett, 1989), these were polarised into opposites:

authoritarian v. *democratic*
instrumental v. *expressive*
bureaucratic v. *human relations*
hierarchical v. *collegiate*

But a continuum seems more appropriate. Tannenbaum's and Schmidt's model (1973) suggests the range of approaches possible (Figure 6.9), and research by Warner (1984) derived three management

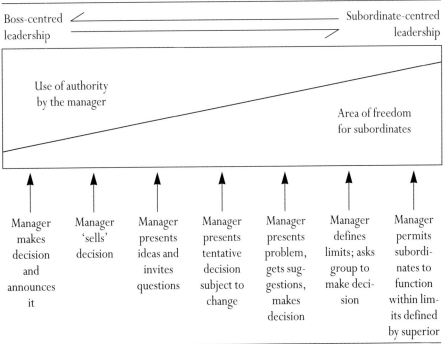

Figure 6.9 Choosing a leadership style

styles – authoritarian, participatory, and somewhere in between – based on in-depth interviews with heads of department.

Team-building is considered by many to be a vital part of a middle manager's role. Bailey (1989) explained that there are a number of advantages in working together as a team. The team members can:

- know more together than one person can know
- have a wider and more varied professional experience than is possible for any one member
- exchange and discuss information and ideas about pupils' progress, about developments in their subject and ways of teaching it, and about wider curriculum matters
- share tasks
- rotate tasks
- specialise
- instruct and support one another
- be in more than one place at once.

The advantages are usually described as $1 + 1 + 1 = 4$! In other words, three people working together can have the effect of four working separately. Adair (1985) suggests that the team process can be seen as three overlapping elements – see Figure 6.10. Lessons from industry are much in line with this model, according to Kemp (1989), since:

- team-building requires planned effort, and may not be a painless process
- once a team has been built it needs to be maintained
- a successful team builds on the strengths of individual members by identifying how individuals can best contribute
- membership of a team should not stifle individuality.

Underlying all this perhaps is the necessity for heads of department to understand the psychology of their staff. In particular, as Maslow (1943) suggests, they should be aware of the higher needs which influence the behaviour of people at work. These include social needs (social activity, sense of belonging, affection); self-esteem needs (status, self-respect); and self-fulfilment needs (growth, personal development, accomplishment). The danger, Maslow argues, is that without such fulfilment of

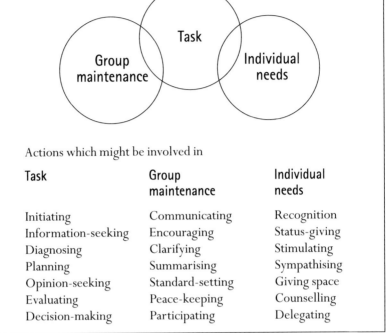

Actions which might be involved in

Task	Group maintenance	Individual needs
Initiating	Communicating	Recognition
Information-seeking	Encouraging	Status-giving
Diagnosing	Clarifying	Stimulating
Planning	Summarising	Sympathising
Opinion-seeking	Standard-setting	Giving space
Evaluating	Peace-keeping	Counselling
Decision-making	Participating	Delegating

Source: After Adair, 1985

Figure 6.10 The team process

needs, employees may exhibit aggression, non-co-operation, apathy and/or alienation.

Finally, as far as team-building is concerned, heads of department probably need to recognise what stage their own team-building has reached. Brown (1979) suggests there are four stages:

1 *Forming*   When the group comes together, there may be low trust and high anxiety among group members; the group is often leader-dependent.

2 *Storming*   A critical stage when group members begin to establish individual roles; issues of power and control may be prominent; a frequent characteristic is challenge to the leadership.

3 *Norming*   The group has sorted out issues of power and control and is freed to develop trust and cohesion; part of the process is the establishment of norms or accepted ways of doing things.

4 *Performing*   At this point the team can begin using the skills and potential of its members; it is characterised by openness and trust, and a greater willingness to take risks and consider change.

Policy-forming and review is another vital element of a head of department's work. Nowadays policy is expected to be written up and is part of an ever-growing collection of subject documentation. The subject documentation checklist in Figure 6.7 illustrates rather well the nature of that task, and could act as an *aide-mémoire* for a head of department engaged in self-evaluation. Such documentation is a useful 'indicator' of the 'success' or 'effectiveness' of a department and can be used as a framework for evaluation and for the departmental handbook which informs pupils, parents and staff about geography in the school. Kent (1990) offers a range of suggestions for those engaged in informing and marketing the subject through handbooks or other devices. The subject handbook forms an important item of evidence in an OFSTED inspection.

Reviewing a department's working is a key part of the brief of a head of department. This author engaged (as an outsider) in a similar review a few years ago, and generated the questions listed in Figure 6.11, which amounts to his agenda for a 'good' department. In a wider sense perhaps an 'effective' department is merely a microcosm of an 'effective' school, and therefore Figure 6.12 is an equally appropriate evaluatory model.

Staff appraisal

Staff appraisal has become an important part of the school system in the last few years. Appraisal has always gone on, though the term is relatively new in common parlance, but nowadays it is more systematic and formalised. It has both developmental elements – whereby it allows a person to realise full potential – and accountability elements. Proponents see it as a continuous and systematic process intended to help individual teachers with their professional development. Seen like this it raises the credibility of teachers with their 'customers' (pupils and parents), improves teacher professionalism and enhances job satisfaction. It is seen as beneficial, valid, practicable, fair, open and comprehensive. However, many teachers have

1 **Workings of the department**   Can the curriculum be negotiated by the 'team'? Can this be done on a regular basis? Should meetings be held on a more regular/formal basis at which concerns can be aired/shared? Is there potential for more division of labour relating to responsibilities of the staff (for instance, staff given responsibility for a year group including the end-of-year/term assessment)?

2 **Staff development**   Can opportunities be given for INSET and other elements of professional development?

3 **Scheme of work**   At present it seems a 'bitty' statement, rather lacking in coherence. Ideally, it should be negotiated/developed as a departmental team. See guidance on curriculum statements in 5–16 document (HMI); Weigand's book *Managing the Geography Department*; and GA *Handbook for Geography Teachers*.

4 This all relates to need for **departmental policies**.   What about homework policy? Marking policy? In the case of the latter, there is variety in the department from '5/5' to 'B+' with or without comments. Some work is unmarked for long periods. Is there a distinction between effort and achievement? Agreed policy would remove uncertainty for both staff and pupils. What about departmental anti-racist policy?

5 Is there a **fieldwork policy**?   Whole Year 10 residential is wonderful, as is lower sixth to Lake District, but what about integrating half or full-day field-work experiences across the ages, not least in Year 9 in contrast to the (apparently) successful history trip to Flanders? Occasional weekend possibilities here? Possible joint fieldwork with adjoining schools? Incidentally, I have a booklet on fieldwork in and around Llandudno which I helped write – you might find it useful.

6 **Resources**   You have the beginnings of a most useful resource collection in sixth-form room and main geography room. Might it be possible to formalise this collection by creating a database (on paper and on micro such as a cheap Amstrad kept in sixth-form room and usable for word-processing by students as well), so that staff and students know what is available? Videos, magazines, journals, maps, books, newspaper cuttings, etc. could all be put onto the database, perhaps under 'theme' or 'topic'. This is a piece of IT awareness/skills which sixth-formers could help you with. Similarly film strips could be made into slides and more slides purchased? Generally perhaps more overtly label and encourage use of such resources in the sixth-form room? This room could, even more than now, become a lively hub of geography activity. One former colleague of mine manages his resources by having the help of several sixth-formers on a regular basis (Friday afternoons).

7 Potential/more overt use could be made of **overseas knowledge/experiences** of children?

8 **Grades at GCSE** have more Ds and Es than I would have expected even given the ability of the intake to geography. Why is that?

9 Can you appeal to the *more able* at GCSE and A level? There is no reason

why geography cannot stretch and be valuable for the careers of the brightest. There are lots of strategies to **'market the subject'** a little more strongly, such as producing a departmental pamphlet. I thought your ideas of a video based around the Queen's speech was brilliant! Why not do the same thing but based around the local papers and issues worthy of consideration by geography? Sources of ideas such as departmental logos, parents' evenings, etc. are abundant in Weigand's *Managing the Geography Department*, and my own GA publication, *Selling Geography*.

10 Where are the **atlases** in the department, and which ones are used? Given the likely geography National Curriculum, their use will have to be more systematic.

11 Is the **video** used across the staff and classes taught by the department?

12 **Years 7–9** are strongly tied to the textbooks, but without detailed schemes of work won't the curriculum being offered to different classes (by different staff) be therefore very different? This, I imagine, makes setting an end-of-year exam a problem.

13 What is the **scale** (local/global) and **regional** (first/third world) **balance** of the geography curriculum across the years?

14 **IT in geography education** is about to take off because of the requirements (in part) of the IT Capability element of the National Curriculum. Geography has a real contribution to make here. A terminal to the main computer lab would make sense, and having your own micro such as a Nimbus. Not least why not start by purchasing the 'Learning Geography with Computers' INSET pack, which now costs £75 from NCET but is marvellous value?

15 Do you have sets of **OS maps**, at different scales, for the local area?

16 Do you have an area/bookshelf for **teachers' books/textbooks** for use by staff?

17 One of your colleagues has a filed set of **worksheets**. Should a wider range across the curriculum be filed and made available to all staff?

18 Taking on board **Geography 16–19 A level** could boost A-level numbers and staff interest.

19 **Gradual evolution of your geography curriculum** to mirror the National Curriculum could be the basis of your ongoing departmental curriculum development.

20 Do you have strategies for **slow learners** in geography, not least in the lower school?

21 Are pupils 'let in on' the mysteries of the **syllabuses** across the year groups?

22 Is your **budget** sufficient? Isn't there an argument in all the above for one or two years of extraordinary extra injections of money to help develop the geography curriculum? This in turn is likely to make the subject more popular and successful than it obviously already is.

Figure 6.11 Issues raised by a departmental review

Source: After Stoll and Fink, 1992

Figure 6.12 Characteristics of effective schools

a different view and regard appraisal with apprehension. They see it as another element of the private sector being imposed upon them, and fear that it will be linked somehow with payment and/or potential dismissal. It is this author's view that the very word 'appraisal' bears unfortunate connotations; 'staff development' or another less threatening and emotive phrase could replace it.

To succeed, all staff need to be committed to the system being used. It should be based on evidence, not on assertion, and action should result. However, there are many obstacles in the way of an effective appraisal system. These include the lack of skill of an appraiser; a lack of commitment in staff and senior management; a lack of openness; no clear criteria; too little time and scope for follow-up activity.

The history of appraisal sits firmly within the recent school and teacher improvement movement which in the UK can arguably be said to have begun with Callaghan's Ruskin College speech in 1976, which raised a concern over standards and accountability. Based on six LEA-based pilot appraisal projects, a national framework for teacher appraisal was published in 1989 (Circular 12/91) and came into statutory force in August 1991. All appraisals of teachers in post in September 1991 were to be completed by the summer of 1995. As the bill said, 'Appraisal must operate and be seen to operate, fairly and equitably for all school teachers' (12/91). Subsequently, since 1989, many LEAs and schools have developed their own schemes based upon the 1989 framework.

This legal necessity has unsurprisingly generated a good deal of support literature. Fidler and Cooper (1992) and Bennett et al. (1992) are but two examples. Two extremes of appraisal systems have appeared: on the one hand managerial/hierarchical and on the other hand participative/democratic. The systems developed probably mirror the management style of schools. Based on Bennett et al. (1992), all appraisal systems should have the following elements and usually in this order:

- a system developed with or without approval/involvement of staff
- related administrative systems established
- appointment and training of appraisers
- initial meeting of appraiser and appraisee with an agreement reached on the process
- assembling information by both appraiser and appraisee
- self-appraisal form filled in
- observation of appraisee in classroom or other work situation(s)
- appraisal interview generating a report(s)
- action taken
- review meeting, reviewing action.

One of the critical elements of all this is the interview, and Bailey (1989) has suggested a possible outline for an interview with a head of department (Figure 6.13).

Such systems, outlined overtly and in plan, do not necessarily lead to teacher and school improvement. That needs more than a formal evaluative system which can too readily be treated as a 'game' to 'win'. Clearly, action needs to be based upon the appraisal, and in any case teacher self-evaluation has been and remains one of the most effective long-term ways of securing educational improvement. So, for instance, Figure 6.14 might cause more change on the part of a reflective practitioner than an elaborate appraisal mechanism!

---

1   I read that your subject has changed very much in recent years. Can you tell me briefly how it has changed, and how this affects what you teach and how you teach it?

2   How do you plan your courses? Do you do it personally?

3   On what principles do you deploy your departmental colleagues?

4   How do you know what your colleagues are doing; and how do they know what you are doing as head of department?

5   What do you do yourself in a typical week or weeks? What are your key tasks? Are they to do with the subject, or with pupil control, for example?

6   What provision do you make for broadening the professional experience of your colleagues and yourself?

7   How do you support your colleagues?

8   Do you hold departmental meetings? What is the purpose of such meetings? Do they work?

9   What are your requisition and stock control arrangements? Have you a long-term requisitions policy? What are its details? Do you discuss these with your colleagues? Do you all agree?

10 What provision do you make departmentally to support probationers, and to help them to contribute?

11 How do you help students doing their teaching practice under your supervision?

12 What have you done in your department this year that is new? Who suggested it? Have you dropped anything to make room for it?

13 What can you tell me about the learning problems of your pupils? What or who causes problems? What are you doing to deal with these problems, in so far as this lies within your capacity? How does your department deal with specially gifted pupils?

14 Is yours a 'productive' department?

15 What can I do, as head of school, to help you in this coming year?

Source: Bailey, 1989

Figure 6.13 Possible outline for an appraisal interview with a head of department, for example by the headteacher

According to Postman and Weingartner, the enquiry teacher displays the following behaviour:

1 Rarely tells students what he/she thinks they ought to know.

2 Is largely interested in helping students learn to learn.

3 Stresses, by example, that education is a process of finding answers.

4 Uses questioning as the basic mode of discourse with students.

5 Encourages openness to alternative perspectives and rarely accepts a single viewpoint as an answer to an enquiry.

6 Encourages student–student interaction as opposed to student–teacher interaction.

7 Develops lessons from the interests and responses of students and not from a previously determined plan for the way the enquiry should proceed.

How often do you display these behaviours? Are you an enquiry teacher? Here is a self-evaluation checklist. Tick the spaces that correspond with the frequency with which you display the following behaviours. So, are you an enquiry teacher? The scoring system shown here is very unscientific – but will provide a fairly accurate answer to the question. Total the number of responses of each frequency. Enter the results in the table on pages 165–6. Calculate your sub-totals using the designated multiplier (for example, your 'Nearly always' score is to be multiplied by 4). Finally, calculate your total score. This will be a score out of 80.

	Nearly always	Frequently	Sometimes	Rarely
1 I opt for flexible seating, student movement and the maximum interaction between students.				
2 I make available a wide range of resources and materials for student use.				
3 My introductory lessons on a unit of work present a problem, issue, question or contradiction to stimulate student thinking.				
4 In doing so, I encourage students to react freely with little direction from me. The course of the enquiry becomes theirs to plan.				
5 The students talk more than I do during classroom enquiry work.				
6 When I talk, I question, not 'tell'.				
7 I consciously use the ideas raised by students and base my next questions on them.				
8 I redirect student questions in such a way that students are encouraged to seek their own answers.				
9 My questions encourage students to test the validity of their ideas in the broad context of experience.				
10 Class dialogue is conducted in a fashion that emphasises courtesy and openness to divergent views.				

	Nearly always	Frequently	Sometimes	Rarely
11 Skills are developed and practised as they are required during an enquiry, not as a separate set of activities.				
12 I encourage a rigorous questioning of the grounds upon which statements are made.				
13 I encourage students to explore the implications of holding alternative value and policy positions.				
14 I make students aware of personal, social and political bases for diversity in attitude, values and policies.				
15 I encourage students to arrive at value and policy positions of their own that they can understand and defend.				
16 I use evaluation in the classroom as a means to improve learning and not to judge people.				
17 The results of evaluation help me make amendments to existing enquiry procedures with students.				
18 I evaluate students on growth in many aspects of the learning experience, rather than simply on the knowledge acquired.				
19 I share the results of evaluation with students, identifying strengths as well as areas where we both need to improve.				
20 I make my students aware that I am involved in my own geographical enquiries, and that learning need not stop when one leaves school.				

Responses	No.	Multiplier	Sub-total
Nearly always		x4	=
Frequently		x3	=
Sometimes		x2	=
Rarely		x1	=
Total			

Are you an enquiry teacher? Here is another unscientific guide. If you scored:

65–80
Yes you are. You are consciously looking for ways to promote student enquiry and are aware of your role in maintaining an atmosphere of enquiry in your classroom.

45–64
You are convinced of the value of enquiry teaching and use it where and when appropriate issues and materials are available. You could try a little harder to create more such opportunities.

35–44
Maybe you should try a lot harder – but I am convinced that all is not lost …!

Less than 34
Well now …!

Contributed by John Fien, Visiting Lecturer at the Institute of Education, London.

Source: Fien, 1980

Figure 6.14 Am I an enquiry teacher?

Evaluating curricula

Nowadays it is expected that schemes of work will be provided by teachers as essential curriculum documents. Until recently there were two terms in common parlance. A *teaching syllabus* (HMI, 1986) was a formal statement which described the rationale and framework for an education programme; gave guidance on the content and methods which could be used; indicated the resources which were available; and outlined the actions which were necessary for effective implementation. The second commonly used term was *examination syllabus* – that is, the content, understanding and skills which were to be examined, but not how these were to be taught. Essentially the *scheme of work* is a curriculum document rather than a syllabus. In fact HMI (1986) stated that teaching syllabuses should include information on goals, content, methods, structure, resources, differentiation, assessment and record keeping, evaluation, and time allocation. This is a very similar list to that of the Curriculum Council for Wales (1991) which mentions: a rationale, sequencing, teaching approaches and learning activities, differentiation, and assessment. That document argues that schemes of work are the interpretation of the National Curriculum as structured programmes of learning experience which relate to the policies, resources and circumstances of each individual school.

> Two layers of schemes of work will be required: the first to cover the whole of a key stage; the second, in more detail, to cover the teaching units/topics which together make up the work for the key stage. Schemes of work are indispensable elements in a school's documentation of its policies and procedures. They show how curriculum policy (school, LEA and government) can be translated into effective and enjoyable teaching and learning experiences.
>
> Curriculum Council for Wales, 1991

A scheme of work is regarded as important because it reflects:
- the aspirations and needs of the students
- the current good practice in the school
- resources (human and material)
- the collective experience and vision of the department.

One can evaluate schemes of work alongside the above expectations and characteristics, or one can use specific evaluation criteria for courses. As Hacking (1992) suggested:

- Was there a coherence to each unit?
- Were pupils able to build on the skills and understanding of previous units?
- Did pupils develop their attitudes and values through successive units?
- Are pupils enjoying and involved in the learning programme?
- Are all pupils achieving positively within their ability?

Brown and Slater (1993) 'distilled' the criteria that experts used to evaluate a particular curriculum document. The following emerged:

- Purpose
- Curriculum view
- Audience
- Elements of the curriculum document
- Internal consistency of the document
- Practicality/utility
- Style of communication
- Presentation
- Overall judgement.

Balance is another criterion for judging a curriculum. A useful device is the curriculum matrix (see Figure 6.15), devised by the Geography 16–19 Project to assess balance across scales and regional examples used. Equally important is the range of teaching strategies used, for instance across the range listed in Figure 6.16.

Evaluating resources

The key resource in any department is, of course, the staff, but almost as vital are the 'fixed' resources such as teaching rooms, library and computer laboratory and the 'movable' resources such as books, paper, furniture, videos and computer software, which have to be purchased regularly. Managing these movable items effectively is an important task for a head of a geography department. Hindson (1990) offered a list of questions to consider when devising such a resource strategy (Figure 6.17). Part of such a strategy is to identify resource strengths and weaknesses (Figure 6.18).

Environments and systems	Dominantly natural environments and ⟷ systems		Dominantly human environments and systems	
Themes / Scales	Theme 1	Theme 2	Theme 3	Theme 4
Small and local scale				
Intermediate scale				
Global scale				

The main emphases of any teaching syllabus based on the Geography 16–19 framework should be plotted on the curriculum matrix so that coverage of scales can be identified and considered.

Note:

Small and local scale = Small-scale case study, e.g. town, farm, factory, village. Local study.

Intermediate scale = Small regional scale, e.g. UK planning region. Sub-national scale, e.g. SE England. National. Major province. Major natural region. Continental.

Global = World patterns and distributions.

Source: Naish, Rawling and Hart, 1987

Figure 6.15 The curriculum matrix

Evaluation is an essential element of the resource management task, which also includes purchasing resources, particularly books, and takes up a large proportion of a department's budget. Careful evaluation and judicious purchase are especially important where a large proportion of geography lessons are taught by non-specialists or relatively out-of-touch specialists who rely (understandably) a good deal on the support of a text-book. There are hazards in the process, since it is often a rushed exercise undertaken towards the end of the summer term, and there is a danger of making snap judgements on curriculum resources based on word of mouth or a superficial contact with the resource. There are two particular challenges in all this for geography teachers.

	Often	**Occasionally**	**Never**
The teacher talks and students respond.			
The teacher talks, students respond and make notes.			
The teacher talks, uses whiteboard/ blackboard and students make notes.			
The teacher dictates notes to students.			
The teacher hands out printed notes, talks and students listen.			
The teacher lectures, students make notes.			
The teacher organises a discussion involving the whole class.			
The teacher organises group discussions.			
The students organise a whole class discussion; teacher joins in.			
The students organise group discussions; teacher joins in.			
The students prepare and distribute sets of notes for each other.			
The students prepare and present lecturettes to the class.			
The teacher sets individual written assignments in class.			
The teacher sets small group assign- ments (written) in class (e.g. reports of group discussions).			
The teacher sets small group assignments (practical) in class (e.g. mapping or graphing).			
The teacher sets students a structured information-gathering exercise.			
The teacher sets students an open- ended enquiry (i.e. students make decisions, teacher advises, end result not known).			

	Often	**Occasionally**	**Never**
The teacher involves pupils in a geographical classroom game.	✓		
The teacher involves students in a role-play.			
The teacher involves students in a simulation.			
Students are involved in a decision-making exercise.			
Students are involved in a problem-solving exercise.			
The teacher organises a video/tape/TV/slides; students watch/listen and make notes.			
The teacher organises a video/tape/TV/slides; students watch/listen only.			
Students make use of video/tape/slides/TV for personal research.			
The teacher sets a short answer test.			
The teacher sets an essay test without books and/or notes.			
The teacher sets a practical test, e.g. map interpretation.			
Students write an essay with the help of books and/or notes.			
The teacher organises an outside speaker to give a lecture.			
The teacher organises an outside speaker for question/answer session.			
The teacher organises an outside visit.			
Other (specify)			
Other (specify)			

Source: Based on a questionnaire devised by the Geography 16–19 Project in 1976

Figure 6.16 Teaching strategies that can be observed in geography classrooms

This is simply a list of stimulus questions you might like to consider when devising a resource strategy. It is by no means exhaustive.

1 How is money allocated within the school and/or faculty?
   • Per capita?
   • Per pupil contact hours?
   • Estimation?
   • Historic need?

2 How is money allocated within the department?
   • Per year group?
   • Per resource area?

3 How are departmental priorities identified?
   • How much is allocated to departmental administration?
   • What kind of resource balance is aimed for?
   • Should any groups/areas be given additional help?

4 How is an ongoing purchase policy to be worked out?
   • Are textbooks and maps going to be given a certain lifespan?
   • Is money going to be allocated to replace lost or damaged books?

5 Are certain items within the department going to be charged for?
   • Do students have to purchase certain items themselves?

6 How are resources to be evaluated before purchase?
   • Are review copies to be ordered?
   • Who is responsible for the final purchase decision?

7 How are resources to be allocated amongst students?
   • Are students given a book each?
   • Are books purchased assuming that students will share them?
   • Are students allowed to take books home?

8 Is money available from external sources?
   • Can PTA money be used – if so, how much each year?
   • Is sponsorship available from local businesses?
   • Can expensive resources be shared with other departments/schools?

9 What does a department have to pay for from its money allocation?

10 Should any money be kept in reserve?
   • Does all the money allocated to a department have to be spent in one year?

Source: Hindson and Dilkes, 1990

Figure 6.17 Key questions for devising a resource strategy

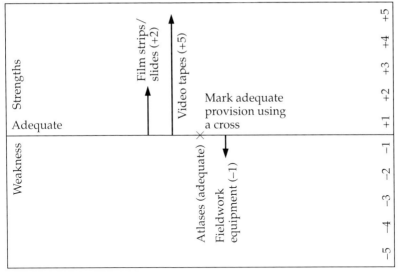

Figure 6.18 Resource strengths and weaknesses

First, to see all the curriculum resources is nigh on impossible, except perhaps at the annual conference of the Geographical Association, which not everyone can attend, while the inspection-copy process is tedious and limiting. Secondly, there is a massive range of products on offer, giving a confusing task to a head of department. However, careful evaluation and subsequent purchase of appropriate resources is vital and expensive. Perhaps the task's importance is underplayed? It is certainly this author's experience that some schools purchase textbooks which seemed superficially at first to suit their purposes but are found subsequently to have severe limitations.

A certain amount of geography education research has focused on the evaluation of curriculum resources and the ways they are used with children. Some examples are MA dissertations at the Institute of Education such as Lidstone (1977), an evaluation of a curriculum based on the Oxford Geography Project books; Gill (1980), partly a critique of GYSL from a radical perspective; and Rider (1986), the use of graphics in textbooks. Lidstone continued his interest in textbooks through his PhD thesis, and his diagram which is reproduced in figure 6.19 illustrates how various areas of research can illuminate the role of textbooks in geography teaching.

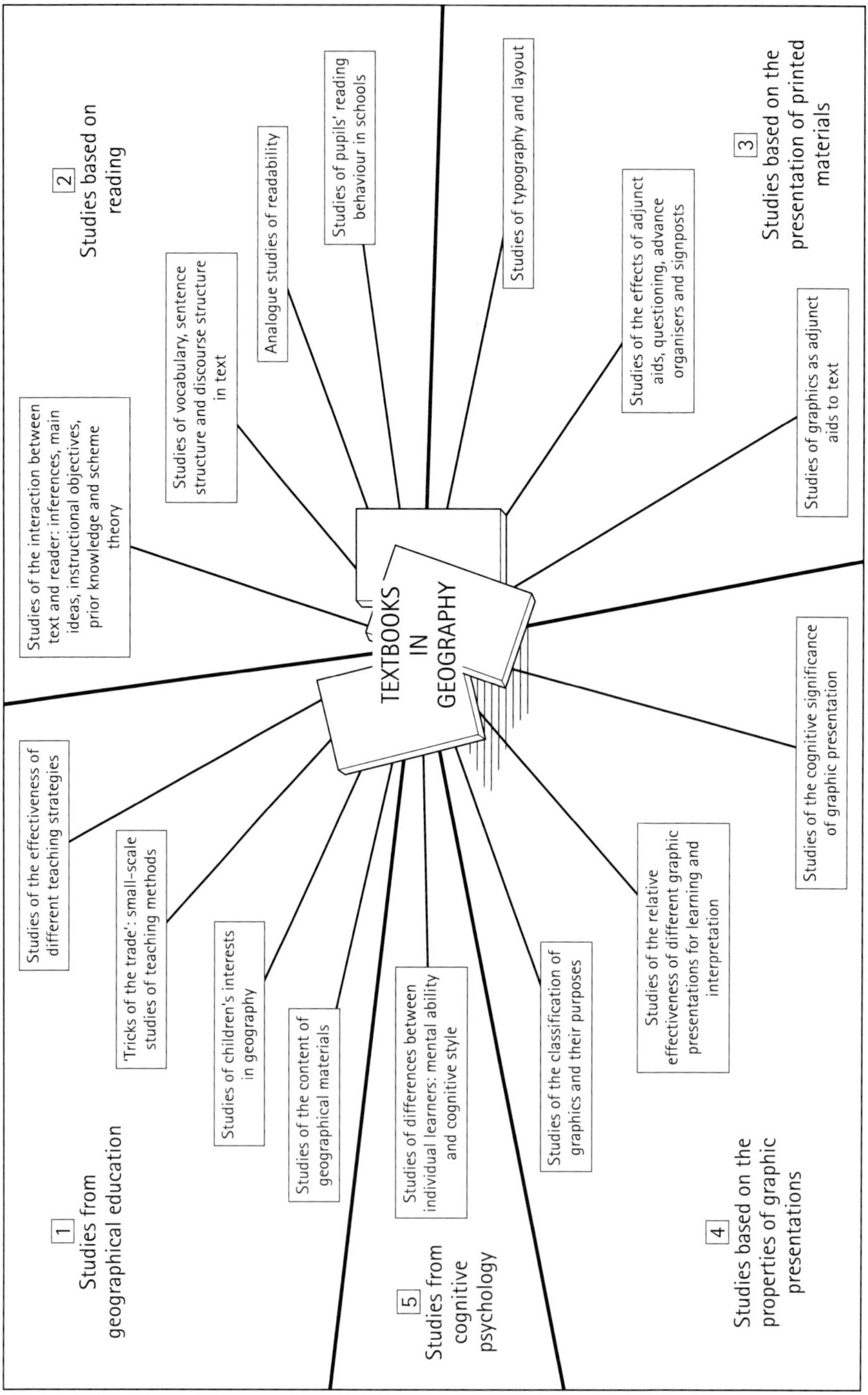

Figure 6.19 The areas of research that contribute to a study of the role of textbooks in geography teaching

Source: Lidstone, 1985

Wright has had a long-standing interest in the evaluation of textbooks and in 1986 suggested ten questions to ask when evaluating a book:

1 What is the true cost of the book?
2 Is the language appropriate?
3 Is the book up to date?
4 Are the themes and topics interesting and relevant?
5 Are the pupil activities varied and appropriate?
6 Does the book have full-colour printing?
7 Is the design and printing clear and attractive?
8 Are the maps and diagrams comprehensible and interesting?
9 Is the value-system of the book acceptable?
10 Does the book suit me and my pupils?

Over the years several checklists and evaluation sheets have been devised against which to judge the quality of curriculum resources, and not just for textbooks. A useful example is the list of criteria used by the Geographical Association for reviewers of teaching resources (Figure 6.20). This author has added two further categories. A similar set of

---

GA categories for review of teaching resources

Content   Is geographical content up to date, rigorous and accurate?

Design   Is the product attractive, robust, well presented?

Originality   Is the concept/content approach original?

Appropriateness   Is it suitable for the pupils it is designed for?

Significance   Does it make a significant contribution to the geographical education of pupils?

Cost/value for money   Would you buy it?

Also consider:

Bias – gender?
       – race/cultural?
       – examples used?

Pupils' views – does it interest/involve them?

Source: Based on a checklist used by Geographical Association reviewers of teaching resources

Figure 6.20 Broad evaluation criteria for textbook resources

A simple sheet to help organise initial thinking on textbook resources		
Title		
Author		
Publisher		

Category	Positive	Negative
Claims made by publisher		
How are contents organised and expressed?		
How is text presented and organised?		
How clearly are key concepts, themes or ideas signposted?		
How successfully are photos and artwork used?		
What forms of exercises and activities have been designed?		
What appears to be the 'ethos' of the book?		
How attractive is the book to young readers?		
Other?		

Source: Devised by David Lambert for the PGCE Geography course at the Institute of Education, University of London

Figure 6.21 Evaluation of published resources for Key Stage 3

guidelines is used at the Institute of Education to help PGCE students to begin thinking about such evaluation (Figure 6.21). An elaborate evaluation of trial teaching materials was devised by the Geography 16–19 Project team, and sections 5 and 6 are shown in Figure 6.22.

5. Your views on these materials

Please indicate your views on this section of the materials by scoring the points set out below.

(a) *Student resources*	very good	quite good	satis- factory	poor	very poor	no comment
Variety of resources incorporated						
Resources in suitable form for 16–19 use						
Resources stimulating and interesting						
Resources well presented						
(b) *Student exercises*						
Guidance given to students						
Clarity of language						
Sequencing of exercises						
Skills appropriate to target group						
Level of conceptual understanding demanded too high/too low (*please indicate*)						
Facilities for able students to extend themselves						
Incorporation of enquiry approach to learning						
People–environment approach to geography put across successfully						
Potential for arousing student enjoyment						
Potential for arousing student interest						
Student achievement of objectives stated						

(c) *Teacher's notes*	very good	quite good	satis- factory	poor	very poor	no comment
Clarity of guidance	☐	☐	☐	☐	☐	☐
Clarity of explanation	☐	☐	☐	☐	☐	☐
Clarity of statement of aims/objectives	☐	☐	☐	☐	☐	☐
Notes clearly related to student exercises and resources	☐	☐	☐	☐	☐	☐

(d) *Quantity and timing of materials*	too much/ too many	just right	too little/ too few	no comment
Number of student resources	☐	☐	☐	☐
Number of student exercises	☐	☐	☐	☐
Number and range of skills included	☐	☐	☐	☐
Amount of teacher guidance	☐	☐	☐	☐
Time allocation	☐	☐	☐	☐

6. Other comments

Please use the space below to make any further comments you wish with regard to this section of the materials (e.g. to elaborate a statement ticked above, to suggest how you would improve the materials, to comment on extra resources used etc.) Thank you!

Source: Geography 16–19 Project

Figure 6.22 Evaluation of trial teaching materials

Sometimes a particular aspect of a curriculum resource is evaluated, such as photographs – for example, Wiegand (1982) and Wright (1986). The latter posed ten questions for evaluating photographs in textbooks:

1   Are the photographs big enough?
2   Are they sharp enough?
3   Is the tone satisfactory?

4   Are the views hackneyed?

5   Are they merely free propaganda?

6   Do most of the photographs show relationships?

7   Do most of them show people?

8   Is there a good variety of types of photographs?

9   Do they encourage varied work?

10 Are they up to date?

To these questions one might add, 'Is there bias (gender, race, age) in the selection of subjects photographed?'

The development perspective was the focus of the work of the Centre for World Development Education (the predecessor of Worldaware) in 1979 when it evaluated seventy-one textbooks aimed at 11 to 16-year-olds against a list of sixteen questions (Figure 6.23) by 'weighting' the extent to which each book answered each question, in the following ways:

0 – no reference of any kind

1 – topic or aspect was referred to

2 – topic is reasonably fully dealt with.

Other checklists focus on bias in various respects. Walford (1985) has a detailed and helpful checklist for geography teachers to become more aware of the role of geography in educating children for a multicultural society. The following questions give a flavour of his later and more detailed checklist:

- Do you teach about inequality on both a local and world scale?
- Do your departmental aims refer specifically to teaching about current social/economic/political issues in their geographical context?
- Have you examined your textbooks for racist stereotypes?
- Are you developing techniques to deal with racist comments made by pupils?

Publishers are now becoming increasingly (and rightly!) sensitive to allegations to bias in their products, and so offer guidance to authors.

Gender bias has also been a concern and Connolly (1984, 1993) has written on this theme. Figures 6.24 and 6.25 give some interesting examples of efforts to 'gender' geography, and how effective they have been.

Does the book

1   deal with spatial variations in the levels of human welfare, measured on a variety of scales? Does it consider the validity of measures of human welfare, e.g. GNP?

2   indicate ethnic and cultural diversity and the plural nature of many societies?

3   show any awareness of the cultural achievements of developing countries and the cultural debts that industrialised countries owe to them?

4   discuss the physical environment in terms of constraints upon, and opportunities for, development?

5   deal with the history of the developing countries concerned, with reference to their colonial background?

6   deal with the world distribution of resources and production?

7   deal with the content and direction of international trade, its changing patterns and the ways in which it affects the internal structure of developing countries?

8   discuss occupational structures and the kinds of work that people do?

9   present a range of agricultural situations in developing countries, and discuss questions of land ownership and land reform?

10 deal with population increase rates, age structures and densities? Does it explain the causes of change?

11 look at migration flows within developing countries (e.g. urbanisation) and at international migration, past and present?

12 discuss different types of human settlements and their characteristics and functions?

13 discuss the nature of aid relationships?

14 look at alternative strategies for development?

15 examine the economic, social and cultural effects of tourism?

16 include any discussion of the role of large multinational corporations?

Source: Centre for World Development Education, 1979

Figure 6.23 An assessment of the coverage of development in textbooks

1 Illustrations

Are women shown in illustrations?

What is the role of women where they are shown?

2 Language

Does the language indicate sexist bias, e.g. the use of 'man', 'he', etc.?

3 Roles in role-play exercises

To what extent and in what way are women included in role-play exercises?

4 Omissions

Are any themes omitted that may result in discrimination against women?

5 Women as an identifiable group

Are there any instances where women are singled out as an identifiable group? What is the nature of such instances?

Source: ILEA (1984), Geography Bulletin No.19

Figure 6.24 Criteria for checking the gender bias of school textbooks

Common usage	Unbiased terms
man's search for knowledge	people have continually sought knowledge
man, mankind	people, humanity, humankind
manpower	workforce, personnel, human resources
mothering	parenting, nurturing

Source: Women and Geography Study Group/Institute of British Geographers (1989), *Area*, 21 (2), June.

Figure 6.25 Changing language to achieve accurate, unbiased communication

Naturally, textbooks are not the only resource requiring careful evaluation. If and when computer software becomes omnipresent in geography classrooms, it too will need to come under scrutiny. Figure 6.26 shows a computer-assisted learning evaluation checklist written up in Gold *et al.* (1991).

A final short-cut for teachers considering purchasing teaching resources is to study reviews, for example in *Teaching Geography* and *Geography*, where books, software and other resources are regularly evaluated.

Evaluating lessons

The core of the curriculum process is of course the geography lesson, and so it is not surprising that lesson observations are at the heart of the OFSTED inspection system. Classrooms are complex places, and unravelling and understanding them from infrequent visits is fraught with difficulties. The presence of an outsider can immediately change the classroom environment and relationships.

There are many approaches to observing classrooms. At one extreme an observer notes down the happenings, events, circumstances that she/he feels are significant, and the feedback is in the form of unstructured prose out of which structure could be imposed. At the other extreme is the more quantitative Flanders-type scheme such as that shown in Figure 6.27, where the observation intervals can vary from a few seconds to a few minutes. In between these qualitative/quantitative extremes are broad headings structuring the observation. The OFSTED lesson observation proforma (Figure 6.1) is of this type, as are the assessment categories used by the Institute of Education with PGCE students on teaching practice (Figure 6.28).

Another approach to evaluating lessons is to consider the range of teaching strategies used. Figure 6.16 is based on the Geography 16–19 Project's questionnaire devised to determine teaching strategies used by teachers of 16 to 19-year-olds. It is now used for student teachers to consider the range of strategies they may observe in their teaching-practice school. Another checklist was provided by the Curriculum Council for Wales (1991) as both a planning and evaluation tool (Figure 6.29).

Criteria	Quality		Importance	

Subject matter content

Criteria	Quality	Importance
Definition of key concepts	1 2 3 4 5	A B C D
Discussion of underlying assumptions	1 2 3 4 5	A B C D
Validity of theories, principles, techniques, facts	1 2 3 4 5	A B C D
Guide to relevant literature	1 2 3 4 5	A B C D
Overall quality of subject matter content	1 2 3 4 5	A B C D

User documentation

Criteria	Quality	Importance
Clarity of presentation	1 2 3 4 5	A B C D
Completeness	1 2 3 4 5	A B C D
Adequacy of instructions for operating the software	1 2 3 4 5	A B C D
Documentation for different users (e.g. teachers, students)	1 2 3 4 5	A B C D
Worksheets and other teaching materials	1 2 3 4 5	A B C D
Consistency with the accompanying program	1 2 3 4 5	A B C D
Overall quality of documentation	1 2 3 4 5	A B C D

Educational support

Criteria	Quality	Importance
Ease of integration with teaching and learning styles	1 2 3 4 5	A B C D
Potential for improving grasp of principles and theories	1 2 3 4 5	A B C D
Potential for improving facility with methods and techniques	1 2 3 4 5	A B C D
Potential for improving retention and recall of knowledge	1 2 3 4 5	A B C D
Overall quality of educational support	1 2 3 4 5	A B C D

Student motivation

Criteria	Quality	Importance
Potential for capturing student interest	1 2 3 4 5	A B C D
Ability to stimulate student creativity	1 2 3 4 5	A B C D
Appropriateness for student-centred work	1 2 3 4 5	A B C D
Overall quality for student motivation	1 2 3 4 5	A B C D

Software

Criteria	Quality	Importance
Freedom from errors	1 2 3 4 5	A B C D
Ease of use	1 2 3 4 5	A B C D
Compatibility with available computer hardware	1 2 3 4 5	A B C D
Completeness of technical documentation	1 2 3 4 5	A B C D
Overall quality of software	1 2 3 4 5	A B C D
Overall evaluation	1 2 3 4 5	A B C D

Quality ratings: 1 excellent; 2 very good; 3 average; 4 poor; 5 bad
Importance ratings: A critical; B important; C optional; D inappropriate

Source: Gold *et al.*, 1991

Figure 6.26 A computer-assisted learning evaluation checklist

Observation intervals

Teacher activity

Teacher asking questions involving:

1   recalling facts and ideas
2   understanding ideas
3   offering hypotheses
4   making value-judgements
5   pupil tasks
6   routine classroom matters

Teacher making statements about:

1   facts
2   ideas
3   values and attitudes
4   what to do (instructions)
5   routine classroom matters
6   small talk

Pupil activity

Pupil(s) answering solicited questions involving:

1   recalling facts and ideas
2   understanding ideas
3   offering hypotheses
4   making value-judgements
5   pupil tasks
6   routine classroom matters

Pupils making unsolicited statements about:

1   facts
2   ideas
3   hypotheses
4   value-judgements
5   pupil tasks
6   routine classroom matters

Silence during oral work

Transition between activities

Pupils engaged in written work

Source: Boydell, 1974

Figure 6.27 Observation schedule for recording teacher and pupil activity in a lesson (the schedule given here is an adaptation of two schedules originally designed for use in primary classrooms)

Beginning teacher _____   Subject _____

School _____   Area _____

Areas of development	1	2	3	4	Comments
Subject knowledge e.g. relevant subject knowledge and under-standing of the material taught					
Planning, preparation e.g. lesson planning and preparation					
Teaching and learning e.g. creating a learning environment; involving pupils in purposeful learning; communication skills					
Classroom organisation e.g. individual, group and whole class management; management of resources					
Assessment and record keeping e.g. marking and feedback to pupils					
Observation and evaluation e.g. lessons; units; resources; own performance					
Professional relationships e.g. with pupils; with staff in school					
Personal qualities and presentation e.g. attendance; promptness; enthusiasm					

Figure 6.28 PGCE: example of end of first teaching practice interim report and self-assessment

Activity	✓	Experienced in _____ unit of work
Fieldwork		
Mapwork/atlas		
Data/diagram analysis		
Photograph interpretation		
Interpret written material		
Library research		
IT		
Reading		
Discussion: Class		
Group		
Pair		
Writing: Creative		
Analytical		
Notes		
Teacher exposition		
Visitor/outside speaker		
Design/art work		
Response to slides/video		
Response to literature/music		
Simulation		
Role play		
Others		

This can be used as a tool for both planning and evaluating a piece of work.

Figure 6.29 Teaching/learning activity matrix

Source: Curriculum Council for Wales, 1991

Checklists can additionally focus on a particular element of a lesson or a particular teaching skill. In the case of the latter, Hay (1994) provides a checklist to evaluate spoken presentations (Figure 6.30) and although geared to higher education, it can easily be applied to schools. Arguably, however, more important in long-term impact on the quality of geography teaching, is a teacher's own evaluation and thereby improvement of lessons. Figures 6.31 and 6.32 are examples of such self-evaluation sheets devised by former PGCE students at the Institute of Education.

	Pass	Fail
Objective: To successfully deliver a spoken presentation		
Aspect 1 Speaker appearance and other first impressions		
Dressed appropriately; tidy and free of distracting features		
Relaxed and comfortable poise		
Speaker appeared confident and purposeful before starting to speak		
Speaker attracted audience's attention from the outset		
Little or no fidgeting and few distracting mannerisms		
Aspect 2 Presentation structure		
Introduction		
Title/topic made clear		
Purpose of the presentation clear		
Organisational framework made known to audience		
Unusual terms defined adequately		
Body of presentation		
Main points stated clearly		
Sufficient information and detail provided		
Sufficient periodic recapitulation		
Appropriate and adequate use of examples/anecdotes		
Correspondence of presentation content to introductory framework		
Discussion flowed logically		
Conclusion		
Ending of presentation signalled adequately		
Main points summarised adequately/ideas brought to fruition		
Conclusion linked to opening		
Final message clear and easy to remember		

	Pass	Fail
Aspect 3 Coping with questions		
Whole audience searched for questions		
Questions addressed in order		
Questions handled adeptly		
Full audience addressed with answers		
Speaker maintained control of discussion		
Aspect 4 Delivery		
Speech clear and audible to entire audience		
Suitable vocabulary (few clichés, little jargon and repetition)		
Interesting variety in tone of voice		
Little false or excessive use of spoken emphasis		
Short, comprehensible sentences		
Few unfinished sentences		
Presentation directed to all parts of audience		
Eye contact held with audience throughout presentation		
Meaningful gestures appropriately used		
Full text not read		
Speaker kept to time-limit		
Good use of time without rushing at end		
Pace neither too fast nor too slow		
Aspect 5 Visual aids and handouts		
Visual aids clearly visible to entire audience		
Overhead and slide projectors etc. operated correctly		
Speaker familiar with own visual aids, e.g. OHPs, blackboard diagrams		
Visual aids well prepared		
Effective use made of handouts and/or visual aids		
Handouts well prepared and useful		
Aspect 6 Target and audience		
Presentation met level of knowledge for audience		
Presentation met need for knowledge of audience		

Source: Journal of Geography in Higher Education, 18, 1994

Figure 6.30 Oral presentation assessment schedule

Questions	1	2	3	4	5
How well have the lesson objectives been achieved?					
How varied are the resources?					
How up-to-date are the resources?					
How well is the work linked to the ATs stated?					
How easy will it be to measure pupil achievement of the ATs from the class work completed?					
How well did I link this session to others?					
How well did I introduce this session?					
How well did I make the aims of the lesson clear?					
How well did I make the lesson progression clear?					
How well did I emphasise key points?					
How well did I summarise effectively?					
How well did I handle problems of inattention?					
How well did I cope with the ability range?					
How well did I handle student questions/responses?					
How well did I keep the material relevant?					
How well did I use my voice/body movements?					
How well did I convey my enthusiasm?					
How well did I maintain student interest?					
How well did I plan and prepare the lesson?					
How well did I produce good clear materials?					
How well did I handle control problems?					
How well did I make contact with individuals?					

Source: Joanne Clark, PGCE student, 1993

Figure 6.31 Individual lesson self-evaluation sheet for teachers

How well did I…?	G	R	C
Link this session with others			
Introduce this session			
Make the aims of the lesson clear			
Make the lesson progression clear			
Emphasise key points			
Summarise effectively			
Pace the lesson appropriately			
Handle problems of inattention			
Cope with the ability range			
Handle student questions and responses			
Keep the material relevant			
Use my voice, body movements			
Convey my enthusiasm			
Maintain student interest			
Plan and prepare the lesson			
Produce good, clear materials			
Handle control problems			
Make contact with individual students			
G = good R = reasonable C = could do better			

Source: Jane Herrington, PGCE student, 1989

Figure 6.32 Teacher self-assessment of a curriculum unit

In Chapter 7, Frances Slater offers a selection of questions to define the ideological stance taken about a lesson or unit of work.

Listening to students

Finally, most fundamental of all, but often neglected, is the impact of geography lessons on students and what they feel. As Walford rightly said in 1979, 'It's no good a teacher claiming that his or her teaching is successful if the students don't corroborate the claim'.

The student perception of teacher style (SPOTS) test was devised with that in mind. This test was administered to students in a range of countries and the results were then presented for international comparison (Stoltman, 1976).

Students are not often asked what they feel about lessons, so the study conducted by Dalton (1988) was an encouraging change. He compared two geography classes, one following a relatively progressive Mode 111 CSE and the other a more conventional syllabus. Figure 6.33 illustrates one set of his results.

Student teachers are encouraged to collect pupil evaluation data, and Figure 6.34 is an example of a form given to pupils after a study of Kenya. Other strategies, of course, involve conversing with students, individually or in groups, as to how they found their geography lesson(s).

	5B	**5D** (GYSL)
Films	5	1
Worksheets	1	3
Teacher talking	9	7
Textbooks	4	0
Resource sheets	0	5
No reply	4	3

Comment
Here the replacement of textbooks in 5D is clearly reflected by the scoring on resource sheets. There is a similar weighting for teacher talking in both classes, and a slightly stronger score in the GYSL group on worksheets. Films appear to have made a greater impression on 5B.

Source: After Dalton, 1988

Figure 6.33 A comparison of geography teaching in two classes

Class:

1 How much did you enjoy the study of Kenya?

	Not at all	Very little	Okay	Enjoyed it	Really enjoyed it
Topic as a whole					
Perceptions of Kenya					
Maasai people					
Kikuyu people					
Population distribution					
Nairobi					

2 How much do you think you learned about the following:

	Nothing	A little	Quite a lot	A great deal
Perceptions of Kenya				
Maasai people				
Kikuyu people				
Population distribution				
Nairobi				

3 How much do you think you learnt from:

	Nothing	A little	Quite a lot	A great deal
Individual work?				
Pair work?				
Group work?				
Class discussion?				
Using textbooks?				
Using photographs?				
Using slides?				
Using a video?				
Using maps/atlases?				
Building clay huts?				
Using worksheets?				

4 Please make any general comments, favourable or unfavourable, on any part of the unit, if you wish.

Source: Karmjit Natt, PGCE student, 1994

Figure 6.34 Pupil evaluation

Regardless of the approach, the 'clients' should be an integral part of the evaluation.

Conclusion

Not unlike principles of curriculum planning and development, evaluation is a somewhat neglected element of the professional development of geography teachers. The aim of this chapter has been to discuss the latest trends in evaluation, but specifically to focus on the level of work of a department. In a world of accountability and restricted resources, it is hoped that the sections on managing a department, OFSTED inspections and departmental review, staff appraisal, evaluating curricula and resources, evaluating lessons, and listening to students, are of immediate practical value. The chapter has a considerable number of checklists and proformas which should help to achieve that intention.

BIBLIOGRAPHY

Adair, J. (1985) *Action-centred Leadership*, McGraw-Hill.

Bailey, P. (1989) 'Leading the geography department: style and task', in Bailey, P. (ed.) *Managing the Geography Department*, Geographical Association.

Bayne-Jardin, C.C. and Hannam, C. (1972) 'Heads of department?', *Forum* 15(1).

Bennett, H. *et al.* (1992) *Teacher Appraisal: Survival and Beyond*, Longman.

Bird, M. (1992) *Effective Leadership. A Practical Guide to Leading your Team to Success*, BBC Books.

Boydell, D. (1974) 'Teacher– pupil contact in junior classrooms', *British Journal of Education Psychology*, 44(3):313–18.

Brighouse, T. (1991) *What Makes a Good School?*, Network Educational Press.

Brown, A. (1979) *Group Work*, Heinemann.

Brown, S.P. and Slater, F.A. (1993) 'Evaluating a Curriculum Document', *Geographical Education* 7(1).

Bruner, J. (1966) *Towards a Theory of Instruction*, Harvard University Press.

Carr, B. (1990) 'The role of the head of department', in Hindson, J. and Dilkes, J. (eds) *INSET Pack*, Geographical Association.

Centre for World Development Education (1979) *The Changing World and Geography: Suggestions for Teachers*, CWDE.

Connolly, J. (1984) *Geography Bulletin*, No 19 Spring, ILEA.

(1993) 'Gender balanced geography: have we got it right yet?', *Teaching Geography*, 8(2), April.

Curriculum Council for Wales (1991) *Non-Statutory Guidance for Teachers*, July, CCW.

Dalton, T.H. (1988) *The Challenge of Curriculum Innovation*, The Falmer Press.

Fidler, B. and Cooper, R. (1992) *Staff Appraisal and Staff Management in Schools and Colleges: A Guide to Implementation*, Longman.

Fien, J. (1980) *Geography 16–19 Project Newsletter*, No. 11.

Gill, D. (1980) 'Social Inequality: Spatial Form. Ideology in Geography', unpublished MA dissertation, Institute of Education, University of London.

Gold, J.R. *et al.* (1991) *Teaching Geography in Higher Education: A Manual of Good Practice*, Basil Blackwell.

Hacking, E. (1992) *Geography into Practice*, Longman.

Hay, J. (1994) 'Justifying and applying oral presentations in geographical education', *Journal of Geography in Higher Education* 18(1).

Hindson, J. and Dilkes, J. (eds) (1990) *INSET Pack*, Geographical Association.

HMI (1986) *Geography from 5 to 16*, Curriculum Matters 7, HMSO.

Hopkins, D. (1989) *Evaluation for School Development*, Open University Press.

House, E.R. (1986) *New Directions in Education Evaluation*, The Falmer Press.
(1993) *Professional Evaluation Social Impact and Political Consequences*, Sage Publications.

Juett, C. (1989) 'The head of department as a manager', in Wiegand, P. (ed.) *Managing the Geography Department*, Geographical Association.

Kemp, R. (1989) 'A sense of team', in *Managing the Geography Department*, Geographical Association.

Kent, W.A. (1990) *Selling Geography*, Geographical Association.

Lidstone, J. (1977) 'An evaluation of the geography curriculum offered to second and third year pupils in a south London junior high school based on volumes two and three of the Oxford Geography Project textbooks', unpublished MA dissertation, Institute of Education, University of London.

Marsden, W.E. (1976) *Evaluating the Geography Curriculum*, Oliver and Boyd.

Maslow, A.H. (1943) *Motivation and Personality*, Harper and Row.

Naish, M. , Rawling, E. and Hart, C. (1987) *Geography 16–19. The Contribution of a Curriculum Project to 16–19 Education*, Longman.

OFSTED (1994) *Handbook for the Inspection of Schools*, first published August 1993, amended May 1994, Office for Standards in Education.

Ormston, M. and Shaw, M. (1993) *Inspection: A Preparatory Guide for Schools*, Longman.

Rider, M.D. (1986) 'Perspectives on the use of graphics in geography textbooks designed for 11–16 year old pupils', unpublished MA dissertation, Institute of Education, University of London.

Scriven, M.S. (1991) *Evaluation Thesaurus* (4th edn), Sage Publications.

Skilbeck, M. (1984) *School-based Curriculum Development*, Harper and Row.

Stoll, L. and Fink, D. (1992) 'Effecting school change: the Halton approach', *School Effectiveness and Improvement*, 3(1): 19–41.

Stoltman, J. (1976) *International Research in Geographical Education*, Western Michigan University.

Tannenbaum, R. and Schmidt, W. (1973) 'How to choose a leadership pattern', *Harvard Business Review*, 51, May–June.

Walford, R. (1979) 'Listening to the Learner', in *Journal of Geography in Higher Education*, 3(1), Carfax.

—— (1985) *Geographical Education for a Multi-Cultural Society*, Geographical Association.

Warner, P. (1984) 'Curriculum planning in 11–14 Geography', unpublished MA dissertation, Institute of Education, University of London.

Wiegand, P. (1982) 'A biased view', in Kent, W.A. (ed.) *Bias in Geographical Education*, Institute of Education, University of London.

Wheeler, D.K. (1967) *Curriculum Process*, University of London Press.

Woods, D. and Orlik, S. (1994) *School Review and Inspection*, Kogan Page.

Wright, D.R. (1986) 'Evaluating textbooks', in Boardman, D. (ed.) *Handbook for Geography Teachers*, Geographical Association.

SECTION THREE | The Geography Curriculum – Issues and Concerns

In this section we identify a number of themes which emerge from the consideration of the curriculum, and explore them in detail. The identification of which themes to take in this way could be interpreted as an expression of a viewpoint: is the discussion of attitudes and values of more importance to geography educators than, say, information technology or vocational qualifications? Is assessment of greater significance than, say, fieldwork? It would be tendentious to argue such a case and yet decisions have to be made. There are many issues concerning the geography curriculum, and a single volume, especially one attempting to achieve a certain depth and provoke debate, cannot cover them all in the manner of a handbook or teachers' guides. The selection that has been made certainly reflects to some extent the priorities of the editors and authors and it is possible that in a different time and place a different selection would have been made. On the other hand, the three chapters in this section each, to a greater or lesser extent, encompass a range of issues faced by teachers. Moreover, they interrelate with each other and, from different perspectives, provide a rich discussion of *classroom processes* in geography.

As Frances Slater points out elsewhere, one of the interesting features of classroom related discussions is the tension of which geographers know much – between the general and the particular (Slater, 1994). Beginning teachers soon find out about the intellectual challenges they face in relating general principles to unique contexts; and the inherent dangers in attempting generalisations from individual experiences. Each of the chapters in Section Three are not, therefore, prescriptive in any sense. What they attempt to do is to offer some frameworks which may help and guide individual reflection. Slater's contribution (Chapter 7) is explicit in this way, starting out with the analogy of the framework as a map. Her intention is to map the locations of values in geographical education. This is a large and complex task which leads her to suggest that 'I may have given myself too large a brief'. However, as a piece of cartography, geography teachers at all levels will find much here both to challenge the cognitive maps we use in our day-to-day professional lives and, more to her point, provide a number of possible directions which might be taken to explore further the implications of making more visible the occurrence of values in geography education. Her discussion expands around the notion of teachers and curriculum planners distinguishing between means and ends, and encompasses a wide literature, from over two or three decades, providing philosophical, psychological and sociological perspectives within a strong and clearly articulated theory of curriculum. No aspect of geography in education is left untouched by her analysis, including fieldwork which commonly becomes, she argues, 'a particular kind of masculine endeavour'. As she notes more than once, 'educational endeavours are shot through with values', and this chapter, at the very least, provides a number of starting points for teachers and researchers to enter a conversation ultimately to enhance the value of learning through geography.

In Chapter 8, Margaret Roberts examines pedagogy in geography within the context of legislation which has brought about greater 'standardisation' of the curriculum. She argues that although the aims and content of geography education have been centrally controlled to an unprecedented degree in England and Wales, the question of how it is to be taught and learned still rests with teachers. On the other hand she cites evidence that the conditions under which teachers now operate may have constrained choice, with greater numbers opting for more 'closed' as opposed to more 'open' teaching strategies. She is careful not to make judgements on this, and takes steps to distance herself from researchers and commentators in the past who have tended to 'place more value on one style over another, either because they believed it to be more effective or because it was related to their particular educational aims and philosophy' (p.234). Her message is more that individual teachers or departments adopt a framework to enable them to interpret for themselves the styles and strategies that they have adopted and the implications of these. After reviewing writing and research on the theme she then provides an analytical framework which teachers can adopt. It is practical and revealing, lucidly illustrated by examples, and will form an excellent basis for teachers in initial training onwards for their enquiries and investigations into classroom processes.

Lambert takes a different approach in exploring one of the veritable growth areas in geography education — assessment. In common with the foregoing contributions, he provides what he terms a *landscape sketch*, akin to a 'map' or 'framework'. This sets out, in broad-brush terms, the aims of assessment, what it involves, and a contextual account which attempts to show the origin of some of the influences and attitudes that have helped shape the assessment landscape. More than Roberts, he is concerned with clarifying some key concepts which inform the assessment debate. Chapter 9 self-consciously argues that teachers — until recently not always the recipients of good advice and training in this area of their professional lives — must be equipped and be prepared to argue the educational ratio- nale. There are traps and dangers for the unwary or ill-prepared, result- ing in poor assessment practices which could be damaging to pupils — just as good assessment, principled and fair with clearly expressed purpose, can enhance pupils' curriculum experience. Thus although external examinations form part of the context in which all secondary teachers have to work, it is discussion of internal, 'formative' assessment that occupies the bulk of the chapter.

In relation to this Lambert tries to distinguish detailed day-to-day assessment ('marking') from the more synoptic 'teacher assessment' which, throughout the period since the establishment of the ten-level TGAT scale of attainment, has resisted easy definition.

REFERENCE
Slater, F. (1994) 'Do our definitions exist? Research in geography education', in *Reporting Research in Geography Education*, Monograph No.1, Institute of Education, University of London.

7 Values: towards mapping their locations in a geography education

Frances Slater

If I were preparing a workshop on the very general theme of what have come to be designated the values-related aspects of geography education, and if I had the opportunity to communicate with participants a week or so prior to the workshop, I would ask them to prepare by reading an article (or two) pertinent to the topic and close to their interest in geography. My aim would be simply to create through a common reading, a common experience for a discussion. On a number of just such occasions I have chosen to alert people to Julian Wolpert's article, 'The decision process in a spatial context' (Wolpert, 1964). There are many other pieces of writing which could serve as background reading to a workshop on values, some closely geographical, others more closely educational. In fact it could be said that any article within the field of geography or geography education would do to set a group of us talking about the values in our subject (geography) and in our endeavours (educational). Indeed, it seems self-evidently true to say that geography and education are 'shot through with values', to use a phrase one often comes across in reading. Yet perhaps it is also a somewhat trite point. We rather take it for granted, nod wisely and pass on. In the workshops embedded in this essay, I shall try to illustrate some but by no means all of the ways in which geography and geography education are 'shot through with values'. Significant distinctions should emerge which help us to be clearer about what is involved in thinking and talking about values.

Values and the disciplines of geography

Wolpert published his article in the *Annals* in 1964 giving us an account of research undertaken prior to that. He was working in the period of the quantitative revolution. What intrigues me particularly about the article is that he was even then calling some of the revolution's fundamental assumptions into question, and he chose to do this in relation to farming patterns in Middle Sweden.

OPTIMISERS OR SATISFICERS

Wolpert spells out the notion of economic man (*sic*) as a normative, inventive concept. Economic man (*sic*) behaves according to a set of norms or assumptions. Under the assumptions or conditions of possessing a single profit goal, omniscient powers of perception and reasoning, and having perfect knowledge and predictive abilities, economic humans ideally organise themselves, live and make decisions that lead to an optimum use of resources in space, and a pattern of land use which maximises output and economic return. Using the concept of economic beings we can predict what ought to be or what should be the case under certain economically determined conditions. Wolpert feels, however, that a behavioural concept – that of bounded rationality – might be very useful for describing and explaining variations in economic behaviour. Accordingly, he sets out to test the farming outcomes of the decisions of a sample of Middle Sweden's farmers against the assumptions contained within economic man (*sic*) and bounded rationality.

Wolpert has a theoretical perspective and an hypothesis. He proceeds in what we recognise to be a scientific manner and evaluates the results statistically. Variables which determine performance levels in farming are defined, selected and measured. Farming productivity, the result of a decision process farmers go through, is represented in Wolpert's article by three mapped spatial distributions. We have, first, the actual productivity average per farm and, secondly, the potential productivity average per farm or the surface which would result if the application of all resources including the farmer's knowledge were optimal. There is, thirdly, the possibility of producing a surface of the ratio of actual to potential productivity. A comparison of the three maps illustrates that the farmers do not achieve optimal production: that is, there are gaps between actual and potential productivity.

As one would expect, Wolpert feels he is establishing the possibility that the prerequisites to economic rationality (perfect knowledge and optimising behaviour) are absent. Without detailing here the entire argument, Wolpert reaches a position where he suggests that of the alternative concepts, 'optimiser' and 'satisficer', the latter may best describe and explain the goal orientation of the sample of farmers.

Before stating such a conclusion more firmly, Wolpert examines and discusses further the variables of knowledge and information available to the farmers, the environments of uncertainty they are operating in, their goals and resources. That is, he examines carefully the assumptions of the theory, and the possibilities of their holding true in Middle Sweden against evidence he has collected. He concludes that 'the individual is adaptively or intendedly rational rather than omnisciently rational'. Farmers make a range of decisions based on an uneven surface of knowledge, capital and other factors, which means there are spatial variations in decision environments. Farmers make choices based on imperfect knowledge.

A SIGNIFICANT ARTICLE

The fact that I have picked out this article suggests that I find it significant and worthwhile. To me it seems an important article both for its own sake, for what it says, its *substance* and when it was said, and for its potential to illustrate a number of points in this chapter. I value the article for a number of reasons. Obviously I preferred to choose it, rather than another. I like its subject matter and in this case the way the research is conducted. I like its questioning of assumptions, its enquiry-style scientific mode of investigation. It's one of a number of good ways to proceed, in my opinion. It extends my knowledge and understanding and capacity to think about spatial variations in farming patterns. I believe that in reading it, I have learned something. I rank it highly as a piece of research in geography and I have held this opinion of it for rather a long time now. I doubt that I would change my mind about it easily or readily. I value it because it seems to me to illuminate, to give perspective, to speak of matters concerning the 'real world' broadly. In addition, its concepts and ideas are useful in thinking and to thinking.

ATTACHING WORTHWHILENESS

I have tried above to give a sense of what I think we mean when we say that we value something. We are attaching worthwhileness to it. We are giving something a stamp of approval. We evaluate an object or idea and place a value on it in the process. I value Wolpert's article for its *content*, or the knowledge contained and developed within it. I have also suggested that I value it for the way he sets up the research and how he *proceeds* with it.

The procedures of organisation, data collection, analysis, respect for evidence, and reflection are all attributes one has learned are appropriate, worthwhile ways of going about an enquiry. Over the years one has come to internalise a strong belief in such procedures and ways of viewing, among other possibilities. One has been socialised into these procedures as a form of intellectual endeavour and behaviour. My response to an article on farmers in Middle Sweden is informed by my values. Others may not have such a response. Their values, sense of worthwhileness, what is significant, important and interesting may be very different. I value, *in this instance*, what I think is a worthwhile process of investigation in a worthwhile area of geography. This is not to say I do not equally value other stances and ways of proceeding. And to a greater or lesser extent I know that there is a group of geographers (not necessarily all) out there who will share my valuation, my preference, attitude, opinion.

A THINKING EXERCISE

To value seems to be synonymous with finding worthwhileness and significance. My values inform my attitude to the article and my values are not held implicitly. I cognitively and consciously, here at any rate, recognise my values. Valuing is a thinking exercise.

Philosophers make this point. And had I been a philosopher rather than a geographer in education I would have begun this piece of writing very differently perhaps. I may well have placed a discussion of values in the context of the cognitive (thinking) side and the affective (emotional) side of education. Reid and others write of the division in society and education generally between 'objective' knowledge and 'subjective' feelings, and the need to bring the two together as illustrated in Figure 7.1. I have recently tried to relate his position (Slater, 1994) to geography education and cannot repeat the whole discussion here, important though it is for us to understand Reid's position. Peters (1974), in contrast to Reid, tended to come down more strongly on the side of the cognitive aims of education, ascribing a more subservient role to emotions. Others, for example Hepburn (1972) and Dunlop (1984), take a different emphasis, giving a

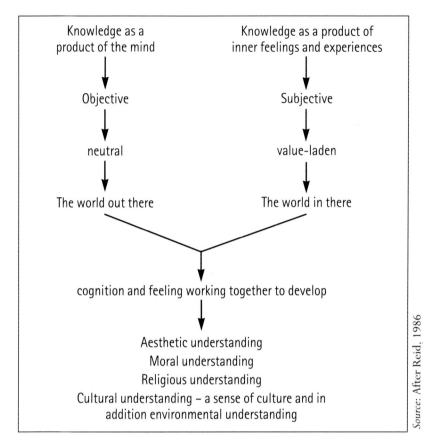

Figure 7.1 Ways of knowing and understanding

more significant role to emotions. Dunlop, in fact, suggests that we cannot differentiate between facts and values since we need information on which to make value judgements. Reid (1986) argues the necessity of the interaction of fact and value for the development of certain kinds of understanding. These philosophical discussions are important areas of exploration for perspectives beyond the usual ones from within geography only.

WOLPERT'S VALUES

In the above paragraphs I have attempted to establish a sense of what we mean when we say we value something. The fact that I selected Wolpert's article to begin with implies a value judgement, just as when we choose to put a particular subject on the curriculum – geography – or decide that urban structure/form needs to be taught within geography, implies a valuing of that subject and topic. At the heart of ascribing value to something and making a value judgement is the act of making a decision about its value, as values education strategies demonstrate over and over again.

Wolpert, one might presuppose, prior to his engagement in his research, had made a value judgement about the worthwhileness of geography. He decided to study geography and then at some later date it seemed worthwhile to him to investigate possible explanations for land use and resulting productivities in Middle Sweden. He collected and weighed up evidence in his search for explanation. There is something here – knowledge and understanding of a spatial distribution – which Wolpert is valuing for itself, and something which he is valuing as a worthwhile and desirable means to a worthwhile and desirable end. He judges it worth while to examine and extend a state of knowledge about farming outcomes, and he is valuing the necessity to collect evidence in the search for explanation for its own sake within the context of competing sets of ideas about people's decision-making behaviours. And in addition, the context is a centrally geographical one, explaining a pattern of rural land use, a mapped spatial distribution.

Two of Wolpert's values cohere around evidence (the need for it and the need to respect it) and explanation (of people's behaviours in their societies and environments). A third is his questioning of the state of knowledge and understanding about farmers' decisions and what influences them.

Classifying values

Earlier literature on the values dimension in geography education relates frequently to a three-fold classification of values as substantive, procedural and behavioural (Fenton, 1967; Blachford, 1972). Substantive values are judged by Fenton to be fundamental and content laden. They are concerned with holding as worth while, let us say in curriculum terms, a particular subject, for example geography, and the studying of its *knowledge base* concerning, for example, rural land use or ecosystems or cities.

Alongside valuing the knowledge base goes the valuing of certain ways of *proceeding*, perhaps adopting an enquiry approach, identifying a question, collecting and respecting evidence, and so on. Valuing an understanding of farmers' land use decision-making or of ecosystems is knowing that area of study and its content rather than another, while using enquiry or problem solving is valuing fundamentally a procedure, a 'knowing how'. Matters to do with 'knowing that' and 'knowing how' can both be counted as fundamental, substantive values which inform our reactions to, our acceptance of and evaluations of, a body of knowledge and its method. Substantive and procedural values may be seen to overlap. Behavioural values, defined as acceptable social behaviour to facilitating a task, could also be seen to overlap with procedural values. So while useful for attempting to make certain distinctions, Fenton's three categories are not exclusive and may even be confusing and open to misinterpretation. An interesting essay by R.I. Smith (1986) looks at some of the difficulties of Fenton's classification from the point of view of history teaching. In the same book, Patrick Wiegand (1986) gives an overview of values in geography in education.

Other ways of thinking about differences amongst values are available. Perhaps the simplest is just to make an end and means distinction or, as Rokeach (1973) puts it, classify on the basis of instrumental and terminal values. Instrumental values are those we adopt in order to reach the goal (the terminus). In this way we can think about politeness in discussion (Smith (1986) challenges this assumption) and using a scientific method as means towards the end of developing knowledge and understanding of a certain kind – a generalisation-generating, predictive kind.

MEANS AND END, PROCESS AND PRODUCT

It would be worth while to add to a means/end or a process/product classification a category specifying values presupposed in engaging in a particular study or activity. We are challenged by such a category to sort out prior values – i.e. values informing and explaining our engagement, for example – that we believe it important to describe and explain land use patterns. We can then analyse the engagement in terms of how it is carried through, towards what end. Cowie (1978) made this distinction in her work. I have tabulated Cowie's scheme and her examples to some extent in Figure 7.2, as one which speaks to geography teachers.

Values presupposed by a voluntary engagement in geography	Values present in content	Values present in geographical methodology (means/processes)	Values present in classroom teaching (means/processes)
• Significance of earth's distributions, patterns, processes and interactions to people • Importance placed on the development of material and cultural resources for human well-being • Significance of monitoring and improving environmental quality through preservation • Significance of people's conscience in relation to population growth, malnutrition and human survival	• Spatial expression of religious values, e.g. self-sufficient nucleated Mennonite villages in Manitoba • Spatial expression of social values, e.g. New Towns in Britain attracting people away from higher-density areas • Spatial expression of economic values, illustrated by population distributions and structure of cities	• Curiosity • Independent rational thought • Flexibility • Disposition towards systematic work • Spatial recording • Fieldwork	•Through choice of approaches, e.g. ideographic or nomothetic • Through choice of teaching strategies, e.g. simulations, or more formal approaches

Source: After Cowie, 1978

Figure 7.2 Cowie's classification of values (with selected examples)

As a conclusion to these matters I have sketched out an analysis both inferred and derived from my reading of Wolpert's article. Figure 7.3 is set out in the context of geographical studies of a scientific kind. It illustrates that prior values are necessary to the means/end values. Note also that raising matters of classification like this is done with the purpose of becoming clearer about what we mean by values. Sorting out Wolpert's article in this way is possibly the kind of exercise which could be given to a class after some discussion of the article and values.

Prior to, presupposed	Means/process	Ends/products
General ←————————————————————→ Particular		
Recognition of importance of studying: – society – people – environment – relationships – interactions, impacts	Question raising Hypothesis testing Gathering evidence Analysing variables statistically Evaluating evidence Reflecting Developing possible generalisations and conclusions to be held tentatively	Knowledge (of patterns, processes and decision-making behaviour) Understanding Explanation Theory modification and development

Source: After Cowie, 1978

Figure 7.3 A reading of Wolpert's values

Had I chosen a piece of research other than Wolpert's, standing at the turning point of quantitative and behavioural geography, especially one in a different tradition, Figure 7.3 would contain somewhat different descriptions of presupposed and means/ends values and value-laden activities. Research like Roger Hart's (1979) on the behavioural/humanistic interface, or David Seamon's (1992) work rather firmly in a humanistic tradition, presupposes an alternative view of geography as a study of society – people – environment interactions and impacts. Again a values analysis of a piece of work from the radical tradition would reveal contrasting prior beliefs and values. Different geographers take up different value positions or ideologies. The different positions serve rather different ends, and postmodernism calls all into question, as Morgan illustrates in Chapter 3.

Values in ideologies

Different ideological positions have been conceptualised as contrasting paradigms or ideologies, bundles of beliefs, values and concepts which are compatible in terms of means and ends or methodologies, philosophies or general outlook and guiding principles. These matters have been relatively recently talked through (for example Slater, 1992). Figure 7.4 illustrates the means and end emphasis of each position, including the postmodern. A piece of research in that paradigm which is sometimes judged to be postmodern is Soja's description of Los Angeles (Soja, 1989), although it has been criticised and questions have been raised about its validity as being postmodern, which I go along with (Marden, 1992).

Viewpoint – the presupposed values	Ends – the overriding aim or focus	Means – ways to explanation and understanding
Scientific	Space, spatial patterns, spatial relationships, spatial processes	Analysis, prediction/modelling, generalising/seeking laws, mathematical deduction, hypothesis testing, problem-solving
Behavioural	Patterns, relationships, people/environment interactions	Analysing perceptions and decision-taking, generalising people environmental behaviour, developing models, hypothesis testing
Humanistic	Place, people and places, sense of place, spirit of place, authenticity	Personal understanding, individual meaning, interpretation, making meaning, reflecting, empathetic stances, being pre-suppositionless, insider/outsider positioning, analysis of personal reactions
Social welfare, liberal, radical and social-historical	Society, organisations, structures, pressure groups, place and society, power, vested interests in time and place	Critical analysis, critical theory, social theories and analysis, social and political analysis, interpretation, critical reflection
Postmodern	Understanding the multiple realities of places, spatial practices, landscape as text, places in transition, celebrating difference, places and developing identities	Critical analysis, interpretation, reflection, un-patterning and re-patterning, reassembling, deconstructing, recognising many realities and representations of space

Figure 7.4 Means and ends in geography

- Care for the environment
- Human rights
- Justice – social/political/economic
- Appropriateness to a culture/society
- Respect for other cultures
- Preserving landscape quality
- Use/misuse/sustainability
- Absence of exploitation
- Empathy for cultures and environments
- Responsibility towards the environment

Figure 7.5 Values in geography as listed by a group of geography teachers

While a recognition of ideological value positions is important, it is interesting to note that a group of geography teachers when asked to list value positions in the subject did not think at the general geographical ideological level but raised environmental and development positions and concerns as listed in Figure 7.5. In that list, matters like the scientific method or respect for evidence are not mentioned. Some of our academic values are held more explicitly than others, apparently.

ENVIRONMENTAL AND DEVELOPMENT IDEOLOGIES

It seems possible, if Figure 7.5 is admitted as evidence, that in relation to school geography an appreciation of geography's ideological/paradigm approaches may be less consciously held than an appreciation of environmental and development ideologies. Issues associated with both are at the core of geography's content today. Environmental 'green' matters, development matters (unequal worlds) and how they interact might be judged to be among the most important concerns that exist out there in the 'real' world for geographers and others to study. Because of the importance of these matters, I have sketched out views on development and environment based on recent writing by O'Riordan (1992). (A more detailed review of recent writing is to be found in Chapter 2 of this current volume.) The four sets of views, each ideologically coloured, need to be keenly appreciated by geography teachers as different and contrasting value positions which enter into their environmental and development lessons. The different messages on the meaning of sustainability held by each are significant in many contexts in geography.

Figure 7.6, then, presents in some detail the different value positions taken by different groups in society, both nationally and globally, in relation to environmental and development issues. It is a table for discussion, and I suggest that a particular issue in the news should be taken as a concrete example and the table used to test the range of values and opinions being expressed. Are they all represented? Who does not have a voice? Which is likely to be the strongest voice? The figure may be related to Figure 2.1. In Figure 7.6, the first two views may be labelled 'technocentric', the second two 'ecocentric'.

UNDERSTANDING VALUES EMBEDDED IN VIEWS ON ENVIRONMENT AND DEVELOPMENT

The headings labelled 'Social beliefs' and 'Attitudes to science' may be thought of as values being held prior to an engagement in the issues, as these will colour environmental and development attitudes. Development priorities and environmental stances are the means and end part of the equation, and vice versa. The one informs the other. Which environmental stance builds big dams, for example? The range of values and positions may be used to analyse real-world examples and in role plays which address environmental and development issues, to develop in students an understanding of how people's values affect decisions and have an impact upon policies and outcomes. While such teaching strategies widen our vision of explanation and distance us from environmental determinism and other one-variable explanations, there is also the danger of stereotyping and seeing and evaluating problems from a range of fixed perspectives. That can be countered by an ever-present respect for and acknowledged need for evidence, but always questioning the evidence for its provenance, its ideological slant and its intended audience. Our colleagues in history are very strongly aware of the place of evidence, and the need to interrogate it. Perhaps there is a tendency for geographers at times to focus more on gathering and organising data than on questioning it, although John Huckle (1983 and onwards), for example, has long asked for a more critical perspective on our endeavours.

1

Political orientation	• Extreme Right • Dry Green
Social beliefs (prior values)	• Cult of the individual • Market forces • People can always find a way out of any difficulties • Unbridled optimism
Attitudes to science (prior values)	• A set of physical and chemical processes and systems, the understanding of which holds the key to global manipulation • Science first
Development priorities (means/ends)	• Promotion of growth to higher and higher levels • The North as a model of resources use and social development • Pro-growth goals justify policies and projects • Suspicion of participation and discussion
Environmental stances (means/ends)	• Cornucopian • People own the earth • Landlord not tenant
Meaning of sustainability (long-term goal/end)	• 'We're forever sustainable' • No limits to growth • Always more resources to be discovered or invented • Sustainable growth

2

Political orientation	• Liberal • Shallow Green
Social beliefs (prior values)	• Belief in national and environmental accounting and auditing • A controlled market • Belief in discussion and consensus • Belief in regulation and inspection
Attitudes to science (prior values)	• A set of natural functions protecting human survival and contentment
Development priorities (means/ends)	• Growth and resource exploitation can continue, assuming suitable taxes and fees • Legal rights to a minimum of environmental quality • Compensation for adverse environmental and/or social effects
Environmental stances (means/ends)	• Environmental managers • Designing with nature as stewards of the earth • Ecological auditing • Managing in harmony with needs • Planning with nature
Meaning of sustainability (long-term goal/end)	• Limits to growth • People managing sustainability and growth through the greening of production

3

Political orientation	•	Green, Liberal, Humanist, Marxist, Red Green
Social beliefs (prior values)	• • • •	Emphasis on local communities and sense of community Changing present lifestyles based on want not need, and the pursuit of material goods Seeking other means of self-fulfilment and satisfaction Generally, a critical view of the status quo
Attitudes to science (prior values)	• •	Commitment to ecology Varying degrees of suspicion of science serving high-tech ends
Development priori- ties (means/ends)	• • • • •	Critical of many development projects and policies Small-scale, intermediate technological solutions advocated Distrust of large-scale economic growth, large companies and centralised state control Equalising living standards North/South Developing renewable resources
Environmental stances (means/ends)	• • • •	Self-reliance, soft technologies Designing with nature on a small scale Working within ecosystems Being sensitive to cultural values and views
Meaning of sus- tainability (long- term goal/end)	•	Moving to sustainable *development*

4

Political orientation	•	Deep Green, Anarchist, Gaian, Libertarian
Social beliefs (prior values)	• • •	Ecological laws dictate human morality Bio rights of endangered species and unique landscapes Communal sharing
Attitudes to science (prior values)	• • •	Acceptance of ecological concepts; interdependence of physical and biological systems Gaian science, i.e. the earth adjusts to change by self-regulation to enable life to continue Life continues as long as it does not threaten life support systems
Development priori- ties (means/ends)	• •	Experimentation in sustainable development Development consistent with the natural functioning of the biosphere
Environmental stances (means/ends)	• • •	Earth-centred, Earth-nurturing People as tenants of the earth Living in nature
Meaning of sus- tainability (long- term goal/end)	•	Subsistence and communal sharing

Source: After O'Riordan, 1992

Figure 7.6 Four views on development and environment – different means to different ends

A SUBJECT-BASED VIEW

In beginning this chapter with an article from geography and using it to illustrate something of what we mean when we talk about values in the subject, I may be being very traditional in a teaching sense. Perhaps I demonstrate how I work out from the subject and that this can be a narrow base and viewpoint. It's not always a conscious position but it may be so. Someone else may well have started with perhaps an article on the environment or development, analysed values from that context, and moved on. There are geographers who have stepped very vigorously outside their subject, committed themselves to issues like environment and futures and gone on to develop curricula which, while owing something to geography, set themselves and the curricula in a different context. John Huckle, David Hicks (1995) and Stephen Sterling are three examples, and John Fien is a fourth, Australian-based, example. Huckle, Sterling and Fien have recent essays in Fien (1993). All were early concerned with values education and I think ideologically that they would describe themselves as reconstructionists with the concerns of radical geographers. Their work should be examined closely to gain a more detailed sense of their positions and their values. I think it is part of a creative tension within a subject that there are people who stand on its edges. They jolt us out of the subjects and viewpoints into which we have socialised ourselves. It is a process bringing renewal and fresh development to geography, though of course it is not the only source of change and renewal. Undoubtedly, too, there are people who stand firmly within the subject who speak of environmental education but always I think in a slightly different tone. Where we choose to locate ourselves powerfully affects the voices with which we speak.

It should not be assumed, however, that geographers, geography teachers and their associates always value or welcome 'prophets'. Ivor Goodson (1983) has written of the ideological struggle between geography and environmental education. It now seems that Sir Ron Dearing may have been responsible for tipping the power balance in favour of geography's having to take on environmental education, among other concerns, as a cross-curricular responsibility. In referring to Goodson, I call the attention of the reader very briefly to another dimension of values in geography's history and development. Looking at the history and sociology of clashes of values between insiders and outsiders as to what constitutes core values is a not uninteresting way to explore geography's values.

Aims and objectives encapsulate values

I hope that at this point readers will feel that the locations of some of the sources of values in geography have been established. Another way of opening up a discussion of values in geography and values in geography education in particular is to reflect on stated aims and objectives. Some readers may like to pursue this way in to an appreciation of the values embedded in the subject and in its contribution to education. In order to illustrate more fully what I mean I shall use an attempt I made some time ago (Slater, 1982) at placing aims and objectives within the context of the general and particular literacies, numeracies and graphicacies which an education in geography develops and promotes. Using literacy in an unextended sense to mean the exercise of reading and writing skills and in an extended sense to embrace the understanding developed by learning through geography, I have sketched out in Figure 7.7 the general and particular learning encouraged by geography. This includes a pointing towards and a recognition of values in geography education and the interlinking with political literacy inevitable in the study of social, economic, physical or environmental topics or issues.

Others, too, have spelled out aims and objectives, and their work can be examined for the values explicit and embedded. Graves (1971) may be re-read. A later case has been made by Bailey, Binns and others (Bailey and Binns, 1987). More general classifications of aims and objectives, like Bloom's taxonomy of the cognitive and affective, map out our priorities in relation to intellectual, rational and cognitive endeavours and our education of the emotions and feelings.

A consideration of aims and objectives leads to the realisation that they also stand in as justifications for a subject. We can also begin to feel that aims and objectives can be informed by prior stances taken in relation to the general aims and purposes of education. Just as Wolpert acknowledged that the concept economic man (*sic*) is a normative one, an inventive one, so we need to be reminded by Terence Moore (1974) and others

General aims or ends	Specific objectives or means	Outcomes or ends
• Understanding of society –people– environment relationships	to read with knowledge, under-standing and valuing, to interro-gate with a critical discernment	
leads to the develop-ment of		
• literacies (at surface and at increasingly more sophisticated and critical levels)	finding meaning in, for exam-ple, landscapes, places, regions, observable patterns and spatial impacts, written texts, video materials, issues and concepts, theories and models, choices and preferences, decision-mak-ing, attitudes and values, feel-ings, cultural differences ...	the ability to express and demonstrate knowledge, understand-ing, feeling and a critical discernment of matters generally considered to be geograph-ical in an increasingly sophisticated and interrog-ative way so as to be able to engage thoughtfully and with intellectual discrimina-tion in 'real' world issues and problems
• numeracies (simple		
complex	finding meaning in, for example, statistical and mathematical concepts	
critical)		
• graphicacies (specific		
general	finding meaning in maps, diagrams and other graphical forms of presentation and com-munication	
critical)		

Source: After Slater, 1982

Figure 7.7 Values explicit in statements of aims and objectives

that we also take educational theory and its ideologies to be normative; that is, they are expressions of opinion, ideals and beliefs rather than of evidence and the results of experiments of a scientific kind.

LOOKING AT ASSUMPTIONS

Within education theory and ideology, certain assumptions which are value laden are made about the nature of children (as eager and enquiring perhaps) or about how best to introduce them to knowledge (through subjects, areas of experience, or through allowing them to follow their own interests). The purposes of education may be assumed to be about the passing on of a culture, a heritage, or be directed towards critiquing and reconstructing society or yet again be about training for employment. A range of different attitudes and beliefs about the means and ends of education can be found wrapped up in ideological positions and educational theory. We can examine readily enough our own ideological positions by analysing a recent lesson we have taught, and judging where in the attitudes and values we brought to the lesson and where in the procedures we used during the lesson it fits in to any or some or all of the ideologies listed in Figure 7.8. Figure 7.9 suggests questions which may be used to get a sense of ideological position. The lesson needs first of all to be written up carefully in terms of aims and objectives, teacher activities, pupil activities and learning outcomes. The dimensions of knowing 'how' and knowing 'that', the means and end to greater and lesser degrees, vary with the ideological stances.

The aim of an exercise like this is to have us think more deeply about the meaning of the concepts and where our own pedagogical practice fits. It is likely that at the end of such an activity not only will concepts be clarified and practice be made more explicit but the reality of the main ideological positions existing as watertight compartments may also be called into question. Many of the concepts and values separated out in different ideological positions may well be part of the theory on which we stand our pedagogical practice as we integrate ideas from each.

REPHRASING IDEOLOGICAL POSITIONS

Other classifications of educational aims and practices exist. Martin McLean (1990), from a comparative view, has recently evaluated

Ideology	Focus	Means	End
Progressive	Child centred	• experience • discovery • active learning • relevance • integration • personal expression and meaning making	• valuing development of the whole person
Liberal	Subject centred	• studying subjects • passing on the culture • receiving interpretations • cognitive development • rational thinking • achieving excellence	• valuing development of the mind
Utilitarian	Work centred	• development of skills • processing information • learning 'how'	• valuing 'payoff'
Reconstructionist	Society centred	• questioning the status quo • developing a critical consciousness • understanding the operations of power and vested interests • awareness of alternative viewpoints	• valuing social change

Figure 7.8 Values contained in different educational ideologies

educational systems in Europe. He uses a three-fold classification of ency-clopaedic, humanist and naturalistic traditions to analyse European sys-tems. Paddy Walsh's (1993) work also gives a fresh view of established ideological positions. He separates out four values which can be applied to education as a whole which he calls the possessive (yielding wealth, sta-tus, power), the experiential (Dewey), the ethical (Peters and a rational approach) and the ecstatic (a romantic viewpoint basing the justification for the study on the supposition that what is being investigated is awe-some, wonderful, beautiful). These two recent perspectives enrich our

- Who initiated the study of the topic?
- Did the topic relate to other topics or concepts?
- What room within the lesson or unit of work existed for pupil initiative or creativity? To whom or what was the work relevant?
- How could the work be said to have contributed to the development of the whole person?
- Could this lesson be judged to be passing on something of our culture, our heritage?
- Was the work done squarely within a subject discipline?
- What skills were developed to what end?
- In what ways could the topic be said to contribute to intellectual growth and cognitive development?
- To what extent were the knowledge and skills developed in the lesson likely to be useful in a job? How was the knowledge 'processed'?
- Was there any questioning of the status quo?
- To what extent did the topic and way of studying it raise questions of justice or draw attention to vested interests and power?
- Was there any likelihood or evidence of pupils becoming critical?
- To what extent was political literacy being developed?

Figure 7.9 A selection of questions to ask about a lesson or unit of work to define ideological stance

understanding of ideologies, I think, the one giving a classification based on views of knowledge and the other expressing conventional ideologies freshly.

Wolpert called into question the normative, inventive concept of economic man (*sic*). In a study which repays further study, Gerald Grace (1978) established through interviews with teachers in inner-city schools (dominantly working-class schools) the curriculum constructs and pedagogic forms used in their teaching practice. His research explores the extent to which generally accepted ideologies exist. I shall not give a full account of Grace's work and his findings here, yet I want to give some sense of it since it spells out again the degree to which work in education is shot through with values and beliefs about what ought to be, what is best, what is to be aimed for. Particularly in the last chapter of his book we can read direct quotations of interviews with teachers which express their beliefs and values about education and teaching. Often for workshops I

Traditional	Progressive	Developing alternatives
• Passing on 'the best that has been thought and known' through traditional subjects • A belief in a need for structure	• Being relevant • Being interesting • Being integrated • Breaking down barriers • Changing the world	• Developing understanding • Developing fraternity • Developing criticism

Source: After Grace, 1978

Figure 7.10 Ideologies in urban schools

have compiled a page of quotations from that chapter as a way in to a recognition and discussion of the values fuelling educational endeavours. In this way we can gain a sense of the beliefs and motivations of some inner-city teachers in the 1970s, compare them with our own, and attempt a classification. My attempt, based on a whole reading of the chapter, is set out in Figure 7.10.

Curriculum and pedagogy

Grace calls his penultimate chapter 'Curriculum and Pedagogy', and I wish to use that as a signal of the fact that not only do values enter our teaching from our views of our subject and from our educational stances but also from the curriculum orientations which have been responsible for forming curricula and syllabus statements in our subject. The three Schools Council Projects in geography all approached the subject differently. Some of the differences arise, of course, from the different age and ability groups they were addressing. The title, *Geography for the Young School Leaver* (those leaving at 16) explains itself. Generally speaking, its purpose was to devise a curriculum relevant to urban children, and we hear this again in the titles of the three curriculum units 'Man (*sic*), Land and Leisure', 'People, Place and Work' and 'Cities and People'. Bristol's responsibilities extended from ages 14 to 18 and – as I see it – they adopted a more 'academic', systematic view of geography influenced by quantification, models and systems. With their view of learners and education (as promoting questioning) they tried to match subject and pupil, albeit from a different viewpoint from GYSL.

Geography 16–19, working for an older group, very strongly espoused geography as a medium for education and developed a framework and aims and objectives accordingly. Geography 16–19 most explicitly built in a framework for values enquiry as well as factual enquiry. The two ran side by side in their diagrams. This implies either a separation of fact and value or an equal emphasis on each. As in my own work, the latter was intended.

VALUES, BIAS, PREJUDICE

From the very fact that values inform our views and actions, it follows that values can bias and turn our views and actions in a particular direction. As a result of beliefs and values we can select one thing rather than another, go one way rather than another. This can be illustrated in relation to the means of selection used by the different projects in order to sample geography as a subject for ordering into a curriculum form. We have to select from the whole in order to break down the subject into units of study, modules, call them what you will, to manage a teaching process which extends over a finite time, and so what we select reflects our values.

VALUES FILTERING

In my view the geography taught within the different projects, partly differs according to the selection filters used. Age and ability acted as one set of filters, as already noted. For selecting geography, GYSL chose its broad themes and then, working around the peak of the scientific revolution in British geography, concepts like accessibility were isolated as key themes. It is interesting that in the hands of inner-city teachers and others working with young school leavers, the GYSL curriculum as it developed over the years took on a stronger critical, even radical stance. Today, under countervailing and more traditional pressures, it has incorporated a physical geography unit within the curriculum as a whole.

The Bristol Project in the end seemed to value a scientific geography and a systematic view of the subject. Later, the development of a geography National Curriculum seemed to be fuelled by a deficit view of geography teaching and a somewhat nostalgic one too. It is a curious document now slimmed down.

Geography 16–19 gave priority to, valued, a people–environment approach, taking behavioural geography seriously. It then set up a nested hierarchy of filters or selection devices under the people–environment umbrella. The emphasis on issues as one selection device is important in bringing controversy into geographical study.

In what might seem to be a recent move on from the Geography 16–19 curriculum, the concept of change has been taken as a very significant selection filter in a new NEAB syllabus. Important geography topics are judged to be those where change can be illustrated. It may be significant to note that change is a concept frequently chosen as an overarching concept in social studies curricula worldwide.

In relation to curricula, as to many other things, we know what we value by what we select. But do we always select as reflectively, deliberately and carefully as content was selected for those three geography projects? We can have our prior intentions, our aims, and we can then set out to achieve them. How often is what we do and the outcome of what we do congruent with our ideals? R. J. Gilbert's (1984) research contests congruence between aims and outcomes. He found a mismatch between aims and outcomes, status quo values infusing what gets taught in geography, as he saw it. The image of social subjects like history, geography and economics to illustrate society is not fulfilled. Henley (1989) writes similarly on language. The language of humanistic geography is not socially critical. The postmodern questioning of whether the real world can be mirrored in geographical studies adds another dimension to this problem of congruence and ideological filtering.

Education and society

We are getting close here to a question of whose values lead and whose values follow, which might be put like this: 'Does education lead society or does society lead education?' It is a stimulating seminar question and at this point the reader could look again at Figure 7.8 to evaluate sources of values outside education informing educational endeavours.

In terms of curriculum, Fashion Phiri (1987) addressed this question in his PhD work. He developed four explicitly value-laden geography units for Grades 10–12 in Zambia. The issues were filtered from amongst many for their close relationship to Zambia's socio-economic development aspirations and were related to rural–urban migration, foreign aid, regional co-operation and wildlife. Phiri argued that units which were congruent with development aspirations were likely to contribute to the development of Zambia. Values education strategies were at the core of learning activities provided in the units. Phiri held that strategies able to generate learning outcomes such as decision-making, political literacy and values and attitudes awareness and understanding are likely to promote critical understanding of Zambia's socio-economic development. A curriculum, it was further argued, that includes critical questioning of such issues is a prerequisite to developing Zambia socially, politically and economically. Phiri tries to match Zambian society's development and development aspirations with a geography curriculum. He sees society and education as closely related, interacting reflexively.

Any geography curriculum from any country could be analysed and compared with others for the value it places on congruence with 'real' world, local, national and global issues. I think it could be demonstrated that curricula range from those very closely oriented to the subject of geography in whatever ideological guise, and those more closely oriented to the society in which the education is being received. The Geographic Inquiry for Global Issues Project is a recent, values-sensitive US curriculum development project which could be analysed and compared with others along these lines (Hill et al., 1992). It would, however, be a complex topic to research and require much teasing out of definitions and meanings. I have not delved into the question either of whose cultural values may be informing geography and geography in education. Another Zambian, Charles Namafe (1992) has raised this issue in relation to floods, and our culturally derived perceptions of them. His arguments have been fleshed out more fully in Chapter 10 of this present text. His work, challenging our cultural perceptions, is a reminder, however, of the limited extent to which I have spelled out academic geography's values in this chapter.

Besides Phiri's work and Namafe's, the point I want to make in this chapter relating to the question of the interaction between education and society (as I move into some final areas raised by a consideration of values in geographical education), is that society and education surely do not exist as separate entities and that there is likely to be an interchange between the two. This has implications for what gets taught in geography as geography.

SOCIETY'S VALUES

If society, let us suppose, is racist and sexist, then the books, resources and other materials we use in geography classrooms can hardly be expected to be free of such bias or presumably undesirable values. Values embedded in society's values – the valuing of white people and their cultures and achievements more highly than other human beings and cultures, the valuing of men and their work more highly than women and theirs – will be there, present in our teaching just as much as the social or political viewpoints we bring into a classroom in environmental issues or whatever.

In the same way that I have used Wolpert's article to introduce matters of value in what I might think of as a first workshop on values, I would now, in a third or fourth workshop, ask people to come having read Marsden's (1989) ' "All in a good cause", geography history and the politicization of the curriculum in nineteenth and twentieth century England'. As I see it, this article reinforces and expands on a number of concerns already raised here. The relationship between society and education is addressed and interpreted within a concept of politicisation defined as:

> using the curriculum and informal channels of education to serve the ends of significant power groups, whether the church, the state, or some other body, even the 'educational establishment', so that explicitly or implicitly employed techniques of inculcation, indoctrination, and loaded selection of material, dictate the content, values, attitudes and beliefs to be transmitted.

Marsden quotes extensively to demonstrate the social purposes for which power groups were using education. He also demonstrates how content and pedagogy were loaded with values. I draw attention to the paper because it can be used as a touchstone to see if such influences might still be around in education and in geography education today. If Mackinder (as quoted in Marsden), revealing values presupposed in studying geography, held to the statement below, who is making equally loaded statements today, and what effect are they having?

> Let our teaching be from the British standpoint, so that finally we see the world as a theatre for British activity. This, no doubt, is to deviate from the cold and impartial ways of science. When we teach the millions, however, we are not training scientific investigators, but the practical striving citizens of an empire which has to hold its place through the universal law of survival through efficiency and effort.
>
> Mackinder, 1911:79–80

In addressing value-related issues in geography one cannot leave out considerations like these. Dawn Gill (1983) had no doubt that geography curricula in schools continued to have racist overtones; nor did David Wright (1985) in relation to textbooks. Yoram Bar-Gal (1994) gives a further recent example. Roger Robinson's (1987) research has revealed the imbalances of sympathy and empathy likely to be part of the values and attitudes children bring to school and have reinforced there. Eurocentric cultural attitudes lie exposed. The education of feelings addressed by Reid (Reid, 1986) needs to be considered if empathy is to grow and develop more in geography classrooms. It is an area which geographers in education address from time to time.

Recent work on multicultural matters and the idea of conversations as a way of encouraging a re-negotiation of meanings may prove fruitful in the geography classroom (Haydon, 1987; Jones, 1987; Lambert and Slater, 1992). The negotiation of areas of agreement and meaning through conversation is I think a postmodern move to respect difference and different values and yet explore differences positively.

GEOGRAPHY'S MASCULINITY

Jane Connolly (1993) with the GEON network and others have addressed the persistence and problem of sexism. A recent book by Gillian Rose (1993), bearing the subtitle 'The limits of geographical knowledge', offers an analysis of geography's paradigms, procedures and content which finds the feminist view and influence lacking or marginalised. Where Carol Gilligan (1982), from specific psychological research, raised general questions which could be used to evaluate geography education's aims and content, Gillian Rose, a geographer, gives arguments and evidence from within our own subject to illustrate its masculinity. She argues that geography's view of Nature derives from a very strong masculinist and cultural split between Nature and Culture. Her analysis opens up new ways of seeing, and for those who have already intuitively felt much of what she says, there are now arguments set up which need to be discussed. 'Field trips instil the ethos of the discipline into students and it is an heroic ethos' and, as Rose adds several sentences later, 'a drinking one, one where the consumption of alcohol is important'. To quote further: 'Geographers become stronger men by challenging Nature . . . and the real geographer faces wild Nature for the sake of knowledge, even though it may on occasion mean taking risks, living dangerously'. Rose notes that the tough heroism of what Stoddart has uncritically called 'militant geography' establishes fieldwork as a particular kind of masculine endeavour. A case has been made, a good enough case I think to need reflecting on, and it is now in print and therefore much more visible and present. Educational endeavours are shot through with values. One set of resources we probably do not look at critically enough for bias and undesirable attitudes is film and video. They must constitute alongside texts one of the big image-forming factors.

TEACHING METHODS

In writing a chapter as a series of possible workshops locating values, cognitive and attitudinal, means and ends, geographical, environmental, developmental, social, cultural, political ... I may have given myself too large a brief for one essay. Some areas I have written on more extensively than others. In all cases I have tried to give signposts for further investigation. One area I have left untouched is that of teaching strategies for values on the grounds that knowledge of these is more widespread than once it was. Again, sources exist and I have recently revised and updated *Learning Through Geography* which in Chapter 4 looks again at teaching strategies and examples (Slater, 1993). Earlier discussions on strategies include Huckle (1983) for a radical critique and Fien and Slater (1981) arguing for a more in-depth values appreciation.

CONTROVERSY

Where values are involved and open to dispute, controversy cannot be far behind. The teaching of controversial issues is an area which is invaluable to us for its insights and ways through hesitancy, anxiety and fear of indoctrination. Stradling and others (1984) wrote some time ago and took us into the field of political education, another area close to and leading on from values and geographical education. Fry (1987) in a Masters dissertation, like others had addressed political literacy through geography. Porter (1986) has clear arguments to overcome indoctrination, suggesting students be given exercises in creating bias, detecting bias and correcting bias. For that matter Snook (1972) and other philosophers have also looked at this problem. Very recently Lester (forthcoming) has challenged the overt indoctrination of well-meaning materials and resources on apartheid and constructed a text using principles derived from research on reading which aims to move students towards an appreciation of academic discourse and argument as a more desirable educational outcome. This chapter may be ending as exploration into fields speaking to geography in education could begin.

Conclusion

I have chosen here to try to locate and define values in geography and geography education as they have been in the last twenty or thirty years. This may enable us to identify and recognise values, not only to be surer about our recognition but also to enable us to accept the fact that values are around and ever present. Recognising and accepting values takes us a long way towards further exploring values and the value-laden nature of learning, at the same time as learning a great deal more through geography as our awareness of value positions is enhanced alongside our enquiry, problem-solving and critical capacities.

BIBLIOGRAPHY
Bailey, P. and Binns, T. (eds) (1987) *A Case for Geography*, Geographical Association.
Bar-Gal, Y. (1994) 'The image of the "Palestinian" in geography textbooks in Israel', *Journal of Geography*, 93(5) Sept/Oct:224–32.
Blachford, K. (1972) 'Values and Geography', *Geographical Education*, 1(4):319–30.
Connolly, J. (1993) 'Gender-balanced geography: have we got it right yet?' *Teaching Geography*, 18(2) April:61–4.
Cowie, P.M. (1978) 'Geography: a value-laden subject in education', *Geographical Education*, 3(2):133–46.

Dunlop, F. (1984) *The Education of Feeling and Emotion,* Allen and Unwin.

Eisner, E. (1979) *The Educational Imagination*, Macmillan.

Fenton, E. (1967) *The New Social Studies*, Holt, Rinehart and Winston.

Fien, J. (1993) *Environmental Education: A Pathway to Sustainability*, Deakin UP.

Fien, J. and Slater, F. (1981) 'Four strategies for values education in geography', *Geographical Education*, 4(1): 39–52.

Fien, J. and Trainer, T. (1993) 'Education for sustainability', in Fien, J. (ed.) *Environmental Education: A Pathway to Sustainability*, Deakin UP.

Fry, P.J. (1987) 'Dealing with political bias through geographical education', unpublished MA dissertation, Institute of Education, University of London.

Gilbert, R.J. (1984) *The Impotent Image: Reflections of Ideology in the Secondary School Curriculum*, The Falmer Press.

Gill, D. (1983) 'Education for a multi-cultural society, the constraints of existing O level and CSE geography syllabuses', *Racist Society Geography Curriculum*, Conference proceedings, Institute of Education, University of London.

Gilligan, C. (1982) *In a Different Voice*, Harvard University Press.

Goodson, I. (1983) *School Subjects and Curriculum Change*, Croom Helm.

Grace, G. (1978) *Teachers, Ideology and Control*, RKP.

Graves, N.J. (1971) 'Objectives in teaching particular subjects with special reference to the teaching of geography', *Bulletin of the University of London*, Institute of Education, NS No. 23.

Hart, R. (1979) *Children's Experience of Place*, Irvington.

Haydon, G. (1987) 'Towards a framework of commonly accepted values', in Haydon, G. (ed.) *Education for a Pluralist Society*, Bedford Way Paper 30, Institute of Education and Turnaround Distribution Ltd.

Henley, R. (1989) 'The ideology of geographical discourse', in Slater, F.A. (ed.) *Language and Learning in the Teaching of Geography*, RKP.

Hepburn, R.W. (1972) 'The arts in the education of feeling and emotions', in Hirst, P.D. and Peters, R.S. (eds) *Education and the Development of Reason*, Routledge and Kegan Paul.

Hicks, D. and Holden, C. (1995) 'Envisioning the future: the missing dimension in environmental education', *Environmental Education Research* 1(2).

Hill, A.D. *et al.* (1992) 'The Geographic Inquiry into Global Issues Project: rationale, development and evaluation', in A.D. Hill (ed.) *International Perspectives on Geographic Education*, Center for Geographic Education, Department of Geography, University of Colorado at Boulder.

Huckle, J. (1983) 'Values education through geography: a radical critique', *Journal of Geography*, 82:59–63.

(1993) 'Environmental education and sustainability: a view from critical theory', in Fien, J. (ed.) *Environmental Education: A Pathway to Sustainability*, Deakin UP.

Jones, M. (1987) 'Prejudice', in Haydon, G. (ed.) *Education for a Pluralist Society*, Bedford Way Paper 30, Institute of Education and Turnaround Distribution Ltd.

Lambert, D. and Slater, F.A. (1992) 'Sharing our sense of the world', in Hill, D. (ed.) *International Perspectives on Education*, Center for Geographic Education, University of Colorado at Boulder.

Lester, A. (forthcoming) 'Conceptualising social formation: producing a textbook on South Africa', forthcoming PhD thesis, Institute of Education, University of London.

Mackinder, H.J. (1911) 'The teaching of geography from the imperial point of view and the use which could and should be made of visual instruction', *Geographical Teacher*, 6(30):79–86.

Marden, P. (1992) 'The deconstructionist tendencies of postmodern geographies: a compelling logic?' – *Progress in Human Geography*, 16(1):41–57.

Marsden, W. (1989) '"All in a good cause": geography, history and the politicization of the curriculum in nineteenth and twentieth century England', *Journal of Curriculum Studies*, 21(6):509–26.

McLean, M. (1990) *Britain and a Single Market Europe*, Bedford Way Series, Institute of Education, University of London / Kogan Page.

Moore, T. (1974) *Educational Theory: An Introduction*, RKP.

Namafe, C. (1992) 'An exercise in environmental education: Investigating, disseminating and evaluating two contrasting floodwater metaphors', unpublished PhD thesis, Institute of Education, University of London.

Northern Examinations and Assessment Board (n.d.) *General Certificate of Education, Syllabuses for 1995, Geography*.

O'Riordan, T. (1992) 'The environment', in Cloke, P. (ed.) *Policy and Change in Thatcher's Britain*, Pergamon.

Peters, R.S. (1974) 'The education of the emotions', in Peters, R.S. (ed.) *Psychology and Ethical Development*, Allen and Unwin.

Phiri, F. (1987) 'The development and evaluation of value-laden geography units and lessons congruent with Zambia's educational policy and its ideological and socio-economic development issues', unpublished PhD thesis, Institute of Education, University of London.

Porter, A. (1986) 'Political bias and political education', *Teaching Politics*, September: 371–84.

Reid, L.A. (1986) *Ways of Understanding and Education*, Heinemann.

Robinson, R. (1987) 'Exploring students' images of the developing world', *Geographical Education*, 5(3):48–52.

Rokeach, M. (1973) *The Nature of Human Values*, Free Press.

Rose, G. (1993) *Feminism and Geography*, Polity.

Seamon, D. (1992) 'A diary interpretation of place: artist Frederic Church's Olana', in Janelle, D.J. (ed.) *Geographical Snapshots of North America*, The Guilford Press.

Slater, F.A. (1982) 'Literacy, numeracy and graphicacy', in Graves, N.J. *et al.* *Geography in Education Now,* Bedford Way Paper 13, Institute of Education and Turnaround Distribution Ltd.

Slater, F.A. (ed.) (1989) *Language and Learning in the Teaching of Geography*, RKP.
  (1992) '... to travel with a different view', in Naish, M. (ed.) *Geography and Education*, Institute of Education, University of London.
  (1993) *Learning Through Geography*, National Council for Geographic Education.
  (1994) 'Education through geography: knowledge, understanding, values and culture', *Geography*, 79(2) No.343:147–63.

Smith, R.I. (1986) 'Values in history and social studies', in Tomlinson, P. and Quinton, M. (eds) *Values Across the Curriculum*, The Falmer Press.

Snook, I. (1972) *Indoctrination and Education*, RKP.

Soja, E. (1989) *Postmodern Geographies: The Reassertion of Space in Critical Social Theory*, Verso Press.

Sterling, S. (1993) 'Environmental education and sustainability: a view from holistic ethic', in Fien, J. (ed.) *Environmental Education: A Pathway to Sustainability*, Deakin UP.

Stradling, R. *et al.* (1984) *Teaching Controversial Issues*, Arnold.

Walsh, P. (1993) *Education and Meaning*, Cassell.

Wiegand, P. (1986) 'Values in geographical education', in Tomlinson, P. and Quinton, M. (eds) *Values Across the Curriculum*, The Falmer Press.

Wolpert, J. (1964) 'The decision process in a spatial context', *Annals of the Association of American Geographers*, 54(4):537–58.

Wright, D. (1985) 'In black and white: racist bias in textbooks', *Geographical Education*, 5(1):8–10.

8

Teaching styles and strategies

Margaret Roberts

One of the challenges facing teacher professionalism and geographical education in England and Wales in the 1990s comes from the standardisation of the curriculum. The Education Reform Act of 1988 included in its measures a National Curriculum with geography as one of the foundation subjects. The Geography National Curriculum (DES, 1991) lays down to a considerable extent what is taught between the ages of 5 and 14, even in its somewhat reduced state since the revisions made in 1994 (SCAA, 1994). Criteria for the GCSE provide a standard framework for the geography curriculum for pupils aged 14 to 16, and subject core proposals for geography, published by SCAA in 1993, indicate what has to be incorporated in all A/AS syllabuses with the title 'geography' (SCAA, 1993).

Standardisation of *aims* and *content* of geographical education from 5 to 19 is not accompanied, explicitly at least, with any suggestion of standardisation of *how* geography is to be taught. On the contrary, during the consultation phase of the geography National Curriculum, teachers were reassured that the decision on how to teach was theirs. Sir Leslie Fielding's letter which introduced the Proposals for Geography 5–16 states: 'the choice of specific teaching strategies and learning activities and the balance of their use is left to the individual teacher' (DES, 1990). This reinforced for geographers what had already been stated generally during the introduction of the National Curriculum. One of the points made in the DES booklet *From Policy to Practice* signalled clearly that what was specified in the attainment targets and programmes of study 'will allow teachers considerable freedom in the way in which they teach, examples and materials used, selection of content and context, use of textbooks, etc. The legislation does not allow particular textbooks or teaching methods to be prescribed as part of a programme of study' (DES, 1989).

The context of geographical education in the mid-1990s, then, is a curriculum from 5 to 19 in a standardised framework for content, but with apparent freedom for teachers to decide how they are going to teach and how their pupils are going to learn. Classrooms all over England and Wales provide evidence of the diversity of ways in which pupils learn geography. Glimpses into geography classrooms might catch a teacher giving a talk and pupils taking notes, pupils copying notes from overhead transparencies, pupils working individually from worksheets and resources, pupils working at computers, pupils working in small groups having heated discussions, a whole class taking part in a mock public inquiry, and others preparing questionnaires for a fieldwork visit.

This chapter is about an aspect of teachers' work where they can still exercise considerable professional judgement: how they teach. It discusses the ways in which variety of practice in the classroom has been described and categorised by researchers and writers, and relates these categories to the approaches promoted by the geography projects of the 1970s. Finally it applies and explores a framework, initially used to evaluate TVEI, to the teaching and learning of geography.

Attempts to classify classroom practice

One of the problems in writing about the variety of practice taking place in our classrooms is the range of vocabulary used by different researchers to describe what they are talking about (Naish, 1988). Each of the different words has a slightly different meaning, but the vocabulary seems to fall into two groups. There are words such as 'methods', 'manner', 'techniques', 'tactics', 'models' and 'strategies', which relate to how teachers work at particular times. There is a second group of words, such as 'styles', 'approaches', 'perspectives', 'types', which suggest a consistent set of practices used by teachers throughout their teaching. Interest in the details of how teachers teach – that is, methods or strategies – has provided the focus of much initial teacher education this century and of many books and articles on teaching geography. Research interest in describing and categorising the overall set of practices used by teachers, i.e. style, developed from the 1970s.

One of the earliest research studies was Bennett's study in 1976 of primary school teachers. He categorised their teaching approaches using a questionnaire, analysing the results by cluster analysis. He identified twelve 'types', ranging across a continuum from formal to informal. At the informal end of the spectrum were teachers who favoured integration of subject matter, and allowed pupils choice of work and who thought that motivation should be intrinsic to the work. At the formal end of the spectrum were teachers who favoured a separate subject approach with class teaching, individual work and no choice for pupils. Extrinsic motivation was favoured. Bennett compared the relative progress of pupils working with different types of teachers, but the validity of his method and findings have been much criticised (Gray and Satterly, 1981).

The ORACLE project (Galton, 1982) also studied primary school teachers but through detailed observation of teachers and pupils in fifty-eight junior school classes instead of through questionnaires. Galton devised a typology of teaching 'styles' based on the way teachers organised their classrooms, planned their curriculum and the way they instructed the children. The project identified four styles: individual monitors; teachers engaged in class-directed enquiry; group instructors; and style changers. The last category acknowledged the difficulty of slotting teachers into categories; many teachers showed characteristics of different styles.

Hammersley (1977) wrote about different teaching 'perspectives' to describe the diversity of practice. He identified four types: discipline-based teaching, where learning is seen as an individual, competitive activity based on reproducing segments of the teacher's knowledge; programmed teaching in which learning is individual and in response to stimuli provided by the teacher; progressive teaching characterised by a concern with process and a low degree of control over pupil action; and radical non-interventionism. He recognised these perspectives as shorthand summary devices, but regarded analysis of practice along various separate dimensions as the crucial analytical tool.

Berlak and Berlak (1981) thought that the terms 'formal' and 'informal' describing teaching styles obscured too many distinctions among teachers. They identified sets of dilemmas that faced teachers in their interaction with children, e.g. dilemmas of control (teacher control versus child control) and dilemmas of curriculum (knowledge as content versus knowledge as process). They thought that there were 'merely differences in emphasis on particular dilemmas' between formal and informal styles rather than distinct categories.

All these studies, which attempted to categorise teaching styles taking many factors into account, recognised the problems of fitting classroom practice into distinct categories. Bennett had many different 'types' between his formal and informal categories. Galton had a category of teachers who used several styles. Hammersley, and Berlak and Berlak, placed more importance on the separate criteria used as a basis of classification.

Some studies related style to underlying philosophies. Fenstermacher and Soltis (1986) define three different 'approaches' to teaching: executive, using the best skills and techniques available; therapist, in which the teacher promotes self-actualisation and understanding; and liberationist, in which the teacher aims to produce autonomous rational and moral human beings. Each approach is related to different values.

Hall's (1976) 'simple fieldwork classification in geography' defined four styles of fieldwork: field demonstration; field study; field testing; and field discovery. The categories were based on the processes involved in the work, the type of structure provided by the teacher, teacher–pupil relationships and the outcome of the fieldwork. Each style of fieldwork had different aims and philosophies.

Walford (1981) also suggested a relationship between teaching style and four ideological traditions: the liberal humanitarian tradition with its aims of passing on the cultural heritage; the child-centred tradition with its concern for personal development; the utilitarian tradition with its emphasis on the acquisition of knowledge and skills useful for society; and the reconstructionist tradition with its emphasis on changing society. The precise implications of these traditions for teaching style were not developed, however.

Naish (1988) was also interested in the relationship between styles and aims and the extent to which different styles could enhance the effectiveness of student learning. He stated a need for more research into teaching styles in relation to the teaching of geography. In the same volume, Slater (1988) examined the relationship between personality and style in a case study of student teachers' lessons. She was concerned with variables such as 'presence' and 'charisma' and how they contributed to style. She recognised the problems of defining style and relating it to the variety of strategies used within each lesson.

There has perhaps always been a tendency for researchers and commentators to place more value on one style over another, either because they believed it to be more effective or because it was related to their particular educational aims and philosophy. The Schools Council geography projects which were initiated in the 1970s and which have continued to develop into the 1990s have all advocated and valued particular styles of teaching in preference to other styles.

In *The Essentials of GYSL*, Renwick (1985) states that the Geography for the Young School Leaver Project syllabus 'needs to be taught in a variety of ways'. He also makes the point that the project:

> encouraged the move away from didactic methods of teaching to experiential learning … the project particularly encourages the move towards a discovery/investigative approach in situations well structured by the teacher. The teacher is encouraged to be a guide and stimulus, and to abandon the traditional expository approach in favour of more 'open learning'.

The project promoted this style of teaching and learning initially through resource packs produced for the project and later through the methods used to assess the examination syllabuses based on the project.

Another Schools Council geography project for this age group, the 14–18 Bristol Project, now a GCSE syllabus, also wanted to influence teaching style. The project handbook (Tolley and Reynolds, 1977) identified three styles of classroom interaction (Figure 8.1) but the project indicated a preference for style 3, an interactionist style of classroom geography. The dangers of the transmission style of style 1 and the structured exercises of style 2 are pointed out, leaving only style 3 uncriticised in the handbook. The Bristol project wanted to make teachers more aware of teaching styles through a process of school-based curriculum development, part of what they called the new professionalism (Hickman *et al.*, 1973).

The Schools Council 16–19 Geography Project likewise advocated a particular 'approach' which it termed 'enquiry-based teaching and learning'. Naish, Rawling and Hart (1987) indicate in their account of the project that they are thinking about 'style' along a dimension (Figure 8.2) rather than in distinct categories. In spite of the project approach providing 'scope for an effective balance of both teacher-directed work and

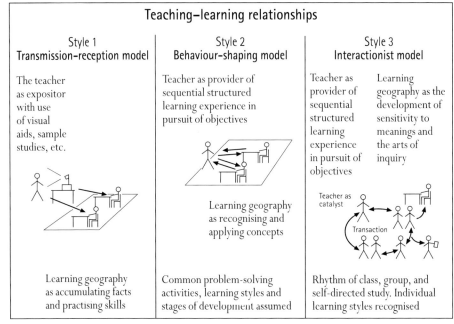

Figure 8.1 Alternative styles of classroom geography

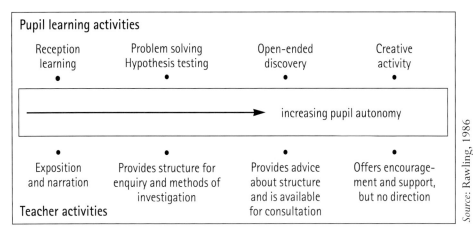

Figure 8.2 The teaching–learning continuum

more independent student enquiry' (Rawling, 1986) and 'the possibility of using a range of teaching methods and approaches', clearly some styles are more approved of than others. Rawling writes about the teacher encouraging students to enquire 'actively into questions, issues and problems rather than merely to accept passively the conclusions and research of others'. In a light-hearted questionnaire published by the project, high scores were obtained only if the responses indicated that the enquiry approach was used 'nearly always' (see pp. 165–6). The serious suggestion was that a consistent style was approved by the project. The 16–19 project attempted to promote this style through an enquiry framework and through the methods of assessment (Naish, Rawling and Hart, 1987).

Since the 1970s there has been a shift in thinking about teaching styles. Initially the interest focused on the effectiveness of different styles. Later the emphasis was on relating styles to underlying philosophies and purposes. Teachers adopted different 'styles' because they wanted pupils to learn different things or because they had different views of the overall aims of education. It was therefore difficult to compare effectiveness, because the aims of the teaching were different. Schools Council geography projects promoted particular styles or approaches not because research had found them to be more effective but because in changing the aims of geographical education they wanted pupils to know, be aware of and be able to do different things from what they had achieved previously.

Research has shown that there was a gap between the ideals of the curriculum projects of the 1970s and actual practice (for example, Steadman et al., 1980; MacDonald and Walker, 1976). *How* teachers teach is not so easily influenced as *what* they teach. Teachers adapt their styles and strategies to the cultures and subcultures in schools and indeed to meet their own needs of coping with the day-to-day demands of being a teacher (Woods, 1980). As Slater's (1988) reflections suggest, there is no reason to expect consistency in a teacher's day-to-day practice. Research in the 1980s and 1990s is appropriately focused more on attempting to understand, rather than on labelling what is taking place in the classroom (e.g. Stones, 1992).

The increasing recognition by educational researchers of the complexity of classroom processes is at variance with the way teaching methods are sometimes presented in the media. The labels of the 1970s – 'progressive', 'traditional', 'back to basics', 'child-centred', 'formal methods', etc. – have become value-laden terms which are used, often in place of analysis and argument, to approve or disapprove of styles which in practice are not so consistent as the terms suggest. For example, a newspaper report (*Daily Mail*, 1994) of the findings of inspectors of primary schools, uses a particular way to interpret the report for its readers. It refers to 'trendy teaching methods' and to 'progressive educational theories of the 1960s and '70s' taking hold, and it mentions approvingly 'traditional teaching methods' and 'formal teaching'. The newspaper report is doubly misleading: it highlights negative aspects of the inspectors' report, ignoring the fact that a large majority of lessons were found to be satisfactory or better; and it ignores the evidence of the range of practices that are used in almost all primary schools. Those involved in education recognise the complexities of teaching and learning processes. Improvement is unlikely to follow a highly simplified and misleading attack on professional methods. More constructive is to encourage teachers to analyse and engage critically with their own practice. The next section suggests a new way of looking at style. It introduces a framework which can be used as an analytical tool to identify 'styles' of teaching, but can also be used to show how teachers can adapt their strategies operating across different styles according to the context in which they are working.

A new framework for thinking about style and strategy

The framework introduced in this chapter is based on a categorisation tentatively suggested by Barnes *et al.* (1987) in an interim report evaluating the TVEI curriculum in twelve case-study schools. The report suggests three 'styles' of teaching and learning: closed; framed; and negotiated. Although these categories are placed along a continuum, the characteristics of various aspects of three different 'styles' are noted in the TVEI report table (Figure 8.3). In this classification the main factor used to determine style is the amount of control teachers maintain over subject content and activities. At one end of the spectrum teachers maintain tight control over all aspects of the subject knowledge. At the other extreme there is maximum learner participation in the construction of knowledge.

The participation dimension, ranging from closed through framed to negotiated, can be adapted and applied usefully to geographical education

	◄─────── Closed ───────	Framed ───────	Negotiated ─►
Content	Tightly controlled by teacher. Not negotiable	Teacher controls topic, frames of reference and tasks; criteria made explicit	Discussed at each point; joint decisions
Focus	Authoritative knowledge and skills; simplified, monolithic	Stress on empirical testing; processes chosen by teacher; some legitimation of student ideas	Search for justifications and principles; strong legitimation of student ideas
Students' role	Acceptance; routine performance; little access to principles	Join in teacher's thinking; make hypotheses, set up tests; operate teacher's frame	Discuss goals and methods critically; share responsibility for frame and criteria
Key concepts	'Authority': the proper procedures and the right answers	'Access': to skills, processes, criteria	'Relevance': critical discussion of students' priorities
Methods	Exposition; worksheets (closed); note-giving; individual exercises; routine practical work. Teacher evaluates	Exposition, with discussion eliciting suggestions; individual/ group problem solving; lists of tasks given; discussion of outcomes, but teacher adjudicates	Group and class discussion and decision-making about goals and criteria. Students plan and carry out work, make presentations, evaluate success

Source: Barnes et al., 1987

Figure 8.3 The participation dimension

(Figure 8.4). The original headings are used at the top of the framework denoting different 'styles'. Down the side are headings related to a simplified teaching and learning sequence appropriate for geography: questions; data; interpretation; conclusions.

What would each of these styles mean in terms of teaching and learning geography, and what would lessons consistent with one particular style be like? Each of the styles is summarised in the table, but the meaning of the table can best be explained by some examples of lessons and fieldwork activities.

Stage of teaching and learning	Closed	Framed	Negotiated
Questions	Questions not explicit or questions remain the teacher's questions	Questions explicit, activities planned to make pupils ask questions	Pupils decide what they want to investigate under guidance from teacher
Data	Data selected by teacher, presented as authoritative, not to be challenged	Variety of data selected by teacher, presented as evidence to be interpreted	Pupils are helped to find their own data from sources in and out of school
Interpretation	Teacher decides what is to be done with data, pupils follow instructions	Methods of interpretation are open to discussion and choice	Pupils choose methods of analysis and interpretation in consultation with teacher
Conclusions	Key ideas presented, generalisations are predicted, not open to debate	Pupils reach conclusions from data, different interpretations are expected	Pupils reach own conclusions and evaluate them
Summary	The teacher controls the knowledge by making all decisions about data, activities, conclusions. Pupils are not expected to challenge what is presented	The teacher inducts pupils into ways in which geographical knowledge is constructed, so that they are enabled to use these ways to construct knowledge themselves. Pupils are made aware of choices and are encouraged to be critical	Pupils are enabled by the teacher to investigate questions of concern and interest to themselves

Figure 8.4 A geography framework

A CLOSED STYLE OF TEACHING AND LEARNING (FIGURE 8.5)

Questions

In the closed style the teacher keeps control over the content of the work by choosing the content and introducing it in a direct way to the learners. The theme or topic might be presented entirely without reference to the questions which generated the geographical knowledge. The distribution of volcanoes, for example, could be introduced without explicit reference to the questions, 'Where are volcanoes situated in the world?' and 'Why

---

Year 10

Questions

The teacher chooses the focus of the fieldwork – shopping hierarchies – and devises a list of hypotheses to be tested. These are given to pupils.

Data

The teacher decides which shopping centres will be visited to collect data, and designs a questionnaire for pupils to use at each centre. Different groups of pupils go to each centre and are told how many questionnaires to get completed.

Interpretation

The teacher collects in the data from groups and makes all the data available to the whole class. The teacher selects a different type of graph for each question on the questionnaire and gives the pupils instructions on how to do the graphs, including an appropriate scale.

Conclusions

The findings are written up by the class after some discussion. The findings are what was expected. Not much attention is given to rogue figures (they may have even been laundered by the teacher in between the data and interpretation stages!).

Comment

This fieldwork provides a model for the pupils of fieldwork based on hypothesis testing. It can be done reasonably quickly as there is no discussion of alternatives. Pupils do not consider alternative hypotheses, survey questions, methods of graphical representation or conclusions. It is straightforward for pupils and can be managed by pupils achieving at lower levels. The role of pupils is to follow instructions. They learn how to carry out the teacher's enquiry and are introduced to survey and graphical techniques.

Figure 8.5 Example of fieldwork conducted in a closed style

is there this uneven pattern?' Distribution maps could be given to pupils. They could be told about the distribution and reasons for it without the questions ever being asked. Alternatively, the teacher might state some questions as a framework. Yet if the pupils do not puzzle over the questions themselves and ask further questions they remain the teacher's questions and are categorised as closed. In this category the pupils' role is to accept the knowledge or the questions given by the teacher as valid, rather than to challenge why this particular topic is being taught, why these questions are being asked, or to add questions which they personally might be interested in.

Data

The data in the closed category are chosen by the teacher and are presented as authoritative knowledge. The data might be a piece of text, a photograph, a video, some statistics, or a map. Fieldwork data might be obtained by following precise instructions. The pupils' role is to accept the data as valid and to learn what is presented in them. This might involve the learning of facts, the learning about relationships, or the understanding of ideas. Data are in this closed category if they are presented as unproblematic, and if they are not expected to be challenged. The sources of the information are not probed.

Interpretation

In the closed style of working the teacher decides how the data are to be investigated. There is no choice of method of analysis, and the reason for the choice of method is not open to discussion. Pupils are expected to follow the procedures given, e.g. to answer specific questions, orally or in writing, or to draw graphs or complete tables, etc. in prescribed ways. This stage of the sequence can be considered closed whether pupils are following instructions as a whole class or working individually from worksheets or textbooks. Resource-based learning in which pupils follow tight instructions can be as closed and controlled by teachers as whole-class teaching. Individualised worksheet learning, for example, is sometimes misleadingly referred to as 'child-centred learning' when in fact everything to be learned has been predetermined by the teacher.

Conclusions

The final stage of the sequence is categorised as closed when the teacher keeps control over the summary of what has been learned. The general-isations, evaluations or conclusions reached at the end of a period of study can be predicted at the start and are not open to debate. The key ideas are presented to be accepted as they are. Some lessons or sections in text-books teach topics entirely through a series of generalisations without ref-erence to the questions, the data and the interpretations on which those generalisations are based. These would be categorised as closed.

A FRAMED STYLE OF TEACHING AND LEARNING (FIGURE 8.6)

Questions

In the framed style the theme or focus is still decided by the teacher. The questions which guide the geography are, however, always explicit and the curriculum is planned to encourage pupils to make the questions their own and to ask further questions themselves. The teacher creates, by var-ious strategies, 'a need to know' among the pupils. This can be achieved in several ways: by giving the pupils a problem to solve or a decision to make; by asking pupils to speculate about facts, reasons, viewpoints before the data are given so that pupils will want to check their precon-ceptions against the presented data; or by the teacher successfully convey-ing a sense of curiosity at the start of a lesson. The essential feature is that the pupils make the questions their own. The way in which teachers pro-voke pupils into asking their own questions is worth investigating. Most research into questioning has concentrated on teachers' questions, rather than on the strategies that encourage pupils' questioning.

Data

The teacher still selects the data in a framed style of learning geography but it is more varied than in the closed style, often presented as 'evidence' to be interpreted and evaluated rather than as hard information to be accepted without question. There could be several pieces of text on the same theme but giving a different emphasis either in the selection of fac-tual information or in the presentation of different viewpoints. Factual data can be as subjective and open to scrutiny as information about atti-tudes and values. There could be several photographs giving different images of the same topic. There could be different sets of statistics. In addition to pupils being expected to know and understand what is in the

Year 8

Questions

The teacher devises a decision-making exercise in which pupils have to decide whether to locate a computer component company in the Lower Don Valley, Sheffield, and if so which of three sites is best. The teacher has already consulted Sheffield Development Corporation (SDC) and has been given maps and background information on three sites by the SDC suggested for the activity. In setting the fieldwork task, the teacher devises only the initial question of which site to choose. The pupils cannot carry out the fieldwork without asking additional questions of their own.

Data

The teacher puts pupils into small groups, competing for the contract to develop a site for the company. Each group already has some information about each site. They discuss what they need to find out about each site during the visit and agree, within their group, on the criteria to be used to make their decision. They decide what scale they will use to rate the criteria. A blank grid is given to the group on which it fills in the criteria to be assessed and the rating scale. The teacher has framed the activity, by deciding that they will need criteria and a rating scale, but has left some decisions to the groups. During the visit each group uses its own criteria to assess each site.

Interpretation

Pupils discuss their findings in groups and use them to select a site for their company. They present their interpretations of the data to the rest of the group in a public meeting.

Conclusions

The meeting decides a) whether to locate in London or the Lower Don Valley, b) which site is most appropriate, and c) which company wins the contract. The findings of each group are open to scrutiny and debate. There is no predictable outcome.

Comment

The teacher has devised a hypothetical situation. The initial question is the teacher's and might not engage the interest of all pupils. They are, however, obliged by the activity to ask further questions of their own. They have to make decisions about criteria and ranking methods: about which site to choose or whether to choose Sheffield at all. They have to decide how to interpret their findings and how to present their case. The techniques used are open to discussion and criticism. There is more scope for pupil participation than in the closed fieldwork but the work as a whole has been framed by the teacher.

Figure 8.6 Example of fieldwork carried out in the framed style

data, they are introduced to the ideas of selection, bias, fact and opinion. The data are open to question under the guidance of the teacher.

Interpretation

In the framed style of working, teachers induct pupils into the techniques and principles of geography. These constitute the frame which the teacher controls. The role of the teacher is to enable pupils to understand the principles and make choices within the frame. Pupils might have to choose between several different ways of representing or analysing data and become aware of their merits and drawbacks. Data might give conflicting information or conflicting opinions which need to be explored in discussion. Role play, whole class and small group discussion can give opportunity for interpretations to be shared and ideas discussed.

Conclusions

What is learned by individual pupils is less predictable than in the closed style. Pupils could come to different conclusions from examining the data and their views could be tested, and challenged. The extent to which the data supported a key idea or generalisation would be open to discussion.

A NEGOTIATED STYLE OF TEACHING AND LEARNING (FIGURE 8.7)

Questions

In this style the broad area of study might be chosen by the teacher or by the requirements of an examination syllabus, but the questions which guide the study are asked by the pupils themselves. For example, the focus of study might be the local village and its population which is introduced to a whole class by the teacher. The pupils discuss, individually or in groups, what aspects of this theme to investigate. They negotiate the questions to be studied with the teacher. Another example might be project work on a theme such as volcanoes or on a country such as Italy, where pupils are allowed to negotiate what aspects to study. The essence of the start of the negotiated sequence is that the questions which form the basis of subsequent study come from the learners.

Data

The data for the negotiated style are provided by the learner, either as a result of a guided search through available school or library resources, or

Year 12/13

Question

An A-level student is looking for a subject for an individual enquiry for 16–19 Geography A-level. He is uncertain what to study, but is interested in a local newspaper report about a public inquiry into an application by Tesco to build a hypermarket on the outskirts of Sheffield. This catches his attention partly because he has seen all the campaign posters against Tesco on his route to football training. His first question is, should Tesco be allowed to go ahead? This generates other questions. What are their plans? Why do they want this site? Who is in favour of the plan and why? Who is against the plan and why? These are all his own questions, which he has to negotiate with his teacher and then with the moderator. As his study proceeds, however, other questions become important. Why are there two action groups? Why was the application unsuccessful?

Data

The student has to decide what primary data to collect, and how. He has accumulated much secondary data from the public inquiry. He has to devise his own methods of data collection, devise his own questionnaires, decide his own sampling procedures, and decide whom to interview.

Interpretation

The student has to interpret the data he has collected. He has to decide how to deal with the problem of inadequate data from the parties in favour of the application. He has to decide what value to place on survey data, and transcripts from interviews. He has to decide how to present the data.

Conclusions

The student has to suggest reasons why the planning application was unsuccessful and the role of the different parties in influencing this decision. He has to decide what he feels about the application. At the start of the enquiry neither the outcome of Tesco's application nor the conclusions to be drawn from the enquiry were predictable.

Comment

The student has had to devise an enquiry which could be done within a reasonable amount of time and where there would be access to data. The data were more complex than any presented to him at school. He had to decide what was relevant and what was not. There were conflicting data in relation to both 'facts' and opinions. The situation was changing as he studied it. In addition to learning some geography and some techniques he was learning about public inquiries, how to contact and interview adults, and something about local politics.

Figure 8.7 Example of fieldwork carried out in a negotiated style

by consulting other people, or from first-hand collection of data. The learner makes the choices, with advice, about what data are appropriate to answer the questions to be investigated.

Interpretation

In the negotiated style of learning the responsibility for choosing methods of analysis and interpretation rests with the pupils. The teacher's role is as consultant.

Conclusions

In concluding the work the final outcomes may not be known in advance or be predictable. They may be open to criticism because of the data selected or because of the methods of analysis. Both learners and teachers evaluate the success of the work.

CHOICE OF STYLES?

It was suggested at the start of this chapter that within the standardised framework of content for geography 5–19, teachers are free to choose how they teach. Early research suggested that choices were made on the basis of what was thought to be the most effective strategy. Later research concentrated more upon clarifying links between teaching styles and teachers' aims and philosophy. It is now recognised that how teachers teach is not simply a matter of efficiency or philosophy. They teach in particular schools, in particular departments, with particular pupils and with limited resources. At each stage of teaching and learning there are factors which would shift the teaching either to the closed end or to the negotiated end of the spectrum.

Questions

Teachers are not completely free to choose whether they operate at the closed, framed or negotiated end of the spectrum at the start of a sequence of work. The National Curriculum, syllabuses for external examinations, textbooks and time constraints all affect their freedom. For much of the time teachers are working with prescribed content and cannot give pupils freedom to decide which aspects of topics or places to study. This has some advantages as pupils are introduced through the curriculum to new areas of experience and interest. The geography curriculum can be planned to provide balance in terms of different aspects of geography, different scales of study and different areas of the world. A student-centred negotiated geography could easily lack balance in any of these respects. So for the majority of timetabled time, teachers are left with a choice of designing a scheme of work in a closed or a framed manner. There seem to be few arguments in favour of the closed end of the spectrum at this stage of the sequence. Unless there is an assumption that the learners are very motivated or can internalise the questions on which a study is based, it would seem better to plan teaching and learning so that the questions which underpin the subject knowledge are made explicit. A 10-year-old once commented, 'School is boring, I hate being told things I don't want to know'. There seems to be every reason to stimulate pupils to want to know and for teachers to create a need to know.

Some textbooks are much more helpful in this respect than others. Many operate at the closed end. For example, a popular Key Stage 3 geography textbook, *Foundations* (Waugh and Bushell, 1991), starts each theme and each double-page spread with a question, but there is then no attempt to involve the learner, making this question his or her own. One section has a heading, 'Why are there different land use patterns in towns?' (*ibid*:52) and the text immediately proceeds to tell the pupils the answer. This section is at the closed end of the spectrum and it is up to the teacher to open it up so that the question becomes the pupils' question. The activities at the end of the section ask the pupils to repeat in a different form the information contained in the section, not to puzzle about the question for themselves. Although every section in this series starts with a question as a title, these questions remain the authors' questions. They act as statements of content.

A very different approach is adopted by *Society Pieces*, published by Cambridge University Press as part of the Cambridge Geography Project. In contrast to *Foundations*, not all sections have questions as titles. One section has the title, 'Living a Life of Leisure'. It starts by asking pupils to list popular holiday locations and then to classify them into groups. Although the title does not have a question-mark, pupils immediately have to ask themselves questions. Another section, 'Brazil — a Land of Opportunity?' starts by asking pupils to look at pictures of Brazil and to speculate on what caused these areas to be like this. The introductions to topics in this series are in the framed style because pupils participate by speculating, brainstorming and other activities which encourage them to be involved in the questions on which the section is based. Of course, teachers are 'free' to use textbooks as they wish. How they use particular books might depend on how they interpret their role in relation to the National Curriculum. Daugherty and Lambert's (1984) investigation into teacher assessment at Key Stage 3 suggests that teachers interpret their roles in significantly different ways. On the other hand, it would be interesting to know whether in fact the different approaches of the two textbooks lead to significant differences in the way themes are introduced.

Assuming that textbooks could have some influence on style, it would be interesting to analyse books produced for the geography National Curriculum using the framework in this chapter. To what extent are they controlling pupils' geographical knowledge, to what extent are they framing knowledge, giving access to principles of constructing knowledge, and offering support for pupils to carry out their own investigations?

Examination syllabuses, like textbooks, can influence teaching styles, as the Schools Council geography projects were fully aware. The nature of coursework requirements can influence whether the questions pupils investigate are controlled by the teacher, framed by the teacher, or negotiated with the teacher. All categories of style are possible for the GCSE Geography syllabus D of the NEAB. It allows for Teacher Planned Enquiries (TPE) in which the teacher selects the focus and the questions to be investigated, and for Student Planned Enquiries (SPE) where the individual student identifies a question or issue to investigate. The TPEs could be closed if they are so tightly controlled that the role of the students is simply to follow instructions, or they could be framed if the questions to be investigated become the students'. The Geography 16–19 Project A Level offered by the University of London requires an individual enquiry which falls into the negotiated category, as the questions which form the basis of the study have to be decided by the students.

Though it appears that textbooks, curriculum frameworks and examination syllabuses do not influence teaching style overtly in any one direction, there seems to be little encouragement below the examination years for teachers to negotiate the content, or questions to be studied, with pupils.

There are, however, opportunities during every year of geographical education for pupils to ask their own questions and pursue their own interests on even a small scale, and evidence exists (Roberts, 1995) that future benefits can accrue in terms of independent study skills. The 1995 reduction of content in the Geography National Curriculum (SCAA, 1995) for ages 5–14 might make this a more attractive proposition than during the period of the overcrowded, original Statutory Order (DES, 1991). The 1995 Order makes negotiated content possible in several ways (SCAA, 1995). First, the proposed programmes of study are far less detailed in terms of content than the original Statutory Orders, so there is some scope to negotiate with pupils, if teachers choose to do so, exactly what is to be studied in each theme. Secondly, the places to be studied are no longer prescribed. This gives teachers, or possibly pupils, a wider choice of countries to be studied. Thirdly, the changes plan a geography curriculum which can be studied in 45 hours per year in each of years 7, 8 and 9. Most geography departments have more time than this at present (Roberts, 1992). They would argue strongly to retain this, partly because of the contribution geography can make to cross-curricular themes and partly because for many pupils geographical education will cease at the end of Key Stage 3. Thus, in offering teachers a reduced and less prescriptive content, the post-Dearing geography National Curriculum is also offering them the possibility of choosing from a greater variety of strategies.

Data

When it comes to geographical data there are advantages and disadvantages relating to each of the styles. Using one piece of text, one photograph, one set of figures, one representation of reality is more straightforward for learners initially than the possible confusion of many sources of data and conflicting ideas. Basic skills of interpretation of maps, graphs, photographs and text can be learned from one data source. It is more economical and more manageable to limit resources presented to learners. Some information is fairly uncontentious and can be represented adequately with one piece of data.

At some time, however, it is important that pupils encounter different perceptions and conflicting viewpoints. Sir Keith Joseph, the then

Secretary of State for Education, voiced this view strongly in 1985 in relation to controversial issues: 'teachers do no service to their pupils if they give the impression that such problems are easily defined'. He thought it was part of the 'professional responsibility of teachers to ensure that alternative views are presented' (Joseph, 1985).

The negotiated style encourages pupils to be less dependent on the teacher as a source of data and to become confident in using the wide range of resources available in libraries and from many other sources outside school. Knowing where to find information, being confident to do so, and being aware of how to judge its validity, are important twenty-first century life skills.

Interpretation

There may be occasions when it is entirely appropriate for students to follow precise instructions and to be initiated into established routines of investigations, e.g. learning how to use a computer database, or learning a graphical or statistical technique. Closed procedures can model good practice and introduce new techniques. If, however, all interpretation and analysis is at the closed end of the spectrum, learners remain dependent on following instructions and being told what to do. At some stage they need to be able to choose between different techniques and to have activities framed to give them this choice.

Another reason for teachers varying their style is related to differentiation. More demands are made on pupils in the framed than the closed style, and yet more demands in the negotiated style (see for example Kerry, 1994). The three categories of teaching and learning could in this sense be seen in terms of progression. Indeed the guidance given to teachers for coursework enquiries for GCSE Geography, MEG syllabus A suggests different styles for pupils likely to achieve at different levels (Figure 8.8). Although the complete framework gives ideas on assessment, it also guides teachers in setting it up. This suggests that teachers, rather than thinking in terms of a consistent set of practices (style), need to be able to be flexible in order to meet the needs of different pupils.

Conclusions

There are sound reasons for operating across the spectrum when it comes to generalisations and conclusions. Some generalisations are more

These statements of levels have been included in the syllabus to provide general guidance to teachers in both the setting and assessment of coursework tasks. They are not intended to be definitive, but rather as draft guidelines which may require amendment in the light of experience.

	In a geographical inquiry of a simple nature
Criterion (a) Primary and Secondary Data	**1-4 marks** The candidate has collected and recorded primary data on provided recording material by following precise instructions. The candidate has, where appropriate, selected relevant information from a limited number of secondary sources, given headings for guidance.
Criterion (b) Presentation of Data	**1-4 marks** The candidate has presented and refined the data in a limited but appropriate form as a result of step-by-step instructions.
Criterion (c) Analysis, Interpretation	**1-5 marks** With specific guidance, the candidate has attempted limited analysis of the refined data and shown some simple awareness of the relevance of the values and perceptions of decision makers.
Criterion (d) Conclusions	**1-4 marks** The candidate has presented a commentary expressed basically in descriptive terms, with very limited comment on the application and usefulness of the findings.

Figure 8.8: GCSE Geographical Enquiry: Levels of response

In a geographical inquiry of intermediate complexity	In a geographical inquiry of complex nature
1-8 marks With guidance, the candidate has made geographically appropriate decisions about strategies for collecting and recording data, and has successfully carried them out, including, where appropriate, selecting relevant information from a number of secondary sources.	**1-12 marks** The candidate has shown initiative in deciding what data are required and how to record them appropriately in relation to the objectives of the inquiry. The candidate has received only general guidance and occasional tutoring when sought.
1-8 marks With guidance, the candidate has chosen and used a number of geographically appropriate techniques to process and present the data.	**1-12 marks** Given limited guidance, the candidate has presented and refined the collected data and chosen or devised appropriate graphical, catographical and/or numerical forms.
1-10 marks Given guidance, the candidate has analysed the refined data and used geographical concepts and principles to offer some interpretation, including demonstrating an understanding of the importance of values and perceptions in decision making.	**1-14 marks** The candidate has demonstrated the ability to analyse and interpret data by applying geographical concepts and principles. The candidate has demonstrated an understanding of the role of decision making and the values and perceptions of decision makers in the evolution of patterns in human geography.
1-8 marks The candidate has drawn some conclusions and presented, where appropriate, proposals, justification and evaluations for solutions to geographical problems.	**1-12 marks** The candidate has drawn conclusions and discussed possible implications. The candidate has shown initiative and imagination in drawing up and evaluating proposals for solutions to geographical problems where appropriate.

Source: Midland Examining Group.

powerful and useful than others, some are more accepted and supported by data. The current state of thinking on some aspects of ecology, environmental issues, physical geography, etc. can be represented by key ideas and generalisations. Pupils cannot handle sufficient data to enable them to form their own generalisations about everything themselves.

Most GCSE and A-level syllabuses state the key ideas and generalisations to be understood. There are strong pressures to operate at times at the closed end of the spectrum where the generalisations are presented as knowledge to be accepted and understood rather than opened to debate.

Nevertheless, it is important that from time to time pupils are expected to reach their own conclusions from the interpretation of data, to make their own judgements of the validity of different value positions on an issue, and to form their own opinions. They need opportunities to do this both supported by a teacher in the framed mode of operating and on their own at the negotiated end of the spectrum. Guidelines for some GCSE enquiries encourage maximum credit for pupil participation at this stage of enquiry: 'The candidate has shown initiative and imagination in drawing up and evaluating proposals for solutions to geographical problems' (see Figure 8.8).

There appear to be good reasons for geography teachers to adopt different styles at different stages, at different times, in relation to different age groups, classes and individuals rather than to remain within one style of working. Instead of aiming for consistency it would seem preferable to be able to work confidently in different ways. The examples set out in Figures 8.9–8.11 show how even within the study of one theme teachers might use closed, framed or negotiated strategies at different stages of the study rather than be consistent in style throughout.

Conclusions

These examples are simplifications of what can happen in the complex reality of classroom interaction. During a class discussion or an activity a teacher might shift from one minute to the next through the different styles identified in this chapter. Close analysis of transcripts and video recordings could identify when the shifts take place. They could be

Teaching and learning activities	Closed	Framed	Negotiated
Question The teacher devises a hypothetical problem-solving situation: the school wants to have a small garden with a bench, lawn and flowerbeds. The size of the garden is given. Where should it be located? Small groups of pupils and then the whole class discuss what has to be taken into account. The pupils suggest that they need to know about temperature, wind direction and wind speed at different parts of the school grounds, about soils and about appearance. The teacher limits the questions to those of weather and the visual environment, thus framing their work. The pupils choose some sites for investigation, these are discussed and an agreed list of sites is selected for the whole class.		✓	
Data The teacher tells the pupils how to collect information about temperature and wind and how to complete environmental assessment forms using standard techniques. She gives them no choice of designing their own techniques as this would be time-consuming and might lead to less accurate measurements. She wants them to learn about standardised methods. Data collection is tightly controlled by the teacher and is closed.	✓		
Interpretation The teacher introduces standard ways of representing data on temperature, wind and environmental assessment graphically. She gives the class appropriate scales and gives the class questions which will help pupils write a report on each site. Interpretation is closed, with pupils introduced to standard techniques of analysis.	✓		
Conclusions The teacher asks each group to select a best site from the data available. The pupils are free to reach their own conclusions and can give different values to different factors. They present their views to the rest of the class and some of the work of each group is displayed. The final stage of this work is negotiated.			✓

Figure 8.9 Strategy and style: Year 7 – Microclimates around the school

Teaching and learning activities	Closed	Framed	Negotiated
Question The questions guiding the work are decided by the teacher. What is the difference between developing and developed countries? In which part of the world are these photographs taken? The teacher devises a problem-solving activity to make the pupils speculate about photographs and ask questions of their own.		✓	
Data Seven photographs are used. They give unexpected views of different parts of the world and are presented as evidence to be scrutinised and questioned rather than as authoritative information on those places. Pupils are invited to discuss them in groups.		✓	
Interpretation A structured grid is given to pupils to complete. It has been predetermined by the teacher to make the pupils look at particular aspects of the photographs which the teacher has decided are important. There is no discussion on why these aspects have been chosen. Pupils are expected to fill in the grid.	✓		
Conclusions There is a whole class discussion. Conclusions are reached about which pictures were most accurately recognised, which least, and why this might be so. The key idea of variety in both the 'developed' and 'developing' world is predetermined by the teacher, who wants this conclusion to emerge from the discussion. It is framed by the teacher. Then one pupil claims that the photographs have been selected deliberately to mislead and that they are not fair representations of where they were taken. This is taken up in a whole class discussion and represents a movement towards the negotiated end of the spectrum where pupils make sense of an activity in their own way and where their own meanings are validated by class discussion.		✓	✓

Figure 8.10 Strategy and style: Year 8 – Introduction to development issues

Teaching and learning activities	Closed	Framed	Negotiated
Questions The teacher selects the overall focus: indices of development. The class is presented with a list of indices for which there are data on the GRASS database in a file on development. Pairs of pupils are asked to produce their own hypotheses about which indices will show positive correlations, which will show negative correlations and which will not correlate at all. This stage of the scheme of work is negotiated in that the pupils can set up their own hypotheses to explore during the lesson. It is within the broad frame set up by the teacher, however.		✓	✓
Data The class is given details of what types of information are in the database and what units of measurement are used. The sources of information are not discussed, nor the validity of the data questioned. The data are given as authoritative data.	✓		
Interpretation Pupils are given precise instructions on how to select two variables and draw scattergraphs on the computer. They are expected to follow instructions to use this technique for correlating data. To this extent the interpretation is closed in that there is no choice of methods for correlation. The pupils have to decide, however, from the scattergraph whether they think there is a correlation, and so at this stage are involved in making their own interpretations of the data.	✓		
Conclusions There is a class discussion on the findings of pairs of students and lists are made of indices which correlate positively, those which correlate negatively, and those where there is no correlation. Pupils are invited to speculate on the reasons for their findings.		✓	

Figure 8.11 Strategy and style: Year 10 – Indices of development

interpreted to explore why they took place, and in whose interest was the shift (teacher's or pupils'). Pupils' written work could be analysed to ascertain when it is controlled by the teacher by closed tasks, when the task is framed, and when it is negotiated. Textbooks and examination papers also could be analysed using this same framework.

The National Curriculum and national criteria for public examinations at 16 and 18 have removed some professional decisions from geography teachers, although the implementation of the post-Dearing geography curriculum should restore some of these choices. The prescriptions of aims and content defined by the new Statutory Order and by the new criteria for GCSE and A-level cannot remove the innumerable professional judgements made day in and day out in the classroom about how to teach and how to enable pupils to learn. Teachers can choose from a wide repertoire of strategies and decide when it is appropriate to give pupils more choices and greater autonomy over their learning. Teachers can be aware of when they are making the choices according to pupil needs, and when they are making them because of the constraints of the context in which they are working. Increasing awareness of the nature of these choices and their implications for learners can increase professional freedom and inform a new professionalism.

BIBLIOGRAPHY

Barnes, D., Johnson, G., Jordan, S., Layton, D., Medway, P. and Yeomans, D. (1987) *The TVEI Curriculum 14–16: An Interim Report Based on Case Studies in Twelve Schools*, University of Leeds.

Bennett, S.N. (1976) *Teaching Styles and Pupil Progress*, Open Books.

Berlak, A. and Berlak, H. (1981) *Dilemmas of Teaching*, Methuen.

Daily Mail (1994) 'The dunce at the front of the class', 5 July.

Daugherty, R. and Lambert, D. (1994) 'Teacher assessment and geography in the National Curriculum', *Geography*, 79(4):339–49.

DES (1989) *From Policy to Practice*, HMSO.

(1990) *Geography for Ages 5 to 16*, HMSO.

(1991) *Geography in the National Curriculum*, HMSO.

Fenstermacher, D.G. and Soltis, J.F. (1986) *Approaches to Teaching*, Teachers College Press.

Galton, M. (1982) 'Strategies and tactics in junior school classrooms', in Richards, C. (ed.) *New Directions in Primary Education*, The Falmer Press.

Galton, M. and Simon, B. (eds) (1980) *Progress and Performance in the Primary Classroom*, Routledge and Kegan Paul.

TEACHING STYLES AND STRATEGIES

Gray, J. and Satterly, D. (1981) 'Formal or informal? A re-assessment of the British evidence', *British Journal of Educational Psychology*, 51(2):187–96.

Hall, D. (1976) *Geography and the Geography Teacher*, George Allen and Unwin Ltd.

Hammersley, M. (1977) *Teacher Perspectives*, The Open University Press.
(ed.) (1986) *Case Studies in Classroom Research*, Open University Press.

Hickman, G., Reynolds, J. and Tolley, H. (1973) *A New Professionalism for a Changing Geography*, Schools Council.

Joseph, K. (1985) 'Geography in the school curriculum', *Geography*, 70(4): 290–7.

Kerry, T. (1994) 'Teachers learning differentiation through classroom question-ing skills', in *Journal of Teacher Development*, 2(2):81–93.

MacDonald, B. and Walker, R. (1976) *Changing the Curriculum*, Open Books.

Naish, M. (1988) 'Teaching styles in geographical education', in Gerber, R. and Lidstone, J. (eds) *Developing Skills in Geographical Education*, The Jacaranda Press.

Naish, M., Rawling, E. and Hart, C. (1987) *Geography 16–19: The Contribution of a Curriculum Project to 16–19 Education*, Longman.

Rawling, E. (1986) 'Approaches to teaching and learning', in Boardman, D. (ed.) *Handbook for Geography Teachers*, The Geographical Association.

Renwick, M. (1985) *The Essentials of GYSL*, Sheffield City Polytechnic, GYSL National Centre.

Roberts, M. (1992) 'A case of information overload', *Times Educational Supplement*, 20 November.
(1995) 'Interpretations of the Geography National Curriculum: a common curriculum for all?', *Journal of Curriculum Studies*, 27(2):187–205.

SCAA (1993) *GCE Advanced and Advanced Supplementary Examinations: Subject Core for Geography*, SCAA.
(1994) *Geography in the National Curriculum: Draft Proposals*, HMSO.
(1995) *Geography in the National Curriculum*, HMSO.

Slater, F. (1988) 'Teaching style? A case study of postgraduate teaching students observed', in Gerber, R. and Lidstone, J. (eds) *Developing Skills in Geographical Education*, The Jacaranda Press.

Steadman, S., Parsons, C. and Salter, B. (1980) *A Second Interim Report on the Schools Council*, Schools Council.

Stones, E. (1992) *Quality Teaching: A Sample of Cases*, Routledge.

Tolley, H. and Reynolds, J. (1977) *Geography 14–18: A Handbook for School-based Curriculum Development*, Macmillan Education.

Walford, R. (1981) 'Language, ideologies and geography teaching', in Walford, R. (ed.) *Signposts for Geography Teaching*, Longman.

Waugh, D. and Bushell, T. (1991) *Foundations*, Stanley Thomas.

Woods, P. (ed.) (1980) *Teacher Strategies: Explorations in the Sociology of the School*, Croom Helm.

9

Assessing pupils' attainment and supporting learning

David Lambert

> We are suffering from an excessive development of the competitive system...Education, instead of consisting of a careful and systematic development of the faculties, is in danger of reducing itself to preparing children for a series of spasmodic efforts ...[and] ...the whole theory of education becomes disturbed.
>
> Matthew Arnold, in a letter to the *Pall Mall Gazette*, 5 October 1870, quoted in Andrews, 1994

Educational assessment (see Figure 9.1) is both a generalist and a specialist activity. The generalists include all teachers who undertake it in their day-to-day professional lives, but who do not necessarily see themselves as part of the 'assessment industry'. The specialists comprise that particular community of experts who, with all their technical knowledge and not inconsiderable resources, have produced what can appear to be a separate yet highly influential culture within the education world. The former can readily be described by statements such as 'teachers mark books' or 'teachers know their pupils'. It is a difficult function (making judgements about other people's worth always is), and time consuming, but plays an essential part in the rhythm of teaching, helping to forge the teacher–pupil relationship. The second group includes teachers of course, but is perhaps best characterised by the public examination bodies and by the work of the School Curriculum and Assessment Authority (SCAA), the most recent manifestation (1993) of the government's education policy quango. Dominant considerations here include notions of 'national standards' and common procedures on which to base comparison of teacher and school performance. What has grown up is a national infrastructure of examinations guided primarily by the purpose of *selecting* young people for future educational or employment opportunities (see Daugherty, 1990; 1992; and forthcoming).

Although one is alert to the way memory can sometimes play tricks with the past, it seems that much of the 'modern' period in British

Assessment in education is taken to mean:
'…the process of gathering, interpreting, recording and using information about pupils' responses to educational tasks'.

Assessment in education involves:
a) more formal contexts and procedures including written, timed tests marked under strict conditions, and
b) less formal settings including reading pupils' work and listening to what they have to say.
'Thus assessment encompasses responses to regular work as well as to specially devised tasks.'

Assessment in education requires:
…teachers to make judgements about pupils' responses measured against some standard of expectation. This is either:
a) norm-referenced (set by the average performance of the age group), or
b) criterion-referenced (set by the interpretation, and statement, of the progression of skills, knowledge and understanding which form the objectives of learning for the subject).

The generally agreed roles of assessment in education are:
a) providing feedback to teachers and pupils about progress in order to support future learning: *the formative role*
b) providing information about the level of pupils' achievements at points during and at the end of their school career: *the summative role*
c) providing the means for selection by qualification: *the certification role*
d) contributing to the information on which judgements are made concerning the effectiveness or quality of individuals and institutions in the system as a whole: *the evaluative role.*

Source: After Harlen et al., 1992

Figure 9.1 Assessment in education

education, since the Education Act of 1944, can be described by the simple distinction being drawn here: external tests and examinations on the one hand, and classroom processes on the other. Until very recently, both these activities were considered to be elements of the so-called education 'secret garden', one consequence of which has been that the general level of understanding of assessment and examining processes has been poor; teachers have rarely had to account for their actions in this aspect of their work, and the examinations system has had the characteristics of a black box.

These two sides of education assessment – the external tests and the classroom processes – were not, and are not, hermetically sealed from each other. For one thing, they share issues of great concern and importance, such as the impact of testing on pupils' learning. But the *interests* of each side, what drives or motivates it, are different and it is for this reason that Stiggins (1992) helpfully identifies what he terms the two assessment 'disciplines' (roughly the internal and external assessment cultures outlined above). I intend to develop this idea more fully in this chapter in order to explore recent and current developments in assessment in England and Wales, and to suggest how teachers of geography might respond to them. The intention is not to examine in any great detail the mechanics of assessment practice, but rather to discuss matters of principle, thus contributing to an urgently needed theoretical debate; as Stiggins noted, in the North American context:

> As we proceed through the 1990's, educators at all levels of responsibility, from classroom to board room, remain almost completely illiterate with respect to development and use of sound assessment strategies in educational contexts.
>
> Stiggins, 1992:2

Wiliam, in the context of England and Wales, puts this perception rather differently, but equally powerfully:

> It is my contention that the development of National Curriculum assessment has proceeded in advance of the currently available theory.
>
> Wiliam, 1993:336

Both writers were, in a sense, lamenting the inability of the profession at large (and others, including politicians) to analyse, evaluate and communicate on assessment effectively. Thus, in urging a theoretical debate, I am not after useless abstraction, divorced from reality. I am arguing for theory that clarifies and helps us make sense of our actions, and shows where change may be desirable. It is interesting how resistant practitioners seem to be to this notion of theory. It is almost a century since Professor James Welton advocated theory in education as 'practice become conscious of itself, and practice [as] realised theory' (Welton, 1906, quoted in Marsden, 1976:1).

We need to be able to develop practice ourselves, but also to challenge others, inside and outside education, who may profess to have simple solutions. For example, to narrow down Wiliam's point, he is particularly concerned with the profession at large refining conceptions of 'reliability' and 'validity', which became the touchstones of competence for the agencies involved in writing national test materials (SATs) in the early years of the National Curriculum:

> At the moment, they are used as high-status labels that make a product seem attractive, much in the same way the advertisers use terms like Quartz, Laser and Turbo to describe everything from furniture to footwear.
>
> Wiliam, 1993:348

This is also a discussion to which we shall return later in this chapter.

We are in the midst of unprecedented developments in assessment, and this chapter would date very quickly if my aim were simply to survey or document how far we had come. It is a long and complex story involving at least three distinctive contemporaneous strands which do not always exhibit a harmonious working relationship:

- Legislative effort by the government which, since the Education Reform Act of 1988, has had increasingly direct impact on classroom processes.
- Unparalleled burdens on teachers, not only attempting to implement mandatory change but also continuing grassroots developments such as records of achievement and profiling.
- A range of movements encouraged by agencies outside the traditional territory of education resulting in the rapid development of alternative (vocational) 'pathways' beyond 14 years, such as General National Vocational Qualifications (GNVQ).

What I shall attempt to do in this chapter, then, is interpret recent changes and make judgements about what we have learned. In doing so, I hope to get beneath the surface 'noise' generated by too close a look at policy documents and such-like, and I need to be judiciously selective. My main interest lies in the development of an identifiable professional code, or framework, which articulates the essential role of assessment in teachers' day-to-day work – what is now referred to in England and Wales as *teacher assessment*.

It is not the case that teachers can pursue their own professional goals without reference to policies, or even opinion, outside the classroom. We need to begin, therefore, with a broad (though brief) historical perspective. Where have we come from? What has shaped evolving practice in assessment? The main context for my discussion is mainstream compulsory secondary education. I do not, therefore, examine in any detail A-level or equivalent 'level 3' vocational qualifications, or developments specific to primary schooling. However, readers will find that comments on public examinations and National Curriculum Assessment (NCA) are applicable to the post-16 and primary phases respectively.

The assessment landscape: a sketch

A FAILING SYSTEM

Previous landmark legislation in education, notably the 1944 Education Act which established the framework for the development of comprehensive schools in England and Wales (see Barber, 1994), had little to say about the curriculum or the assessment of children's learning. It simply was not the government's job, as perceived at the time, to become involved in such professional matters. This is an important point because the 'hands-off' tradition profoundly shaped teachers' attitudes both to their role and to that of others contributing to the education service. Arguably, the most significant 'other' consisted of the examination boards, independent of the education policy makers but controlled by the universities. The influence of university academics on examination board committees is of interest in this connection.

The limitations of the post-1944 arrangements are not easy to conceal in retrospect, though they persisted for many years. We have already noted the high profile given to external examinations, access to which was severely rationed, a feature which guaranteed failure for large numbers of young people, year after year. Even after the widespread introduction of the 'less academic' Certificate of Secondary Education (CSE) in 1965, 40 per cent of pupils reaching the end of compulsory schooling were deemed unsuitable for a qualification or certificate. The assessment system was in fact an elaborate mechanism for selecting a minority of pupils considered able to benefit from continuing in formal education.

The assessment, or selection, system failed pupils in other ways too. The introduction of comprehensive schools (revealingly and perhaps damagingly referred to as 'grammar schools for all' by the Prime Minister Harold Wilson) sounded the death knell, over most of the country, of the unloved 'eleven-plus', a narrowly based external test designed to select children for grammar school. Its abolition was, in itself, probably desirable, as was the move towards comprehensive education, but it was risky not to replace it with a dependable means of assessing and reporting pupils' progress at this stage of their education. It was as if the differences between children, including their intellectual capacities, became blurred or not fully acknowledged. Mortimore (*Sunday Times*, 1994) regards this as one reason for the continuing charged debate over reading standards of children entering secondary school. It is also almost certainly one of the reasons for the final acceptance by ministers in the latter half of the 1980s of a national assessment system, though the rationale for assessment within such circles was more to do with evaluating teachers and schools in the marketplace, than any educational or monitoring purposes that Mortimore may have had in mind.

FIGURES TO BLAME

There may be lessons to be learned from this episode. We could interpret these events as an example of what can happen if the profession at large resists or rejects reasonable and proper accountability. If it does, those with the purse strings can become greedy for symbolic figures of blame (the 'education establishment') for any perceived weakness or failure. In these circumstances the truth often becomes grossly over-simplified. Lambert (1994) has examined this discussion in relation to the establishment of the original National Curriculum Order in geography (DES, 1991): 'trendy' curriculum developers of the 1970s were deemed at fault for the apparent failure of geography to teach its share of what has been called 'cultural literacy' (Hirsch, 1987; see also Dowgill and Lambert, 1992). Whether or not one has sympathy for these views is beside the point. The resulting (short-lived) geography National Curriculum Order came to resemble little more than a list of certified knowledge to be learned, and the meaning of the word 'curriculum', and the role of assessment, were left in a severely reduced condition.

In any case it is salutary to remember that notions of national assessment are more recent even than that of a national curriculum. Faith had tended to be placed in the 'gold standard' of the General Certificate of Education (GCE). This was (and remains in the case of A-level) an examination framework designed for an elite section of the school population. Examinations were taken at the end of the course, by which time it was impossible to do anything to remedy difficulties, develop talent and improve performance. Partly as a result, teachers have for many years been particularly sensitive to certain processes associated with the assessment of children's performance which they feel to be harmful. Teachers are wary of supporting 'self-fulfilling prophecies', for example. They are also acutely aware of the dangers of 'labelling' children, and knowledgeable of the barriers to success that examinations often place before children (Marsden, 1976, is still a useful summary of the characteristics, including the deficiencies, of essay questions, multiple-choice testing, etc.; see also Lambert, 1990). Teachers tend, therefore, to be committed to what might be called a 'pure form' of curriculum, untainted by the real or imagined corrupting, 'backwash' effects of assessment. This tradition is perhaps perfectly illustrated by the position adopted by the Institute for Public Policy Research (IPPR) in a critique of the original National Curriculum Assessment (NCA) proposals:

> ...if we wish to see how well the curriculum is working we should directly observe its operation, rather than indirectly trying to infer its effects by measuring the achievements of its students.
>
> Goldstein, 1991:9

Critics of this sentiment would label it as typical of the supposed educational establishment, with its great propensity needlessly to muddy the water. On the other hand, as Lambert and Purnell (1994) argue in the context of international testing of geographical attainment, the curriculum context cannot be ignored if any meaningful comparisons are going to be made of assessment data.

NEW BEGINNINGS?

Turning more specifically to geography, it is this impetus to disengage curriculum and assessment processes that may explain the widespread, but not universal, acceptance of *common* examination papers in the General Certificate of Secondary Education (GCSE) when it replaced the dual system of GCE and CSE in 1986. This encouraged teachers of geography to rely heavily upon 'differentiation by outcome' in their curriculum planning, and allowed them to postpone indefinitely decisions concerning the appropriate level of examination for their pupils. It is a contention well worth exploring that in judging the response of all children to common experiences, rather than attempting to judge the type of experience most suitable to particular learners in the first place, teachers have too often (and probably unwittingly) *lowered* their expectations of pupils in geography lessons, whether academically gifted or academically less able. This, apparently, flies in the face of the received professional wisdom, the orthodoxy which labels the GCSE a success. It need not, for the problems noted at the 'ability' extremes can be consistent with rising average 'pass' rates. Indeed, in many ways the GCSE remains an exemplary case of positive, assessment-led curriculum innovation which, it appears, had had limited, positive impact on classroom processes (Boardman, 1988; Daugherty *et al.*, 1991), making a contribution to breaking the 'vicious circle of curriculum under-development' (Hickman *et al.*, 1973) in which external examinations had been viewed as an obstacle to the realisation of more ambitious learning goals.

On the other hand, it can be argued that the enormous potential of the GCSE has not yet fully been realised (see Daugherty, 1990:294). Furthermore, while attention was turned in recent years to mass standardised testing structures for the National Curriculum, what has been learned from the GCSE was in danger of being lost. It is a touch ironic that the GCSE used methods that are now becoming influential in the USA as an antidote to the traditional widespread use of short, standardised tests which, as Black (1993) notes, are being abandoned there 'because it is evident that they have done nothing to improve education' (p.64). The assessment framework of the GCSE is built upon a design principle which identifies improvement (through rewarding the 'positive achievement' of candidates) as a major concern. In a similar way, influential work in the USA takes the view that

> assessments must be so designed that when you do the natural thing – that is, prepare the students to perform well – they will exercise the kinds of abilities and develop the kinds of skills that are the real goals of educational reform.
>
> Resnick and Resnick, 1992, quoted in Black, 1993:65

Shepard (1992) characterises such approaches to assessment as using 'terms such as "authentic", "direct" and "performance" …to convey the idea that assessments must capture real learning activities if they are to avoid distorting instruction'. The GCSE, through the identification of *assessment objectives* and the accompanying *specification grids*, the insistence on *coursework* assessment components (often including mandatory field-work investigations) and the attempt to spell out 'grade-related criteria' to support 'positive achievement', was a bold reform with exactly these concerns to the fore.

A DECISIVE BREAK WITH THE PAST

The reform which led to the introduction of the GCSE was a long time in coming, the result of discussions and indecision lasting well over a decade. When finally it came (in 1986) it was soon under the shadow cast by the far-reaching 1988 Education Reform Act. This provided an assessment framework for the subject-based National Curriculum, which had been set out in the remarkable report of the so-called Task Group on Assessment and Testing (TGAT) (DES/WO, 1988). This framework ambitiously developed those notions of authentic and direct assessment mentioned above. In addition, it proposed a national assessment system for all children in compulsory schooling, which would involve *teachers* making criterion-referenced judgements of attainment for each distinc-tive domain (or 'attainment target') of the National Curriculum subjects, as well as administering externally produced 'standard assessment tasks' (SATs). Thus was born the National Curriculum Assessment (NCA) sys-tem, based upon the ten-level scale, itself predicated on the notion that progress in learning in geography could be described in terms of progres-sive levels of attainment.

In so far as GCSE geography was concerned, the ten-level scale dealt a decisive blow to 'differentiation by outcome', or at least common exam-ination papers. With GCSE syllabuses and examinations having to be re-written in order to come into line with the National Curriculum levels, tiered papers became the order of the day. The ten-level scale is no longer set to replace GCSE grades, since the government accepted the Dearing review proposals (Dearing, 1994) which effectively abolished Key Stage 4 (the compulsory curriculum for 14 to 16-year-olds), but it is difficult to imagine new GCSEs (for first examination in 1998) without tiered arrangements, as teachers of children from the age of 7 years will be required to report levels of attainment in geography on the national scale.

Progression, then, is an idea which has had to move to the front of teachers' minds. In former times it was a notion which had formed part of the educational planning landscape, but despite noteworthy attempts (Bennetts, 1981) it was difficult to articulate with precision and in a form which teachers could work with. Without sufficient evidence to suggest whether or not it was possible, let alone desirable, the ten-level scale has now forced us to describe progression in distinctive levels; what concentrates the mind further is the assumption that this should acquire national acceptance and agreement.

Though the TGAT report was accepted by the then Secretary of State, Kenneth Baker, it was apparently less wholeheartedly accepted by the Prime Minister, Margaret Thatcher (*The Independent*, 1988). This betrayed the less than uniform approach which existed within government circles to the root and branch educational reforms being pursued. Several ideologies and political viewpoints vied with each other (see Bennetts, 1994; Lambert, 1994), and it is tempting to suggest that the educational principles, and the implications, of the TGAT report were never really understood, let alone widely endorsed. In academic circles also there was some scepticism, one key complaint being that the proposed system attempted too much, thus confusing and dangerously merging the educational (classroom) and bureaucratic (political/administrative) purposes of assessment (Gipps, 1990; Sutton, 1991); mixing up, in other words, Stiggins' two disciplines of assessment.

Almost from the start, then, the features of the proposed NCA system were eroded (see Black, 1993; Lawton, 1992), and it is interesting to note the similarities between this and the process of erosion also beginning to take place on the GCSE. Ministerial comment in the early 1990s was ambiguous, on the one hand taking credit for the sustained improvement in 'pass' rates but on the other questioning the rigour of the examination and its need to be tightened up to improve 'credibility' (Phillips, 1991). Thus, just as the role of teachers making assessments of children against National Curriculum levels was marginalised by the government – very few resources were directed to developing what was becoming known as *teacher assessment* in comparison with the very large sums devoted to the commissioning of 'standard assessment tasks' (SATs) – the role of course-work in the GCSE was significantly reduced in 1992.

What appears to be at the heart of this matter is the level of trust ministers feel that they can place in teachers making assessments of this kind. After all, there is a matter of 'trust' at issue contained within the 'two disciplines' debate: are assessments made by teachers – who may legitimately emphasise the formative purposes of these activities – *reliable* enough to be used in national systems in which evaluative and selection purposes are paramount?

SUMMARY

The purpose of this section has been to identify a number of highly significant influences on the way assessment has developed in England and Wales. Some of these are incontrovertible, 'hard' and prominent in the landscape, while others are 'softer' and more open to judgement and interpretation. Figures 9.2–9.4 summarise much of this. Figure 9.2 lists a number of trends which can be discerned from developments leading to the establishment of the GCSE and, indeed, other 1980s assessment

---

- Concern to clarify assessment objectives and to make these explicit to teachers and learners.

- Less emphasis on end-of-course examinations as the sole assessment opportunity.

- Greater variety of assessment methods appropriate to a range of skills and attributes.

- Greater awareness of bias, both in the content of assessments and in the methods employed.

- Increased understanding of the formative potential of assessments integrated into the teaching and learning process.

- Increased involvement of pupils in their own assessment, often in the context of profiling and compiling records of achievement.

- Development of recording and reporting procedures which offer a fuller description of pupils' achievements

---

Figure 9.2 Recent trends in assessment

- The assessment should provide direct information about pupils' achievements in relation to objectives: they should be *criteria referenced*

- The results should provide the basis for decisions about pupils' future learning needs: the assessments should be capable of being used *formatively*

- The results should provide teachers, pupils and parents with information on which to base comparisons; the assessments should be *moderated*

- The criteria on which assessments are made should express continuity in learning: they should relate to *progression*

Figure 9.3 Guiding criteria of the TGAT framework, 1988

artefacts such as pupil Records of Achievement (ROA) and the Certificate of Prevocational Education (CPVE), an early venture to pull schools into 'competency'-driven vocational education, and which the General National Vocational Qualification (GNVQ) now seeks to extend. Figure 9.3 shows how NCA was designed to build on these developments, albeit in a political climate not altogether conducive to steady incremental change. Nevertheless, the enduring legacy of the TGAT Report has been, in Lawton's (1992) view, substantial, influencing professional and public thinking in three areas:

- Moving the emphasis away from the summative to considerations of formative assessment and its development.
- Moving discussion away from the relatively simplistic and doctrinaire notions of 'absolute standards' to criterion-referencing. This reflects the realisation that no matter how precisely the criteria are framed, purporting to *define* standards, their meaning – and therefore the standards they represent – is provided by those who actually apply them; that is, teachers. 'Standards are not absolutes. Even in a criterion-referenced system grades can only be established by a professional consensus on acceptable levels of performance' (SEC, 1986:7).
- Moving discussion away from age-related 'benchmark' tests (and associated talk of pass/fail tests and *redoublement* – repeating the year) to a more individual and age-free developmental, or ipsative, assessment model.

1991–95	After 1995
Ten-level scale against which attainment is measured and reported for the whole of compulsory schooling (5–16 years)	Eight-level scale against which attainment is measured and reported for Key Stages 1–3 only (5–14 years)*
GCSE, the principal means to assess Key Stage 4 (14–16 years), to be brought into line with the national ten-level scale	GCSE grades A–G reinstated; Key Stage 4 no longer an entitlement, and GCSE Geography optional
Geography to be disaggregated into five domains or attainment targets (ATs)	Geography to be recombined into one AT (Geography)
Level criteria for each AT to be expressed as separate statements of attainment (SoA); Geography acquired 183 SoA, most of which were content-related	Levels to be expressed by single, more holistic, 'level descriptions', not tied to specific content
At the end of Key Stage 3 (14 years), Geography to be subject to two externally set, one-hour pencil-and-paper tests (national pilot 1993)	End-of-key-stage tests shelved; teacher assessment the sole source of knowledge on which to base reports of pupil attainment and progress
Key Stage 1 teachers supported in their assessments with non-mandatory standard assessment tasks (SATs) (SEAC, 1992)	Plans to produce non-mandatory test materials to support teacher assessment, the sole source of evidence on which to base reports of pupil attainment and progress

*The proposals for the remodelled geography curriculum were published for consultation in May 1994. The Secretary of State, while accepting the principle of the national scale, questioned whether levels 9 and 10 were still required for a curriculum that was now to terminate at the end of Key Stage 3.

Figure 9.4 Broad characteristics of National Curriculum Assessment

We will return to these interrelated facets of the TGAT legacy on a number of occasions in this chapter.

Finally, Figure 9.4 summarises in broad terms the post-Dearing (1994) settlement. The geography curriculum has been rationalised, clarified and severely reduced in size; the assessment demands in particular are now a fraction of what they once were, but certain principles remain. What is especially significant is the acceptance by the government that the only alternative to a prohibitively expensive and damagingly bureaucratic assessment system is to entrust teachers with the task of assessing level attainment of children in geography, which, unlike the core subjects of mathematics, science and English, will not be encumbered with external tests at the end of Key Stage 1, 2 or 3. It remains to be seen whether teachers will be supported with proper moderation arrangements, training and exemplar materials, all of which are expensive to provide, but the fact remains that teacher assessment is a key responsibility of geography teachers and it is to these matters we can now turn our attention.

Assessment issues for teachers

A number of issues emerge from the previous discussion. In this section I wish to discuss some of these in more detail, and from the particular point of view of teachers striving to make sense of their as yet ill-defined 'teacher assessment' responsibilities.

WHAT ARE THE STAKES?

The first of these matters was alluded to at the beginning of this chapter with reference to Stiggins' (1992) identification of the 'two disciplines' of assessment, roughly the contrasting internal and external assessment procedures. What seems to have happened during recent years is that trends such as those outlined in Figure 9.2 have been encouraged in such a way that the boundary between the two disciplines has become less distinct. In the early years of the GCSE, for example, a dilemma faced by many teachers undertaking coursework assessment, perhaps for the first time, was the amount of 'help' that legitimately could be given to the pupils. The significance of this problem was, perhaps unwittingly, mentioned in an advice pamphlet at the time, which urged teachers to think of children not only as 'examinees' but as *learners* as well (SEC, undated). More recently, the School Examinations and Assessment Council (SEAC) was also explicit about this conflict. Discussing the impact of NCA on the GCSE it stated:

> It will be essential to hold public confidence in the rigour and fairness of the examination if pupils' achievements are to be fully recognised and valued. Equally, it will be important to provide teachers with the support they need to use assessment to promote better learning and higher standards of attainment within and beyond the national curriculum.
>
> SEAC, 1991: ii

Children are indeed both candidates and learners, but it is possible that the GCSE examination, with its overriding roles of selection and evaluation (the latter given added prominence with the publication of league tables), cannot seriously attend to formative assessment purposes at the same time. To put this differently, if we must have an external examination system which purports to have national currency, then procedures to ensure *reliability* of the results assume overriding importance. Thus, when the *stakes are high*, as undoubtedly they are in the GCSE for pupils, teachers and schools, the tendency is for the administrators (and, I suspect, teachers too) to reduce to the minimum any possibility of external factors affecting the scores. Daugherty and Lambert (1994) report evidence that some teachers have perceived National Curriculum 'teacher assessment' also to have high stakes attached to it, concentrating their energies on devising and managing tests and examinations in preference to more ipsative approaches (see also Lambert and Daugherty, 1993).

But reliability, as Figure 9.5 shows, is only one dimension of assessment that must be addressed. If it is not balanced by other competing considerations, maximising the reliability of an assessment may distort the quality of information yielded by the assessment. Nuttall, (1989), for example, described research in the USA which evaluated low stakes testing designed to support learning, and the impact of *raising* the stakes, which followed test results being used in comparisons of schools, or testing becoming part of the high-school graduation requirements. The evidence suggests that teachers move quickly to a situation in which concentrating on raising scores conflicts with what the researchers considered to be sound educational practice. School administrators acknowledged that the 'devotion to specific, almost game-like ways to raise test scores' was entirely for political reasons, not to improve standards of teaching and learning but to look good. Though we must be careful to avoid drawing simple parallel conclusions in one country based on experiences in another, this research seems instructive, sounding some clear warnings in the

Reliability

This concerns the reduction to a minimum of external influences having impact on performance as measured by the assessment. Such influences include the effect of different markers or raters, the timing and other conditions under which the assessment is conducted, and so on. Making arrangements to ensure 'examination conditions' and administering centrally designed standardised tests accompanied by detailed marking instructions, are ways to maximise reliability.

Validity

This idea can be interpreted in a number of ways. Most straightforwardly, it concerns the extent to which an assessment assesses what it claims or purports to assess. We can see readily that this can become a complex matter: it must include reference to *relevance* of the assessment materials as well as their *completeness*, and also whether or not they contain *bias*.

Fitness for purpose

Assessment has many purposes (see Figure 9.1), and choices have to be made in order that the form of the assessment is appropriate. The principle of fitness for purpose can act as a touchstone against which other decisions, such as those concerned with balancing validity and reliability, can be set.

Manageability

Assessment is an information-gathering exercise, the potential of which is infinite; we can always add to our data about individuals for whom we have responsibility. In other words, assessment can easily become unmanageable. The assessment regime needs control for, apart from any other consideration, there is a point when diminishing returns set in. And yet there is equally a danger in claiming that assessment loads are unmanageable because 'simpler and more manageable' alternatives may sever the essential link between assessment, teaching and learning.

Figure 9.5 Dimensions of assessment

context of the as yet still unsettled NCA system.

As we have seen, the TGAT framework, in its initial manifestation, failed because the proposal to combine formative 'teacher assessment' and summative 'SAT' scores as parts of the same system, was an attempt to square a circle. The proposals brought together forms of educative (low stakes) assessment and tried to harness these with external tests in the highly competitive arrangements required of the Education Reform Act. As the late Desmond Nuttall concluded as early as 1989:

> You cannot combine formative, summative and evaluative purposes in the same assessment system and expect them all to function unaffected by each other. By making the stakes so high we are making sure that the evaluative function predominates and that the pressure for comparability and rigid systems of moderation that will make the system as cheat-proof as possible will drive out good formative practice and the facilitating conditions that allow pupils to put forward their best performance.
>
> Nuttall, 1989:7

The most significant feature of the post-Dearing arrangements for geography, and a major shift since the time when Nuttall wrote the above, is that external standardised tests are no longer a threat to professional judgement (the stakes have in this sense been lowered a little). Teachers can undertake assessments which are valid (authentic to the learning experiences) and fit the purpose of maximising pupil performance. Teachers can concentrate upon their major professional purposes, which are to learn more about individual pupils and to develop ways to design learning activities appropriate to different needs.

Since the Dearing review (1994), there are also signs that the government has relaxed plans for officially published league tables for the National Curriculum attainment levels (though they remain an important element of policy for the GCSE and examinations post-16). This may have the effect of lowering the stakes still further, but the professional point of concern, which remains whether or not results become public in the form of league tables, is the degree to which these data are *dependable* measures of pupil attainment. In being considered dependable, assessment takes on a 'property requiring both reliability and content validity' (Wiliam, 1993:340). In essence, it means that the assessment result is not only reliable, in the sense that the particular test or assessment task was set and administered in such a way as to address this dimension, but also has validity in the sense that the content of the test or task was such that we are able to make reasonable inferences about attainment across a broader field of study and not just that particular content 'covered' by the test or task.

The challenge that faces teachers of geography in Key Stages 1, 2 and 3 is the establishment of such dependable 'teacher assessment' regimes within the National Curriculum framework. This will not be achieved quickly, for we do not expect much in the way of guidance from the centre in the form of past papers, syllabuses containing assessment objectives, or local and regional moderation panels. Furthermore, as Daugherty and Lambert's (1994) research indicates, there is in the minds of teachers a problem of definition of 'teacher assessment', linked to wider concerns including notions of what constitutes 'teacher-work': What are the assessment responsibilities and legal duties of teachers? What is the purpose of 'teacher assessment'? In what ways, and to whom, are teachers accountable, and in what ways does pupil performance play a part in this accountability?

This kind of uncertainty is challenging. However, failure to respond to this challenge would be to miss what only a few years ago was a quite unforeseen opportunity to retain – enhance even – the teacher's role in shaping and developing geography in the National Curriculum.

TOWARDS A CURRICULUM-INTEGRATED ASSESSMENT MODEL

That the curriculum and assessment are linked is a truism; developments in one affect the other. A curriculum-integrated assessment system takes this notion a step further by ensuring that assessment arrangements are explicitly built into the fabric of the curriculum, including the planning, implementation and evaluation stages. This means that teachers think about how to integrate a range of assessment opportunities into schemes of work, which will give pupils a fair chance to show their best performance. Teachers will decide practical strategies which can accommodate such plans in the classroom in a balanced and manageable way. Finally, teachers will decide on how to use the information generated. Figure 9.6 depicts this cyclical process. The problem still remains, however, of how to relate this professional process – which could be interpreted as involving nothing more, or less, than the competent marking of pupils' books – to NCA and the idea of national standards. Put differently, how can teachers achieve, in a technically proficient way, dependable assessments of children's attainments in geography?

The proposal that NCA should be part of the normal curriculum experience of children was, as we have seen, explicit in the TGAT report though, as we have also seen, this component was given little encouragement in comparison with the proposed external SATs, or tests. However, the parameters of the 1991 geography curriculum with 5 attainment targets (ATs) and 183 statements of attainment (SoA), were such that it

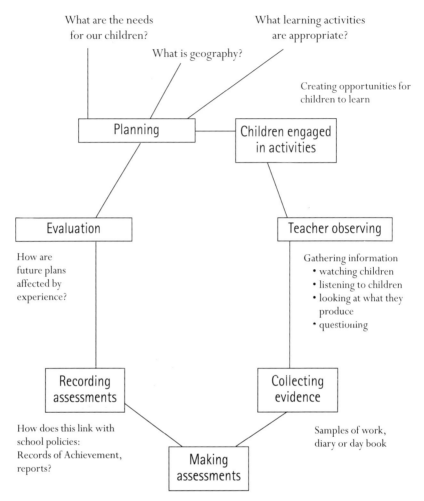

What are the needs
for our children?

What learning activities
are appropriate?

What is geography?

Creating opportunities for
children to learn

Planning

Children engaged
in activities

Evaluation

Teacher observing

How are
future plans
affected by
experience?

Gathering information
• watching children
• listening to children
• looking at what they
produce
• questioning

Recording
assessments

Collecting
evidence

How does this link with
school policies:
Records of Achievement,
reports?

Samples of work,
diary or day book

Making
assessments

Informed judgement based on evidence and NC criteria

Figure 9.6 Assessment: a cyclical process

became accepted by SEAC and the government that assessment which consisted solely of add-on experiences such as tests could not possibly assemble assessment data across the whole curriculum (the 1993 pilot SATs covered just around half the relevant SoA, which, incidentally, seriously compromised the integrity of a supposedly criteria-referenced assessment system). Internal teacher assessment was to supply the rest, but official guidance (SEAC, 1993) did little to assuage teachers' anxieties over how to achieve this, especially as it inferred that pupils should be given the chance to *revisit* specific SoA in order to have the opportunity to improve performance, or to provide 'evidence' appropriate to the whole scope of the statement (see Figure 9.7).

The principle of integrating NCA into day-to-day teaching might be sound, but how to achieve this was a problem to which teachers found no convincing solution. Compromises were reached (as was also the case with the pilot SATs) either on the volume of assessment undertaken or on its quality (see Daugherty and Lambert, 1994).

Once the decision had been taken to express SoA in such *content* terms, proliferation was inevitable. It also brought to a head the more serious technical issues of whether progress in learning in geography *can* be measured in terms of content (see Balderstone and Lambert, 1992).

Similarly, the principles behind the policy to express an assessment-led curriculum in terms of attainment targets (ATs) and statements of attainment (SoA) – that is, to disaggregate achievement into 'domains' or 'components' – was also persuasive in principle. For a curriculum developer, or a writer of course materials, the ATs were useful constructs helping to provide balance and shape to the subject. However, for assessment purposes they presented serious difficulties: were they, as the rhetoric

---

AT1 Geographical Skills: Level 2(d)
Record weather observations over a short period.

AT2 Knowledge and Understanding of Places: Level 6(d)
Compare the general features of the USA, USSR and Japan.

AT3 Physical Geography: Level 4(b)
Describe evidence that materials are eroded, transported and deposited.

AT4 Human Geography: Level 8(c)
Analyse the cause of uneven economic development in and between countries and make an appraisal of actions and policies intended to redress such imbalances.

AT5 Environmental Geography: Level 5(a)
Explain why rivers, lakes, seas and oceans are vulnerable to pollution, and describe ways in which pollution problems have been addressed.

Figure 9.7 Examples of geography statements of attainment from the 1991 Order

tried to insist, discrete *domains* of the subject? If they were, then what was to be assessed of a distinctive nature, say between 'Physical' (AT3) and 'Human' (AT4) geography? Apart from the obvious content differences (and there was a wide range of content variation *within* each would-be domain too, undermining any strong sense of distinctiveness), it is highly questionable whether they possessed inherent properties of sufficient substance to warrant isolating each from the other for assessment purposes.

The assessment problems associated with National Curriculum geography in the first half of the 1990s were, therefore, formidable, containing an interesting mix of practical and theoretical concerns which informed the thinking of the geography advisory group which produced the recommendations for the revised National Curriculum (SCAA, 1994). These proposals advocated a return to a single AT (Geography) with 'level descriptions' in the place of the SoA (see Figure 9.8). The question of whether this reform will make the task of establishing dependable 'teacher assessment' more successful remains to be seen. To be sure, the suggestion that geography is a single unitary domain, however implicit, is less tenable even than the former notion of ATs. But it

---

GEOGRAPHY
LEVEL DESCRIPTIONS

The following level descriptions describe the types and range of performance that pupils working at a particular level should characteristically demonstrate. In deciding on a pupil's level of attainment at the end of the key stage, teachers should judge which description best fits the pupil's performance. Each description should be considered in conjunction with the descriptions for adjacent levels.

Level 3
Pupils describe and make comparisons between the physical and human features of different localities. They offer explanations for the locations of some of those features. They show an awareness that different places may have both similar and different characteristics. They offer reasons for some of their observations and judgements about places. They use skills and sources of evidence to respond to a range of geographical questions.

Level 4
Pupils show their knowledge, understanding and skills in relation to studies of a range of places and themes, at more than one scale. The begin to describe geographical patterns and to appreciate the importance of location in understanding places. They recognise and

---

describe physical and human processes. They begin to show understanding of how these processes can change the features of places, and that these changes affect the lives and activities of people living there. They describe how people can both improve and damage the environment. Pupils draw on their knowledge and understanding to suggest suitable geographical questions for study. They use a range of geographical skills drawn from the Key Stage 2 or Key Stage 3 Programme of Study, and evidence to investigate places and themes. They communicate their findings using appropriate vocabulary.

Level 5

Pupils show their knowledge, understanding and skills in relation to studies of a range of places and themes, at more than one scale. They describe and begin to offer explanations for geographical patterns and for a range of physical and human processes. They describe how these processes can lead to similarities and differences between places. Pupils describe ways in which places are linked through movements of goods and people. They offer explanations for ways in which human activities affect the environment and recognise that people attempt to manage and improve environments. Pupils identify relevant geographical questions. Drawing on their knowledge and understanding, they select and use appropriate skills, from the Key Stage 2 or Key Stage 3 Programme of Study, and evidence to help them investigate places and themes. They reach plausible conclusions and present their findings both graphically and in writing.

Level 6

Pupils show their knowledge, understanding and skills in relation to a wide range of studies of places and themes, at various scales. They explain a range of physical and human processes. They describe ways in which processes operating at different scales create geographical patterns and lead to changes in places. They describe and offer explanations for different approaches to managing environments and appreciate that different approaches have different effects on people and places. Drawing on their knowledge and understanding, pupils identify relevant geographical questions and suggest appropriate sequences of investigation. They select and make effective use of a wide range of skills, from the Key Stage 3 Programme of Study, and evidence in carrying out investigations. They present conclusions that are consistent with the evidence.

Level 7

Pupils show their knowledge, understanding and skills in relation to a wide range of studies of places and themes, at various scales. They describe the interactions within and between physical and human processes. They show how these interactions create geographical patterns and contribute to change in places and patterns. They show understanding that many factors influence decisions made about places, and use this to explain how places change. They appreciate that people's lives and environment in one place are affected by actions and events in other places. They recognise that human actions may have unintended environmental consequences and that change sometimes leads to conflict. With growing independence, pupils draw on their knowledge and understanding to identify geographical questions, establish a sequence of investigation, and select and use accurately a wide range of skills, from the Key Stage 3 Programme of Study, and evidence. They are beginning to reach substantiated conclusions.

Source: SCAA (1995) *Geography in the National Curriculum,* HMSO

Figure 9.8 Geography level descriptions: the great majority of pupils in Key Stage 3 (11 to 14-year-olds) are expected to perform within the range of levels 3–7, shown here

does have the benefit of simplicity: in the former system teachers had the task of establishing progression, perhaps spuriously, under five headings, whereas now only one, holistic series of steps is required. This also conveniently overcomes the technical difficulty of how to aggregate attainment levels from separate domains to make a single subject level for reporting purposes; a single AT, or domain, requires that the assessments themselves are made in the round, or 'synoptically' as SCAA describes it (SCAA, 1994:i), almost certainly over a period of time, but not atomistically, requiring some form of *post hoc* aggregation procedure which could have been further complicated by having different weightings for each domain.

Research conducted in the early 1980s revealed, in the context of 16+ examinations (a prelude to the GCSE), the difficulty in achieving a clear profile of the performance of candidates at any one grade level in the examination (Massey, 1983). Such findings cast serious doubts on the feasibility of describing 'grade-related criteria' for the new GCSE examinations. Nevertheless, such criteria were written for A, C and F grades, although – probably for the reasons that Massey identified – these have not acquired a prominent place in teachers' minds. On the other hand, broad criteria have been used successfully in order to grade coursework. This has not become an exact science and has depended on an external moderation process in order to provide an acceptable level of reliability to teachers' judgements.

Level descriptions such as those in the revised geography curriculum offer the prospect of a similar process. They are not binary 'switches' as the earlier SoA seemed to be – that is, detailed statements against which we were to judge pass or fail according to the evidence presented to us by pupils. They are more 'best-fit' guidelines by which, over a period of time and on the basis of a range of evidence presented in a variety of modes and contexts, we can place pupils at an appropriate level. The evidence assessed may not have covered all possible aspects of a level and will often display an unsettling variety of particular strengths and weaknesses between pupils. The proposals recognised this and, in a realistic move to eradicate or relax real or imagined hurdles to reported progress, they required teachers to examine performance in relation to the level descriptions only intermittently:

> We have concluded that it is the programmes of study which should guide the planning, teaching and day-to-day assessment of pupils' work. The essential function of the level descriptions is to assist in the making of summary judgements about pupils' achievements as a basis for reporting at the end of a key stage.
>
> SCAA, 1994:i

This note was not included in the final geography Orders (SCAA, 1995).

The School Curriculum and Assessment Authority (SCAA) appears, then, to make a distinction between day-to-day 'marking' and 'teacher assessment', the latter being more summative in nature. This may yet prove to be a useful distinction, but it is difficult to imagine such summative judgements being accurately applied without regular informal assessments (on which the summative judgements will be based) also set in the framework of the level descriptions. This is entirely plausible and could serve to enhance the diagnostic role of 'marking'. Gradually, teachers will adapt their interpretations of pupils' work *so that* the system of levels makes sense (Wiliam, 1993:343). It is likely that a 'canonical' interpretation of level descriptions will emerge as more experience is gained and a kind of 'case law' is accumulated. It is perhaps this process which prompted Angoff's remark that just beneath the surface of any criterion-referenced assessment lies a norm-referenced set of assumptions (Angoff, 1974, referred to in Wiliam, *ibid*:342).

The process being outlined here depends on teachers sharing with each other their interpretations of pupils' work. There needs to be more than mark lists and summary comments passed around, but unlike the GCSE there is unlikely to be a funded moderation system put in place. It seems, therefore, that the pupil portfolio could play a very significant role. This is an occasionally updated selection of pupils' best work which will form a useful record of evidence, not to 'prove' a particular level of attainment, but to indicate the grounds on which the level has been judged to be appropriate. The portfolio, which to remain manageable need never contain more than, say, five or six pieces of work, could follow the pupil through the school and form a crucial record to pass on to new teachers and for use at parents' evenings. Managing portfolios in this kind of regime could become a termly or half-termly classroom activity for pupils and a regular item on departmental meeting agendas, and it is through this process that a 'case law' will begin to build. In this way we have the makings of a meaningful curriculum-integrated assessment regime. To enable *national* standards to be interpreted, understood and applied through such a system will, however, require substantial central support.

Conclusion

The teacher assessment regime being proposed here puts a premium on professional artistry. The assessment process, in other words, is not an exact, 'hard' science and resembles much more closely a 'softer' art form in which judgements are always contingent on new information and perspectives. Reduced to its absolute fundamentals, assessment is concerned with making a dependable judgement of a pupil's *performance*. This judgement is the basis on which we extrapolate the pupil's level of *attainment* in the subject. This in turn, we assume, relates to the child's *ability*, but we have learned enough about the complexities of the teaching and learning interface to know that the relationship is not a simple one. NCA does not directly measure children's 'ability', but it can serve teachers in getting to know what circumstances enable pupils to perform well, what blocks or hinders them, what helps them make progress, and so on. Much of this professional activity may look like 'marking'; teachers do, and will continue to, mark pupils' work. But it will be substantially more technically proficient than that which often passed for marking in former times. It will be more than checking for work done. It will be targeted in accordance with both curriculum criteria and the needs of individual learners. Teachers' judgements (the marks) will be guided by assessment criteria specified by teachers which themselves will relate to the national framework set out by the level descriptions. These level descriptions look to be more suggestive of assessment objectives (the balance of knowledge, understanding and skills) than the original statements of attainment, and this is helpful.

It remains to be seen whether the ten-level (subsequently reduced to eight-level) 'national grid' will have currency in geography; that is, whether it assists in the process of assessing progress between the ages of 5 and 14. Daugherty (1995) has expressed some doubts, but in their serious attempt to find out, geography teachers are likely to continue to learn a great deal more about children learning and how to structure the curriculum with appropriate learning and assessment opportunities. They are likely to improve yet further their technical ability in making criteria-referenced assessments without being dazzled by the temptation of simple (or over-elaborate) mechanistic solutions based on the myth of objective, externally set standards applied, in Matthew Arnold’s (1870) phrase, via ‘a series of spasmodic efforts’.

BIBLIOGRAPHY

Andrews, R. (1994) *International Dimensions of the National Curriculum*, Trentham Books.

Angoff, W.H. (1974) ‘Criterion-referencing, norm-referencing and the SAT’, *College Board Review*, 92:2–5.

Balderstone, D. and Lambert, D. (eds) (1992) *Assessment Matters*, Geographical Association.

Barber, M. (1994) *The Making of the 1944 Education Act*, Cassell Educational.

Bennetts, T. (1981) ‘Progression in the geography curriculum’, in Walford, R. (ed.) *Signposts for Geography Teaching*, Longman.

(1994) ‘Reflections on the development of geography in the National Curriculum’, in Walford, R. and Machon, P. (eds) *Challenging Times: Implementing the National Curriculum in Geography*, Cambridge Publishing Services.

Black, P. (1993) ‘The shifting scenery of the National Curriculum’, in O’Hear, P. and White, J. (eds) *Assessing the National Curriculum*, Paul Chapman Publishing.

Boardman, D. (1988) *The Impact of a Curriculum Project: Geography for the Young School Leaver*, University of Birmingham.

Daugherty, R. (1990) ‘Assessment in the geography curriculum’, *Geography*, 75(4):289–301.

(1992) ‘The role of assessment in geographical education: a comparative analysis’, in Hill, D. (ed.) *International Perspectives on Geographical Education*, Center for Geographic Education, University of Colorado at Boulder.

(1995) *National Curriculum Assessment: A Review of Policy, 1988–1994*, Falmer.

(forthcoming) ‘Assessment in geographical education’, in Williams, M. (ed.) *Understanding Geographical and Environmental Education*, Cassell.

Daugherty, R. and Lambert, D. (1994) ‘Teacher assessment and geography in the National Curriculum’, *Geography*, 79(4):339–49.

Daugherty, R. *et al.* (1991) *GCSE in Wales*, Welsh Office Education Department.

Dearing, R. (1994) *The National Curriculum and its Assessment: Final Report*, SCAA.

DES (1991) *Geography in the National Curriculum (England)*, HMSO.

DES/WO (1988) *Task Group on Assessment and Testing: A Report*, HMSO.

Dowgill, P. and Lambert, D. (1992) 'Cultural literacy and school geography', *Geography*, 77(2):143–51.

Gipps, C. (1990) *Assessment: A Teacher's Guide to the Issues*, Hodder and Stoughton.

Goldstein, H. (1991) *Assessment in Schools: An Alternative Framework,* Education and Training Paper No. 5, Institute for Public Policy Research.

Harlen, W., Gipps, C., Broadfoot, P. and Nuttall, D. (1992) 'Assessment and the improvement of education', *The Curriculum Journal*, 3(3):215–30.

Hickman, G., Reynolds, J. and Tolley, H. (1973) *A New Professionalism for a Changing Geography*, Schools Council.

Hirsch, E.D. (1987) *Cultural Literacy: What Every American Needs to Know*, Houghton Mifflin.

Independent, The (1988) Letter from Paul Gray (Prime Minister's Private Secretary) to Tom Baker (Education Secretary's Private Secretary), 10 March.

Lambert, D. (1990) *Geography Assessment*, Cambridge University Press.
 (1994) 'The National Curriculum: what shall we do with it?', *Geography*, 79(1):65–76.

Lambert, D. and Daugherty, R. (1993) 'Teacher assessment: a snapshot of practice', *Teaching Geography*, 18(3):113–15.

Lambert, D. and Purnell, K. (1994) 'International testing in geography: comparing students' achievements within and between countries', *Assessment in Education*, 1(2):167–79.

Lawton, D. (1992) 'Whatever happened to the TGAT Report?', in Gipps, C. (ed.) *Developing Assessment for the National Curriculum*, Kogan Page.

Marsden, W. (1976) *Evaluating the Geography Curriculum*, Oliver and Boyd.

Massey, A.J. (1983) 'Grades and performance in 16+ geography', *CORE*, 7(1):F8,C5.

Nuttall, D. (1989) 'National Assessment: Will Reality Match Aspirations?', paper delivered as part of the conference 'Testing Times', organised by Macmillan Education, 8 March 1989.

Phillips, M. (1991) 'Fiddling in the laboratory', *The Guardian*, 22 November.

SCAA (1994) *Geography: Draft Proposals*, May, HMSO.
 (1995) *Geography in the National Curriculum*, HMSO

SEAC (1991) *Coursework: Learning from GCSE Experience*, School Examinations and Assessment Council.
 (1992) *Geography Standard Assessment Tasks: Key Stage 1*, School Examinations and Assessment Council.

(1993) *Pupils' Work Assessed*, School Examinations and Assessment Council.

SEC (1986) *Policy and Practice in School-based Assessment*, Working Paper 3, Secondary Examinations Council.

(undated) *Managing GCSE Coursework in Schools and Colleges*, Working Paper 6, Secondary Examinations Council.

Shepard, L.A. (1992) 'Commentary: what policy makers who mandate tests should know about the new psychology of intellectual ability and learning', in Gifford, B.R. and O'Connor, M.C. (eds) *Changing Assessments: Alternative Views of Aptitude, Achievement and Instruction*, Kluwer.

Stiggins, R.J. (1992) 'Two disciplines of educational assessment', paper given at the Education Commission of the States Assessment Conference, Boulder, Colorado, USA, June 1992.

Sunday Times (1994) Hymas, C. and Cohen, J. 'Lost for Words: the scandal of children who never learned to read', *Sunday Times,* 12 June:13.

Sutton, R. (1991) *Assessment: A Framework for Teachers*, NFER/Nelson.

Wiliam, D. (1993) 'Validity, dependability and reliability in National Curriculum assessment', *The Curriculum Journal*, 4(3):335–50.

SECTION FOUR | Research and Research Methods

Research in geography education is sometimes thought to be problematic and open to critique. One area for criticism might be that there is simply too little research in geography education; funding for research is limited generally and usually available only for areas of the curriculum regarded by funding bodies to be essential. The main group of people who undertake research in geographical education in the UK are students, like those taking the Master of Arts course in Geographical Education at the University of London Institute of Education, who are required to complete a dissertation or thesis. The research is therefore likely to be personal, undertaken in order to enhance qualifications, and constrained by time and cost.

These characteristics may influence the style of the research, which is more often 'soft' than 'hard', illuminative rather than quantified, and therefore does not always have the ability to offer predictive qualities. Most of the research is small-scale and tends to focus on case studies so that the data gathering will actually be manageable in the time available to the researcher, who is normally a practising full-time teacher. There is a lack of large-scale research that is likely to offer the kind of data from which findings can be generalised to the whole population.

Too few completed research projects are published. There are not enough examples of promising research being followed up, either by taking the earlier research to provide *a priori* ideas for further research, or simply by replication in new places, at other times, by different researchers.

Teachers tend to be sceptical of the value of research and have too little time to take note of it, especially when what is published is in relatively inaccessible journals or books. The educational revolutionary can tactically ignore such research and experience as does exist, in order to carry through reforms – as we have witnessed to our cost in recent years.

This final section of the book offers a more considered view than this of the value of research. The authors, each with a commitment to research, explore its significance for pupils and teachers, for the way teachers and students interrelate, and for their learning in geography.

Working from her experience over many years as a researcher in her own right and a supervising tutor for other people's research, Frances Slater provides a professional view of the research output of the Geography Section of the Institute of Education. She discusses classifications and groupings of research, and selects three 'research paradigms' – positivist (scientific) research, interpretative research, and action research – to provide a framework for her critical review. In her conclusion, she reflects on the overlapping nature of ideologies and the way in which our frameworks for classification 'dissolve and re-form' over time.

Michael Naish focuses in on one of Slater's research paradigms, action research. He draws out certain characteristics of this genre from a collection of examples of completed research. He then moves on to trace the origins and development of action research, before discussing how it is undertaken. Some problems associated with this research approach are considered. In conclusion, he points up the significance of action research as a means of professional enhancement.

In the final chapter, Anthony Ghaye takes these ideas further in his autobiographical account of his experiences of improving practice through research. In doing this, he develops and broadens our understanding of what it means to be involved in action research, or, in his expression, 'practitioner research'. Anthony's basic premise is that there is a close relationship between the way he thinks and the way he acts. If we apply that to ourselves, it follows that reflection on the way we think is important if we are to develop our own responsibility for our approaches to tackling professional problems and challenges.

In tracing his journey as a practitioner researcher, Anthony illuminates important ideas about children learning and the complex interrelationship between teacher and learner. He also proposes significant questions for the teacher who wishes to research her or his own practice in order to improve children's learning and enhance the quality of that relationship.

Anthony ends with a call for more writing of this nature, setting out to reflect a 'discourse of lived cultures' based on sustained analysis of pedagogy and understanding of the political and cultural nature of our situation as teachers.

10 Illustrating research in geography education

Frances Slater

A departmental focus

People come with their own experience, interests, priorities and ways of seeing to undertake a piece of research in geography education within the context of a higher degree. In this chapter, I attempt to give a sense of the range and styles of research which students, most often practising geography teachers, have realised in one department. This is an illustration of the research produced for either an MA in geography education, or the more recent MEd in Educational Studies with a major in geography education, or a PhD focused on geography education.

I have chosen to try to put together a montage of the work of the department I know best, and one which in the last twenty-five years or so has produced a goodly proportion of the published and unpublished research in geography education in the United Kingdom and elsewhere.

I am immediately aware of how that seems to be defining research and what is being left out in terms of worldwide definition and product – a good deal, in a number of senses.

WHAT IS LEFT OUT

First, I am leaving out the work which beginning teachers, and teachers in their early years of teaching, do in their learning process. By inspiration, trial and error, from example and suggestions, beginning teachers experiment with teaching geography to children and young adults at all ranges of abilities. They read, talk and reflect. They search for ideas, models and resources. They work in a context and work themselves into a context. They accept and reject and refine. They prepare lesson plans and curriculum units, and complete other assignments which bring together geography as an academic discipline and geography as an educational endeavour.

We do not generally in any strong sense accept this experience of searching and re-searching processes as research to be recorded. To put it another way, we may be somewhat weak in our research in geography education, as in other disciplines, in encouraging the recording and the structuring of personal experience by those undergoing the experience. To some extent this is partially redressed where diary-keeping or log-keeping is encouraged by some departments and disciplines for various reasons, usually as a key to developing the reflective practitioner. Inevitably, then, I leave out of this chapter what is not actually recorded as research but which I know – from conversation with students and from the evidence of their assignment writing – to be a process of research. It is interesting that Tony Ghaye's initial paragraphs in Chapter 12 add to that evidence.

SEARCHING AND RE-SEARCHING

I also leave out any account of the research that is done by those of us employed in higher education and which I could have partially included in an account of the research of a department. Had I chosen to review the personal and funded research of even one department, I would have rapidly come up against the problem of drawing a line between research and scholarship. I leave out not only the staff departmental research, in the more narrowly accepted meaning of the term, but to some extent writing and research of the reflective mode also – but not entirely, since some student dissertations and theses have elements of the reflectively investigative.

Definitions of research begin to emerge from my sense of what I am leaving out and what I shall soon begin to review and give an account of. People come to undertake a piece of research out of something contained within their experience, an experience which then becomes particularly focused and organised in an explicit way. It is about a process of searching and re-searching experience which is usually thought to be rather outside ourselves, though paradoxically it has at least to be part of ourselves, our experience and observation if we are to identify it as a 'problem' to be researched. It certainly becomes part of ourselves in the process and final-ly the product. What we define as research is open to question, as the development of consciously different ideologies and methodologies like action research, and more recently accepted techniques like diary-keep-ing, attest to. Research as it is generally accepted seems to be defined by a deliberately selected or chosen starting point, a set period of time in which the study is undertaken using accepted frameworks and techniques, and a point at which we say the investigation, the thinking, the focused effort, is finished, handed in, written up.

Research is what researchers do

Let's say at the level of a working definition that research in geography education is what researching students have produced (some will hear an echo of 'geography is what geographers do'). Such a definition allows me to illustrate, from among a number of dissertations, a version of the meaning and light and shade in the phrase 'doing research'.

In earlier days of the MA in geography education, research was classified into work belonging to philosophical, historical, sociological, psychological and general curriculum concerns. Those categories are still useful for revealing the academic context, focus and purpose of research. Certainly they are rather clear-cut areas and there are not many problems in assigning dissertations to the appropriate category. A more recent development attendant upon developments in thinking within educational research generally is to classify research according to its ideological/methodological stance. Since the early 1980s I have been aware of students taking up a research stance more consciously, and explicitly identifying it and writing themselves into its context. As a light aside, one might be permitted to mention that this may or may not follow on from the publication of a much-quoted and accessible book on research methods in education by Cohen and Manion (1980).

I deliberately write 'ideological/methodological' since it seems to me that useful and real as the distinctions are in educational research, the different stances are often embraced with some passion, and views can become very fixed on the absolute worthwhileness of one stance over another. Useful shorthand terms like *hard* (scientific and quantitative) and *soft* (illuminative, qualitative) have been coined to describe two different approaches. I was somewhat surprised to find myself berated when I used the latter term, 'soft', about ten years ago to describe a research approach to a well-known case-study researcher. My purpose had been to convey the fact that our students were working in the paradigm. She objected very vehemently at such terminology, taking it as a criticism. 'You try doing some', I was told. I then realised to what an extent research stances had become ideological positions, matters of belief not only about appropriate views and methods, but also about absolutely right views and methods to save educational research from itself. It is surely very helpful, interesting and important to have different views of research and its purposes and goals, and to choose appropriately from among them. Having refined purposes and goals, then to move into a research position seems to be a sensible way of ordering activity, as long as this is open to critical discussion. I say this at the risk of appearing to be conservative and not open to change. I do not think this to be the case. I believe 'hard' and 'soft' offer different ways into problems and produce qualitatively different kinds of understanding. If a choice is made to adopt the scientific paradigm or vision with its methodological framework and techniques, the understanding outcomes will be of a different order from that produced by action research. And, for the meantime, the latter seems to have excited teachers and helped them to look at their practice, evaluate it and change it. The development of teachers as researchers as well as reflective practitioners must be something to be valued.

I have mentioned two research paradigms or viewpoints or ideologies but that is to leave out a third category – the interpretative – and perhaps even a fourth – the postmodern. Students find useful the summary sketches (Figure 10.1a–c) of research positions by Bassey (1990), as indeed I do. A postmodern sketch is added (Figure 10.1d). I wish to emphasise that the sketches are for debate and discussion and not necessarily for believing. They emphasise the assumed relationships between reality and researchers. Scientific investigations (Figure 10.1a) are held to treat the world as objective. Interpretative and action researchers (Figure 10.1b and c) see reality as subjective, and depending on interpretation and purpose their procedures for examining and organising observations are also different. Postmodern research (Figure 10.1d) goes beyond these in its emphasis on multiple realities. I have tabulated the aims, methodology and techniques of the research paradigms in Figure 10.2. A postmodern researcher, while inhabiting the same world as you and me, seems to be questioning all established categories and concepts, descriptions and languages, to unpack and deconstruct presently received

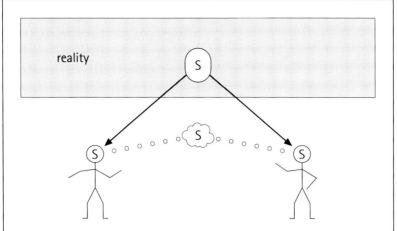

Positivist researchers seek, systematically, critically and self-critically, to describe and explain phenomena which they take to be 'out there in reality' and which therefore they can study without disturbing. One positivist researcher will have the same perceptions of phenomena as another. In this diagram, sense data (S) is received from 'out there' by the two researchers, both of whom perceive an 'S' and store it in their memories. When they describe it, the same thought is conjured up by both.

(a) Data collection by positivist researchers

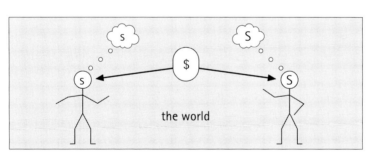

Interpretive researchers seek systematically, critically and self-critically, to describe and interpret phenomena which they take to be in the same world that they inhabit and which therefore may be disturbed when they try to investigate it. One interpretive researcher may not have quite the same perceptions of phenomena as another. In this diagram, data from the '$' is received by the two researchers, one of whom perceives it as an 's' and the other as an 'S', and as such it is stored in their memories. When they describe it, one has the thought 's' and the other the thought 'S'.

(b) Data collection by interpretive researchers

Figure 10.1 Research paradigms sketched

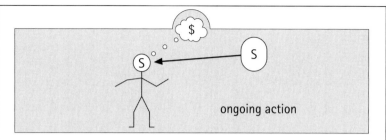

Action researchers seek systematically, critically and self-critically, to describe and interpret the phenomena of the action in which they are engaged, in order to improve it. In this diagram the researcher, having described an 'S', changes it into an 'S' – which s/he deems more worthwhile – and thus changes the ongoing action.

(c) Data collection by action researchers

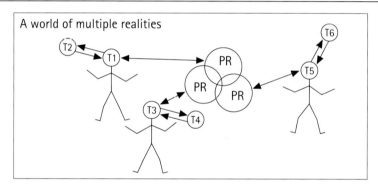

Postmodern researchers draw attention to the notion that their research text is not simply a faithful representation of a reality outside the text. They seek to write research that is 'reflexive' – recognising that since the activity of the researcher always influences what is known, nothing can be known except through those activities. Postmodern research tends to highlight that our descriptions of reality are in fact inscriptions, by using language which avoids the appearance of an objective meaning. Data is regarded as material for telling a story where the challenge becomes to *vivify* interpretation rather than to 'support' or 'prove'. Postmodern researchers recognise that all research methods have a political content and that who speaks for whom becomes a central question. Postmodern researchers try to break down the distinction between researcher and researched by producing a collaborative analysis that avoids imposing the researcher's understanding of reality.

In this diagram, the researchers have perceived realities (PR) and produce texts (T) which seek to record that interpretation. The researcher is aware of the 'reflexive' nature of his/her account and attempts to deconstruct the text.

(d) Data handling by postmodern researchers

Sources: (a)–(c) Bassey, 1990; (d) author in discussion with John Morgan

knowledge and set up new descriptions of ways of seeing. This appears to go beyond the action researcher's desire to engage in change at a fairly practical 'let's make a difference' level.

It is almost certainly accurate to say that of the topics chosen by our MA students up until the 1993/94 academic year all fall into one or more of the first three research stances described above. To greater and lesser degrees it should be noted that apparently neutral and/or biased and critical voices may be adopted within each of the stances. Scientific, so-called objective work, let us remember, as well as interpretative work and action research, can be the springboard for critical and positive

Framework	Aim	Methodology	Techniques
Scientific	To test relationships among variables, to understand interrelationships, to describe, explain, predict	Inductive or deductive, hypothesis formulation	Experimental, testing, pre-test, post-test formulae, hypothesis testing, observation and survey
Interpretative	To find meaning, to illuminate meaning in written and spoken accounts, past and present events and situations and interactions among people, to portray, to paint a picture	Anthropological, ethnographic, phenomenological, case study, context respecting	Observation, note-taking, interviewing, (structured and unstructured, semi-structured), conversation, diary-keeping, illuminative descriptions, thick descriptions
Action	To effect an improvement by action within a situation alone or with others	Critical stance, working within a situation	Acting, observing, refining and replanning
Postmodern	To highlight the 'constructedness' or contingency of knowledge, to draw attention to the hidden agendas of knowledge claims	Working within a situation, case study, ethnographic, critical stance, self-reflexive, foregrounding of researcher subjectivity	Experiments with writing that blur the boundary between facts and fiction, textual analysis, collaborative research and collective authorship of research texts

Figure 10.2 Research paradigms tabulated: '...no approach prescribes nor rejects any particular methods' (Bell, 1993)

comments; I think it rather important to remember this, as competing research viewpoints make their claims for their particular orientations and strengths.

THREE EXAMPLES

I take as an introductory example of our departmental research three recent dissertations, by Acheson, Hemingway and Dunkerley respectively, which may be seen to fall into each of the three research categories sketched by Bassey (1990) and generously interpreted. A dissertation by David Acheson (1992, 1994) may be classified as a piece of traditional positivist research. David takes as his study population – to use a term from positive research – a selection of school texts for which, using content analysis, he identifies viewpoints. He aims to discover what viewpoints dominate and as a result of his analysis he is able to isolate seven viewpoints and two concerns, the green and the feminist. Another person analysing the same texts, using the same key words in content analysis, would come up with very similar results. The study falls within the category of replicable, verifiable and so-called objective research in the positivist tradition. Into this David writes his own context and views, to a certain extent.

A second dissertation written in the same year by Judith Hemingway (1992, 1994) is an analytically interpretative exercise. Judith chose to delve into accounts of anarchism and libertarian pedagogy and the historical connections between them, in order to understand better their possible contributions to geography and teaching. It is perhaps surprising that this topic had not been tackled earlier. Now, it fills a gap. In examining the work of notable anarchists, Judith seeks to understand their thinking on pedagogy, and attitudes to children, and then relates these to the aims of geography teaching. The differences between libertarian pedagogy and progressive education are described, and an account is given of experiments in libertarian education. Within anarchism and libertarian education, it is noted how place and people's connections to place are given importance. In a final section of the essay these connections are made more explicit. Judith Hemingway's interpretation of anarchism and libertarian pedagogy to some extent knocks down stereotypes of those concepts and related ideas and draws in more positive connotations than those perhaps commonly held.

The art of interpretation

Judith's research is an investigation in a strongly analytical mode. She is analysing the meaning of concepts and people's writing around certain ideas. The art of interpretation is at its centre. At this centre it is acknowledged that how we read a text or a situation is a subjective business and may not accord with another person's reading of the same document or event. People can approach research which is essentially interpretative in different ways using different frameworks. Some take an historical perspective and may investigate, for example, an aspect of geography in primary schools over a number of decades. Another person may take a comparative approach and analyse the aims and objectives of geography in different school systems. Still others adopt philosophical approaches and perhaps try to evaluate meaning of trends, concepts or positions in geography. This often happens at time of change as a student tries to make sense of new thought. More recently, interpretative research has described experiences of people in their workplaces and sought to elucidate and illuminate meanings grounded in workplace contexts. All these endeavours search deeper and wider perspectives and theoretical insights on their chosen topic. All want to understand something better by interpreting or reinterpreting it. All, in essence, search for meaning rather than generalisation. It should be noted that I am using here a broad definition of interpretative research and not one confined to recent definitions. I deliberately use, too, *interpretative* rather than *interpretive* to signal the wider meaning I am using. I am not restricting the term to case study and classroom research, as sometimes happens.

Today, running alongside positivist, interpretative and the beginnings of postmodern research, action research has established itself as a valuable stance in geography education from which to undertake research (Fien, 1992). However, action research is seen by some to be the only really 'with-it' and valid way of tackling educational research. It is described as the research stance which gets into classrooms, it describes the teachers as teacher and researcher. Action researchers participate in and initiate action in order to try to effect some improvement in the educational enterprise. Their aim is to be part of the research, to understand better what is going on, to bring about change and to evaluate that change. To bring about change in the process of teaching and researching is what makes research worthwhile for them. It is what validates the research. In action research it is not generalisations which are sought but description of the singular, the particular, the unique. Since, however, action research is subject to a chapter of its own in this book (see Chapter 11), I will not go into more detail here but rather describe a piece of action research written up in the same year as Acheson's and Hemingway's work.

Choosing a case to study

Having absorbed the action research stance, the characteristics of which she enumerates in her essay, Susan Dunkerley (1992, 1994) chose her case to study. She then set to work with and was involved with a school staff to facilitate and effect change in the geography curriculum as required by the geography National Curriculum. In her essay she tells the story of her involvement, a story which contributes to our knowledge of the process of curriculum change at the same time as her work in the school contributed to curriculum development. Once more the difficulties of changing curricula without providing sufficient or additional resources of time, personnel and materials are demonstrated. The pressures created by change are clear in the instances recounted. It is generally accepted that action research adopts a critical voice. Susan Dunkerley does not take up a strongly critical stance in her research using her own personal voice. She adopts as a stylish device the use of quotations from educational daily and weekly newspapers being published at the same time as the research was in progress. The quotations are interspersed with her own writing as a chorus which may be heard as critical and ironic. It reads effectively. One hears the gap between reality and criticism. (See also Chapter 11.)

RESEARCH CLUSTERS

The three dissertations I have just described and classified within contrasting research paradigms happen to have been written up in the same academic year. Looking back over the years, it is possible to find clusters of research on similar topics which may be classified as positivist and interpretative. There are fewer examples of action research *explicitly* and *consciously* adopted, though people's *intentions* have often been of an action research nature in that they hoped to effect change as a result of their investigation. And it seems to me they may well have succeeded. Interviewing teachers on, say, mixed ability teaching may have brought about a reflection and a rethinking which caused people to see things differently and perhaps changed their aims and/or practices and outcomes. Dissertations in a *conscious* and *explicit* action research paradigm are likely to increase, however. It will be interesting, in addition, to learn in which year a genuinely postmodern piece of research occurs.

BLURRING BOUNDARIES

Having established that there are distinct categories of research endeavour, I could now begin to blur those boundaries and point out that being aware of change, wanting to understand change – changing ideas, concepts and practices – has always been a characteristic of the content of conversations one has had with students. They very often come to undertake a piece of research because they see the topic they are beginning to grapple with as something which is or has changed and so is significant and worthwhile for their own understanding as teachers, their understanding of children, their understanding of schools and their understanding of newer or even older ideas and concepts. In the general task and associated pressure of teaching and supervising research students, one has not systematically gathered data on initial motivations and interest, stated aims and objectives, changing and developing ideas and stances. I have missed that research opportunity and have only recollections to draw upon. A belief that the research will be involved in bringing about changes in themselves or in other elements in the education process is present, and certainly most students hope that their work will in some way make a difference.

I will resist the desire to further blur boundaries, however, and continue to describe another cluster of dissertations. I should say that I have no method I can make explicit for selecting the dissertations, apart from the fact that they illustrate a range of methodologies. The ones I mention here I simply know perhaps better than some others, or I have known the writers better than others of our students, or I have been more particularly interested in the topics. I am conscious of not being able to review all the research produced and so some important work is left aside. Perhaps there will yet be opportunities for placing it in the 'published world'.

Teaching mixed ability

Three more dissertations which may be contrasted and compared like the three by Acheson, Hemingway and Dunkerley are focused on aspects of mixed ability teaching. Mixed ability teaching has been a widespread practice in the educational systems of England and Wales over the last twenty-five years, and is associated with the rise of the comprehensive school. It is now being questioned but I leave aside that aspect here.

AN EXPERIMENTAL APPROACH

J.C. Maton (1975) was interested in effective methods/strategies for teaching mixed ability classes. He found a lack of conclusive evidence on the effectiveness of different teaching methods used in mixed ability classes and stated that 'At present our knowledge of the effectiveness of different teaching methods is limited to observation' (p.19). A survey of research on mixed ability teaching is followed in his dissertation by a summary of selected research findings in classroom methods in geography. If the first indicated an inconclusiveness, the second pointed to the need for teachers to maintain verbal control in the classroom, and to verbal interaction between teacher and pupils being important in promoting factual retention and understanding by pupils. The surveys provide Maton with a context for his research and at the same time allow him to narrow his investigation to a comparison of two methods which he designates as (1) the conventional secondary teacher's discussion method and (2) the worksheet method supplemented by verbal interaction both with individual pupils and the whole class.

To gauge the effectiveness of the two methods, Maton adopted an experimental approach. In other words, he placed himself within the scientific paradigm, sometimes called the agricultural, engineering paradigm. If pesticide A is spread over one crop of wheat of variety Y, is the yield higher than in the case of a second field of variety Y which is not treated? A whole series of 'what ifs' can then arise. What if the wheat variety is not exactly the same in the untreated field? What if the physical conditions experienced are not exactly the same? What if indeed the incidence of pests is different? And so on. Experimental methods are logically tight and characterised by 'controls'. An early example of experimental research in geography education is that by H. Verduin-

Muller, who investigated the learning effects of two versions of a film (Verduin-Muller, 1964, 1991). More recent examples of experimental research have been published where contributors world-wide give accounts of their work (Schrettenbrunner and Van Westrhenen, 1992).

In the field or in the classroom, there is a need to control variables which might intervene between the variables under examination to affect test results. John Maton, fully aware of the need for control and reducing differences between classes and teachers, set out a summary of his experimental design. Each point made is related to the need to set up as controlled an experiment as possible. Technically speaking the experimental design chosen for the research is known as the 'Post test only control group design', as described by Campbell and Stanley (1966). It takes the form of

$$R \; x \; O_1$$
$$R \quad O_2$$

where R represents a randomly assigned group, x represents the exposure of the group to an experimental variable, the effects of which are to be measured, and O_1 refers to the measurements taken as a result of the effects of the worksheet method, compared with measurement O_2 which represents the test results obtained by the discussion method.

Statistical testing

The experiment is set up so as to make it appropriate for statistical testing, and the test results were subject to a number of tests assuming certain conditions. Statistically significant interaction or difference was found to exist between teachers and methods at the 5% level using an analysis of variance test. Consequently, the results for all the classes using worksheets could be analysed teacher by teacher only. A variance ratio test gave a significant difference between marks obtained under different teachers for the discussion lessons but not for the worksheet lessons.

In a teacher-by-teacher comparison of marks, the marks for only one teacher showed a significant difference, the test scores being higher for his discussion lesson. Otherwise, there was not a statistically significant difference in test scores between discussion and worksheet methods. This suggests that there is a more variable reaction to teachers than to worksheets. In other words, the difference between the variance estimates for the discussion-based lesson marks indicates that individual pupils do significantly better or worse when taught by different teachers. In discussion with the teachers, John Maton found they were not in complete agreement after the experiment as to which method was most appropriate to mixed ability classes. The discussion method was considered to be more successful than worksheets in capturing pupil interest and understanding. Worksheets, on the other hand, offered an 'individualised' approach, where the teacher was free to move around the classroom in order to follow and support the progress of each pupil. The teachers considered that the weakness of the discussion method was to be found in the difficulty of asking questions and providing information which extended the able and at the same time ensured that the less able understood.

A QUALITATIVE APPROACH

I have given a fairly full account of Maton's way of organising his research within the scientific paradigm. In 1984, Michael Milton (1984) investigated mixed ability teaching, again motivated, like Maton, by his own experience. He chose, however, to view, to observe, to look at the activity through case-study methodology – a distinctly qualitative approach to research. McElroy (1980) had been a pioneer of the case-study method in the department as he sought insights into the processes and constraints on school-based curriculum development. His reviewed chapter, like Milton's on the case-study method, provides a sound account of a then developing qualitative methodology which I place within the general category of interpretative research.

Qualitative research, as Milton describes it in his review of the genre, aims to illuminate the area being studied not through the positivist, experimental approach but by preserving context and complexity and assembling data through close contact with the people involved in their setting, classroom or otherwise. Rather than working with hypotheses and statistical tests, case-study researchers aim at observing the totality of a situation with the intention of painting a picture, portraying features for a reader which have become significant to the observer with his or her set of interests. However, the researcher is enjoined to be as detached as possible, to be free of presuppositions, and to come to the research as ready to be open to the event or situation and its contexts as it is humanly possible to be. The researcher becomes an anthropologist for educational purposes – the careful, 'culture-free', considerate, percipient observer. As Milton points out in his review of case-study research, the researcher may be both participant and non-participant observer, getting involved or not in those activities that he or she sets out to observe. No standard methodology characterises case-study research. Observation, interviewing, video recording, field note-taking and document collection may all be important. Discussing the accuracy of an account with informants or others may be used as an approach to triangulation and preserving validity while acknowledging the multi-faceted nature of interpretation. Case-study research aims to illuminate, and this allows a reader to interpret his or her own situation. A classroom case study provides information and description/interpretation but not necessarily generalisation, although hypotheses might develop out of one's reading of a case study.

Key authors

Milton, like others, refers to a number of key authors at that time on case-study method, including Adelman, Burgess, Walker, Elliott, Simons and McElroy (in geography education) and a number of others as he builds up an account of the case-study method, including its key features, strengths and weaknesses, and research techniques. Different writers tend to emphasise and colour aspects differently within the general category of case study. The significance of *interpretation* – the observer interpreting, the reader of the study interpreting, those being observed interpreting – is acknowledged by all, and the elements of subjectivity in the endeavour recognised. These features are seen to be as much strengths as weaknesses in developing the overall picture. The amount of detail in the description of schools, lessons and teachers in Michael Milton's fourth and fifth chapters, where he gives an account of his observations and meetings with teachers in the two schools in which he chose to work, contrast markedly with John Maton's description of statistical tests and levels of significance. This is inevitable given the different stances taken by the researchers. In the case-study research we learn something of the school as a whole – its policies and ethos, and the conduct and development of lessons – though context, it may be emphasised, is not entirely absent from Maton's write-up. Milton in his final chapter presents tentative interpretations in line with case-study philosophy.

DEVELOPMENT OF CASE-STUDY RESEARCH

A third dissertation on mixed ability, by Michael Tompkinson (1987), focuses and refocuses some of the aims and concerns of Maton and Milton. Michael Tompkinson also chooses a case-study approach belonging to that branch of the interpretative paradigm which is situated in classrooms. This research aims to explain actions and interactions by conveying a culturally appropriate understanding of them. Three years on from Milton, it is interesting to note from Tompkinson's review of methodology, a mention of concepts like 'grounded theory' and 'thick descriptions' coming through. It is obvious that case-study research was developing and expanding its language and concepts, justifications and claims, as time went by. While this may be true of all research paradigms, it seems particularly visible in relation to case study as I've observed it in the past twenty years.

Tompkinson added to his two case studies, ten unstructured but not unfocused conversations with teachers, in order to come to some understanding of how teachers talked about their teaching and their approach to mixed ability.

Selection of material is naturally a very marked feature of case-study interpretative research. Along with author description, comment and interpretation, quotations from conversations are included in the research write-up. With the detailed plans and accounts of lessons given in all three dissertations, readers can to a large extent draw their own conclusions and form their own interpretation of the fitness and effectiveness of mixed ability teaching. In both case-study dissertations the researchers withheld any comments of their own until the final chapter. Both stressed the tentativeness of their interpretations, and Michael Tompkinson draws out his general comments by writing a description of the two teachers and their teaching which he had most closely observed. This leaves us to tease out our own understanding of the responses they were making to the mixed ability class.

Environmental concerns

Another group of dissertations – a rather larger group – can be compared in the same way. These dissertations loosely group around environmental concerns. Like Maton, Kelly (1978), within the context of exploring values and attitudes towards the environment, undertook a small-scale empirical study with pupils. A thoroughly scientific pre-test/post-test design was used to evaluate an experiment in teaching environmental problems involving values clarification. The results suggested that some value change took place. Verbal commitment to doing something about environmental problems increased but there was no significant increase in actual commitment to doing anything about the problem.

If I now try to place other dissertations in this group along a line stretching away from the most strictly scientific with its agreed statistically verifiable procedures, then Calland (1973) and Cribb (1981) are a little distant from Kelly. Both, to my mind, adopt a broadly scientific approach. I make a claim for Cribb's work as scientific on the basis that he constructs principles of environmental education which he uses as a yardstick to evaluate environmental education in Hertfordshire schools. Calland's procedure is somewhat similar. He uses categories established by Lynch (1960) to examine children's perceptions of their local environment. Calland's work was to some extent the precursor of a number of dissertations which took findings on children's perceptions from the literature and used established techniques with groups of children whom the researcher was teaching or had contact with. All these dissertations of a behavioural/humanistic geography mould, I classify as scientific in organisation if strongly humanistic in spirit and intention. Diane Simmonds (1982), R. Newham (1985), W.G. Harrisson (1987) and Sharon Pratt (1990) all wrote dissertations around pupils' perceptions. Research philosophies and research methodologies intermix and overlap in these dissertations, and where the term 'case study' is used, it is more a case study meaning a *sample* than a fully developed case-study approach as described and adopted by Milton and Tompkinson, for example.

A more recent dissertation by Cox (1993) in the environmental group, espouses an interpretative, ethnographic methodology on the grounds that in school-based research like his, the distance between 'researcher' and subject is reduced. In contrast to Kelly's pre-test/post-test design, Cox used structured and semi-structured interviews within his overall research design to explore the question: 'To what extent does environmental concern influence the culture and lifestyle of A-level geography students?' The investigation has a scientific feel to it. And yet, as the in-depth interviews with students probe their lifestyles, environmental attitudes and actions and no doubt cause them to reflect on their responses, we are approaching a form of action research at the same time as Martin Cox selects and interprets his findings. Cox draws on all three of the research paradigms I have defined in this essay. He is Kelly writ larger.

AN INTEREST IN VALUES

As might be expected, the environmental interest is often intertwined with an interest in values in geography education. While Kelly worked with children in an experimental way, Hartley's (1980) work may be contrasted methodologically with that of Kelly and Cox. Hartley's dissertation reviews approaches in values education. He reviews and interprets the literature. It is an example of an interpretative survey-type dissertation. Cowie's (1974) earlier work could also be so classified – reviewing, reflecting, and coming up with her understandings and interpretations for the subject of geography in education. Interpretation, a search for meaning, plays its part in the writing-up of all these dissertations whether focused on literature, subject or children. Descriptions and interpretations leading to conclusions and generalisations are characteristic.

Huckle's work (1976) is another which stands as a clear example, like Hemingway's and others already mentioned, of an investigation of a body of literature. In Huckle's case it is literature to do with values, environment and ethics, out of which meaning for geography in education can be drawn. There are many dissertations which fit this description. Some have become rather well-known and have been reported in articles. Cowie (1974), Fien (1978), Henley (1986) and Morgan (1993) are but four examples of reflective, interpretative research. To these four many others could be added including Kilburn's (1974) philosophically oriented enquiry, Hartley's (1980) values review, Gill's (1980) social inequality enquiry, Jones' (1986) work on structuralism – and so the list grows.

Geography teachers do not always choose to examine geographical concepts. They do, for example, look outside the subject and explore ideas of citizenship (Welsh, 1978) and economic understanding (Starkey, 1987). By reference to the dissertations, readers could decide whether they agree with the categories I am adopting. A full listing of the department's dissertations up to 1988 is to be found in Graves *et al.* (1989), and from 1989 to 1994 in Slater (1994).

Just as with interpretative studies, so a further listing of scientific studies having a strong empirical content could be made. One investigating map-using abilities (Walker, 1978), and another on spatial ability and cognition (Tierney, 1985), set up experiments with children from the results of which conclusions are drawn. In structure and intent they are close to Maton and Kelly. As I examine the department's dissertations I debate more uneasily with myself about the strength of a methodological classification. Some dissertations fall strongly within one category or another, while others blur the definitions of scientific, interpretative and action research.

However, I turn now to action research, of which I have already given a working example through Dunkerley's work. I first became acquainted with action research at a practical level when Tony Ghaye (1984) began his PhD work in 1978 and introduced me to the idea of action research and techniques like concept mapping and diary-keeping. These were then passed on to other PGCE and MA students (e.g. Robinson (1986), Ghaye and Robinson (1989) and Dowgill (1989)). Ghaye's account of his research history in Chapter 12 complements the present chapter as a personal account of research aims and styles. I shall now elaborate further on such aims and styles in a general fashion.

Action research oriented studies

In order to do this, I find myself contemplating Graham Butt's (1991) *action* research oriented dissertation, partly because it pleased me that he took up ideas I had long identified as needing research and indeed which I had researched in a preliminary fashion (Slater, 1989). However, I also remember clearly his saying in conversation at an early stage that he wanted his investigation to be characterised by rigour of a *scientific* kind.

Graham Butt researched the question: 'Does audience make a difference to children's writing and learning in geography?' The literature out of which this question arises need not be reviewed here, though of course it is discussed in the dissertation. From his review of the literature Butt, as scientist, frames as a working hypothesis 'that by introducing a wide variety of audiences into their work children will improve their writing, talking and learning in geography'. This hypothesis is subsequently restricted to 'an examination of the effect of audience on some written work'. In order to move on and select a way through the question raised, Butt briefly reviews approaches to research in education and significantly quotes some of the broadest definitions available of action research. He quotes Hopkins (1985) who describes action research as 'a personal attempt at understanding whilst engaged in the process of improvement and reform', and Kemmis (1982) is cited as describing action research as a process of 'self-reflective enquiry'. The ensuing research guided by an hypothesis is a 'personal attempt at understanding'. If we stopped there, probably all research could be seen as action research.

Butt's research methodology and style contains strong elements of scientific, case-study and action research. The classes available for the 'experiment', each making up a 'case to study' and for whom it was conjectured that the experimental work would make a difference to their learning, were split randomly into two groups. The first group experienced what might be called a standard lesson, and the second group was given an audience-centred exercise on a roughly parallel theme.

Presenting results

Once the children's responses are obtained, some style for presenting the children's work has to be adopted. A selection of quotations could have been given, presumably rather in the case-study style of painting a picture and in the manner of Milton, Tompkinson and McElroy. However, scientific lessons learned by the author have an influence here, I think, and the writing is given a 'stronger' frame. A matrix is set up, and children's work is interpreted against certain descriptions characterising the matrix's elements. In addition, examples from the children's work are set alongside and one can read from description to example. Then follow accounts of the lessons and the children's responses. Evaluations and interpretations are offered on all seven lessons, and important further observations made and issues raised. The complexity of examining the initial hypothesis is filled out in the commentary and in the final chapter of conclusions. Butt is prepared to write 'there are indications that by changing the audience for which children write there is a notable effect on the learning process-es they experience'. Finally, he seeks to illuminate and to generalise the strengths and problems arising from providing audience-centred writing.

I think with Butt's dissertation, as with others, we have an example of action research guided by scientific frameworks and supplemented by interpretation and analysis. Butt himself in his dissertation states that he wants to adopt an appropriately flexible style which would accommodate the observation he wanted to undertake, the teaching strategy he wanted to monitor and the evaluation he wanted to make. He considered action research to provide the broadly qualitative context he felt suited the question. His interpretation of action research allowed a scientific framing. When I discussed my interpretation of his research with Graham Butt in the course of writing this chapter, he acknowledged that he felt he had a fairly clear idea of what he wanted to do and how he wanted to do it, and then he went on to think about appropriate research paradigms. I am sure this is not an unusual sequence of events.

Running alongside the task of writing this chapter, I have been reading a dissertation by David Balderstone (1994) which is clearly in the tradition of a mixed framework. He uses the phrase 'controlled action research' (p. 35) to describe his methodology. A very valuable hybrid research tradi-tion is evolving, as theory and practice from different paradigms interact and 'talk' to each other. It reminds one of old debates in teacher educa-tion. It certainly confirms Bell's idea that 'no approach prescribes nor rejects any particular methods'.

TOWARDS ACTION RESEARCH

I believe that a detailed analysis of a number of other dissertations would enable one to find action research elements where researchers work with children to study their learning and their responses, with a view to under-standing better, making a difference, or analysing a situation in order to change it. Dissertations by Rupar (1982), Haile (1988), Bogdin (1980), Owen-Jones (1987) and Palfrey (1984), just to mention a few, could be so classified. Phiri's work for a PhD (see Chapter 7 of this book) is another example of curriculum development as a form of action research.

Then there have been curriculum development exercises undertaken with the express purpose of addressing the problem of the gender imbalance in curriculum materials. Franchi (1987) and Kayes (1992) undoubtedly intended to make a difference both through trialling materials and disseminating them. So surely did Fry (1987) and Lam (1984). The same might be said of Carter (1980) and Okpala (1983) in their evaluations. Indeed, it seems to me that any dissertation which is at heart evaluative, approaches that part of action research which wants to illuminate and improve, to bring about change. Trevor Hones (1988) set out to analyse problems in his department with a view to improvement. The same I think can be said of Brown (1991), Keats (1986), Malindine (1987), Osakwe (1983) or Stephens (1988). If one adopts Fien's (1992) analysis that the 'critical' dimension of critical action research relates to its concern to critique, challenge and change, then these dissertations fall into a category of action research.

MIXED FRAMEWORKS

A recent PhD thesis by Namafe (1992) is another example of a mixed framework investigation, to coin a phrase. Namafe raises questions about attitudes deeply embedded in cultures. I have a hunch that if readers of this chapter were asked to describe floods as friends or enemies, the majority would plump for enemies, recognising floods as hazards troublesome and destructive. Yet Namafe challenges such an interpretation of all floods and brings in evidence from his own culture where floods were or are received as friends. Within a broadly scientific enquiry framework and embedded in a literature review, Namafe interprets and reinterprets attitudes to floods in different cultures. Through a pamphlet and a skeletal video script he gets people to interpret and react to messages about floods. By using this form of data collection and analysis he is seeking to make a difference to the way his respondents and the readers of the thesis view floods. In his conclusion he remodels his original opposing views of floods and suggests a 'both/and' view. Predicated on the action research thread of his thesis is the assumption that university research must be disseminated into the community to modify, challenge or change it. Had the money been available, the skeletal video script would have become a fully formed video and the vehicle for disseminating the message. Namafe's thesis interestingly can cause us to change our perceptions and views of reality. Science, interpretation, and impact or action run alongside each other.

Do our definitions exist?

Some time ago I discussed with David Acheson, Judith Hemingway and Sue Dunkerley the preparation of their respective essays for a departmental research publication (Slater, 1994). As I thought more carefully about their work and the range of dissertations in the department, I was reminded of an earlier situation. Several years ago, I had two PGCE students in one geography department in the same school (Slater, 1988). On each visit, I observed them within an hour or two of each other. This became a stimulus to thinking about the meaning of the concept of teaching style, and I was provoked into thoughts about whether the concept exists as defined or whether the concept can be defined. Perhaps the paper I wrote around the students as I had observed them, and concepts like personality, strategy, class organisation and activities and style, became a word game. I do know that what I wrote was based on experience. I was trying to unravel how unique individuals worked in classrooms and how they played their roles differently using different personalities, different strategies, different activities in different mixes.

It seems reasonably clear that individual differences and particularities exist and general concepts also exist, the one informing the other. The general concepts cannot convey all of the light and shade and complexity of the individual instance. The general concept picks out certain features and helps to focus our thought and observation. We can move between particular and general in a useful way. The general concept stimulated my thinking. Here, one is commenting on one of the functions of language. Words are definitions of experience, but in the very process of codifying they cannot encapsulate all. And as I had asked questions about teaching style and the concepts used to define it alongside research styles expressed in dissertations, I asked again: 'Do our definitions exist?'

OVERLAPPING IDEOLOGIES

I think pondering the question helps soften the rhetoric used by the different stances, points to the overlap among them and strengthens our awareness of the aims and purposes and possible achievements of different research endeavours. Out of this brief and unavoidably selective view of a department's research, classified in the way I have chosen, I think that we are reminded that categories act as conveniences for thinking. These categories, reasonably enough, need to be re-examined from time to time for the evolution of the meanings and their appropriateness for our research purposes and needs. Part of the educational world has moved in the last decade from a predilection for case-study research to an advocacy of action research, and from illumination to action (Ghaye and Isaac, 1989). One can detect an evolution in the thinking of some qualitative researchers as they have moved from concerns of defining and observing teachers as professionals in curriculum development and teaching practice to defining teachers as researchers, researching and refining their own practice. The one emphasises the detached, observing case-study approach, the other a critical active stance taken with the intention of bringing about change. The one stands back and documents and interprets a process; the other is in there assisting change. Somewhere here, there is a dissertation to examine the evolution more fully. The published literature is indicating that some early advocates of case-study research now write on action research – for example John Elliott (1991).

I have attempted here to take note not just of the differences between scientific, interpretative and action research but also of what one adds to the other and how elements of each do and can exist in the same work. Recent guides to and overviews of qualitative research confirm my conclusion here (Bell, 1993; Miles and Huberman, 1994). I could repeat Figure 10.2 at this place in the text and add a fifth category named 'mixed frame' or 'controlled action' research, or other words intended to convey a fusion of scientific, interpretative and action research traditions.

Conventions and paradigms exist to help clarify thinking and suggest an overall view and set of procedures. Tutors can meet students, talk and discuss, get alongside, lend an ear, share experience, refocus experience, turn their own ideas upside down with their students, listen and listen again. Usually we are finally given work which may stand identifiably in one tradition while not being entirely unsupported by others which are there too. Definitions to some extent do exist. We create them. They can keep us thinking. They both shape our experience and in turn are shaped by it. Our frameworks, our languages, our definitions need discussion.

We might say that out of the discussion encapsulated in this essay we arrive at broader and narrower or stronger and weaker definitions of science and scientific procedures and research and research paradigms. We realise too that recent definitions of interpretative research in classrooms – that is, case-study research – may be put in the context of age-long exercises in interpretation. In addition, changing definitions of qualitative research as it has shifted from descriptive case studies to action for change may be better appreciated. Our frameworks dissolve and re-form as we wish, as we develop and as we learn to evolve traditions and meanings for different purposes.

BIBLIOGRAPHY
Acheson,D. (1992) 'An analysis of how changing viewpoints in geography at university level have influenced school textbooks at GCSE and 'A' level', unpublished MA dissertation, Institute of Education, University of London.
   (1994) 'An analysis of how changing viewpoints in geography at university level have influenced school textbooks at GCSE and 'A' level', in Slater, F. (ed.) *Reporting Research in Geography Education*, Monograph No. 1, Department of Economics, Geography and Business Education, Institute of Education, University of London, in association with Collins Educational.
Balderstone, D. (1994) 'An evaluation of the impact of a range of learning experiences on concept acquisition in physical geography', unpublished MA dissertation, Institute of Education, University of London.
Bassey, M. (1990) 'On the nature of research in education (part 2)', *Research Intelligence*, Bera Newsletter, Autumn: 39–44.
Bell, J. (1993) *Doing Your Research Project*, Open University.
Bogdin, D. (1980) 'An investigation into the understanding of selected concepts experienced in geographical field studies by pupils aged 15+ to 17+', unpublished MA dissertation, Institute of Education, University of London.
Brown, S. (1991) 'An evaluation of a curriculum document: the P-10 social education framework from Queensland, Australia', unpublished MA dissertation, Institute of Education, University of London.
Brown, S. and Slater, F. (1993) 'Evaluating a curriculum document', *Geographical Education*, 7(1):45–50.

Butt, G.W. (1991) 'An investigation into the effects of audience-centred teaching on children's writing in geography', unpublished MA dissertation, Institute of Education, University of London.

——(1993) 'The effects of "audience centred" teaching on children's writing in Geography', *International Research in Geographical and Environmental Education*, 2(1) March:11–24.

Calland, A. (1973) 'An investigation into the images held by a small sample of primary school children of their local environment', unpublished MA dissertation, Institute of Education, University of London.

Campbell, D. and Stanley, J. (1966) *Experimental and Quasi-experimental Design for Research*, Rand McNally.

Carter, P. (1980) 'A critical study of the geographical education elements in PGCE courses in selected British universities and a brief comparison with similar Australian courses', unpublished MA dissertation, Institute of Education, University of London.

Cohen, L. and Manion, L. (1980) *Research Methods in Education*, Croom Helm.

Cowie, P. (1974) 'Value teaching and geographical education', unpublished MA dissertation, Institute of Education, University of London.

——(1978) 'Geography: a value-laden subject in education', *Geographical Education*, 3(2):133–46.

Cox, M. (1993) 'To what extent does environmental concern influence the culture and lifestyle of A-level geography students?', unpublished MA dissertation, Institute of Education, University of London.

Cribb, M. (1981) 'Geography and environmental education: an investigation into the contribution of geography to environmental education with reference to Hertfordshire secondary schools', unpublished MA dissertation, Institute of Education, University of London.

Dowgill, P. (1989) 'GCSE Geography: a case study of classroom experience', unpublished MA dissertation, Institute of Education, University of London.

Dunkerley, S. (1992) 'The implementation of National Curriculum geography in one primary school', unpublished MA dissertation, Institute of Education, University of London.

——(1994) 'The implementation of National Curriculum geography in one primary school', in Slater, F. (ed.) *Reporting Research in Geography Education*, Monograph No. 1, Department of Economics, Geography and Business Education, Institute of Education, University of London, in association with Collins Educational.

Elliott, J. (1991) *Action Research for Educational Change*, Open University.

Fien, J. (1978) 'Geographical and private geography: the humanistic perspectives in geographical education', unpublished MA dissertation, Institute of Education, University of London.

——(1979) 'Towards a humanistic perspective in geographical education',

Geographical Education, 3(2):407–21.

(1992) 'What kind of research for what kind of teaching? Towards research in geographical education as critical social science', in Hill, D. (ed.) *International Perspectives in Geographic Education*, Center for Geographic Education, Department of Geography, University of Colorado at Boulder.

Franchi, N. (1987) 'An investigation into the potential role of geography in the political education of sixth formers', unpublished MA dissertation, Institute of Education, University of London.

Fry, P. (1987) 'Dealing with political bias through geographical education', unpublished MA dissertation, Institute of Education, University of London.

Ghaye, A. (1978) 'The identification and arrangement of certain geographical concepts for the 11–14 year age range', unpublished MA dissertation, Institute of Education, University of London.

(1984) 'Discovering geographical mindscapes: a participant observation study of children in the middle years of schooling', unpublished PhD thesis, Institute of Education, University of London.

Ghaye, A. and Isaac, J. (eds) (1989) *From Illumination to Improvement*, CARN Bulletin.

Ghaye, A. and Robinson, E. (1989) 'Concept maps and children's thinking', in Slater, F. (ed.) *Language and Learning in the Teaching of Geography*, Routledge.

Gill, D. (1980) 'Social inequality: spatial form – ideology in geography', unpublished MA dissertation, Institute of Education, University of London.

Graves, N., Kent, A., Lambert, D., Naish, M. and Slater, F. (1989) *Research in Geography Education: MA dissertations 1968–1988, Institute of Education, University of London*, Geography Section, Institute of Education, University of London.

Haile, D. (1988) 'Thinking into another's environment – an investigation into learner response to pictures of village scenes in Africa', unpublished MA dissertation, Institute of Education, University of London.

Harrisson, W.G. (1987) 'Young people's perception of spatial injustice in cities', unpublished MA dissertation, Institute of Education, University of London.

Hartley, R. (1980) 'Values and values education in geography teaching: the trend towards social action', unpublished MA dissertation, Institute of Education, University of London.

Hemingway, J. (1992) 'Libertarian pedagogy and the urban environment: a geographical exploration', unpublished MA dissertation, Institute of Education, University of London.

(1994) 'Libertarian pedagogy: a geographical perspective', in Slater, F. (ed.) *Reporting Research in Geography Education*, Monograph No. 1, Department of Economics, Geography and Business Education, Institute of Education, University of London, in association with Collins Educational.

Henley, R. (1986) 'Ideology in school geography: a consideration of methodology and languages', unpublished MA dissertation, Institute of Education,

University of London.

(1989) 'The ideology of geographical language', in Slater, F. (ed.) *Language and Learning in the Teaching of Geography*, Routledge.

Hopkins, D. (1985) *A Teacher's Guide to Classroom Research*, Open University.

Hones, T. (1988) 'An in-school evaluation of a specific problem in geography and other humanities subjects at advanced level', unpublished MA dissertation, Institute of Education, University of London.

Huckle, J. (1976) 'A consideration of some curriculum problems involved in developing an environmental ethic within geographical education', unpublished MA dissertation, Institute of Education, University of London.

Jones, A. (1986) 'Structuralism and geographical education: some inferences and implications for A-level teaching and learning', unpublished MA dissertation, Institute of Education, University of London.

Kayes, J. (1992) 'Taking equal opportunities in school a step further: an evaluation of a subject-focused response', unpublished MA dissertation, Institute of Education, University of London.

Keats, G. (1986) 'An evaluation of curriculum change – the T.E.D.'s new high school geography curriculum', unpublished MA dissertation, Institute of Education, University of London.

Kelly, P. (1978) 'Values and attitudes in geographical education with special reference to environmental problems', unpublished MA dissertation, Institute of Education, University of London.

Kemmis, S. (1982) 'Action research', in Husen, T. and Postlethwaite, T.H. (eds) *International Encyclopaedia of Education: Research and Studies*, Pergamon.

Kilburn, E. (1974) 'A critical assessment of the concept of reality in geography in education', unpublished MA dissertation, Institute of Education, University of London.

Lam, C.C. (1984) 'Value education in high school geography in Hong Kong', unpublished MA dissertation, Institute of Education, University of London.

(1988) 'Problems of new town development – using values in geography lessons', in Gerber, R. and Lidstone, J. (eds) *Developing Skills in Geographical Education*, International Geographical Union Commission of Geographical Education with Jacaranda Press.

Lynch, K. (1960) *The Image of the City*, MIT Press.

Malindine, D. (1987) 'An investigation and evaluation of the contribution to geographical education of independently produced video materials', unpublished MA dissertation, Institute of Education, University of London.

Maton, J.C. (1975) 'An experimental investigation of two methods of teaching geography in mixed-ability classes in a comprehensive school', unpublished MA dissertation, Institute of Education, University of London.

McElroy, B. (1980) 'School-based curriculum development – an investigation into teachers' perceptions of their role, the major constraints and the in-service teacher education implications in this form of curriculum development', unpublished MA dissertation, Institute of Education, University of London.

Miles, M.L. and Huberman, A.M. (1994) *Qualitative Data Analysis*, 2nd edition, Sage.

Milton, M. (1984) 'A case study of mixed ability teaching in some geography and integrated studies classes at two comprehensive schools', unpublished MA dissertation, Institute of Education, University of London.

Morgan, J.W. (1993) 'Disputed places: the postmodern challenge and geography education', unpublished MA dissertation, Institute of Education, University of London.

Namafe, C. (1992) 'An exercise in environmental education: investigating, disseminating and evaluating two contrasting floodwater metaphors', unpublished PhD thesis, Institute of Education, University of London.

Newham, R. (1985) 'A study of urban secondary school pupils of diverse ethnic backgrounds, and their perceptions of a rural locality whilst engaged in geographical fieldwork', unpublished MA dissertation, Institute of Education, University of London.

Okpala, J. (1983) 'The link between teacher education and the teaching of geography in Nigerian secondary schools', unpublished MA dissertation, Institute of Education, University of London.

Osakwe, E. (1983) 'The need for curriculum renewal in Nigerian school geography', unpublished MA dissertation, Institute of Education, University of London.

Owen-Jones, G. (1987) 'Values education through fieldwork', unpublished MA dissertation, Institute of Education, University of London.

Palfrey, R. (1984) 'Teaching radical geography: an evaluation of student reaction to Marxist perspectives on urban housing', unpublished MA dissertation, Institute of Education, University of London.

Phiri, F. (1987) 'The development and evaluation of value-laden geography units and lessons congruent with Zambia's educational policy and its ideological and socio-economic development issues', unpublished PhD thesis, Institute of Education, University of London.

(1988) 'Geography, decision-making and socio-economic development issues in Zambia', in Gerber, R. and Lidstone, J. (eds) *Developing Skills in Geographical Education*, International Geographical Union Commission on Geographical Education with Jacaranda Press.

Pratt, S. (1990) 'Young people's perceptions of their environment', unpublished MA dissertation, Institute of Education, University of London.

Robinson, E. (1986) 'The teaching and learning of geographical structures: a small-scale investigation', unpublished MA dissertation, Institute of

Education, University of London.

Rupar, T. (1982) 'Middle-class images of the Third World', unpublished MA dissertation, Institute of Education, University of London.

Schrettenbrunner, H. and Van Westrhenen, J. (eds) (1992) *Empirical Research and Geography Teaching*, Netherlands Geographical Studies, 142 Centrum Voor Educatieve Geografie Vrije Universiteit Amsterdam.

Simmonds, D. (1982) 'Adolescents' experience of their environment: a case study – Manor School, Cambridge', unpublished MA dissertation, Institute of Education, University of London.

Slater, F. (1988) 'Teaching Styles? A case study of post-graduate teaching students observed', in Gerber, R. and Lidstone, J. (eds) *Developing Skills in Geographical Education*, IGU and Jacaranda.

(1989) *Language and Learning in the Teaching of Geography*, Routledge.

(ed.) (1994) *Reporting Research in Geography Education*, Monograph No. 1, Department of Economics, Geography and Business Education, Institute of Education, University of London, in association with Collins Educational.

Starkey, R. (1987) 'An assessment of geography's contribution to economic understanding in the school curriculum', unpublished MA dissertation, Institute of Education, University of London.

Stephens, P. (1988) 'An enquiry into the extent to which the Geography 16–19 project has fulfilled its objectives with regard to its enquiry approach to learning and its distinctive approach to geographical education', unpublished MA dissertation, Institute of Education, University of London.

Tierney, G. (1985) 'The development of spatial cognition and ability in the primary and secondary school', unpublished MA dissertation, Institute of Education, University of London.

Tompkinson, M. (1987) 'An investigation into the way geography teachers cope with range of ability in pupils', unpublished MA dissertation, Institute of Education, University of London.

Verduin-Muller, H. (1964) *Leren met beelden* (*Learning with Visual Images*), Groningen: Wolters.

(1991) 'Serving the knowledge-based society: research on knowledge products', *Netherlands Geographical Studies*, 123.

Walker, R. (1978) 'An investigation into the development of map-using abilities in primary school children', unpublished MA dissertation, Institute of Education, University of London.

(1980) 'Map-using abilities of 5 to 9 year old children', *Geographical Education*, 3(4):545–54.

Welsh, A. (1978) 'The contribution of geography to citizenship education', unpublished MA dissertation, Institute of Education, University of London.

11 Action research for a new professionalism in geography education

Michael Naish

What is the use of research?

Teachers commonly have a healthy scepticism about research. Research is what goes on elsewhere, outside and beyond school. It is undertaken by experts who make use of teachers, schools and children to undertake their research. The research thus undertaken is directed at enhancing the qualifications of the student researcher or improving the curriculum vitae of the academic researcher. It is commonly perceived to be largely irrelevant to the needs of the practising teacher and is usually reported in somewhat inaccessible journals and books, not normally the everyday reading matter of hard-pressed teachers.

Fien (1992) points out that most research in geography education is of the empirical, process–product type. In empirical research the researcher is the actor, who poses hypotheses to be tested by the setting up of controlled experimental situations. Empirical research is positivistic in style and concerned with the processes of teaching and learning and the product of such processes. There is, as Fien points out, rather less of the interpretive mode of research in geographical education. In interpretive research, the ethnographic researcher observes the subjects of the research – the actors, often using a case-study approach in her or his search for illuminative evidence and information. In Fien's view, such research could offer 'rich descriptions of the thoughts, practices and problems of teachers' (op.cit. p.267).

A third style of research, educational action research, developed in the UK and elsewhere from the mid-1970s, offers the possibility of research activity which is yet more immediately relevant to the needs of teachers and students and can thus contribute directly to the professional standing of teachers and teaching and to enhancement of the education of our students.

What is educational action research?

Educational action research is research undertaken by the practising teacher as a response to an issue or problem that is a matter of concern to that teacher. The purpose of undertaking the research is to try to get at the nature of the issue or problem, to explore its roots and causes and to plan and implement possible ways and means of dealing with it. The effects of implementing these ways and means are then evaluated and this may lead on to further attempts to refine the action, further reflection on the issue or problem and so on. Thus one could say that the basic characteristics are that it is undertaken by the practitioner and is mainly concerned to produce an effective action plan to deal with a situation or condition. Some examples may help to develop these ideas.

EXAMPLE 1: DEVELOPING A TEACHING UNIT

Jeannette Kayes was dissatisfied with the part of her GCSE (General Certificate of Secondary Education) course for 14 to 16 year-old students (Kayes, 1992). In particular, she was concerned 'that the Work and Employment part of the course was male biased, concentrating on manufacturing industry and traditionally male jobs. When teaching this it felt "other worldly" even to me and I was very conscious that I was not teaching it as well as the rest of the course' (p.18). Kayes felt that she had little personal interest in this aspect of the course from an academic point of view, and she therefore set out to develop the unit to include more interesting, more demanding work for the pupils and to stimulate her own interest.

She decided to focus the unit on women's work in the global economy. She prepared the unit and taught it to her class while monitoring the experience to enable her to reflect on a series of questions for investigation. These were:

(a) In terms of pupils:
    (i)   Do pupils learn the subject content and therefore become more aware of the work women do?
    (ii) How do pupils react to the feminist content, and does there seem to be a difference in how girls and boys react?
    (iii) Do pupils' reactions to the feminist content change from the beginning to the end of the work?

(iv) Does the subject content affect their performance in examination terms?

(b) In terms of the unit:

(i) Was the unit successful in terms of the pupils' results, and was there any gender pattern in the results?

(ii) Was the unit successful in terms of the pupils' interest and enjoyment?

(c) In terms of the rest of the GCSE:

(i) What recommendations can be made to improve the rest of the GCSE course, especially the Work and Employment section?

(ii) How can feminist geography be used in schools in the light of examination syllabuses and the National Curriculum?

In addition to analysis of the pupils' performance in assessment terms, a participant observer role was adopted in investigating and reflecting upon these questions, and the teacher kept a diary for a term, administered questionnaires to the pupils and interviewed pupils. She found that pupils had become more aware of the work women do. Four of the twenty pupils changed their opinions during the course of the work. Three boys became more positive about the role of women in the world of work, while one girl became rather negative towards equal opportunities issues. The majority of the boys expressed positive outcomes and the girls increased in confidence in class during the work. The study strengthened the researcher's resolve to develop more enquiry approaches in her teaching and learning strategies, and she gained in confidence with regard to integrating some aspects of feminist geography into the GCSE course.

EXAMPLE 2: DEVELOPING THE ROLE OF HOMEWORK

P. J. Sweasey (1989) was concerned about the nature and role of homework in her large, mixed comprehensive school. Her feeling was that not enough care went into the setting of homework and that it was not being used to its full potential for the educational benefit of the students.

The researcher reviewed the literature on the topic and investigated current views using questionnaires to be completed by children, parents and fellow teachers. She also interviewed a number of families, a deputy headteacher and the head of geography in the school. The homework policies of some neighbouring schools were also examined.

Homework was seen to be occasionally irrelevant, frequently boring, often poorly designed and sloppily executed. It was seen as a chore to complete and a chore to mark. It was thought to appeal to the brightest students and to alienate the weakest. Homework set to improve individual study skills was done best by those who needed least improvement. Homework could provide the opportunity for the ability gap to be widened by the varying levels of support in the home.

As a response to these findings, the researcher produced a trial local studies unit with an integral homework scheme. The work was divided into sections and students in Year 7 (11 to 12 year-olds) were required to select their own route through the unit. Thus they were given an element of choice as to the order in which they undertook the sections and whether they treated them as classwork or homework. Pupils were expected to undertake at least thirty minutes of homework per week. Instructions and resources were provided for the work. Six teachers were involved with the large mixed-ability group of children, and pupils recorded their progress on specially prepared sheets.

The unit was carefully evaluated and a generally positive response was noted from the pupils, but the work did raise other issues, such as how to support the less able in this freely structured work. An increased level of competitiveness between pupils was noted and the researcher wished to go on to question whether this was (a) desirable and (b) beneficial for all pupils.

EXAMPLE 3: IMPLEMENTING THE NATIONAL CURRICULUM
The Education Reform Act of 1988 established a National Curriculum for England and Wales. The National Curriculum was fundamentally subject-based and geography was included as one of the Foundation Subjects, to be taught to all children from age 5 to 16. Subject Working Groups were set up, which recommended to the Secretary of State for Education the programmes of study (PoS) and statements of attainment (SoA) for each subject. The PoS basically set out what was to be taught and the SoA listed what was to be assessed. The Secretary of State, working through the National Curriculum Council, had the last word on the final details of

the PoS and SoA which were published as Statutory Orders for each sub-ject (DES, 1991).

The challenge for teachers was the translation of the Orders into a working curriculum for their particular school and pupil situation. For primary school teachers in particular, this was no mean task, since many lacked subject expertise for a number of the subjects included in the cur-riculum, and most lacked knowledge and experience of curriculum plan-ning, development and evaluation.

Sue Dunkerley, studying at the time for a Master's degree in geography education, set out to monitor the implementation of the geography National Curriculum in a primary school (Dunkerley, 1992 – see also Chapter 10). She was strongly supported by the school in this endeavour and adopted the role of an external consultant or facilitator. Thus she was able to develop her research role as participant observer. She collected background information on the school and its catchment area, attended relevant staff meetings at the school when the geography element of the curriculum was being discussed, and worked with the teacher whose role it was to lead the development of the geography curriculum in line with the Statutory Orders. She also made a collection of media cuttings at this time of rapid change, and attended meetings, such as those organised by the Geographical Association, which were relevant to the task.

During this work, the researcher mounted a simple questionnaire sur-vey of the level of geographical background of the staff and their view of the nature of geography and its educational value. She maintained a jour-nal in which she reflected on the process of developing the geography cur-riculum, audio-taped the meetings, and encouraged the teacher responsible also to maintain a journal.

In her review of her findings, the researcher noted the significance of the fact that the whole school staff had been involved in the development through the staff meetings. The value of adopting a whole-school approach was clear. The level of awareness of the role and potential of geography in the curriculum had increased as a result of the need to imple-ment the National Curriculum requirements. The level and quality of resourcing, in terms of learning resources, had also improved. Dunkerley noted that the role of the participant observer, taking an active role in the development from an external perspective, required great sensitivity.

EXAMPLE 4: DEVELOPING THE CURRICULUM AT A NATIONAL SCALE

The Geography 16–19 Project was a national project, funded for most of its lifetime (1976–85) by the Schools Council. The project worked with teachers and students in England, Wales and Northern Ireland to develop the geography curriculum for 16 to 19 year-olds (Naish et al., 1987). It was set up as a direct response to analysis of the nature of the geography curriculum in the mid-1970s, since it appeared that that curriculum was not fulfilling the educational potential of the subject. In particular, there was concern about the content of the subject in the 16 to 19 curriculum, where it tended to be largely influenced by and dependent upon developments in academic geography at higher education level. The tendency was for a significant time-lag between changes at the research frontier and changes at 16 to 19 level. These changes were largely mediated through examination boards, which were subject to institutional and historical inertia.

A second major concern was that the pedagogy of geography courses for 16 to 19 year-olds was largely expository, thus limiting the range of skills being developed by students. Thirdly, the significance of attitudes and values in decisions about the use of space was largely unrecognised in geography courses for the age group, as was the educational potential of involving students in active values enquiry into issues, questions and problems about the use of space. Thus the potential of geography as a medium for the education of young people was seen to be largely unfulfilled and in need of consideration and development.

From the very beginning, it was the intention of the project to work with practising teachers in developing the geography curriculum. Such intentions are encapsulated in the aims of the project, which were:

- to involve teachers and lecturers in a reconsideration of the objectives, content and teaching methods of geography courses for the 16 to 19 age group; and
- by means of this involvement, to help them appreciate their role as curriculum developers.

In order to further these aims, the project team set up what they called 'a system for involvement' in the earliest stages of the project. Working through the Schools Council, pilot groups of teachers were set up in thirteen local authorities in England and Wales. These groups consisted of teachers from a range of establishments within each authority and they were led by a co-ordinator, usually from higher education and supported by their headteacher or principal and by the local authority advisory service. Some funding was made available to ensure that teachers could have reprographic facilities and travel to meetings locally and nationally. Each member of the three-person central project team was allocated a selection of these pilot groups and travelled regularly to work with the groups. At a later stage, single associate schools or colleges were nominated in a further twelve authorities, including two schools in Northern Ireland.

Working with this system for involvement, the project conducted an analysis of the current situation within geography education for 16 to 19 year-olds, researched the needs of the students, and reviewed the significant rapid changes taking place in the subject at the time (late 1970s). On the basis of this research phase, they put forward broad aims for geography in the 16 to 19 age range. In order to put these aims into operation, the system of team and teachers moved on to produce a framework for the geography curriculum designed to help promote the construction of syllabuses and the preparation of teaching materials to support such syllabuses. The framework proposed an approach to geography, dubbed by the project 'the people–environment approach', an active, enquiry-based approach to teaching and learning, to include values enquiry, and guidelines on selection of content and scale of study.

Continuing to work with its system of involved teachers, the project moved on to produce innovative courses for the Advanced level of the General Certificate of Education and other national examinations for 17, 18 or 19 year-olds, all based on the curriculum framework. Teachers engaged with the team in the production of pilot materials to support these courses and undertook trials of the materials. The teachers were also critically involved in the development of the courses, their implementation and evaluation. When it came to the further dissemination of the project, the pilot teachers played a key role in conferences designed to introduce colleagues to what the project had to offer. Their role as change agents continued significantly in helping to establish and develop working groups of teachers in local areas meeting to discuss issues, develop materials and assessment items, and generally enhance each other's professional development.

Characteristics of action research

These examples demonstrate some further characteristics of educational action research. The first is that action research is often *collaborative*. In the case of Examples 1 and 2, the researchers were students on a post-graduate degree course, working with a university-based supervisor and having the opportunity to share their ideas with fellow students in both formal and informal situations. In Example 3, the researcher, in addition to working with her supervisor and fellow students, also worked with the staff of the school and with one teacher in particular. In Example 4, the project team established its network of involved schools and colleges in order to undertake a large-scale collaborative action research enterprise.

The second characteristic is that the research in each of the examples was of a *critical* nature. In Example 1, it was concerned with problems of gender bias as this is commonly manifested in mixed classes in mixed-sex schools. For example, adolescent boys may frequently dominate lessons in such classes, demanding the attention of both male and female teachers and excluding girls from oral participation in the lesson. The research arose through a critical appraisal of this situation. It was also critical of the content of the unit, which previously to the research development had been mainly concerned with a view of work that states that most work and the most important work is undertaken by men. In Example 2, the research was based on a critique of the nature and quality of homework being set and undertaken in geography. In Example 3, the nature of the geography Orders in the National Curriculum became subject to critical analysis by the researcher and the teachers. In Example 4, a critique of the quality of geography in the 16–19 curriculum and of the failure of geography to achieve its educational potential was the starting point for the large-scale project.

The third characteristic is that the research was *concerned with social situations*, the nature of such situations and ways in which conditions might be changed for the better. In Example 1, the social situation is that of the mixed-sex classroom, where certain gender characteristics were observed and questioned. In Example 2, the experimental unit questioned the conventional roles of teachers and pupils and the role of the home in the development of learning and as a place for learning. In Example 3, the critical role of the whole staff in the primary school was considered and the significance of whole staff involvement in curriculum renewal was emphasised. Journal entries in the reporting of the research opened up many important points about the nature of collaborative work. In Example 4, the role of teachers as curriculum developers and therefore the power of teachers relative to other elements of the education system was fundamentally under examination and development as teachers were involved in key areas of the work of the project.

The fourth characteristic is that the examples illustrate well the thinking of *reflective teachers* (Schön,1983). In Example 1, the researcher was aware of the limitations of her original approach to the unit, of the social situation in her classroom, and of the gender bias which can pervade much of the geographical content of the school curriculum. She set up an experimental situation which enabled her to reflect further on these situations and develop a possible approach to dealing with some of these. Her reflection upon the actual research led her on to recognise further issues and questions for analysis and possible treatment. Similar reflective activity on the part of the teacher can be observed in Examples 2 and 3, while in Example 4, reflection upon the process and product of the geography curriculum for 16 to 19 year-olds was deliberately called for by the project team and stimulated by the situation of team members and teachers working together on all aspects of the project's development.

A fifth characteristic is that, in each of the examples, the research was *systematic*, divided into clear phases, which included planning, implementation, reflection, analysis and reporting (through a dissertation or through publications). It is this systematic approach to action research, together with the fact that such research is *made public*, or shared through discussion with others, that distinguishes action research from simply what teachers do as a matter of good practice. Of course it *is* good practice to take a critical view of what one is doing, to develop new units or fresh approaches to units and to evaluate these in terms of student and teacher activity and involvement. To undertake such activities in purposeful, explicitly acknowledged, systematic research of the kind described above, may be a productive way of helping to develop the reflective skills of the professional teacher.

This notion of the reflective practitioner and of the teacher as researcher takes us on to a consideration of the origins and development of action research in education.

The origins and development of action research

In recent years a great deal has been written about action research. It is clearly a fashionable mode of research and its popularity is reflected in the number of books and articles produced through the 1980s and early '90s. Many writers trace the origins of the genre to the work of social psychologists in group dynamics, and of Kurt Lewin in particular (Lewin, 1948), stressing his concern for practical situations of social conflict. Lewin felt that where a community was prepared to study the results of its own social action, remedial efforts could be introduced. The notion of action following study is clear at this early stage and Lewin developed change experiments to allow groups, with the guidance of external consultants, to develop objective and detached means of examining the foundations of their own biases. Basic to his approach was the idea of action cycles which include analysis, fact finding, conceptualisation, planning, implementation and evaluation of action (McKernan, 1991). Lewin pulled together ideas about the process of scientific enquiry developed in the late nineteenth century (Buckingham, 1926) and the work of John Dewey on stages in reflective thinking (Dewey, 1910, 1929, 1938) to develop a credible theory of action research so that it began to be recognised as an innovation in social inquiry. For Lewin, research should help solve social problems and 'research that produces nothing but books will not suffice' (Lewin, 1948: 203).

It was Stephen Corey who led the post-war drive for educational action research as part of the movement for social reconstruction that characterised the years following the Second World War (Corey, 1953). Corey believed that curriculum practice could be significantly developed and improved if teachers themselves were involved in research and devel-

opment. The enthusiastic drive to use action research as the general strategy for curriculum change and development in the 1950s, characterised
by teachers and schools co-operating with outside researchers, was overtaken in the 1960s by the research, development and dissemination movement which tended to isolate teachers from the process and involve them
only as potential targets of the dissemination.

In the 1970s, the work of Lawrence Stenhouse (Stenhouse, 1975) led
to a renaissance of the action research approach through his promotion of
the idea of the teacher as researcher. Stenhouse directed the Humanities
Curriculum project (1967–72) which was concerned with a process
model of curriculum with profound implications for the role of the
teacher in the discussion of controversial issues amongst groups of adolescent students. In the process model, the curriculum is not 'a body of
predetermined static content, to be reproduced via the pedagogical
process. Rather it is the selection and organisation of content within a
dynamic and reflective pedagogical process and is therefore constantly
evolved and developed through it' (Elliott, 1991: 16). Thus the role of the
teacher, working with a particular group of students, is paramount in
determining the day-to-day, week-to-week character of the curriculum.
With the dominance of content provision removed, the door is opened
for consideration of important questions such as the relative roles of
teacher and learner and the appropriateness, relevance and significance of
the content being considered at any particular time.

Under pressure of time, the Humanities Curriculum project team
devised packs of resource materials to act as evidence to be fed into student discussions. The team then began to study the pedagogical situation
within which the materials were being used by teachers. The importance
of fostering self-reflection on the part of the teachers soon became clear
if they were to gain in confidence and competence in developing an appropriate pedagogy rather than rely upon the critique provided by the outsiders – the project team. The potential of self-reflective practice for the
generation of theory from the basis of practice became clear, and the
importance of reflection upon practice as an element of professionalism
received a further boost (Elliott, 1991). On the basis of his experience
with the Humanities project, Stenhouse clarified his view of the teacher
as researcher. This is clearly stated in his influential book *An Introduction to*

Curriculum Research and Development (1975) where his thesis is that teaching ought to be based on research undertaken by the teacher, who develops the curriculum by means of study of and evaluation of teaching episodes and approaches, thus improving her or his own work as understanding develops.

John Elliott, who was a member of Stenhouse's Humanities Curriculum Development Project team, has since played a leading role in proselytising educational action research. From 1973 to 1975, he and Clem Adelman led the Ford Teaching Project, sponsored by the Ford Foundation (Elliott and Adelman, 1976). In this project, forty teachers in twelve schools undertook action research into the problems of implementing enquiry approaches in their classrooms. In Elliott's view (Elliott, 1991), most curriculum projects in the 1960s and 1970s had espoused an enquiry approach to learning but had assumed that all that was needed to implement such an approach was the provision of supporting curriculum materials. His experience on the Humanities Project had suggested that this was far from the case, and the Ford Project offered teachers the opportunity to explore the issues through their own teaching and thus to generate 'diagnostic and practical hypotheses' which would help to develop a pedagogical theory. Triangulation approaches were employed in reflecting upon the practices of the teachers as Elliott and Adelman recorded lessons on tape or tape/slide and then interviewed the teachers and a sample of students about the recorded lessons. The interviews themselves were recorded and these recordings then discussed again with the teachers and students. Hypotheses generated through this triangulation approach were then circulated to other teachers involved in the project and used as the basis of discussion in meetings across project personnel. This led to further experimentation as teachers went on to try to assess how far the hypotheses could stand up to scrutiny from the perspective of their own teaching. Thus the teachers were encouraged to reflect on their practices in the light of the theory they had themselves helped to generate.

Efforts to create networks of researchers interested in action research and to disseminate ideas are illustrated by the setting up of CARN (the Classroom Action Research Network) in 1976 and of NARTAR (the National Association for Race Relations Teaching and Action Research).

In 1990, the first world congress on action research, action learning and process management was held in Australia. The number and frequency of publications on action research have increased dramatically in recent years and attempts have been made to restructure award-bearing courses for teachers to support and encourage action research in schools (Elliott, 1981).

How is action research undertaken?

Several writers offer advice on how to undertake action research. Some helpful examples are Elliott (1991), who includes a chapter entitled 'A practical guide to action research' in his interesting general review of the genre. Jean McNiff's *Action Research. Principles and Practice* (1988) contains sections on 'How to start an action research study' and on 'Making sense of the data' (McNiff, 1988). James McKernan's comprehensive book *Curriculum Action Research* (1991) is a *Handbook of Methods and Resources for the Reflective Practitioner*.

Most writers make considerable play of elegant models of action research, each refining the other in efforts to encapsulate the essence of the process. All stress the cyclical nature of the endeavour, from the simplicity of McNiff's attempt to model Lewin's approach (Figure 11.1), to the more complex efforts of Elliott (1991) (Figure 11.2). The four basic activities in Lewin's approach are planning, acting, observing and reflecting, and this can lead on to revised planning, further action, observation and reflection, as indicated in Figure 11.1.

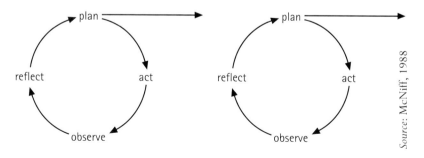

Figure 11.1 Action research cycles

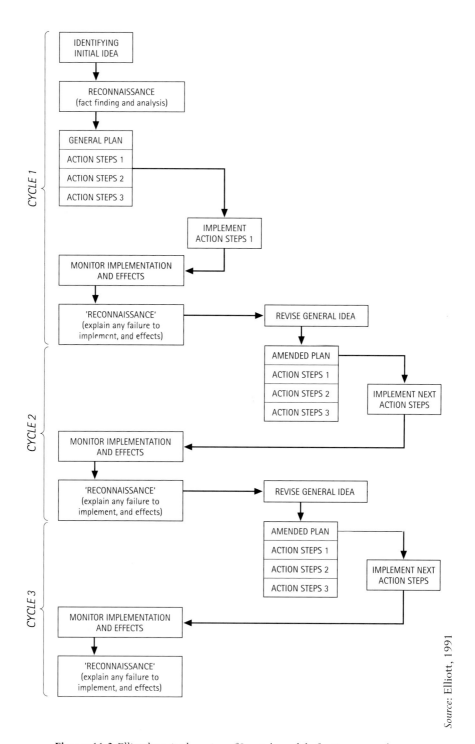

Figure 11.2 Elliott's revised version of Lewin's model of action research

Source: Elliott, 1991

Kemmis (1980) elaborated Lewin's simple model, suggesting that research begins from an initial idea which is subjected to reconnaissance largely consisting of fact finding. This leads to the statement of a general plan which can be broken down into a series of steps for action. The first action step is implemented and then evaluated and this can lead to an amended plan with related steps. The researcher then spirals into implementation of action step 2, evaluation of step 2 and reconsideration in an amended plan, and so on – the cyclical, spiral process continues.

Elliott (1991) wished to refine this model by acknowledging that completion of the first cycle may cause a shift in the initial, or general idea. He considers that reconnaissance should be analytical as well as concerned with fact finding, and that each action step should be monitored as it is undertaken as well as being subjected to subsequent evaluation. These considerations led him to propose the model shown in Figure 11.2.

At this stage it may help to consider a hypothetical example of the application of this model.

Identifying the initial idea   The teacher is concerned that students at an early stage in her 16–19 course in geography are reluctant to talk. The amount, level and quality of their oral contributions is limited.

Reconnaissance   In order to be more clear about the situation, the teacher analyses the situation further and feels that:
- students' oral responses are poor when she poses questions in class
- students have little to contribute towards discussion
- students' oral responses are short and undeveloped
- oral work is normally expected in whole-class situations
- better performance is noted when students are in small groups.

She undertakes some reading on group work and language in learning. She puts forward hypotheses that:

Oral/discussion work will improve and make more of a contribution to student learning if:
- students are put into more challenging situations
- students are encouraged to develop a fuller knowledge base
- students are given more stimulating tasks to complete
- students are given access to appropriate and relevant evidence in the form of learning resources and data.

Preparing the general plan The teacher now re-states the initial idea with more clarity – she is anxious to improve students' oral work since she believes that student talk is vital for effective learning. Her general plan is to try to devise activities that will motivate the students to make more effective use of spoken language in their geographical studies.

She plans action steps:

Action step 1   Set up a groupwork situation where students have to investigate certain aspects of an issue and report back on the completion of the task.

Action step 2   Involve students in a role play which will enable them to take on a particular role in order to discuss an issue of spatial and environmental significance.

Action step 3   Involve the students in the production of a video-taped report on a local people–environment issue.

The teacher considers what resources she will need to implement these action steps, decides who else may be involved in the activity, for example the media resources officer and the general public in Action step 3. She thinks into the question of whether any ethical questions may be raised by the activities which could require sensitive attention.

Implementation of action step 1 The teacher plans the group work, decides how to monitor and evaluate it and then puts it into practice with the group of students.

Monitoring the implementation The teacher monitors the implementation of Action step 1 by keeping a log of her work in preparation, of the actual teaching of the session and the students' learning, and of the evidence of their learning. During the teaching sessions she stands back from the groups at work and records her observations as a participant observer. She also records groups at work on audio tape.

At the end of the teaching sessions, she evaluates the work by analysis of the tapes, by using a student questionnaire and interviews, and by her own subjective evaluation of the events.

Reconnaissance   The teacher uses the evidence gained from the monitoring exercise to consider the positive and negative elements of the experiment. She uses this analysis to help revise the general idea and moves on to amend the plan and proceed with Action step 2.

An enormous range of techniques is available for the teacher-researcher to employ in the monitoring, analysis and evaluation stages of an episode of action research. McKernan (1991) describes forty-eight techniques, classified and grouped into the following:

- Observational and narrative research methods, e.g. participant observation, case studies, diaries, journals, photography, video/audio taping, rating scales.
- Non-observational, survey and self-report techniques, e.g. questionnaires, interviews, attitude scales.
- Discourse analysis and problem-solving methods, e.g. content analysis, document analysis, episode analysis, brainstorming, group discussions.
- Critical-reflective and evaluative research methods, e.g. triangulation, lesson profiles, student/teacher evaluation forms, critical trialling.

Elliott (1991) offers a simpler list consisting of diaries, profiles (e.g. lesson profiles), document analysis, photographic evidence, tape/video recordings and transcripts, using an outside observer, interviewing, running commentary, shadow studies (shadowing a participant), checklists, questionnaires, inventories, triangulation and analytic memos recorded at critical stages.

An important element of action research is sharing the experience and findings with colleagues, and this may be done informally, within the context of the researcher's institution, or more formally as a publication or a presentation at a conference or meeting. McNiff makes the point that the evidence in the form of tapes, photographs, videos or written reporting is available for consultation, and the teacher can say 'Look, I have evidence!' (McNiff, 1988).

One of the key problems of action research is the question of how teachers are to find the occasion and the time to undertake activities that will distinguish their research from the kind of good practice which one would normally expect of teachers who evaluate their teaching in a reflective manner and reorganise their work on the basis of such evaluation. A study by Kwan and Lee (1994) invited geography teachers in Brisbane and Hong Kong to respond to a questionnaire survey investigating their knowledge of and involvement in action research. Only nine teachers responded, thus suggesting that action research is a low priority for them. Of the nine who responded, only four claimed to be undertaking action research, and it was clear that they had only recently discovered the idea. Three of the four provided only brief descriptions of the salient characteristics of action research while the fourth provided a fair description. The nine teachers described the main barriers to undertaking action research as:

- time constraints
- heavy workload
- lack of familiarity with techniques
- lack of support and recognition from the school.

In the United Kingdom, the radical revolution in education undertaken by the Conservative governments of the 1980s and '90s has placed new demands on teachers which have increased their workload considerably, especially in the amount of paperwork which has to be undertaken. Such bureaucratic demands militate against the proper activity of the reflective practitioner and it is the commonplace view of many teachers that it is difficult in the present situation to find time for the preparation and evaluation of their teaching. The phenomenon is by no means limited to the United Kingdom, as is indicated in Lidstone's (1994) reflections on becoming professional.

There is little doubt that at present, action research takes place mainly where teachers are released from normal teaching and administrative duties in some way, such as for in-service activities, or where the occasion is provided, usually through enrolment on a course in higher education, often at diploma and Master's level.

There is also little doubt that a key opportunity for action research is provided by in-service activities, including both short courses and award-bearing courses. Good practice would involve the in-service provider and the teacher in working together to isolate key issues and problems in the teacher's practice. This would lead to the setting up of action research activities to investigate these issues and problems and to endeavour to improve practice. It is increasingly common to find in-service courses of this nature developing. The key feature is to ensure that any required coursework is related to this kind of enquiry.

A new professionalism

The notion that involvement in critical action research may lead to an enhanced professionalism for teachers has been with us for some time. The Schools Council Geography 14–18 project team embraced the idea in the structure of their work, which involved the setting up of groups of teachers in various parts of the country, who worked on an analysis of the contemporary situation of the geography curriculum (Hickman *et al.*, 1973). The thesis was developed that the main gatekeeper militating against improvement of the curriculum was the style and approach of public examinations. A cycle of curriculum underdevelopment was described in which teachers taught to achieve maximum success for their students in public examinations. If such examinations demanded mainly recall of factual information as a measure of success in learning geography, then this militated against the development of more enquiry-based approaches to teaching and learning such as might broaden the range of skills and abilities being developed by students through their geographical studies. It followed that curriculum change should be approached through a drive for new approaches in the design and requirements of the public examination syllabuses and an experimental examination for 16 year-olds became the main focus of the project's work.

The involvement of teachers in the discussions which led to this approach and then in the development of school-based elements of the courses, their trial and evaluation, was seen as a key element of the professional teacher's role, and to develop this role would lead to a new professionalism for the geography teacher.

These ideas are taken forward in Fien's important paper of 1992, where he calls for involvement of geography teachers in critical action research of a collaborative nature, the collaboration being with university-based tutors who would act as 'critical friends, sponsors and co-participants' of the teacher-researcher. The research would be critical in the sense put forward by Carr and Kemmis (1986), influenced by the kind of critical social science envisaged by Habermas (1972; see also McCarthy, 1978). It would have, as its central concern, the role of providing a critique of and challenge to 'the personal beliefs and the ideological and structural contexts that constrain desirable practices in teaching'

(Fien, 1992:268). The ultimate aim would be to make such desirable practices more possible to achieve.

Some writers concerned to discuss the nature of professionalism emphasise the potential of action research to enhance professional behaviour. Kemp (1977) analyses the competencies required in occupations, such as teaching, that require problem solving and decision making in complex situations. He suggests that learning from reflection upon experience is a key cognitive competence. In a group of competencies concerned with motivation, eliciting feedback on one's own performance is seen as a key ability. Action research is likely to enhance such abilities or competencies and thus form a vital element in maintaining and developing the professional status of teachers.

Carr and Kemmis (1986) suggest the following three distinctive features of professionalism:

1 Professions base methods and procedures on theoretical knowledge and research.

2 Members of a profession have dominant commitment to the well-being of their clients.

3 Members have the individual and collective right to make autonomous, independent judgements regardless of external, non-professional controls and constraints with regard to particular decisions in particular situations.

At the time of writing, the professional status of teachers as viewed within this definition is under prolonged and active attack in the United Kingdom through the legislation of the Education Reform Act and through the National Curriculum that forms the central element of the Act. While nothing can be done to diminish the commitment of teachers to the well-being of their students, theoretical knowledge and research is being disregarded and teachers are being denied their individual and collective right to make autonomous, independent judgements regardless of external controls. Movements to control the training of new teachers also militate against the professional status of teachers. A key element of the professions is normally considered to be the links with higher education in the training of members of the profession, yet at the present time we witness attempts to break the link with higher education in the training of teachers and base such training entirely in schools. In the National Curriculum the role of the teacher is reduced to that of 'delivery' of the prescribed curriculum. The content of the curriculum is set out in the programmes of study contained in the Statutory Orders for each of the subjects that make up the National Curriculum. Teachers have little choice in the selection of content, while in the assessment of the pupils, stress is placed on externally set Statutory Assessment Tasks (SATs).

For the teacher committed to action research and thus to enhanced professionalism, this Fordist, conveyor belt, strait-jacket curriculum can offer little hope of an enabling education for our children. The review undertaken by the School Curriculum and Assessment Authority (SCAA) in 1993–94 (Dearing, 1994) offers little scope for fundamental improvement of this situation, although marginal improvements are included. The professional role of teachers will need to be reconsidered radically if education that will genuinely offer the opportunity for the development of autonomous thinking individuals is to be re-established. The effective growth of action research as a means to a new professionalism should assist considerably in this process and should help to provide the opportunity for geography to begin to move towards the achievement of its true educational potential once again.

BIBLIOGRAPHY

Alexander, R.J. and Ellis, J.W. (eds) (1981) *Advanced Study for Teachers*, Teacher Education Study Group, Society for Research into Higher Education, distributed by Naferton Books.

Buckingham, R.B. (1926) *Research for Teachers*, Silver Burdett Co.

Carr, W. and Kemmis, S. (1986) *Becoming Critical: Education, Knowledge and Action Research*, The Falmer Press.

Corey, S. (1953) *Action Research to Improve School Practices*, Columbia University, Teachers' College Press.

Dearing, R. (1994) *The National Curriculum and Assessment. Final Report*, School Curriculum and Assessment Authority.

DES (1991) *Geography in the National Curriculum (England)*, Department of Education and Science, HMSO.

Dewey, J. (1910) *How We Think*, D.C. Heath.

(1929) *The Sources of a Science of Education*, Horace Liveright.

(1938) *Logic: The Theory of Inquiry*, Henry Holt.

Dunkerley, S.M. (1992) 'The implementation of National Curriculum Geography in one primary school', unpublished MA dissertation, Institute of Education, University of London.

Elliott, J. (1981) 'The teacher as researcher within award-bearing courses', in Alexander, R.J. and Ellis, J.W. (eds) *Advanced Study for Teachers*, Teacher Education Study Group, Society for Research into Higher Education, distributed by Naferton Books.

— (1991) *Action Research for Educational Change*, Open University Press.

Elliott, J. and Adelman, C. (1976) *Innovation at the Classroom Level: A Case Study of the Ford Teaching Project*, Open University Press.

Fien, J. (1992) 'What kind of research for what kind of teaching? Towards research in geographical education as a critical social science', in Hill, D. (ed.) *International Perspectives on Geographic Education*, Center for Geographic Education, University of Colorado at Boulder/Rand McNally.

Habermas, J. (1972) *Knowledge and Human Interests*, Heinemann.

Haubrich, H. (ed.) (1994) *Europe and the World in Geography Education*, Papers for the International Geographical Union Commission on Geographical Education Meetings in Berlin and Prague, 1994, Geographiedidaktische Forschungen Band 25, Hochschulverband für Geographie und ihre Didaktik e. V. (Selbstverlag).

Hickman, G., Reynolds, J. and Tolley, H. (1973) *A New Professionalism for a Changing Geography*, Schools Council Geography 14–18 Project, Schools Council.

Hill, D. (ed.) (1992) *International Perspectives on Geographic Education*, Center for Geographic Education, University of Colorado at Boulder/Rand McNally.

Kayes, J. (1992) 'Taking equal opportunities in school a step further: an evaluation of a subject-focused response', unpublished MA dissertation, Institute of Education, University of London.

Kemmis, S. (1980) 'Action research in retrospect and prospect', mimeo presented at the Annual General Meeting of the Australian Association for Research in Education, Sydney.

Klemp, G.O. (1977) *Three Factors of Success in the World of Work: Implications for Curriculum in Higher Education*, McBer & Co.

Kwan, T. and Lee, J. (1994) 'A reflective report on an action research towards understanding conceptions of action research held by geography teachers', in Haubrich, H. (ed.) *Europe and the World in Geography Education*, Geographiedidaktische Forschungen Band 25, Hochschulverband für Geographie und ihre Didaktik e. V. (Selbstverlag).

Lewin, K. (1948) *Resolving Social Conflicts*, Harper.

Lidstone, J. (1994) 'Becoming professional: geographers and environmental education', keynote address delivered at International Geographical Union Regional Conference, Prague, 1994.

McCarthy, C. (1978) *The Critical Theory of Jürgen Habermas*, Hutchinson.

McKernan, J. (1991) *Curriculum Action Research. A Handbook of Methods and Resources for the Reflective Practitioner,* Kogan Page.

McNiff, J. (1988) *Action Research. Principles and Practice*, Macmillan Education.

Naish, M., Rawling, E. and Hart, C. (1987) *Geography 16–19: The Contribution of a Curriculum Project to 16–19 Education*, Longman.

Stenhouse, L. (1975) *An Introduction to Curriculum Research and Development*, Heinemann.

Schön, D. (1983) *The Reflective Practitioner*, Temple Smith.

Sweasey, P. J. (1989) ' "Homework with Humanity". A study of homework in geography and humanities in secondary schools', unpublished MA dissertation, Institute of Education, University of London.

12 Improving practice through practitioner research: learning to account for myself

Anthony Ghaye

This chapter represents an account of my own educational development since 1974. It is not the whole story but rather some snapshots which relate to researching my own practice, with a view to trying to improve the quality of education for those with whom I have been working.

> 'But you must not accept my story as gospel, you know it is only a retelling, in parts.'
> 'It's a story', said Mrs Clemency equably, 'that's the point.'
>
> Hill, 1978:130

For the purpose of this book I will illustrate some of what I shall claim to be my major ways of thinking, ways of doing and seeing and how these have shifted over time, with examples, where appropriate, drawn from children's learning through geography. Over the last twenty years as a practitioner-researcher I have come to appreciate that if I always think the way I have always thought, then things will happen the way they have always happened. I have also learned that in order to improve my thinking about my practice, my practice itself and the social context in which it is situated, I have needed both intellectual and affective support (Day, 1985:138). In this chapter I focus primarily on the major sources of intellectual support and inspiration which I believe have, over time, enabled me to become more confident and competent in confronting questions of the kind, 'How can I improve my practice in order to enhance the quality of learning in my classroom?'

I have crafted this account with the hope that readers will find what I have to say educationally significant. More specifically these hopes are fivefold:

- I hope my value positions are clear. They have changed over time. Educational values are not always fixed entities. They shift and move and change in character and emphasis as we develop and as we are buffeted by the turbulence of educational change.

- I hope you feel that this is a passionate account (Ghaye, 1990). I use the word 'passionate' deliberately because I want to convey to you a sense of those things I have really cared for and have been concerned about in my professional practice.
- I also hope that what I say here is useful to you in some way, that my account has the potential to make some significant impact on your thinking about your teaching of geography.
- Related to this I hope that some of you might feel empowered to act, to do something as a consequence of reading this account.
- Finally, I hope that you feel you can trust my story. I want to address this criterion by attempting to support the claims I make with evidence drawn from my practice and from the work of others.

I would like you to judge the validity of my claim to know with reference to these five aspirations.

> I realise that I have more than begun, I have plunged on too far ahead. I have already lost any sense of pattern. But that is right, that cannot be as bad as the pompous, meaningless attempt at a formal beginning...
>
> Hill, 1972:13

To make some sense of aspects of twenty years as a teacher I have drawn upon the notion of a professional life cycle and in particular I have construed my life as a 'career' (Huberman, 1993). The main advantage of using the concept of *career* is that it will enable me to add a sense of selectivity, focus and boundedness to what I have to say about my attempts at doing practitioner research with the intention of improving the quality of my geography teaching with those in my care. I use here four of Huberman's career phases and then go inside each one in order to set out my educational values and the way these gave a shape, form and purpose to what I did. Actions and reflections will then be added. The four main career phases are these:

1 *Painful beginnings*   Feeling my way into the profession as a geography teacher.

2 *A period of transition*   Where I felt that I had to engage in some in-service education.

3 *Stabilisation*   Being clearer about that to which I was committed.

4 *Activism*   A desire to increase the impact of my practice beyond the confines of the classroom.

Painful beginnings

I was trained as a teacher of geography and physical education in a college of higher education. I left after four years of study with a Bachelor of Education degree, supposedly equipped to teach children from 8 to 13 years of age. My first job was in a school in Leicestershire where I taught geography to children between the ages of 11 and 13 years. It was a period of survival but it was also a time of discovery. One of my major preoccupations of that time was the question, 'How can I support and facilitate learning when I am somewhat bewildered and uncertain about what was actually happening in my geography classroom?' Some of my reflections on my practice went like this. This is a reconstruction based on my own lived experiences.

> I left college thinking that I should have a healthy respect for those robust and complicated things called theories. Lengthy lectures about Ausubelian advanced organisers, Piagetian stages, Brunerian spirals, Gagné's types of learning, Rumelhart and Norman's information processing, about Freud and Jung, and so on, led me to believe that educational theory was related to educational practice, my practice. Additionally, because I believed that these bodies of knowledge were put together systematically and over time by respected academics, then they would have the power to explain what was happening in my classroom. As you can hear, I put a lot of faith and trust in them.
>
> But very soon things started to happen which initially led me to think that something was seriously wrong either with me, the children, the activities or, even worse, the whole learning milieu in my classroom. For example, I was finding that some children were very good at solving practical science-type problems when working on the topics of rock and soils, but much less good at understanding that places were located in both space and time. I found that some children were very good at creative writing when we were exploring the experiences of those living in hazardous environments and yet they were still counting on their fingers when we were doing exercises requiring graphicacy and numeracy. I found that some children wanted the freedom to learn and to express themselves in their own way when we were exploring the neighbourhood but wanted lots of structure and guidance in order to be able to follow my oral explanations in class. And what about my own geography teaching? In short, when I appealed to theory and tried to relate it to what was actually going on in my classroom to help me to explain the learning I thought was going on – a classroom full of unpredictability, multidimensionality and simultaneity, I discovered two things. First, the theory did not fit my particular situation. Even if I tried to force-fit it, it did not fit. Second, it did not help to explain my practice,

to enable me to offer explanations for what was going on. As a newly qualified teacher I needed to feel confident that the profession, which had just acquired a new member, possessed educational theory which could relate directly to educational practice in classrooms. For the first five years of my career as a geography teacher I had a crisis of confidence. All this so-called 'knowledge' seemed to have no direct relevance to my practical everyday pedagogical problems. (See Eraut, 1994, for some very useful insights into the acquisition and use of theory by beginning teachers: 59–74.)

I want to extend and elaborate upon some of the things I claim I learned from these early and very formative 'beginning' years as a geography teacher. I held a number of debilitating beliefs. First I had too much respect for the knowledge generated by others. I did not question it. By implication I devalued my own knowledge. I can remember asking myself the question, 'So why doesn't my knowledge count as much as yours?' I was beginning to learn that knowledge was 'positioned' (Hollingsworth, 1994). There seemed to be a kind of high-status knowledge and then there was my knowledge. I felt that my knowledge did not count as much as that knowledge I was reading about in books and written largely by people working in institutions of higher education. Second, I did not believe that knowledge could be seen as a 'contested terrain'. Perhaps rather naively I thought knowledge from 'outside' was relevant and appropriate. If it did not appear to be so then the problem rested with me, not with the nature of this knowledge. Third, I believed that I could facilitate children's learning through geography even though I could not claim to understand and enhance my own learning. This was misguided and presumptuous. Fourth, I believed that because I felt able to explain things clearly to children, I could naturally talk clearly about my practice to other teachers. I was in fact very inarticulate and unable to explain my most sacred and cherished geographical work patterns and values when called upon to do so. I was unable to transform contextualised experience into decontextualised discourse. Finally, I believed that if I looked at my pupils I would understand what they were learning. On reflection I needed to shift from looking and to make more effort to listen to my pupils. The conflict I experienced between my beliefs and my practice gave me the motivation to go back to do some more specific learning about my teaching of geography.

A period of transition

In 1976 I enrolled as a part-time MA student at the Institute of Education, University of London. My course was in geography education. The first year was organised around a number of themes such as those to do with the development of geography as a discipline, new subject 'frontiers', geography curriculum planning and evaluation, and the development of children's geographic knowledge, skills and sensitivities. I wrote a number of essays. The second year was devoted to writing a dissertation. I wrote mine on 'the identification and arrangement of certain geographical concepts for the 11–14 age range' (Ghaye, 1978). It was essentially a piece of practitioner research which attempted to build a curriculum that emphasised the teaching and learning of geographic concepts, for I believed at that time (1977–78) – and still do – that concepts are the building blocks for all learning. I managed to get some of my early ideas about conceptual development and curriculum construction published (Ghaye, 1977 and, after my dissertation, Ghaye, 1983). I went public with my ideas not out of some deep-felt value position that this is what novice practitioner-researchers *should* do! I did it to see if anyone might be interested in the kind of knowledge I had constructed. To my surprise and delight someone 'out there' was.

I was on a very steep learning curve between 1976 and 1978. In the essays that I wrote during the first year, I was slowly moving away from the detached teacher-as-observer of learning and moving towards a position that I could increasingly defend as a teacher 'reconstructing from within the inherent logic of the situation as perceived and experienced by the actors themselves...' (Crozier and Friedberg, 1977:262). Increasingly I began to feel good about this. Having taken the plunge, new insights and discoveries were made. New beliefs began to emerge. For example, I began to wake up to the fact that it was legitimate for me to focus upon my pupils' learning, my own learning and the context in which it took place. I began to get really interested in three questions. First, 'What does learning look like in my classroom?' Second, 'How do the children in my class learn most effectively?' And third, 'How am I as a teacher learning about my practice?' Since this moment in my career I have always had a fascination for learning and I am always on the lookout for it. For example:

It is 10.30 am and the time for Charlotte to finish her lesson with her class of thirty Year 5 children. She has been working on the topic of canals. Charlotte recalls:

'After this morning's lesson, during playtime, I asked some of the children if they had learned anything from the lesson. Some politely conceded having learned a bit, others confessed to having learned nothing! The most memorable response came from Billy when I asked, "Well, what have you learned from the lesson, Billy?" His reply was, "Eh, something Miss, but I can't remember what it was."'

Ghaye, Johnstone and Jones, 1992:19

I was also coming to know two other values which were rapidly giving my practice a new form and purpose. I was waking up to the fact that I had a responsibility for my own learning and a responsibility to be able to account for myself. This has stayed with me (Ghaye, 1994a, 1994b). Additionally I began to believe that if I was to enhance the quality of learning I had to begin at the interface between me and my pupils. It was here that I had to begin to interrogate my practice.

Stabilisation and commitment

Huberman (1993) characterises this period as one in which a teacher 'sets about mastering more systematically the various aspects of the job. This may include a specific focus or specialization . . . For others, stabilization may lead to added responsibility, with attendant increments of prestige and financial rewards' (p.3). For me this period marks the time when I began to choose a certain professional identity for myself. It was also a period of pedagogical consolidation. I had worked in a number of schools in the UK and abroad, held posts of responsibility, and decided that a post in higher education would be an appropriate niche for me where, initially, I would be teaching undergraduate-level geography *per se* and also enabling students to teach geography in primary and secondary schools. It was in the early 1980s that I believe I came of age. Moving from schools as workplaces to a college of higher education as my workplace was a huge rite of passage. I want to claim that I learned two main things in that period with regard to classroom-based research to support and enhance children's learning.

1 That we first need to research our own practice if we want to

enhance it and improve the quality of the educative relationships we have with our pupils.

2 That I had to learn to research my own practice and the context in which it took place in a systematic, rigorous and disciplined way.

I want to open up each of these claims now to share a number of things that I have learned about the interplay between practitioner research in classrooms and enhancing children's learning.

CLAIM ONE: THAT I RESEARCHED MY OWN PRACTICE WITH A VIEW TO ENHANCING IT

With hindsight two things contributed to this. First, I registered to do a PhD degree. I stayed with the Institute of Education. I liked their style and I knew some of the staff. Amongst other things I wanted to do a PhD because I thought it might give me some added incentive to structure and disseminate action and reflections on my geography teaching. Second, and because of my particular professional role in the early 1980s, I had the opportunity to get into school to teach but also to recover my own exteriority by being able to work in the college. Being able to oscillate between being an insider and an outsider, between being close in and more detached, is important when trying to gain a sense of perspective on our role as facilitators of learning.

My PhD was generally a joy to undertake (Ghaye, 1984) because I was committed to the central research question, which was: 'How can I improve my practice of teaching geography in order to enhance the quality of the learning of the children in my class?' But I want to make something clear. This question is a retrospective reconstruction of what it was that I was doing. Put another way, this was what I was examining but I did not fully appreciate it at the time! Finding a significant research question is a crucial step. I suggest that you 'test' your commitment to your research question and its significance as follows:

- *How far is it utility focused?*   i.e. how far will your research be useful to you and the people you work with?
- *How far is it feasibility conscious?*   i.e. how feasible will your research be in relation to the pragmatics and socio-political context in which your research is located?

- *How far is it propriety oriented?* i.e. how far do you feel that researching your question can be done justly and ethically?
- *How far is it empirical?* i.e. how far can you bring data to bear upon it?
- *How far is it prospective?* i.e. how far does your question suggest that you wish to bring about some improvement in the future?
- *How far is it of personal interest?* i.e. how far do you care about it, feel passionate about it and committed to exploring it?

I completed my PhD in 1984 and went to my first conference. More by luck than judgement I picked a good one. It was a Classroom Action Research Network (CARN) conference on 'Collaborative Action Research' at the Cambridge Institute of Education. I presented a conference paper, my first, which was an account of my classroom-based research. It was subsequently published in a CARN Bulletin (Ghaye, 1986a). I am still attracted to the title of it because it reflects another deep-seated value position that I hold. In order to facilitate children's learning I believe it is fundamental to look closely at the match between what teachers say and what they do, on the one hand, and what children say about learning and what they are actually learning on the other. In the introduction to the paper I explain why I undertook this piece of practitioner research and some of the hallmarks of it. Part of the introduction is reproduced in Figure 12.1.

I would like to begin by reading to you a short extract from Tom Stoppard's work, 'Albert's Bridge' because it helps to contextualize in a vivid way the research project I want to describe to you this evening. Embedded in this short extract is a reason why I became involved in the project and two important hallmarks of it, namely that of seeing things from the participant's point of view, and the critical role that 'perspective' plays in making sense of the world around us.

Fraser goes up on to Albert's Bridge in order to commit suicide and says:

'I couldn't bear the noise and the chaos. I couldn't get free of it, the enormity of that disorder, so dependent on a chance sequence of action and reaction. So I started to climb, to get some height you know, enough height to drop from to be sure, and the higher I climbed the more I saw and the less I heard.

And look now. I've been up here for hours, looking down, and all it is is dots and bricks, giving out a gentle hum. Quite safe. Quite small after all. Quite ordered, seen from above. Laid out in squares, each square a function, each dot a functionary. Yes, from this vantage point things do look different.'

And so it was that two years ago I

began working for one day each week, for three terms, in a four-form entry comprehensive school, with a teacher and a class of thirty 11–12 year-old children.

For me, a full-time lecturer in a college of higher education, it was an opportunity to continue with some actual classroom teaching, to be responsible for teaching one class, in one school department, for a year, and at the same time pursue my interest in classroom based research, particularly that which explores the quality of individual pupil learning experiences. For the teacher, a head of department, it was a chance to look closely and in a sustained way at the humanities curriculum on offer to pupils, a chance which could not be passed over in view of the fact that he was 'confused by the noise and chaos', by 'the enormity of the disorder' brought about largely by local authority secondary reorganisation.

Before any attempts were made to alter the curriculum we decided we should undertake a thorough investigation of the nature of what was currently on offer, the aim being to identify and understand those aspects of classroom life which helped or hindered learning. Our work rested primarily upon five assumptions. The first was that ethnography with its cognisance of context, its quest for understanding the perspectives of the people under study and way of observing their activities in everyday life, provided an appropriate platform of principles and procedures necessary to come to an adequate understanding of the professional issue we were to examine for three school terms. The issue was:

'How does a body of knowledge develop in a pupil's mind and how might a busy teacher monitor, assess and account for a pupil's developing conception in terms of the changes that occur in both the amount and quality of what is learned?'

Three other assumptions are embedded in this issue. One was our belief that college lecturer, school teacher and pupils had to be collaborators in an illuminative process. Another was that the principle of triangulation had to be used in data collection to promote ecological validity. Additionally we proceeded on the assumption that access to the kinds of evidence collected – the control and confidentiality of it – had to be explored fully with all the participants.

We gathered evidence using a variety of techniques such as questionnaires, pupil semantic structure diagrams, pupil self-reports, schoolteacher field-notes, transcripts of classroom discourse, and video-recordings of lessons followed by researcher–pupil focused interviews. It is here that the fifth and last assumption is located. We believe that each method used has not only to serve a teaching function (to claim quality as a teaching procedure) but serve a research purpose also.

This evening I would like to disclose some of the more important things we (and I include the pupils here) learned about ourselves, about each other and about the dynamic interplay between pupil–teacher–task and the situation in which they are found. To do this I have divided what follows into two parts. The first part looks at a way of assessing the match between what was taught and learned. The second part considers two ways of supplementing this picture with evidence of the classroom under-life.

Source: Ghaye, 1986a

Figure 12.1 Extract from 'Discovering classroom underlife: a prerequisite for assessing the match between what is taught and learned'

In 1986 I published two further accounts of my work. The first (Ghaye, 1986b) focused on what my pupils and I were learning in our geography lessons when I set up a particular context for learning, namely children working in self-directed groups. Using video tape and video feedback in a catalytic way, I was able to 're-see' and review what was happening in my geography lessons. By showing my pupils the tapes, they were able to 're-experience' and to explicate the rationale upon which their thinking, feelings and actions, in the group, were based. In this paper I tried to set out and support a claim that a more holistic understanding of learning through working together in a group could be achieved when teachers and pupils 'think together' to explore the dynamic, ambiguous and often provisional links that exist between thoughts and actions. The section from this paper on 'gathering evidence' is reproduced in Figure 12.2. Video tape is a powerful and rich source of evidence from which to learn about practice, particularly as our lessons with our children are rather like bubbles of a 'fleeting and ephemeral quality' (Jackson, 1979:31).

Gathering evidence

Evidence was gathered on 24 separate occasions across one school year. Work was based on the environmental topic of 'resources'. Lessons were prepared and taught by me while the school teacher adopted the role in my class of observer-as-participant.

There were occasions throughout the year when pupils worked in small, mixed sex, self-directed groups of six. Pupils were presented with a resource-related problem and were given one hour to formulate an adequate and justified resolution. This meant that they had to work collaboratively and draw upon and apply their collective skills and understanding. Before lessons of this kind the teacher and I decided which one of the five groups we would study. In order to capture and reflect upon what the pupils said and did, and their manner of proceeding, video-recordings were made of these lessons. Later that day, in a quiet reading room, I had a 30-minute focused interview (Merton and Kendall, 1946) with each child in the target group. We were concerned that the children should understand the function of the interview and of keeping diaries to record their group work experiences. We felt they had the right to know. We discussed our motives and intentions principally in relation to differences between a pupil's performance on and understanding of a task, the rewards for being right and being thoughtful and the difference between safe responses and personal ones. In the interview each child was shown the same three-minute video-segment of their group's work. The segments were drawn from the 15, 30 and 45 minute points within the allotted time span. The general intention was to use video-feedback as a catalytic medium to help pupils to re-experience and to explicate the rationale upon which their actions were constructed. These act meanings were audio

---

recorded and subjected to content analysis. We had to constantly cross-check our analyses with each child, being mindful of the fact that what we were claiming was reality in the pupil's mind had to be reality in the same way that they were conceiving it.

The procedure for portraying each child's outer appearance was as follows. After school the teacher and I replayed the video-recording. First we had to locate those parts of the recording which had formed the basis of the interview. The behaviours of one of the six children in the target group were then scrutinised. The teacher and I took turns to try to describe the nature and record the duration of the child's behaviour during each three-minute segment. For example, if the teacher elected to go first he would control the video-recorder. When a particular behaviour began he would say 'Now'. When it appeared that the same behaviour finished he would say 'Stop'. He would then write a description of the behaviour he observed in his notebook. I would sit alongside recording the duration of each behaviour on a stopwatch. The teacher would then simultaneously press Play on the video-recorder and say 'Now' and the procedure described above was repeated. In this way each child's overt behaviour could be viewed frame by frame. At the end of one three-minute segment our roles were reversed. I would attempt to describe the child's behaviour while the teacher operated the stopwatch. We would then compare descriptions and durations, offering each other a justification for what we saw, or thought we saw. This was the process of constructing action meanings. When there was a mismatch of interpretations we reviewed and discussed the appropriate part of the segment until we were able to describe the child's behaviour in a way that satisfied both of us. An example of what would emerge for each child at the end of one three-minute segment is shown in Fig 1.

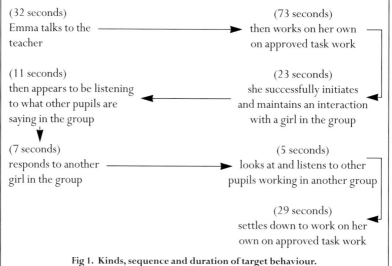

Fig 1. **Kinds, sequence and duration of target behaviour.**

Source: Ghaye, 1986b

Figure 12.2 Extract from 'Outer appearances with inner experiences: towards a more holistic view of group work'

I also want to refer to another paper that was published in the *British Educational Research Journal* (Ghaye, 1986c) because not only is it a reflection of another central belief I hold about supporting children's learning, but the work I did for that paper also had a profound and lasting effect on me. It was a paper based upon the premise that I might become more effective as a geography teacher if I had a better understanding of my pupils' 'states of mind'. The data comprised 434 accounts written by thirty 11 year-old children in my class of their geographical experiences with me. I have included here (Figure 12.3) two short sections from this paper. The one sets the context for 'eliciting pupil accounts' of their learning experiences. The other focuses upon the uses of 'pupil diaries'. I have referred to this account of my practice because it helped me to appreciate that few 'can claim to know themselves in a complete, consistent and uncomplicated way' (Ghaye, 1986c:134).

Pupil Typifications of Topic Work

Eliciting pupil accounts.   For some considerable time teachers and research workers have been eliciting pupil perceptions of school and schooling. Not surprisingly these have been gathered in a variety of ways, for example through interviews and more formal conversations (Becker, 1952; Davies, 1982; Beynon & Atkinson, 1984; Logan, 1984; Measor, 1984; Pollard, 1985), repertory grid tests (Nash, 1976), questionnaires (Woods, 1976) and diaries (Lacey, 1970; Cotterell, 1982). Methods have been combined in various ways often supported by extensive field observations (Furlong, 1984). The utility and authenticity of pupil accounts together with the possible implications of making public that which usually remains unknown to teachers, has also been discoursed about (Hargreaves, 1977; Nisbett & Wilson, 1977; Hammersley & Atkinson, 1983; McKelvey & Kyriacou, 1985).

Despite the attention that has been given to finding ways of making more visible and therefore more understandable those configurations of meaning that comprise consumer knowledge, two significant 'blind spots' remain. We still know very little about the way pupil perceptions of the same school phenomenon change over time. One of the few report studies of this kind is Gannaway (1976). Embedded in this are the neglected distinctions between those accounts that are situation-specific and those which are context independent, and also those which are idiosyncratic or held by those who share a similar world. Hereafter this paper refers to these as transcontextual and transpersonal 'typifications' respectively. Second, the link between awareness of consumer views and teacher reactions to them is inadequately articulated. For example, how might knowledge of pupil typifications of one subject, gathered across one school year, lead to more 'effective teaching' (Kyriacou, 1985) and perhaps improve the quality of the teachers' day-to-day encounters with their pupils?

Typifications have been lucidly discussed by Schutz (1932, 1973), Hargreaves (1977) and Furlong (1977). Hargreaves argues that the way pupils and teachers construe or 'type' each other plays a critical part in our understanding of the nature of classroom life and teacher–pupil relations.

The influence of context on what pupils come to know is well documented (Lunzer, 1965; Entwistle, 1979; Biggs & Collis, 1982). We should therefore be mindful of the influence of contextual variations in the typification process. But for consumer knowledge of this kind to be of real practical use to teachers it has to have an anticipatory quality. In other words it must help teachers anticipate how teaching certain ideas and skills in a certain manner is likely to be construed by their pupils. Two kinds of knowing help with this. First, teachers need to know the critical attributes and thus the dimensionality of pupil typifications in a number of commonly occurring contexts (e.g. in group work, class discussions, silent work). Secondly, they need to know when particular typifications are called upon by certain pupils.

Pupil diaries.   Three interrelated issues are pertinent to this paper. These are the context in which an account is made, its evidential value and its intended audience. Teachers involved in the Ford Teaching Project (Elliott *et al.*, 1975) elicited pupil accounts, some of which were in the form of pupil diaries. The principal *raison d'être* was that a pupil's account could be used by a teacher as a yardstick to judge the degree of congruence between what they espoused and how they were perceived to behave. This reflects a prevailing tendency in that the value of pupil accounts is often seen from the point of view of those who read, rather than those who write them. Some teachers who have tried to elicit accounts in the form of pupil diaries have remained unconvinced as to their value. For example, 'The majority (of teachers) asked students to keep diaries, but reported little evidence of any deeper thinking beyond, "it was a bit boring" or "the lesson was alright" ' (Elliott, 1976, p.8). We have to seek answers to a number of questions in order to understand why this was the case. For example, how did the students perceive the function of keeping a diary? How open did they feel they could be? Were they locked into presenting safe rather than personal responses and if so why? Arguably then what is of most value to teachers are pupil diaries that not only contain honest and open accounts, but those that also include justifications or reasons why pupils interpreted the lesson in the way they did. The problem is how to tease-out these hidden meanings, grasp this inner reality and come to a shared understanding of situations. We must guard against creating an accountability context in the sense of teachers challenging pupils to account for their thoughts and feelings. A way of overcoming this is to see keeping diaries as opportunities for expressive writing (Britton, 1971), where teachers help their pupils to present their 'loaded commentary on the world' and to explain their view of things. By using the diary to ask questions aimed at clarifying participant understandings, a context can be created where pupils feel they can inform and share rather than merely reply. The diary then becomes a dialogue which is not adversarial but, as Socrates expressed it, 'like friends talking together'. This friendly dialogue is a creative experience for both pupil and teacher.

A more developed and elaborated account of this work can be found in Ghaye, 1989.

Source: Ghaye, 1986c

Figure 12.3 Extract from 'Pupil typifications of topic work'

One further illustration is provided here (Figure 12.4) in order to point up four more issues pertinent to facilitating children's geographical

Some reflections. I hope that this short paper at least begins to suggest some of the really important things we might consider with regard to how learning can be enhanced by embedding the microcomputer within it. Looking back on all of this, some twelve months later, I feel that it made me think about the following.

Disembedded work. It seems that computers can be used in many ways to enhance children's and students' learning. What I have learned is that each way rests upon a particular view of how children may be helped to learn (Hughes, 1990). A day such as this where the computer is seen as an integrated and integral part of a learning process seems important. Disembedding it and therefore decontextualising it seems counter-productive. Creating a genuine need to use the computer, in a natural learning context, is probably one of the crucial early moves to make when planning for effective learning to take place.

Thinking skills. The idea that the computer can be used to develop children's thinking skills is not uncommon (Papert, 1980). What I have found is that we have some grounds for suggesting that the computer can facilitate that important cognitive process of metacognition, which Entwistle (1981) calls our 'seventh sense'. In other words this day has, in some small yet important way, helped the children to think about their own thinking that informs what it is that they do. I feel this might be a rich area for future teacher-researchers to explore.

Time to reflect. Reflection is of course a certain kind of thinking. Many have stressed how important it is to know both why reflective thought is important and the different ways to engage in it (Donaldson, 1978: Grimmett and Erickson,1988; Louden 1991; Winter, 1989). This exercise has caused me to think through how computers, if used in this way, can help learners to build meanings, confront them on the screen and rebuild them if necessary. Here the art of critical reflection becomes important for teachers to teach and children to practise.

Feeling in control. Much of the evidence which underscores this paper directly or indirectly refers to feelings of control. Being in control is clearly a highly motivating force in learning, especially where the learning is complex and new. The teachers' theories-of-action which were expressed in their practices suggested that they were adherents of 'learning by discovery'. But they had a particular view of this. Their construction of a context for their children to learn by discovery was not one where children discovered by chance and in a haphazard way. It was underpinned by a clear rationale. The key to a successful day was flexibility within a clear and robust learning framework.

Becoming critical. This case study suggests how meaningful partnerships and significant relationships between schools and colleges, teachers, tutors, students and children, can create a context for a critical review of the process of facilitating quality learning. Through the interview with me, the teacher was able to adopt a critical view of the day. She was able to describe her practice, articulate what underpinned it, begin to confront her assumptions and beliefs and think about what aspects she might change. The evidence from students and children also showed that much can be learned from this critical posture. 'Being critical does not mean being negative, but refers rather to the stance of enabling teachers to see their classroom actions in relation to the historical, social and cultural context in which their teaching is actually embedded' (Smyth, 1991, p. 17).

Source: Ghaye, 1992

Figure 12.4 Extract from 'Tales from the Riverbankers'

learning through practitioner research. In 1992 I published a paper called 'Tales from the Riverbankers: children and teachers becoming critical with the aid of the microcomputer' (Ghaye, 1992), which I subsequently revisited and reconstructed (Ghaye, 1994c). The first point the paper makes is that it reflects my sustained commitment to working closely and in partnership with learners; to try to understand how they think and feel. Second, it illustrates that the questioning of my own practice described earlier (see 'Painful beginnings') is still there in the 1990s but more grounded now, more stable and consolidated.

> To understand what it is we do, we need to see professional action as a form of inquiry underpinned by the adoption of a research posture in our classrooms... Becoming critical is a process. We do not suddenly become critical... The process is supported by a number of skills and strategies. In essence I believe these to be the learners' ability to question what it is they do, gather evidence about their work, and analyse, reflect upon, justify and transform actions and the value system that underpins them. I also believe that this is a process that needs to begin early in the life of every learner.
>
> Ghaye, 1992:22

Third, it reminds us about how important it is in geography teaching for children to see the worlds outside their school as a classroom. In this case the classroom was a riverbank. Finally, it serves as an illustration of how 'technology' can aid geographical learning. I have reproduced here the tailpiece of that paper. I believe it makes a number of statements that I want to press home about facilitating learning in the 'classroom'.

CLAIM TWO: THAT I DID INDEED DEVELOP SOME UNDERSTANDINGS, SKILLS AND SENSITIVITIES WITH REGARD TO UNDERTAKING PRACTITIONER RESEARCH IN A SYSTEMATIC, RIGOROUS AND DISCIPLINED WAY

There have been many people but also many books which have influenced and shaped my thinking as a practitioner-researcher. In the early 1980s one particular text gave me certain insights and a rationale which I believe is worth stating here with regard to the focus of this chapter. Michael Patton's book (1980), *Qualitative Evaluation and Research Methods*, drew my attention to this fundamental premise that 'how you study the world determines what you learn about the world' (p.67). So how can the world of the classroom be studied? The choice is profoundly important. There are many ways to do this and numerous research perspectives to draw upon. Understandably this can seem bewildering. But Patton adds reassuringly that researchers '…must make their own decisions about the relative values of any perspective' (p.89). I believe that this gives practitioner-researchers the opportunity to make a claim that there is no taken-for-granted virtue in conforming to the strictest interpretation of any particular research style or approach, but instead it may be prudent technically, socially, ethically and politically to draw in elements from any approach into an amalgam tailored to the unique circumstances under which you are conducting your enquiry. You will see evidence of this position in my own work cited here.

More recently another text has given me a greater sense of what it was that I had been doing for a number of years. Egon Guba and Yvonna Lincoln (1989), in their book *Fourth Generation Evaluation*, set out the case for 'constructivist' thinking. I can align myself with this mindset – more so when they clarify the constructivist's position in relation to the three fundamental building blocks of any research: ontology, epistemology and methodology. There are three big messages here for those researching issues to do with geography education.

The first is ontology – that is, what is the nature of reality, or what is there that can be known? The constructivist asserts a 'relativist' ontology. In this understanding of 'how things are' there is no such thing as an objective 'truth' out there, waiting to reveal itself to the inquiring mind of the geography teacher. Instead, the only way in which the word 'truth' can have any meaning at all is to define it as 'the most informed and sophisticated construction on which there is a consensus among individuals most competent (not necessarily most powerful) to form such a construction' (p.86). In terms of epistemology – that is, the origin, nature and limits of human knowledge – the constructivist takes a 'monistic' view. The researcher and the subject/s are not separate entities with 'clear water' between the two, so essential for 'uncontaminated research'! The monistic view asserts that the 'inquirer and the inquired-into are interlocked in such a way that the findings of an investigation are the literal creation of the inquiry process' (p.84). When it comes to methodology, the dice are already cast for the geography educator and practitioner-researcher by the ontological approach and epistemological assumptions already advanced. Working in 'sterile' conditions, 'context stripping' to remove the confounding influences is not the constructivist's way. Methodologically constructivists embark upon a hermeneutic (interpretive) cycle of statement, analysis, critique, reiteration and re-analysis until a joint collaborative 'construction' has been achieved.

These are complex issues and I only have space to touch on them briefly. I have learned that it is a relatively simple task to make things complex, but a complex one to make them simple! I am trying to offer the geography practitioner-researcher three things to think about. The first is to sort out where you stand with the assertion that 'reality is a social construction'. There are many 'realities' in any classroom. Secondly that as a practitioner-researcher trying to improve your practice and the quality of the educational experiences of your pupils, you are naturally located in the action, not detached from it. So when you phrase your research question, be clear about where you are positioned in your own research. Finally, try to let your responses to my first two points drive the contents of your toolbox, your ways and means of finding out what it is you wish to know.

And into a phase of activism

During the late 1980s and up to the present I have really been enjoying my work in the field of improving the quality of teaching and learning. I have moved away from mainstream geography education and now have a much broader brief which gives me the opportunity to work with school teachers, police trainers, nurse educators, midwifery tutors, social workers and so on. In Sikes' terms (1985), activism is characterised by a desire to both understand and confront the killer cogs, influences and structures that stifle our creativity in the classroom, dull our ardour and hinder us in our attempts to improve the quality of our pupils' educational experiences. For me this period has been one where I have needed to locate and position my own thinking and practitioner research within the ongoing professional discourse about the technical and socio-political nature of enhancing teaching and learning (Ghaye and Wakefield, 1993; Ghaye, 1994d). Space does not permit me to give a full account here of this

activist phase, so I am going to attempt a compromise. I have tried to pinpoint some of the most important texts for me which I claim have contributed significantly to moving my thinking and my practice forward. I shall cite them and recommend them to you as a good read. I then want to select five of these texts and say something about each one of them that is germane to the title of this chapter.

If you won the National Lottery and had some money to build up a small library of books which would help you to gain the knowledge, skills and sensitivities to become a practitioner-researcher dedicated to improving the quality of your practice for the benefit of the children in your class, and yet wanted to view improvement in teaching and learning within the context of an improving school, I would recommend the following:

between these two constituents and the possibility that a teacher might

Altrichter, Posch and Somekh, 1993	Lomax, 1989
Argyris and Schön, 1976	Louis and Miles, 1992
Calderhead and Gates, 1993	McNiff 1991, 1992, 1993
Colins and Chippendale, 1991	Morgan, 1986
Dalin *et al.*, 1994	Plummer and Edwards, 1993
Donaldson, 1978	Ribbins and Burridge, 1994
Freire, 1990	Sheerens, 1989
Fullan, 1991, 1994	Schön, 1990
Hargreaves, 1994	Silver, 1994
Hargreaves and Hopkins, 1991	Whitehead, 1993
Holly, 1989	Zuber-Skerritt, 1991

FIVE TEXTS AND FIVE MESSAGES

Argyris, C., and Schön, D. (1976) *Theory in Practice: Increasing Professional Effectiveness*, Jossey-Bass

Argyris and Schön suggest that we can explain a person's behaviour by attributing to them 'theories of action'. This perspective on things comes in two parts. What a teacher might say about their practice constitutes their 'espoused theories'. What teachers actually do, how they put into practice what they espouse, constitute their 'theories-in-use'. The match

hold different espoused theories and theories-in-use in different contexts provides a very useful way of understanding what is happening in your geography classroom.

Donaldson, M. (1978) *Children's Minds,* Collins/Fontana

Three things from Donaldson's work are germane to this chapter. First, that when planning some practitioner research in your own classroom it is important to consider the whole child, especially if you are trying to discover what a child understands or is capable of in geography. The second important message is the need to consider learning from the child's point of view. We often lose sight of this. Donaldson also reminds us how important it is to try to improve our practice in such a way that children acquire abstract modes of thought. In her terms this means modes of thought and ways of understanding that are 'disembedded' from the vicissitudes of the immediate context.

Morgan, G. (1986) *Images of Organization*, Sage Publications

The teaching and learning of geography occurs in a number of contexts. The most immediate ones are the context of the classroom and the school. Morgan's work helps us to develop the art of reading and understanding how classrooms and schools are organised. He draws upon different metaphors to help us to understand the complex and paradoxical character of organisational life. Reflecting on my own work I can now see how I have sometimes regarded life in my own classrooms as a 'machine' when I have been preoccupied with ideas and ways of working that were to do with routine, efficiency, reliability and predictability, when I have seen teaching in terms of inputs and outcomes. There are times when I have viewed my classroom more like an 'organism', particularly when I have focused on children's needs and the learning environment. I must admit that for a significant period of my time in school, and when I was working towards my PhD, I tended to see my classroom as a 'brain' because I was influenced, even seduced for a time, by the importance of information processing, with theories of communication and learning, and decision-making with regard to the process of learning and the process of learning to learn. More recently I have been viewing the environments in which I teach in four ways: first as 'cultures' organised by values, beliefs, norms and rituals; second as a 'political system' in which interests, conflicts and

power are positioned and can collide; third as a system in 'flux and transformation'. Doing practitioner research with this in mind requires us to be very clear about the issues of ontology, epistemology and methodology discussed earlier. So how do you undertake research in a systematic and rigorous manner in a turbulent, fluid, pulsating and ever-changing environment? Fourthly I am currently trying to clarify my thinking about the idea that classrooms and schools are 'instruments of domination' where individuals and groups find ways of imposing their will on others. This metaphor is particularly useful for understanding organisational behaviour from the perspective of minority or exploited groups. In our teaching of geography it can help us to appreciate that domination may be intrinsic to the way we organise things and not just an unintended side-effect.

Freire, P. (1990) *Pedagogy of the Oppressed*, Penguin Books

> Freire's passion for justice, for critical knowledge, and for social change stand out . . . when you read his work. For Freire, teaching and learning are human experiences with profound social consequences. Education is not reducible to a mechanical method of instruction. Learning is not a quantity of information to be memorised or a package of skills to be transferred to students. Classrooms die as intellectual centres when they become delivery systems for lifeless bodies of knowledge.
>
> McLaren and Leonard, 1993:25

Freire offers us much food for thought as we help children to learn about and through geography. For example, that education is not a neutral process, that we should decide whether we are educating for domestication or emancipation, and that we should affirm the stories that our pupils tell us, for these can serve as guideposts to liberating praxis. Freire proposes a dialogical pedagogy in which learners and teacher engage in active interaction with knowledge in conditions of mutuality and respect. If you share this value, how can you continue to improve your practice so that you are more able to live out this value in your daily work?

Whitehead, J. (1993) *The Growth of Educational Knowledge: Creating Your Own Living Educational Theories*, Hyde Publications

For twenty years as an academic action researcher, Whitehead has been trying to create a new form of educational theory which can be directly related to the processes of improving the quality of learning and to the educational development of individuals. His idea is that educational theory is being constituted by the descriptions which you and I, as individual learners, are producing for our own educational development as we answer professional questions like, 'How do I improve what I am doing?' (Whitehead, 1992: 1). One implication of this position is that practitioner-researchers must speak for themselves. A further implication is that practitioners must come to know their educational values. The inclusion of the individual 'I' experiencing problems because of the negation of their values is also central to his thesis. He offers us an idea which deserves serious attention; namely that we should regard ourselves as 'living contradictions' when values conflict, collide and are not fully lived out in our practice. Being an effective geography teacher for me rests with our ability to create, critique and validate our own living educational theories.

Accounting for myself

In this chapter I have tried to account for myself by creating a story of aspects of my own professional development as a practitioner-researcher trying to improve the quality of geography education. It may seem rather obvious to say this but I have learned that there has always been a very close relationship between the way I think and the way I have acted. This has had one very important consequence for me. It has encouraged me to take some responsibility for and ownership of the part I have played in tackling the professional problems and challenges with which I have been confronted. I offer you the idea that this kind of acceptance can be empowering. This account has also tried to show how I have attempted to adopt a research-based posture and in doing so create a chance to engage in a meaningful dialogue with the situation I am trying to understand and improve. This kind of approach may help us all to grasp the multiple meanings of the educative nature of classroom life and help us to confront and manage educational contradiction and paradox, rather than to pretend that they do not exist in our daily practice.

In accounting for myself I would wish to claim that I have experienced something of a 'paradigm shift' during the last twenty years in my dual attempts to improve my practice and to increase the quality of learning of

those I have worked with. I believe I have supported this claim with evidence. There are a number of golden threads which weave their way through this account, sometimes more overt and explicit, at other times more embedded and coded. These are presented below in summary form.

- *A move away from perceived needs to a more sustained consideration of 'real' needs*

To improve my practice and the quality of educative relationships, I have had to come to know the real needs of my pupils, students and colleagues. I have also had to learn to express my needs.

- *A move away from striving and searching for stability in my praxis to a position where I view change as learning*

I now know that all change is not improvement. In my most recent research I am looking at the 'impact' of teaching and learning on changes in the quality of student thinking and action. I am trying to deepen my understanding and learn more about what constitutes meaningful change.

- *A move away from a focus on the culture of my classroom to a focus on organisational culture*

Individual and collective improvement needs to be set in the context of school improvement. It is the school's culture which is the major influence on the quality of opportunities.

- *A move away from exclusively celebrating the influence of human agency to a structural and political perspective on improving practice*

In this deepening structural perspective I am trying to understand how hierarchies and positions, roles and dependencies enable or hinder work in schools. For me this has to be coupled with understanding how power and influence are distributed in school, how authority and control is exercised, and the way resources are allocated.

This account is dominated by the 'teacher's voice' because it is an attempt to create my own 'living educational theory' (Whitehead, 1993). It is also an attempt to reflect a *discourse of lived cultures*. By that I mean it is a reflection on and interrogation of how a teacher and pupils have created stories, memories and understandings that posit a sense of ambition, intention and agency. It is an account of our 'lived experience'. By drawing upon the dual method of action and reflection, new concerns, possibilities and struggles emerge. I believe we need more accounts that embrace this spirit of what I want to call the discourse of lived cultures, a discourse which I believe involves sustained pedagogical analysis and an understanding of the way political action and cultural production in our schools have an impact on the quality of learning. Public discourses and knowledge of this kind, for me, represent the voice of hope for making a better world.

ACKNOWLEDGEMENTS

I have been fortunate to have the support and stimulating company of a number of colleagues who have encouraged me to write a paper of this kind. I would like to thank several who have helped me to develop my professionalism and to account for myself.

To my supportive and stimulating friends and colleagues: Roy Ballantyne, Chris Day, Margot Ely, Rod Gerber, Colin Henry, Mary Louise Holly, Tammy Kwan, John Lidstone, Pam Lomax, Jean McNiff, Michael Nott, Chris Pascal, Steve Phillipson, David Prideaux and Peter Wakefield. Additionally I am indebted to my Masters and PhD students, past and present, those in the Worcester Action Research support group, and colleagues in my School of Education who always make me stop and think and who help me sustain my 'passion' for my work.

Frances Slater has been there since 1976 with her wisdom and insights. Through educative dialogues and his stimulating writing, Jack Whitehead has enabled me to celebrate and interrogate the living 'I'. Finally I acknowledge a great debt of thanks to my 'critical friend' Kay Danai who has kindled in me a dream of a better world.

BIBLIOGRAPHY

Altrichter, H., Posch, P. and Somekh, B. (1993) *Teachers Investigate Their Work: An Introduction to the Methods of Action Research*, Routledge.

Argyris, C. and Schön, D. (1976) *Theory in Practice: Increasing Professional Effectiveness*, Jossey-Bass.

Becker, H. (1952) 'Social Class Variations in the Teacher–Pupil Relationship', *Journal of Educational Sociology*, 25:451–65.

Beynon, J. and Atkinson, P. (1984) 'Pupils as data-gatherers: mucking and sussing', in Delamont, S. (ed.) *Readings on Interaction in the Classroom*, Methuen.

Biggs, J. and Collis, K. (1982) *Evaluating the Quality of Learning: The Solo Taxonomy: Structure of the Observed Learning Outcome*, Academic Press.

Britton, J. (1971) 'What's the Use', *Educational Review*, 23:205–19.

Calderhead, J. and Gates, P. (eds) (1993) *Conceptualizing Reflection in Teacher Development*, The Falmer Press.

Colins, C. and Chippendale, P. (eds) (1991) *Action Research and Process Management*, Acorn Publications.

Cotterell, J. (1982) 'Student experiences following entry into Secondary School', *Educational Research*, 24:296–302.

Crozier, M. and Friedberg, E. (1977) *Actors and Systems: The Politics of Collective Action*, University of Chicago Press.

Dalin, P. *et al.* (1994) *How Schools Improve: An International Perspective*, Cassell Publications.

Davies, B. (1982) *Life in the Classroom and the Playground: The Accounts of Primary School Children*, Routledge.

Day, C. (1985) 'Professional learning and research intervention: an action research perspective', *British Educational Research Journal*, 11(2):133–51.

Donaldson, M. (1978) *Children's Minds*, Collins/Fontana.

Elliott, J. (1976) *Developing Hypotheses about Classrooms from Teachers' Practical Constructs*, University of North Dakota Press.

Elliott, J. *et al.* (1975) 'Eliciting pupil accounts in the classroom', *The Ford Teaching Project, Unit 2, Research Methods*, CARE, University of East Anglia.

Entwistle, N. (1979) 'Stages, levels, styles and strategies: dilemmas in the description of thinking', *Educational Review*, 31:123–32.

—— (1981) *Styles of Learning and Teaching*, Wiley.

Eraut, M. (1994) *Developing Professional Knowledge and Competence*, The Falmer Press.

Freire, P. (1990) *Pedagogy of the Oppressed*, Penguin Books.

Fullan, M. (1991) *The New Meaning of Educational Change*, Teachers College Press.

—— (1994) *Change Forces: Probing the Depths of Educational Reform*, The Falmer Press.

Furlong, V. (1977) 'Social interaction in the classroom: a participant observation study of pupils' classroom life', unpublished PhD thesis, The City University, London.

—— (1984) 'Interaction sets in the classroom: towards a study of pupil knowledge', in Hammersley, M. and Woods, P. (eds) *Life in School: The Sociology of Pupil Culture*, Open University Press.

Gannaway, H. (1976) 'Making sense of school', in Stubbs, M. and Delamont, S. (eds) *Explorations in Classroom Observation*, Wiley.

Ghaye, A. (1977) 'Towards good practice in the teaching of geography', *Classroom Geographer*, January:17–21.

—— (1978) 'The identification and arrangement of certain geographical concepts for the 11–14 age range', unpublished thesis for the award of MA(Educ), Institute of Education, University of London.

—— (1983) *Discovering Geography* Books 1–3, Macmillan Education.

—— (1984) 'Discovering geographical mindscapes: a participant observation study of children in the middle years of schooling', unpublished PhD thesis, Institute of Education, University of London.

—— (1986a) 'Discovering classroom underlife: a pre-requisite for assessing the match between what is taught and learned', *CARN Bulletin No. 7*:232–42.

—— (1986b) 'Outer appearances with inner experiences: towards a more holistic view of group work', *Educational Review*, 38(1):45–56.

—— (1986c) 'Pupil typifications of topic work', *British Educational Research Journal*, 12(2):125–35.

—— (1989) 'A Teacher, an Adult or a Friend?', in Slater, F. (ed.) *Language and Learning in the Teaching of Geography*, Routledge.

—— (ed.) (1990) 'Perspectives on professional development: histories, stories and celebrations', *START Occasional Paper No. 3*, WCHE Educational Development Unit, Worcester.

—— (1992) 'Tales from the Riverbankers: children and teachers becoming critical with the aid of the microcomputer', *Developing Information Technology in Teacher Education*, 4:17–33.

—— (1994a) 'Accounting for ourselves: changing the culture for learning in a college of higher education', keynote address: World Congress 3, Action Learning, Action Research and Process Management, University of Bath.

—— (1994b) 'Doing quality practitioner research in the workplace: elephants, mazes, passion and empowerment', keynote address: Scottish Education Research Association, University of Strathclyde.

—— (1994c) 'Information technology on the riverbank: a strategy for learning through critical dialogue', in Somekh, B. and Davis, N. (eds) *Using IT Effectively in Teaching and Learning: Studies in Pre-Service and In-Service Teacher Education*, Routledge.

—— (ed.) (1994d) *Creating Cultures for Improvement: Dialogues, Decisions and Dilemmas*, Hyde Publications.

Ghaye, A., Johnstone, E. and Jones, J. (1992) *Assessment and the Management of Learning*, Scholastic Publications.

Ghaye, A. and Wakefield, P. (eds) (1993) *The Role of Self in Action Research*, Hyde Publications.

Grimmett, P. and Erickson, G. (eds) (1988) *Reflection in Teacher Education*, Teachers College Press.

Guba, E. and Lincoln, Y. (1989) *Fourth Generation Evaluation*, Sage.

Hammersley, M. and Atkinson, P. (1983) *Ethnography: Principles in Practice*, Tavistock Publications.

Hargreaves, A. (1994) *Changing Teachers, Changing Times: Teacher's Work and Culture in the Post-modern Age*, Cassell.

Hargreaves, D. (1977) 'The process of typification in classroom interaction: Models and Methods', *British Journal of Educational Psychology*, 47:274–84.

Hargreaves, D. and Hopkins, D. (1991) *The Empowered School: The Management and Practice of Development Planning*, Cassell.

Hill, S. (1972) *The Bird of Night*, Penguin Books.
    (1978) *Gentleman and Ladies*, Penguin Books.

Hollingsworth, S. (1994) 'Repositioning the teacher in US schools and society: feminist readings of action research', unpublished paper presented at the CARN International Conference, University of Birmingham.

Holly, M.L. (1989) *Writing to Grow: Keeping a Personal-Professional Journal*, Heinemann.

Huberman, M. (1993) *The Lives of Teachers*, Teachers College Press and Cassell.

Hughes, M. (1990) 'Children's computation', in Grieve, R. and Hughes, M. (eds) *Understanding Children*, Basil Blackwell.

Jackson, P. (1979) 'The way teaching is', in Moyles, J. *Self-evaluation – A Primary Teacher's Guide*, NFER.

Kyriacou, C. (1985) 'Conceptualizing research on effective teaching', *British Journal of Educational Psychology*, 55:148–55.

Lacey, C. (1970) *Hightown Grammar*, Manchester University Press.

Logan, T. (1984) 'Learning through interviewing', in Schostak, J. and Logan, T. (eds) *Pupil Experience*, Croom Helm.

Lomax, P. (ed.) (1989) *The Management of Change*, BERA Dialogues No. 1, Multilingual Matters Ltd.

Louden, W. (1991) *Understanding Teaching*, Teachers College Press.

Louis, K. and Miles, M. (1992) *Improving the Urban High School*, Cassell Publications.

Lunzer, E. (1965) 'Problems of formal reasoning in test situations, monograph of the Society for Research', *Child Development*, 100:19–46.

McKelvey, J. and Kyriacou, C. (1985) 'Research on pupils as teacher evaluators', *Educational Studies*, 11:25–31.

McLaren, P. and Leonard, P. (eds) (1993) *Paulo Freire: A Critical Encounter*, Routledge.

McNiff, J. (1991) *Action Research: Principles and Practice*, Macmillan Education.
(1992) *Creating a Good Social Order through Action Research*, Hyde Publications.
(1993) *Teaching as Learning: An Action Research Approach*, Routledge.

Measor, L. (1984) 'Pupil perceptions of subject status', in Goodson, I. and Bull, S. (eds) *Defining the Curriculum: Histories and Ethnographies*, The Falmer Press.

Merton, R. and Kendall, P. (1946) 'The Focussed Interview', *American Journal of Sociology*, 51:541–57.

Morgan, G. (1986) *Images of Organization*, Sage Publications.

Nash, R. (1976) 'Pupils' expectations of their teachers', in Stubbs, M. and Delamont, S. (eds) *Explorations in Classroom Observation*, Wiley.

Nisbett, R. and Wilson, T. (1977) 'Telling more than we can know: verbal reports on mental processes', *Psychological Review*, 85:231–59.

Papert, S. (1980) *Mindstorms*, Harvester.

Patton, M. (1980) *Qualitative Evaluation and Research Methods*, Sage.

Plummer, G. and Edwards, G. (eds) (1993) *Dimensions of Action Research: People, Practice and Power*, Hyde Publications.

Pollard, A. (1985) 'Opportunities and difficulties of a teacher-ethnographer: a personal account', in Burgess, R. (ed.) *Field Methods in the Study of Education*, The Falmer Press.

Ribbins, P. and Burridge, E. (eds) (1994) *Improving Education: Promoting Quality in Schools*, Cassell Publications.

Scheerens, J. (1989) *Effective Schooling: Research, Theory and Practice*, Cassell.

Schön, D. (1990) *Educating the Reflective Practitioner*, Jossey-Bass.

Schutz, A. (1932) *The Phenomenology of the Social World*, Heinemann.
(1973) *The Structures of the Life World*, Heinemann.

Sikes, P. (1985) 'The life cycle of the teacher', in Ball, S. and Goodson, I. (eds) *Teacher's Lives and Careers*, The Falmer Press.

Silver, H. (1994) *Good Schools, Effective Schools: Judgements and their Histories*, Cassell Publications.

Smyth, J. (1991) 'Problematising teaching through a critical approach to clinical supervision', *Curriculum Inquiry,* 21(3):321–52.

Whitehead, J. (1992) *What Significance Does the Action Research and Educational Theory Case Study Collection at the University of Bath Have for the Creation of Living Educational Theories?* School of Education, University of Bath.
(1993) *The Growth of Educational Knowledge: Creating Your Own Living Educational Theories*, Hyde Publications.

Winter, R. (1989) *Learning Through Experience*, The Falmer Press.

Woods, P. (1976) 'Pupils' views of school', *Educational Review*, 28:126–37.

Zuber-Skerritt, O. (ed.) (1991) *Action Learning for Improved Performance*, AEBIS Publishing.

Index